A Treatise of the Soul of Man

by

John Flavel

© 2010 Benediction Classics, Oxford.

Contents

The Epistle Dedicatory	1
The Preface	9
Gen. 2:7	15
Rev. 6:9,10,11	82
Eph. 5:29	118
2 Pet. 1: 13,14	142
Heb. 12:23	159
1 Pet. 3:19	197
Matt. 16:26	224
Eph. 5:16	299

The Epistle Dedicatory

To the much honoured, his dear kinsman, Mr. John Flavel, and Mr. Edward Crispe, of London, Merchants; and the rest of my worthy friends in London, Ratcliffe, Shadwell, and Lymehouse, grace, mercy, and peace.

Dear Friends,

"Among all the creatures in this lower world, none deserves to be styled great, but man; and in man nothing is found worthy of that epithet, but his soul."

The study, and knowledge of his soul was, therefore, always reckoned a rich and necessary improvement of time. All ages have magnified these two words, "Know thyself as an oracle descending from heaven."

"No knowledge, says Bernard, is better than that whereby we know ourselves; leave other matters therefore, and search thyself; run through thyself, make a stand in thyself; let thy thoughts, as it were, circulate, begin and end in thyself; Strain not thy thoughts in vain about other things, thyself being neglected.

The study and knowledge of Jesus Christ must still be allowed to be the most excellent and necessary: But yet the worth and necessity of Christ is unknown to men, till the value, wants, and dangers of their own souls be first discovered to them.

The disaffectedness, and aversion of men to the study of their own souls, are the more to be admired; not only because of the weight and necessity of it, but the alluring pleasure, and sweetness that are found therein. What Cardan speaks, is experimentally felt by many, "That scarce any thing is more pleasant and delectable to the soul of man, than to know what he is, what he may and shall be; and what those divine and supreme things are, which he is to enjoy after death, and the vicissitudes of this present world." For we are creatures conscious to ourselves of an immortal nature, and that we have something about us which must overlive this mortal flesh, and therefore it is ever and anon some way or other hinting and intimating to us its expectations of, and designation for a better life than that it now lives in the body, and that we shall not cease to be, when we cease to breathe.

And certainly, my friends, discourses of the soul, and its immortality; of heaven and of hell, the next, and only receptacles of unbodied spirits, were never more seasonable and necessary than in this atheistical age of the world, wherein all serious piety and thoughts of immortality are ridiculed, and hissed out of the company of many: As if those old condemned Heretics, the "Tnelopsuchitai", who asserted the corruptibility and mortality of the soul as well as the body, had been again revived in our days.

And as the Atheism of some, so the tepidity, and unconcerned carelessness of the most, need and call for such potent remedies, as discourses of this kind do plentifully afford. I dare appeal to your charitable judgements, whether the conversations and discourses of the many, do indeed look like a serious pursuit of heaven, and a flight from hell?

Long have my thoughts bended towards this great and excellent subject, and many earnest desires I have had, (as I believe all thinking persons must needs have) to know what I shall be when I breathe not. But when I had engaged my meditations about it, two great rubs opposed the farther progress of my thoughts therein: Namely,

I. The difficulty of the subject I had chosen: And,

II. The distractions of the times in which I was to write upon it.

I. As for the subject, such is the subtilty and sublimity of its nature, and such the knotty controversies in which it is involved, that it much better deserves that inscription, than Minerva's temple at Saum did, "Never did any mortal reveal me plainly.

"It is but little that the most clear and sharp-sighted do discern of their own souls, now in the state of composition; and what can we positively and distinctly know of the life they live in the state of separation? The darkness in which these things are involved doth greatly exercise, even the greatest wits, and frequently elude and frustrate the most generous attempts." Many great scholars whose natural and acquired abilities singularly furnished and qualified them to make a clearer discovery, have laboured in this field, usque ad sudorem et pallorem, even to sweat and paleness, and done little more but entangle themselves, and the subject more than before; this cannot but discourage new attempts.

And yet, without some knowledge of the inability, and subjective capacity of our souls to enjoy the good of the world to come, even in a state of absence from the body, a principal relief must be cut off from them, under the great and manifold trials they are to encounter in this evil world.

As for myself, I assure you, I am deeply sensible of the inequality of my shoulders to this burden; and have often thought (since I undertook it) of that grave and necessary caution of the poet, to wield and poise the burden as porters use to do, before I undertook it. Zuinglius blamed Carolostadius (as some may do me) for undertaking the controversy of that age; because, says he, Non habet satis humerorum; his shoulders are too weak for it.

And yet I know men's labours prosper not according to the art and elegancy of the composure, but according to the divine blessing which pleaseth to accompany them. Ruffinus tells us of a learned philosopher at the Council of Nice, who stoutly defended his thesis against the greatest wits and scholars there, and yet was at last fairly vanquished by a man of no extraordinary parts: of which con quest the philosopher gave this candid and ingenuous account;— Against words (said he) I opposed words; and what was spoken I overthrew by the art of peaking: But when, instead of words, power came out of the mouth of the speaker, words could no longer withstand truth; nor man oppose the power of God.

O that my weak endeavours might prosper under the influence of the like Spirit, upon the hearts of them that shall read this inartificial, but well meant discourse.

I am little concerned about the contempts and censures of fastidious readers. I have resolved to say nothing that exceeds sobriety, nor to provoke any man, except my dissent from his unproved dictates must be his provocation.

FLAVEL

Perhaps there are some doubts and difficulties relating to this subject which will never fully be solved till we come to heaven. For man, by the fall, being less than himself, doth not understand himself, nor will ever perfectly do so until he be fully restored to himself; which will not be while he dwells in a body of sin and death. And yet it is to me past doubt, that this, as well as other subjects, might have been much more cleared than it is, if instead of the proud contendings of masterly wits for victory, all had humbly and peaceably applied themselves to the impartial search of truth.

Truth, like an orient pearl in the bottom of a river, would have discovered itself by its native lustre and radiancy, had not the feet of Heathen philosophers, cunning Atheists, and daring school divines disturbed and fouled the stream.

II. And as the difficulties of the subject are many, so many have been the interruptions and avocations I have met with, while it was under my hand: which I mention for no other end but to procure a more favourable censure from you, if it appear less exact than you expected to find. Such as it is, I do with much respect and affection tender to your hands, humbly requesting the blessing of the Spirit may accompany it to your hearts. If you will but allow yourselves to think close to the matter before you, I doubt not but you may find somewhat in it apt both to inform your minds and quicken your affections. I know you have a multiplicity of business under your hands, but yet I hope your great concern makes all others daily to give place; and that how clamorous and importunate soever the affairs of the world be, you both can and do find time to sit alone, and bethink yourselves of a much more important business you have to do.

My friends, we are borderers upon eternity, we live upon the confines of the spiritual and immaterial world: we must shortly be associated with bodiless beings, and shall have, after a few days are past, no more concerns for meat, drink, and sleep, buying and selling, habitations and relations, than the angels of God now have. Besides, we live here in a state of trial: Man, (as Scaliger fitly calls him,) is utriusque mendi nexus, One in whom both worlds do meet; his body participates of the lower, his soul of the upper world; Hence it is that he finds such tugging and pulling this way and that way, upward and downward; both worlds, as it were, contending for this invaluable prize, the precious soul. All Christ's ordinances are instituted, and his officers ordained for no other use or end but the salvation of souls.

Books are valuable according to their conducibility to this end: how rich a reward of my labours shall I account it, if this treatise of the soul may but promote the sanctification and salvation of any reader's soul.

To your hands I first tender it: it becomes your property, not only as a debt of justice, the fulfilling of a promise made you long since, upon your joint and earnest desires for the publication of it; but, as an acknowledgement of the many favours I have received from you: To one of you I stand obliged in the bond of relation, and under the sense of many kindnesses, beyond whatever such a degree of relation can be supposed to exact.

You have here a succinct account of the nature, faculties and original of the soul of man, as also of its infusion into the body by God, without intitling himself to the guilt and sin resulting from that their union

You will also find the breath of your nostrils to be the nexus, tie, or bond, which holds our souls and bodies in personal union; and that, while the due crasis and temperament of the body remains, and breath continues, your souls hang, as by a weak and slender thread, over the state of a vast eternity in heaven or in hell; which will inform you both of the value of your breath, and the best way of improving it, while you enjoy it.

The immortality of the soul is here asserted, proved, and vindicated from the most considerable objections; so that it will evidently appear to you, by this discourse, you do not cease to be, when you cease to breathe: and, seeing they will overlive all temporal enjoyments, they must necessarily perish as to all their joys, comforts, and hopes, (which is all the death that can be incident to an immortal spirit,) if they be not in the proper season secured and provided of that never perishing food of souls, God in Christ, their portion for ever.

Here you will find the grounds and reasons of that strong inclination, which you all feel them to have to your bodies, and the necessity notwithstanding that, of their divorce, and separation from their beloved bodies; and that it would manifestly be to their prejudice, if it should be otherwise: and to overcome the unreasonable aversations of believers, and to bring them to a more becoming cheerful submission to the laws of death, whensoever the writ of ejection shall be served upon them; you will here find a representation of that blessed life, comely order, and most delightful employment of the incorporeal people inhabiting the city of God; wherein, beside those sweet meditations which are proper to feast your hungry affections, you will meet with divers unusual, though not vain or unuseful, questions stated and resolved, which will be grateful entertainment to your inquisitive and searching minds.

It is possible they may be censured by some as underminable and unprofitable curiosities, but as I hate a presumptuous intrusion into unrevealed secrets, so I think it is a weakness to be discouraged in the search of truth, so far as it is fit to trace it, by such damping and causeless censures. Nor am I sensible I have in any thing transgressed the bounds of Christian sobriety, to gratify the palate of a nice and delicate reader.

I have also here set before the reader an idea or representation of the state and case of damned souls, that, if it be the will of God, a seasonable discovery of hell may be the means of some men's recovery out of the danger of it; and close up the whole with a demonstration of the invaluable preciousness of souls, and the several dangerous snares and artifices of Satan, their professed enemy, to destroy and cast them away for ever.

This is the design and general scope of the whole, and of the principal parts of this treatise. And, O that God would grant me my heart's desire on your behalf; in the perusal of it! Even that it may prove a sanctified instrument in his hand both to prepare you for, and bring you in love with the unbodied life, to make you look with pleasure into your graves, and die by consent of will, as well as necessity of nature. I remember Dr. Stoughton, in a sermon preached before king James, relates a strange story of a little child in a shipwreck, fast asleep upon its mother's lap, as she sat upon a piece of the wreck amidst the waves; the child being awaked with the noise, asked the mother what those things were? She told it, They were drowning waves to swallow them up. The child, with a pretty smiling countenance, begged a stroke from its mother to beat away those naughty waves, and chide them as if they had been its play-mates. Death will shortly shipwreck your bodies; your souls will sit upon your lips ready to expire, as they upon the wreck ready to go down. Would it not be a comfortable and most becoming frame of mind, to sit there with as little dread, as this little child did among the terrible waves? Surely, it our faith has but first united us with Christ, and ten loosed our hearts off from this enchanting and ensnaring world, we might make a fair step towards this most desirable temper; but unbelief and earthly-mindedness make us loth to venture.

I blush to think, what bold adventures those men made, who, upon the contemplation of the properties of a despicable stone first adventured quite out of sight of land, under its conduct and direction, and securely trusted both their lives and estates to it, when all the eyes of heaven were veiled from them, amidst the dark waters, and thick clouds of the sky, when I either start, or at least give an unwilling shrug, when I think of adventuring out of the sight of this world, under the more sure and steady direction and conduct of faith and the promises. To cure these evils, in my own and the reader's heart these things are written, and in much respect and love tendered to your hands, as a testimony of my gratitude, and deep sense of the many obligations you have put me under. That the blessing of the Spirit may accompany these discourses to your souls, afford you some assistance in your last and difficult work, of putting them off at death with a becoming cheerfulness, saying in that hour, Can I not see God till this flesh be laid aside in the grave? must I die before I can live like myself? then die my body, and go to thy dust, that I may be with Christ. With this design, and with these hearty wishes, dear and honoured cousin, and worthy friends, I put these discourses unto your hands, and remain,

Your most obliged kinsman and servant,
JOHN FLAVEL.

The Preface

Among many other largesses and rich endowments, bestowed by the Creator's bounty upon the soul of man, the sentiments and impressions of the world to come, and the ability of reflection and self-intuition, are peculiar, invaluable, and heavenly gifts. By the former, we have a very great evidence of our own immortality, and designation for nobler employments and enjoyments than this embodied state admits. And by the latter we may discern the agreeableness of our hearts, and therein the validity of our title to that expected blessedness.

But these heavenly gifts are neglected and abused all the world over. Degenerate souls are every where fallen into so deep an oblivion of their excellent original, spiritual and immortal nature, and alliance to the Father of spirits; that (to use the upbraiding expression of a great philosopher) "they seem to be buried in their bodies, as so many silly worms that lurk in their holes, are loth to peep forth, and look abroad.

So powerfully do the cares and pleasures of this world charm all, (except a small remnant of regenerate souls) that nothing but some smart stroke of calamity, or terrible messengers of death can startle them; (and even those are not always able to do it,) and when they do, all the effect is but a transient glance at another, and an unwilling shrug to leave this world, and so to sleep again. And thus the impressions and sentiments of the world to come (which are the natural growth and offspring of the soul) are either stifled and suppressed, as in Atheists; or borne down by impetuous masterly lusts, as in Sensualists.

And for its self reflecting and considering power, it seems in many to be a power received in vain. It is with most souls as it is with the eye, which sees not itself, though it sees all other objects. There be those that have almost finished the course of a long life, (wherein a great part of their time has lain upon their hands, as cheap and useless commodity, which they knew not what to do with) who never yet spent one solemn entire hour in discourse with their own souls. What serious heart doth not melt into compassion over the deluded multitude, who are mocked with dreams, and perpetually busied about trifles? Who are, (after so many frustrated attempts both of their own, and all past ages) eagerly pursuing the fleeting shadows, who torture and rack their brains to find out the natures and qualities of birds, beasts, and plants; indeed any thing rather than their own souls, which are certainly the most excellent creatures that inhabit this world. They know the true value and worth of other things? but are not able to estimate the dignity of that high born spirit that is within them. A spirit which (without the addition of any more natural faculties or powers, if those it has be but sanctified and devoted to God) is capable of the highest perfections and fruitions, even complete conformity to God, and the satisfying visions of God throughout eternity. They herd themselves with beasts, who are capable of an equality with angels. O what compassionate tears must such a consideration as this draw from the eyes of all that understand the worth of souls!

As for me it has been my sin, and is now the matter of my sorrow, that while myriads of souls, (of no higher original than mine) are some of them beholding the highest Majesty in heaven, and others giving all diligence to make sure their salvation on earth, I was carried away so many years in the course of this world, (like a drop with the current of the tide) wholly forgetting my best self, my invaluable soul; while I prodigally wasted the stores of my time and thoughts upon vanities, that long since passed away as the waters which are remembered no more. It shall be no shame to me to confess this folly, since the matter of my confession shall go to the glory of my God. I studied to know many other things, but I knew not myself. It was with me as with a servant to whom the master committed two things, viz. the child, and the child's clothes; the servant is very careful of the clothes' brushes and washes, starches and irons them, and keeps them safe and clean, but the child is forgotten and lost. My body which is but the garment of my soul, I kept and nourished with excessive care, but my soul was long forgotten, and had been lost for ever, as others daily are, had not God roused it, by the convictions of his Spirit, out of that deep oblivion and deadly slumber.

When the God that formed it, out of free grace to the work of his own hands, had thus recovered it to a sense of its own worth and danger, my next work was to get it united with Christ, and thereby secured from the wrath to come; which I found to be a work difficult to effect, if it be yet effected) and a work of time to clear, though but to the degree of good hope through grace.

And since the hopes and evidences of salvation began to spring up in my soul, and settle the state thereof, I found these three great words, viz. Christ, soul, and eternity, to have a far different and more awful sound in my ear, than ever they used to have. I looked on them from that time, as things of the greatest certainty and most awful solemnity. These things have laid some weight upon my thoughts, and I felt, at certain seasons, a strong inclination to sequester myself from all other studies, and spend my last days, and most fixed meditations upon these three great and weighty subjects.

I know the subject matter of my studies and enquiries (be it never so weighty) doth not therefore make my meditations and discourse upon it great and weighty; nor am I such a vain opinionator, as to imagine my discourses every way suitable to the dignity of such subjects; no, no, the more I think and study about them, the more I discern the indistinctness, darkness, crudity, and confusion of my own conceptions, and expression of such great and transcendent things as those; but In magnis voluisse sat st, I resolved to do what I could; and accordingly some years past I finished and published, in two parts, the Doctrine of Christ; and by the acceptation and success the Lord gave that, he has encouraged me to go on in this second part of my work, how unequal soever my shoulders are to the burden of it.

The nature, original, immortality, and capacity, of mine own soul, for the present lodged in and related to this vile body, destined to corruption; together with its existence, employment, perfection, converse with God, and other spirits, both of its own, and of a superior rank and order: when it shall (as I know it shortly must) put off this its tabernacle; these things have a long time been the matters of my limited desires to understand, so far as I could see the pillar of fire (God in his word) enlightening my way to the knowledge of them. Yea, such is the value I have for them, that I have given them the next place in my esteem, to the knowledge of Jesus Christ, and my interest in him.

God has formed me, as he has other men, a prospecting creature. I feel myself yet uncentered, and short of that state of rest and satisfaction to which my soul, in its natural and spiritual capacity, has a designation. I find that I am in a continual motion towards my everlasting abode, and the expense of my time; and many infirmities tell me that I am not far from it: by all which I am strongly prompted to look forward, and acquaint myself as much as I can, with my next place and employment. I look with a greedy and inquisitive eye that way.

Yet would I not be guilty of an unwarrantable curiosity in searching into revealed things; how willing soever I am to put my head by faith into the world above, and to know the things which Jesus Christ has purchased and prepared for me, and all the rest that are waiting for his appearance and kingdom, I feel my curiosity checked and repressed by shat elegant paronomasia, Rom. 12:3. "Me uperfronein par ho dei fronein, alle fronein eis to sofronein," In all things I would be wise unto sobriety. I groan under the effects of Adam's itching ambition to know, and would not by repeating his sin, increase my own misery; nor yet would I be scared, by his example, into the contrary evil of neglecting the means God has afforded me, to know all that I can of his revealed will.

The helps philosophy affords in some parts of this discourse are too great to be despised, and too small to be admired. I confess I read the definition of the soul given by the ancient philosophers with a compassionate smile. When Thales calls it a nature without repose; Asclepiades, an exercitation of sense! Hesiod, a thing composed of earth and water: Parmenides, a thing composed of earth and fire; Galen says it is heat; Hippocrates, a spirit diffused through the body; Plato, a self-moving substance; Aristotle calls it Entelechia, that by which the body is moved: If my opinion should be asked which of all these definitions I like best, I should give the same answer which Theocritus gave an ill poet, repeating many of his verses, and asked which he liked best; Those (said he) which you have omitted. Or if they must have the garland as the prize they have shot for, let them have it upon the some reason that was once given to him that shot wide.—Ditficilius est toties non attingere,—Because it was the greatest difficulty to aim so often at the mark, and never come near it. One word of God gives me more light than a thousand such laborious trifles. As Caesar was best able to write his own commentaries, so God only can give the best account of his own creature, on which he has impressed his own image.

Modern philosophers, assisted by the divine oracles, must needs come closer to the mark, and give us a far better account of the nature of the soul. Yet I have endeavoured not to cloud this subject with their controversies, or abstruse notions; remembering what a smart but deserved check Tertullian gives those, Qui Platonicum et Aristotelicum Christianismum producunt Christianis. Words are but the servants of matter, I value them as merchants do their ships, not by the gilded head and stern, the neatness of their mould, or curious flags and streamers, but by the soundness of their bottom, largeness of their capacity, and richness of their cargo and loading. The quality of the subject necessitates, in many places, the use of scholastic terms, which will be obscure to the vulgar reader: but apt and proper words must not be rejected for their obscurity, except plainer words could be found that fit the subject as well, and are as fully expressive of the matter. The unnecessary I have avoided, and the rest explained as I could.

  The principal fruits I especially aim at, both to my own and the reader's soul, are, That while we contemplate the freedom, pleasure, and satisfaction of that spiritual, incorporeal people, who dwell in the region of light and joy, and are hereby forming to ourselves a true scriptural idea of the blessed state of those disembodied spirits, with whom we are to serve and converse in the temple-worship in heaven; and come more explicitly and distinctly to understand the constitution, order, and delightful employments of those our everlasting associates; we may answerably feel the sound and inordinate love of this animal life sub-acted and wrought down; the frightful vizard of death drop off, and a more pleasing aspect appear; that no upright soul that shall read these discourses may henceforth be convulsed at the name of death, but cheerfully aspire, and with a pleasant expectation wait for the blessed season of its transportation to that blessed assembly. It is certainly our ignorance of the life of heaven, that makes us dote as we do upon the present life. There is a gloom, a thick mist overspreading the next life, and hiding, even from the eyes of believers, the glory that is there. We send forth our thoughts to penetrate this cloud, but they return to us without the desired success. We reinforce them with a sally of new and more vigorous thoughts, but still they come back in confusion and disappointment, as to any perfect account they can bring us from thence; though the oftener and closer we think, still the more we grow up into acquaintance with these excellent things.

  Another benefit I pray for, and expect from these labours, is, that by describing the horrid estate of those souls which go the other way, and shewing to the living the dismal condition of souls departed in their unregenerate state, some may be awakened to a seasonable and effectual consideration of their wretched condition, while they yet continue under the means and among the instruments of their salvation.

Whatever the fruit of this discourse shall be to others, I have cause to bless God for the advantage it has already given me. I begin to find more than ever I have done, in the separate state of sanctified souls, all that is capable of attracting an intellectual nature; and if God will but fix my mind upon this state, and cause my pleased thoughts about it to settle into a steady frame and temper, I hope I shall daily more and more depreciate and despise this common way of existence in a corporeal prison; and when the blessed season of my departure is at hand, I shall take a cheerful farewell of the greater and lesser elementary world, to which my soul has been confined, and have an abundant entrance through the broad gate of assurance, unto the blessed, unembodied inhabitants of the world to come.

Gen. 2:7

And the Lord God formed man out of the dust of the ground, and breathed into his nostrils the breath of life; and man became a living soul.

Three things (says Athanasius) are unknown to men according to their essence, viz. God, angels, and the souls of men." Of the nature of the divine and high-born soul, we may say, as the learned Whitaker doth of the way of its infection by original sin, "it is easier sought than understood, and better understood than explicated." And for is original, the most sagacious and renowned for wisdom amongst the ancient philosophers understood nothing of it. It is said of Democritus, that "there is nothing in the whole workmanship of nature of which he did not write;" and in a more lofty and swelling hyperbole, they stile their eagle-eyed Aristotle, "the rule, yea, and miracle of nature; learning itself, the very son of knowledge:" yet both these are not only said, but proved by Lactantius to be learned idiots. How have the schools of Epicurus, and Aristotle, the Cartesians, and other sects of philosophers abused and troubled the world with a kind of philosophical enthusiasm, and a great many ridiculous fancies about the original of the soul of man! and when all is done three words of God, by the pen of the inspired Moses, enlightens us more than all the subtle notions of he accidential concretion of atoms, their materia subtilis, and anima mundi, and the rest of their unintelligible fancies could ever do.

The account Moses gives us in this context, of the origin of the world, and of man the epitome of it, is full of sense, reason, congruity, and clearness; and such as renders all the essays of all the Heathen philosophers to be vain, inevident, self-repugnant, and inexplicable theories.

The inspired penman gives us, in this context, a compendious narrative of the world's creation, relating more generally the rude, inform, and undigested chaos; and then more particularly the specificating, and diversifying of the various beautiful beings, thence educed by the notion of the Spirit of God upon the face of the waters.

When the first matter was strictly created out of nothing, "the Spirit (as Moses excellently expresseth it, chap. 1:2.) hovered, or moved over it as a bird over her eggs, and, as it were, by way of incubation, cherishing and influencing it, did thereby draw forth all the creatures into their several forms, and distinct particular natures, wherein we now, with delight and admiration, behold them.

In this manner and order was the stately fabric of the world produced and erected; but as yet, it remained as a fair and well furnished house without an inhabitant. God had employed infinite wisdom and power about it, and engraven his name upon the meanest creature in it; but there was no creature yet made (except angels, the inhabitants of another city) to read the name and celebrate the praises of the Almighty Creator.

He therefore thought the world imperfect till there was a creature made that could contemplate, praise, and worship the Maker of it; for this very use and purpose was man created, that he might not only see, but consider the things he saw; discourse, and rationally collect out of them the things he saw not; and both praise, and love the Maker for, and in them all.

The palaces of princes are not beautified and adorned, to the intent men should pay their respects and honours to the walls, but to shew the grandeur and magnificence of the king, to whose person their honour is due, as Athenagoras in his excellent apology for the Christians, speaks. The world is a glorious and magnificent pile, raised designedly to exhibit the wisdom and power of its Creator to the reasonable creature man, that from him God might receive the glory of all his other works. Of this creature man, the master-piece of all the visible world, (and therefore crowned king over it the first moment he was made, Psal. 8:5.) Moses in the next place, gives us the account, both of his original, whence he came, and of his dignity, what he is. "The Lord God formed man out of the dust of the ground, and breathed into his nostrils the breath of life; and man became a living soul." Where we find,

I. The original of the body of man.

II. The original of the soul of man.

I. The original of the body of man: "Formed out of the dust of the ground." "Dust was its original matter; of dust was it made, and into dust it must be resolved, Gen. 3:19. The consideration is humbling, and serves to tame the pride of man", who is apt to dote upon his own beauty. Man's body was not made of heavenly matter, as the radiant sun, and sparkling stars: no, nor yet of the most precious and orient earthly matter: God did not melt down the pure and splendid gold and silver, or powder the precious pearls and sparkling diamonds, but he formed it of the vile and despicable dust.

We find that the sprinkling of dust upon new writing prevents many a foul blot: I am sure, the sprinkling of our original dust upon our minds by serious consideration, is the way to prevent many a proud boast.

However, the baseness of the matter, and coarseness of the stuff, serves to set off the admirable skill of the most wise and powerful Architect, who out of such mean, despicable materials, has fashioned so exact and elegant a piece. "The Lord God formed man out of the dust."

"The Lord God.] The name of God is here set down at full, to set forth the dignity of man," the subject matter wrought upon, as some conceive.

Formed.] Fashioned, or curiously moulded, and figured it. The Hebrew verb, primarily signifies "to press, compress, or squeeze together; and by a metalepsis, by pressing or compressing, to mould or fashion, as the potter doth his clay." The Psalmist useth another word to express the artificial elegancy of the body of man, Psal. 139:15,16. "rakamti", acupictus sum, I am embroidered, painted, or flourished as with a needle. We render it curiously wrought. Whatsoever beauty and comely proportion God has bestowed by creation upon it, "it is all answerable to that excellent idea, or model before conceived in his mind and purpose." All this care and cost was bestowed upon the body of man, which, when all is done, is but the case in which that inestimable jewel, the soul, was to be lodged. This therefore I must lay aside, and come to the more noble subject,

II. The soul of man: about which we have before us four things to ponder in this text, viz.

(1.) The nature and property of the soul of man.
(2.) The descent, and original of the soul of man.
(3.) The manner of infusion of the soul of man.
(4.) The nexus, or bond that unites the soul of man.

(1.) The nature and property of it, a living soul. The word "nefesh" as also the Chaldee Naphsha; and the Greek "psuche", have one and the same etymology, all signifying to breathe, or respire; not that the breath is the soul, but denoting the manner of its infusion by the breath of God, and the means of its continuation in the body, by the breath of our nostrils. God's breath infused it, and our breath continues it in union with the body. It signifies here the rational soul and the Hebrew "nefesh" has a very near affinity with the word "shayamim", the heavens; and indeed there is a nearer affinity betwixt the things, viz. soul and heaven, than there is betwixt the names.

The epithet "chazah" which we translate living, the Arabic renders a rational soul, and indeed, none but a rational deserves the name of a living soul, for all other forms or souls, which are of an earthly extract, do both depend on, and die with the matter out of which they were educed, but this being of another nature, a spiritual and substantial being, is therefore rightly stiled, a living soul.

The Chaldee renders it, a speaking soul. And indeed, it deserves a remark, that the ability of speech is conferred on no other soul but man's. Other creatures have apt and elegant organs; birds can modulate the air, and form it into sweet delicious notes, and charming sounds; but no creature, except man, whose soul is of an heavenly nature and extraction, can articulate the sound, and form it into words, by which the notions and sentiments of one soul are in a noble, apt, and expeditious manner conveyed to the understanding of another soul. And indeed, what should any other creature do with the faculty or power of speech, without a principle of reason to guide and govern it? It is sufficient to them that they discern each others meaning by dumb signs, much after the manner that we traded at first with the Indians; but speech is proper only to a rational, or living soul, however, we render it a living, a rational, or a speaking soul, it distinguishes the soul of man from all other souls.

(2.) We find here the best account that ever was given of the origin of the soul of man, or whence it came, and from whom it derives its being. O, what a dust and pother have the disputes and contests of philosophers raised about this matter! which is cleared in a few words in this scripture; "God breathed into his nostrils the breath of life, and man became a living soul:" which plainly speaks it to be the immediate effect of God's creating power. Not a result from matter; no, results flow e sinu materiae, out of the bosom of matter; but this comes ex halitu divino, from the inspiration of God. That which is born of the flesh, is flesh; but this is a spirit descending from the Father of spirits. God formed it, but not out of any pre-existent matter, whether celestial or terrestrial; much less out of himself, as the Stoics speak; but out of nothing. An high born creature it is, but no particle of the Deity. The invisible and immutable essence of God is utterly repugnant to such notions; and therefore they speak not strictly and warily enough, that are bold to call it a ray or emanation from God.

A spirit it is, and flows by way of creation, immediately from the Father of spirits; but yet is a spirit of another inferior rank and order.

(3.) We have also the account of the way and manner of its in fusion into the body, viz. by the same breath of God which gave it its being. It is therefore a rational, scriptural, and justifiable expression of St. Augustine, Creando infunditur, et infundendo creatur; it is infused in creating, and created in infusing; though Dr. Brown too slightingly calls it a mere rhetorical antimetathesis. Some of the fathers, as Justin, Ireneus, and Tertullian, were of opinion, That the Son of God assumed a human shape at this time, in which afterwards he often appeared to the fathers, as a prelude to his true and real incarnation; and took dust or clay in his hands, out of which he formed the body of man, according to the pattern of that body in which he appeared: and that being done, he afterwards, by breathing, infused the soul into it. But I rather think it is an anthropopathia, or usual figure in speech, by which the Spirit of God stoops to the imbecility of our understandings, "He breathed into his nostrils the breath of life;" Hebrew, lifes. But this plural word "chayim" rather the twofold life of man, in this world, and in that to come; or, "the several faculties and powers belonging to one and the same soul, viz. the intellective, sensitive, and vegetative offices thereof; than that there are more souls than one, "essentially differing, in one and the same man; for that, (as Aquinas truly says,) is impossible." We cannot trace the way of the Spirit, or tell in what manner it was united with this clod of earth. But it is enough, that he who formed it, did also unite, or marry it to the body. This is clear, not by way of natural resultancy from the body, but by way of inspiration from the Lord; not from the warm bosom of matter, but from the breath of its Maker.

4. Lastly, We have here the nexus, copula, the tie or band by which it is united with the body of man, viz. The breath of his (i.e. of man's) nostrils. It is a most astonishing mystery to see heaven and earth married together in one person; the dust of the ground, and an immortal spirit clasping each other with such dear embraces and tender love; such a noble and divine guest to take up its residence within the mean walls of flesh and blood. Alas, how little affinity, and yet what dear affection is found betwixt them!

Now, that which so sweetly links these two different natures together, and bolds them in union, is nothing else but the breath of our nostrils, as the text speaks: it came in with the breath; while breath stays with us, it cannot go from us and as soon as the breath departs, it departs also. All the rich elixirs and cordials in the world cannot persuade it to stay one minute after the breath is gone. One puff of breath will carry away the wisest, holiest, and most desirable soul that ever dwelt in flesh and blood. When our breath is corrupt, our days are extinct, Job 17:1. "Thou takest away their breath, they die, and return to their dust," Psal. 114:19.

Out of the text thus opened, arise two doctrinal propositions, which I shall insist upon, viz.

Doct. 1. That the soul of man is of a divine original, created and inspired immediately by the Lord.

Doct. 2. That the souls and bodies of men are linked, or knit together, by the feeble band of the breath of their nostrils.

In the prosecution of these two propositions, many things will come to our hands, of great use in religion; which I shall labour to lay as clearly and orderly to the reader's understanding, and press as warmly upon his heart as I can. And first,

Doct. 1. That the soul of man is of a divine original, created and inspired immediately by the Lard.

In this first proposition, two things are to be distinctly pondered, viz.

1. The nature of the soul.

2. The original of the soul.

Or, what it is, and from whence it came.

I. The first thing which arrests our thoughts, and requires their attention and exercise, is the nature of the soul, or what kind of being it is.

Those that are most curiously inquisitive into all other beings, and put nature upon the rack to make her confess her secrets, are in the mean time found shamefully slight and negligent in the study of themselves. Few there are that can prevail with themselves to sit down and think close to such questions as these. What manner of being is this soul of mine? whence came it? why was it infused into this body? and where must it abide, when death has dislodged it out of this frail tabernacle? There is a natural aversation in man to such exercises of thought as these, although in the whole universe of beings in this lower world, a more noble creature is not to be found.

The soul is the most wonderful and astonishing piece of divine workmanship; it is no hyperbole to call it the breath of God, the beauty of men, the wonder of angels, and the envy of devils. One soul is of more value than all the bodies in the world.

The nature of it is so spiritual and sublime, that it cannot be perfectly known by the most acute and penetrating understanding, assisted in the search by all the aid philosophy can contribute.

It is not my design in this discourse to treat of the several faculties and powers of the soul, or to give you the rise, natures, or numbers of its affections and passions: but I shall confine my discourse to its general nature and original. And seeing "none can so well discover the nature of it, as he who is the author of it," as Tertullian speaks, I therefore justly expect the best light from his words, though I will not neglect any other aid he is pleased elsewhere to afford.

The soul is variously denominated from its several powers and offices, as the sea from the several shores it washes. I will not spend time about the several names by which it is known to us in scripture, but give you that description of it, with which my understanding is most satisfied, which take thus:

The soul of man is a vital, spiritual, and immortal substance, endowed with an understanding, will, and various affections; created with an inclination to the body, and infused thereinto by the Lord.

In this description we have the two general parts into which I distributed this discourse: viz. its general nature, and divine original. The nature of the soul is expressed to us in these following terms.

I. It is a substance.

That is to say, not a quality, nor an accident inhering in another being, or subject; as whiteness doth in the snow: but a being by itself. Qualities and accidents have no existence of their own. but require another being, or subject to their existence; but the soul of man is a substantial being of itself, which will evidently appear upon the following grounds.

(1.) Because it is, in a strict and proper sense, created by God, "He formeth, or createth the spirit in man," Zech. 12:1: To him we are advised to "commit it, as to a faithful Creator," 1 Pet. 4:19. The substantial nature of the soul is implied in the very notion of its creation; "for whatsoever is created, is a substance, an ens par se. Accidents are not said to be created, but concreated;" the crasis of humours and results of matter are not substances created, but things rising in a natural way from created substances. They flow from, and as to their essence, depend upon pre-existent matter; but the soul was created out of nothing, and infused into the body after it was formed and organised; which evidenceth its substantial nature.

(2.) This evidenceth the soul to be a substance; that it can, and doth exist, and subsist by itself alone, when separated from the body by death, Luke 23:43. "Today shalt thou, (i.e. thy soul) be with me in paradise," and Matt. 10:20. "Fear not them that kill the body, but cannot kill the soul." Were the soul but an accident, a quality, or a result, he that kills the body must needs kill the soul too; as he that casts a snowball into the fire, must needs destroy the whiteness with the snow. Accidents fail and perish with their subjects: but seeing it is plain in these and many other scriptures, the soul doth not fail with the body; nothing can be more plain and evident, than that it is of a substantial nature.

When the Spaniards came first among tile poor Indians, they thought the horse and his rider to be one creature; as many ignorant ones think the soul and body of man to be nothing but breath and body: whereas indeed, they are two distinct creatures, as vastly different in their natures as the rider with his horse, or the bird and his cage. While the man is on horseback, he moves according to the motion of the horse; and while the bird is incaged, he eats and drinks, and sleeps, and hops and sings in his cage. But if the horse fail and die under his rider, or the cage be broken, the man can go on his own feet, and the bird enjoy itself as well, yea, better in the open fields and woods, than in the cage; Neither depend, as to being, or action, on the horse or cage.

(3.) Both scripture and philosophy consent in this, that the soul is the chief, most noble, and principal part of man, from which the whole man is, and ought to be denominated. So Gen. 46:26. "All the souls that came with Jacob into Egypt," i.e. all the persons; as the Latins say, tot capita, so many heads or persons. The apostle, in 2 Cor. 5:8. seems to exclude the body from the notion of personality, when he says, We are willing rather to be absent from the body, and to be present with the Lord: That we, a term of personality is there given to the soul, exclusively of the body, for the body cannot be absent from itself: But we, that is, the souls of believers, may be both absent from it, and present with Christ.

To this we may add, 2 Cor. 4:16. where the soul is called the man, and the inner man too, the body being but the external face, or shadow of the man. And to this philosophers agree. The best philosophers are so far from thinking that the body is the substantial part of man, and the soul a thing dependent on it, that contrarily they affirm, that the body depends upon the soul, and that it is the soul that conserves and sustains it; and that the body s in the soul, rather then the soul in the body, and that which is seen not the man, but that is the man which is invisible, that the body might be killed and the man not hurt; meaning the soul, which only deserves the name of man. Now if it be the chief part of man, and that which is only worthy the name of man, and from which therefore the whole is and ought to be denominated a man; if it be so far from depending on the body, or being contained within the body, that the body rather depends upon it, and is in it, then surely the soul must be, what we describe it to be, a substantial being.

(4.) It is past all controversy, that the soul is a substance, because it is the subject of properties, affections and habits; which is the very strict and formal notion of a substance. All the affections and passions of hope, desire, love, delight, fear, sorrow, and the rest, are all rooted in it, and springing out of it; and for habits, arts and sciences, it is the soul in which they are lodged and seated. Having once gotten a promptitude to act, either by some strong, or by some frequently repeated acting, they abide in the soul, even when the acts are intromitted, as in sleep, a navigator, scribe, or musician, are really artists, when they are neither sailing, or writing, or playing; because the habits still remain in their minds, as is evident in this, that when they awake, they can perform their several works, without learning the rules of their art anew.

II. The soul is a vital substance, i.e.

A substance which has an essential principle of life in itself; a living, active being. A living soul, says Moses in the text; and hereby it is distinguished from, and opposed to matter or body. The soul moves itself and the body too; it has a self-moving virtue or power in itself; whereas the matter, or body is wholly passive, and is moved and acted, not by itself, but by this vital spirit, James 2:26. "The body without the spirit is dead.- It acts not at all, but as it is acted by this invisible spirit. This is so plain, that it admits of sensible proof and demonstration. Take mere matter, and compound or divide it, alter it, and change it how you will, you can never make it see, feel, hear, or act vitally without a quickening and actuating soul. Yet we must still remember, that this active principle, the soul, though it has this vital power in itself, it has it not from itself, but in a constant receptive dependence upon God, the first cause, both of its being and power.

III. It is a spiritual substance.

All substances are not gross, material, visible and palpable substances; but there are spiritual and immaterial, as well as corporeal substances, discernible by sight or touch. To deny this were to turn a downright Sadducee, and to deny the existence of angels and spirits, Acts 23:8. The word substance, as it is applied to the soul of man, puzzles and confounds the dark understandings of some, that know not what to make of an immaterial substance, whereas in this place it is no more than substare accidentibus, i.e. to be a subject in which properties, affections, and habits are seated and subjected. This is a spiritual substance, and is frequently in scripture called a spirit; "Into thy hands I commit my spirit," Luke 23:46. "Lord Jesus receive my spirit," Acts 7:59. and so frequently all over the scriptures. And the spirituality of its nature appears, (1.) By its descent, in a peculiar way, from the Father of spirits. (2.) In that it rejoiceth in the essential properties of a spirit. (3.) That at death it returns to that great Spirit who was its efficient and former.

(1.) It descends, in a peculiar way, from the Father of spirits, as has been shown in the opening of this text. God stiles himself its Father, Heb. 12:9. its former, Zech. 12:1. It is true, he gives to all living things "dzoen kai pneuma", life and breath, Acts 17:25. Other souls are from him, as well as the rational soul; but in a far different way and manner. They flow not immediately from him by creation, as this does. It is said, Gen. 1:21, 27. "Let the earth bring forth the living creature after its kind;" but "God created man in his own image." Which seems plainly to make a specified difference betwixt the reasonable and all other souls.

(2.) It rejoiceth in the essential properties of a spirit: For it is an incorporeal substance, as spirits are. It has not partes extra partes, extension of parts; nor is it divisible, as the body is. It has no dimensions and figures as matter has; but is a most pure, invisible, and (as the acute Dr. Moore expresseth it) indiscernible substance. It has the principle of life and motion in itself, or rather, it is such a principle itself, and is not moved as dull and sluggish matter is, per aliud, by another. Its efficacy is great, though it be unseen, and not liable to the test of our touch, as no spiritual substances are. "A spirit (says Christ) has not flesh and bones," Luke 24:89. We both grant and feel, that the soul has a love and inclination to the body, (which indeed is no more than it is necessary it should have) yet can we no more infer its corporiety from that love to the body, than we can infer the corporiety of angels from their affection and benevolent love to men. It is a spirit of a nature vastly different from the body in which it is immersed. There is (says a learned author) no greater mystery in nature, than the union betwixt soul and body: That a mind and spirit should be so tied and linked to a clod' of clay, that while that remains in a due temper, it cannot by any art or power free itself! What so much a-kin are a mind and a piece of earth, a clod and a thought, that they shall be thus affixed to one another?

Certainly, the heavenly pure bodies do not differ so much from a dunghill, as the soul and body differ. They differ but as more pure and less pure matter; but these, as material, and immaterial. If we consider wherein consists the being of a body, and wherein that of a soul, and then compare them, the matter will be clear.

We cannot come to an apprehension of their beings, but by considering their primary passions and properties, whereby they make discovery of themselves. The first and primary affection of a body (as is rightly observed) is that extension of parts whereof it is compounded, and a capacity of division, upon which, as upon the fundamental mode, the particular dimensions (that is, the figures) and the local motion do depend.

Again, for the being of our souls, if we reflect upon ourselves, we shall find that all our knowledge of them resolves into this, that we are beings conscious to ourselves of several kinds of cogitations; that by our outward senses we apprehend bodily things present; and by our imagination we apprehend things absent; and that we oft recover into our apprehension things past and gone, and, upon our perception of things, we find ourselves variously affected.

Let these two properties of a soul and body be compared, and upon the first view of a considering mind it will appear, that divisibility is not apprehension, or judgement, or desire, or discourse: That to cut a body into several parts, or put it into several shapes, or bring it to several motions, or mix it after several ways, will never bring it to apprehend, or desire. No man can think the combining of fire, and air, and water, and earth, should make the lump of it to know and comprehend, what is done to it, or by it. We see manifestly, that upon the division of the body, the soul remains entire and undivided. It is not the loss of a leg or arm, or eye, that can maim the understanding or the will, or cut off the affections.

Nay, it pervades the body it dwells in, and is whole in the whole, and in every part, which it could never do if it were material. yea, it comprehends, in its understanding, the body or matter in which it is lodged; and more than that, it can, and does form conceptions of pure spiritual and immaterial beings, which have no dimensions or figures; all which shew it to be no corporeal, but spiritual and immaterial substance.

(3.) As it derives its being from the Father of spirits, in a peculiar way, and rejoiceth, in its spiritual properties: So at death it returns to that great Spirit from whence it came. It is not annihilated, or resolved into soft air, or sucked up again by the element of fire, or catched back again into the soul of the world, as some have dreamed; but it returns to God who gave it, to give an account of itself to him, and receive its judgement from him. "Then shall the dust return to the earth as it was, and the spirit shall return to God who gave it" Eccl. 12:7. Each part of man to its like, dust to dust, and spirit to spirit. Not that the soul is resolved into God, as the body is into earth: but as God created it a rational spirit, conscious to itself of moral good and evil, so when it has finished its time in the body, it must appear before the God of the spirits of all flesh, its Arbiter and final Judge.

By all which we see, that as it is elevated too high on the one hand, when it is made a particle of God himself; not only the creature, but a part of God, as Plutarch and Philo Judeus, and others have termed it, (spirit it is, but of another and inferior kind:) So it is degraded too low, when it is affirmed to be matter, though the purest, finest, and most subtle in nature; when approacheth nearest to the nature of spirit. A spirit it is, as much as an angel is a spirit, though it be a spirit of another species. This is the name it is known by throughout the scriptures. In a word, it is void of mixture and composition; there are no jarring qualities, compound elements, or divisible parts in the soul, as there are in bodies; but it is a pure, simple, invisible, and indivisible substance, which proves its spirituality, and brings us to the fourth particular, viz.

IV. It is an immortal substance.

The simplicity and spirituality of its nature, of which I spake before, plainly shews us, that it is in its very nature designed for immortality; for such a being or substance as this has none of the seeds of corruption and death in its nature, as all material and compounded beings have. It has nothing within it tending to dissolution: No jarring elements, no contrary qualities are found in spirits as there are in other creatures of a mixed nature. Physicians and Philosophers have disputed and contended eagerly about the true causes of natural death; "and while they have been contending about the way, they have come to the end." The ingress of the soul is obscure, and its egress not clear. But this seems to be the thing in which they generally centre, that the expense and destruction of the natural moisture, or radical balsam, as others call it, which is the oil that maintains natural light, or the bridle that restrains that flame of life from departing, as others express it: this is the cause of natural death: Others assign the unequal reparation of the parts of the body as the cause of death. But be it one or another, it is evident the soul, which consists neither of contrary qualities, nor of dissimilar parts, must be above the reach and stroke of death. For if the soul die, it must be either from some seeds, and principles of death and corruption within itself, or by some destructive power without itself. In itself you see there is no seed or principle of death; and if it be destroyed by a power without itself, it must be either by the stroke of some creature, or from the hand of God that first formed and created it: But the hand and power of no creature can destroy it; the creature's power reaches no farther than the body, Matt. 10:28. "They cannot kill the soul." And though the Almighty power of God, that created it out of nothing, can as easily reduce it to nothing; yet he will never do so. For besides the designation for eternity, which is discernible in its very nature, (as before was observed) and which speaks the intention of God to perpetuate the threatenings of eternal wrath, and promises of everlasting life, respectively made to the souls of men, as they shall be found in Christ, or out of Christ, puts it beyond all doubt that they shall never die; as will be more fully evidenced in the following discourse.

Well then, I hope so far our way is clear, in the search of the nature of the soul, that it is a substance, a spiritual substance, and being so, it is also an immortal substance. No doubt remains with me as to either of these. Let us then proceed to the consideration of its faculties and powers by which it may be yet more fully known, and we shall find that,

It is a spiritual, and immortal substance, endued with an understanding.

This is the noble leading faculty of the soul: We are not distinguished from brutes by our senses, but by our understanding. As grace sets one man above another, so understanding sets the meanest man above the best of brutes. Strange and wonderful things are performed by the natural instinct and sagacity of beasts; but yet what is said of one, is true of them all, "God has not imparted understanding to them," Job 39:17. This is a jewel which adorns none but rational creatures, men and angels.

The understanding is a faculty of the reasonable soul by which a man apprehends and judges all intelligible things.

The object of it is every being, so far as it is true in itself, and apprehensible by man. It has a twofold use in the life of man, viz.

(1.) To distinguish truth from error and falsehood. By this candle of the Lord, lighted up in the soul of man, he may discern betwixt duty and sin, good and evil: It is the eye of the soul, by which it sees the way in which we should go, and the dangerous precipices that are on either side. It is the soul's taster, and discerns wholesome food from baneful poison, Job 12:11. "Does not the ear (i.e. the understanding by the ear) try words, as the mouth tasteth meat?" It brings all things as it were in the lump before it, and then sorts them, and orderly ranks them into their proper classes of lawful and unlawful, necessary and indifferent, expedient and inexpedient, that the soul may not be damnified by mistaking one for another. And this judgement of discretion every man must be allowed for himself. No man is obliged to shut the eyes of his own understanding, and follow another and blind fold.

(2.) To direct and guide us in our practice. This faculty is by philosophers rightly called "to hegemonikon", the leading faculty; because the will follows its practical dictates. It sits at the helm, and guides the course of the soul; not impelling, or rigorously enforcing its dictates upon the will; for the will cannot be so imposed upon; but by giving it a directive light, or pointing, as it were, with its finger, what it ought to choose, and what to refuse.

To this faculty belong two other excellent and wonderful powers of the soul, viz.

1. Thoughts.

2. Conscience.

1. The power or ability of cogitation; "Thoughts are properly the actings and agitations of the mind, or any actual operation of the understanding." They are the musings of the mind, which are acted in the speculative part of the understanding. It is observable that the Hebrew word "suach", which is used for meditation, or thinking, signifies both to think and to speak in the mind. When the understanding, or mind resolves, and meditates the things that come into it, that very meditation is an inward speaking, or hidden word in the heart, Deut. 15:9. "Beware, lest there be a thought in thy wicked heart," as some render it: In the Hebrew it is "davar im levavech", a word in thy heart. So Matt. 9:3, 4. "eipon ei autois", "they spake within themselves," i.e. "they thought in their hearts." The objects presented to the mind are the companions with whom our hearts talk and converse.

Thoughts are the figments and creatures of the mind: they are formed within it, in multitudes innumerable. The power of cogitation is in the mind, yea, in the spirit of the mind.

"The fancy indeed, while the soul is embodied, ordinarily, and for the most part presents the appearances and likenesses of things to the mind;" but yet it can form thoughts of things which the fancy can present no image of, as when the soul thinks of God, or of itself. This power of cogitation goes with the soul, and is rooted in it when it is separated from the body; and by it we speak to God, and converse with angels, and other spirits in the unbodied state, as will be more fully opened in the process of this discourse.

2. The conscience belongs also to this faculty; for it being the judgement of a man upon himself, with respect or relation to the judgement of God, it must needs belong to the understanding part or faculty. "Thoughts are formed in the speculative, but conscience belongs to the practical understanding." It is a very high and awful power; it is solo Deo mi nor, and rides (as Joseph did) in the second chariot; the next and immediate officer under God. He says of conscience with respect to every man, as he once said of Moses with respect to Pharaoh. "See I have made thee a god to Pharaoh," Exod. 7:1. The voice of conscience is the voice of God; for it is his vicegerent and representative. What it binds on earth, is bound in heaven: and what it looseth on earth is loosed in heaven. It observes records, and bears witness of all our actions; and acquits and condemns, as in the name of God, for them. Its consolations are most sweet, and its condemnations most terrible: so terrible, that some have chosen death, which is the king of terrors, rather than to endure the scorching heat of their own consciences. The greatest deference and obedience is due to its command, and a man had better endure any rack or torture in the world, than incur the torments of it. It accompanies us as our shadow wherever we go: and when all others forsake us, (as at death they will) conscience is then with us, and is then never more active and vigorous than at that time. Nor does it forsake us after death; but where the soul goes, it goes, and will be its companion in the other world for ever. How glad would the damned be if they might but have left their consciences behind them, when they went hence! But as Bernard rightly says, "It is both witness, judge, tormentor, and prison;" it accuseth, judgeth, punisheth, and condemneth.

And thus briefly of the understanding, which has many offices, and as many names from those offices.

It is sometimes called wit, reason, understanding, opinion, wisdom, judgement. And why we bestow so many names upon one and the same faculty, the learned author of that small, but excellent tract "de anima", gives this true and ingenious account.

> *The wit, the pupil of the soul's clear eye,*
> *And in man's world the only shining star,*
> *Looks in the mirror of the fantasy,*
> *Where all the gatherings of the senses are;*
> *And after by discoursing to and fro,*
> *Anticipating and comparing things,*
> *She doth all universal natures know,*
> *And all effects into their causes brings.*
> *When she rates things, and moves from ground to ground,*
> *The name of reason she obtains by this:*
> *But when by reason she the truth hath found,*
> *And standeth fix'd, she understanding is.*
> *When her assent she lightly doth incline*
> *To either part, she is opinion light:*
> *But when she does by principles define*
> *A certain truth, she has true judgement's sight.*
> *And as from senses, reason's work doth spring:*
> *So many reasons understanding gain;*
> *And many understandings knowledge bring,*
> *And by much knowledge wisdom we obtain.*

VI. God has endued the soul of man not only with an understanding to discern, and direct, but also a will to govern, moderate, and over-rule the actions of life.

The will is a faculty of the rational soul, whereby a man either chuseth or refuseth the things which the understanding discerns and knows.

This is a very high and noble power of the soul. The understanding seems to bear the same relation to the will, as a grave counsellor does to a great prince. It glories in two excellencies, viz.

1. Liberty.

2. Dominion.

1. It has a freedom and liberty; it cannot be compelled and forced: Coaction is repugnant to its very nature. In this it differs from the understanding, that the understanding is wrought upon necessarily, but the will acts spontaneously. This liberty of the will respects the choice, or refusal of the means for attaining those ends it prosecutes, according as it finds them more or less conducible thereunto. The liberty of the will must be understood to be in things natural, which are within its own proper sphere, not in things supernatural. It can move, or not move the body, as it pleases, but it cannot move towards Christ, in the way of faith, as it pleaseth; it can open or shut the hand or eye at its pleasure, but not the heart. True, indeed, it is not compelled, or forced to turn to God by supernatural grace, but in a way suitable to its nature, it is determined and drawn to Christ, Psal. 110:3. It is drawn by a mighty power, and yet runs freely; Cant. 1:4. "Draw me, and I will run after thee."

Efficacious grace, and victorious delight, is a thing very different from compulsive force. "Pelagius (as a late author speaks) at first gave all to nature, acknowledged no necessity of divine grace; but when this proud doctrine found little countenance, he called nature by the name of grace; and when that deceit was discovered, he acknowledged no other grace but outward instruction, or the benefit of external revelation, to discourse, and put men in mind of their duty. Being yet driven farther, he acknowledged the grace of pardon; and before a man could do any thing acceptably, there was a necessity of the remission of sin, and then he might obey God perfectly. But that not sufficing, he acknowledged another grace, viz. the example of Christ, which does both secure our rule and encourage our practice. And last of all, his followers owned some kind of internal grace, but they made that to consist in some illumination of the understanding, or moral persuasion, by probable arguments, to excite the will, and this not absolutely necessary, but only for facilitation, as a horse to a journey, which otherwise a man might go on foot. Others grant the secret influences of God's grace, but make the will of man a co-ordinate cause with God, namely, that God doth propound the object, hold forth inducing considerations; give some remote power and assistance; but still there is an indifferency in the will of man, to accept or refuse, as liketh him best." Thus have they been forced to quit and change their ground; but still the pride of nature will not let men see the necessity of divine efficacious influences upon the will, and the consistency thereof with natural liberty.

(2.) Its dignity in its dominion, as well as in its liberty. The will has an empire, and sceptre belonging to it; yea, a double empire, for it rules,

1. Imperium Despoticum, Over the body, imperio despotico, by way of absolute command.
2. Imperium Politicum, Over the other powers and passions of the soul, imperio politico, by way of suasion.

(1.) The will, like an absolute sovereign, reigns over the body, i.e. its external members by way of absolute command. It says, as the centurion did, I am in authority, and God has put the many members of the body in subjection to me; I say to one, move, and it moves; to another, stop, and it stops; and to a third, do this, and it doth it. The obsequious members of the body, like so many servants, have their eyes waiting on the imperial commands of the will, and it is admirable to behold with what dispatch and speed they execute its commands, as if their obedient motions were rather concomitant than subsequent acts to the will's mandates. Let it but command to have the windows of the body, open or shut, and it is done in a moment, in the twink of an eye; and so for the rest of the external senses and members, they pay it most ready obedience. Yet when I say, the will has a despotical, and absolute sovereignty over the members, it must be understood with a double limitation. First, They are only at its beck for use and service; it can use them while well and rightly disposed; but it cannot perpetuate them, or restore them when indisposed. If the soul will the health and life of the body never so intensely and vehemently, it cannot keep off death one moment the longer from it. And, Secondly, Its sovereignty no way intrenches upon, nor interferes with the dominion of providence over the members of the body, and the various motions of them. God has reserved a sovereign, negative voice to himself, whatever decrees the will passes. Jeroboam stretches out his hand against the man of God to smite him; but God puts a remora in the very instant to the loco-motive faculty, that though he would never so fain, he could not pull in his hand again to him, 1 Kings 13:4. The will commands the service of the tongue, and charges it to deliver faithfully such or such words, in which, it may be, the ruin of good men may be imported; and when it comes to do its office, the tongue faulters; and contrary to the command of the will, drops some word that discovers and defeats the design of the will, according to that in Job 12:20. "He removeth away the speech of the trusty." This is its despotical and sovereign power over the external members of the body.

(2.) It has a political power over the faculties and passions of the soul, not by way of absolute command, but by way of suasion and insinuation. Thus it can ofttimes persuade the understanding and thoughts to lay by this or that subject, and apply themselves to the study of another. It can bridle and restrain the affections and passions, but yet it has no absolute command over the inner, as it has over the outward man. Its weakness and inability to govern the inner man appears in two things, more especially remarkable, viz. 1. It cannot, with all its power and skill command and fetch off the thoughts from some subjects, which are set on, at some times, with extraordinary weight upon the soul. However, the thoughts may obsequiously follow its beck at some times, yea, for the most part; yet there are cases and seasons, in which its authority and persuasions cannot disengage one thought.

As (1.) When God has to do with the soul, in the work of conversion, when he convinceth of sin and danger, and sets a man's evils in order before his eyes: These are terrible representations, and fain would the carnal will disengage the thoughts from such sad subjects, and strives by all manner of persuasions and diversions so to do, but all to no purpose, Psal. 2:3. "My sin is ever before me." The thoughts are fixed, and there is no removing of them. It may give them a little interruption, but they return with the more impetuous violence. And instead of gaining them off, they at last, or rather God by them gains over the will also.

(2.) When Satan has to do with the soul, in the way of temptation and hellish suggestion: Look, as the carnal will opposes itself to the thoughts in the former case to no purpose; so that the sanctified will opposes itself to them in this case, oft times with as little effect or success, as he that opposeth his weak breath to the strong current of a mighty river. Well were it, if the sanctified will were now the master of the fantasy, and could control the thoughts of the heart; but, like a mad horse, the fancy takes the bit in its teeth, and runs whither it pleaseth; the will cannot govern it. Think quite another way says the will, turn thy thoughts to other things; but notwithstanding, the soul turneth a deaf ear to its counsels. 2. It cannot quiet and compose a raging conscience, and reduce it at its pleasure to rest and peace. This is the peculiar work of God. He only that stills the stormy seas, can quiet the distressed and tempestuous soul. The impotence of the will, in this case, is known to all that have been in those deeps of trouble. And this is the misery of the devil and the damned, that though they would never so lain, yet they cannot get rid of those tormenting impressions made upon them by their own trembling and condemning consciences. There would not be so many pale, sweating, affrighted consciences on earth, and in hell, if the will had any command or power over them.

Tam frigida mens est.
Criminibus; tacita sudant praecordia culpa.

It is an horrible sight to see such a trembling upon all the members, such a cold sweat upon the panting bosom of a self-condemned, and wrath presaging soul, in which it can, by no means relieve or help itself. These things are exempt from the liberty and dominion of the will of man; but notwithstanding these exemptions, it is a noble faculty, and has a vastly extended empire in the soul of man; it is the door of the soul; at which the Spirit of God knocks for entrance. When this is won, the soul is won to Christ; and if this stand out in rebellion against him, he is barred out of the soul, and can have no saving union with it. The truth of grace is to be judged and discerned by its compliance with his call, and the measure of grace to be estimated by the degree of its subjection to his will.

VII. The soul of man is not only endued with all understanding and will, but also with various affections and passions, which are of great use and service to it, and speak the excellency of its nature. They are originally designed and appointed for the happiness of man, in the promoting and securing its chiefest good, to which purpose they have a natural aptitude: for the true happiness and rest of the soul not being in itself, nor in any other creature, but in God, the soul must necessarily move out of itself, and beyond all other created beings, to find and enjoy its true felicity in him. The soul considered at a distance from God, its true rest and happiness, is furnished and provided with desire and hope to carry it on and quicken its motion towards him. These are the arms it is to stretch out towards him, in a state of absence from him. And seeing it is to meet with many obstacles, enemies, and difficulties, in its course, which hinder its motion, and hazard its fruition of him, God hath planted in it, fear, grief, indignation, jealousy, anger, &c. to grapple with, and break through those intercurrent difficulties and hazards. By these weapons in the hands of grace, it conflicts with that which opposes its passages to God, as the apostle expresseth that holy fret and passion of the Corinthians, and what a fume their souls were in by the gracious motion of the irascible appetite; 2 Cor. 7:11. "For behold this self same thing, that ye sorrowed after a godly sort; what carefulness it wrought in you, yea, what clearing yourselves, yea, what indignation, yea, what fear, yea, what vehement desire, yea, what zeal, yea, what revenge?" Much like the raging and struggling of waters, which are interrupted in their course by some dam or obstacle which they strive to bear down, and sweep away before them.

But the soul considered in full union with and fruition of God, its supreme happiness, is accordingly furnished with affections of love, delight, and joy, whereby it rests in him and enjoys its proper blessedness in his presence for ever. Yea, even in this life, these affections are in an imperfect degree exercised upon God, according to the prelibations and enjoyments it has of him by faith, in its way to heaven. In a word,

The true uses, and most excellent ends for which these affections and passions are bestowed upon the soul of man, are to qualify it, and make it a fit subject to be wrought upon in a moral way of persuasions and allurements, in order to its union with Christ, (for by the affections, as Mr. Fenner rightly observes, the soul becomes marriageable, or capable of being espoused to him) and being so, then to assist it in the prosecution of its full enjoyment in heaven, as we heard but now.

But, alas, how are they corrupted and inverted by sin! The concupiscible appetite greedily fastens upon the creature, not upon God; and the irascible appetite is turned against holiness, not sin. But I must insist no farther on this subject here, it deserves an entire treatise by itself.

VIII. The soul of man has, in the very frame and nature of it, an inclination to the body. There is in it a certain pondus, or inclination which naturally bends or sways it towards matter, or a body. There are three different natures found in living creatures, viz.

    1. The brutal.
    2. The angelical.
    3. The human.

(1.) The soul of a brute is wholly confined to, and dependent on the matter or body with which it is united. It is dependent on it, both in esse et in operari, in its being and working; it is but a material form, which arises from, and perisheth with the body. "The soul of a brute, (says a great person) is no other than a fluid bodily substance, the more lively and refined part of the blood (called spirit) quick in motion, and from the arteries by the branches of the carotides carried to the brain; and from thence conveyed to the nerves and muscles, move the whole frame and mass of the body; and receiving only certain weak impressions from the senses, and of short continuance, hindered and obstructed of its work and motion, vanishes into the soft air.

(2.) An angel is a spirit free from a body, and created without an appetite or inclination to be embodied. The Stoics call the angels "ousias psuchikas", souly substances; and the Peripatetics, formas abstractas, abstract forms. They are spirits free from the fetters and clogs of the body.

"An angel is a perfect soul, and an human soul is an imperfect angel." Yet angels have no such rooted disaffection to, and abhorrence of a body, but they have assumed, and can, in a ready obedience to their Lord's commands, and delight to serve him, assume bodies, for a time, to converse with men in them, i.e. aerial bodies in the figure and shape of human bodies. So we read, Gen. 18:2: three men, i.e. angels in human shape and appearance, stood by Abraham, and talked with him; and at Christ's sepulchre, Luke 24:4 "There appeared two men in shining garments." But they abide in these bodies, as we do in an inn, for a night, or short season; they dwell not in them as our souls in those houses of flesh, which we cannot put on and off at pleasure as they do, but as we walk in our garments, which we can put of without pain.

(3.) The human soul is neither wholly tied to the body, as the brutal soul is; nor created without inclination to a body, as angels are; but loves and inclines to it, though it can both live and act without it, when it is parted from it at death. The proof of this assertion, and the reasons why God created it with such an inclination, will, in their proper place, be more fully spoken to, in the following discourse. All that I shall add is, that in this, as well as in some other respects, our souls are made a little lower than the angels; but when they are unclothed of the body, and have received it again, in a new edition, a spiritual body, then they shall be "isangeloi", equal unto angels, in the way and manner of life and action.

Thus I have, as briefly as I could, dispatched the first thing propounded, viz. the nature of the soul, in the explication of these seven particulars: it is a substance, a vital, spiritual, and immortal substance, a substance endued with understanding, will, affections, and an inclination to the body. And now we are come to the

II. Branch, viz. Its original and infusion.

I. As to its original, I have described it to be immediately from God, in the way of creation: an honour done to no other living creature except angels. The world has been troubled with a great many extravagant and wild notions about the original of the soul of man; a certain mark and argument of its apostasy from God. "Solinus writes of one, who by a wound in the hinder part of his head, fell into such a degree of ignorance and oblivion, that he forgot his own name, and could not tell whether he had any name at all." But oh! what a stunning blow did man receive by the fall, that he should forget the very Author of his being, and rather claim alliance, and derive the being of his soul from any thing than God; though it bears the very marks and characters of its divine Author and Father upon it! The principal errors about the origin of the soul (for that wild notion of Epicurus has been laid so flat by the pens of many learned men, that it is a vanity to strike one blow more at it) may be reduced to these three heads.

(1.) Some affirm it to be by way of traduction, or natural generation from the parents to the child. This opinion is very ancient; Tertullian, and divers of the Western Fathers, closed with it, as judging it the best expedient to solve the difficulties of the soul's taint and defilement with original sin. But antiquity is no passport for errors. The grey hairs of opinion, as one well notes, are then honourable, when they are found in the way of truth. Doctor Brown tells us, "He should rather incline to the creation, than the traduction of the soul, though either opinion (says he) will consist well enough with religion, did not one objection haunt him, and this is a conclusion from the equivocal and monstrous productions by unnatural copulation, as of a man and beast: for, if the soul of man, says he, be not transmitted and transfused in the seed, why are not these productions merely beasts, but have also an impression and tincture of reason in as high a measure as it can evidence itself in those improper organs?

Which way the doctor's judgement had inclined in this controversy, had been of no great consideration to the determination of it; though it is a pity we should lose his consent and company, for the sake of such a beastly objection as this, which haunts his mind: for if there be any such creatures that seem to have a tincture of reason, it is but a tincture, and a seeming, not a real tincture neither, which many other brutes have.

The doctor is too well acquainted with philosophy, and a man of too much reason to allow himself to think that such a production as he speaks of has two natures and essential forms in one body, as of a man and a horse. He knows that every entity has but one special essence, and can have no more, except he will place one and the same thing under divers species in the predicament of substance. And as there cannot be two distinct forms, so neither can there be a mixture of them in the Centaur or monstrous birth: for, ex duobus entibus perse, non fit unum ens per se. But he confesseth this objection was bred among the weeds and tares of his own brain, (a rank soil no doubt) and I am pretty confident he had weeded it out in his latter years; for I find this notion of the Centaurs, (that is, half horse, half man), put into its proper place among his vulgar errors, B. 1. chap. 4. And so I suppose that rub being out of the way, he returned again to us.

(2.) A second opinion was, That they were procreated by angels: and that which gave the ground, such as it is, to this opinion or fancy, is the similitude or resemblance which is found betwixt angels and the souls of men. But this fancy needs not any industry to overthrow it; for though it be certain there is a similitude and resemblance betwixt angels and souls, both being immaterial and spiritual substances, yet angels neither propagate by generation, nor is it in their power to create the least fly or worm in the world, much less the soul of man, the highest and noblest and most excellent being. Great power they have, but no creating power, that is God's incommunicable property; and procreate our souls they did not, for though they are spirits, yet spirits of another species.

(3.) A third sort there are, who deny that souls are created substances, and proceeded from God; but affirm withal, that he created them simul, et semel, together and at once, as the angels were, and not one by one, as men are born into the world. "Of this opinion was Plato, who thought all human souls to be created together before their bodies, and placed in some glorious and suitable mansions, as the stars, till, at last, growing weary of heavenly, and falling in love with earthly things, for a punishment of that crime, they were cast into bodies, as into so many prisons." Origen sucked in this notion of the pre-existence of souls: and upon this supposition it was that Porphyry tells us, in the life of Plotinus, he blushed as often as he thought of his being in a body, as a man that lived in reputation and honour, blushes when he is lodged in a prison. The ground on which the Stoics bottomed their opinion was, the great dignity and excellency of the soul, which inclined them to think they had never been degraded and abased, as they are by dwelling in such vile bodes, but for their faults; and that it was for some former sins of theirs, that they slid down into gross matter, and were caught into a vital union with it; whereas, had they not sinned, they had lived in celestial and splendid habitations, more suitable to their dignity.

But this is a pure creature of fancy; for, (1.) No soul in the world is conscious to itself, of such a pre-existence, nor can remember when it was owner of any other habitation than that it now dwells in. (2.) Nor does the scripture give us the least hint of any such thing. Some indeed would catch hold of that expression, Gen. 2:2. "God rested the seventh day from all the works which he had made;" and it is true, he did so, the work of creation was finished and sealed up, as to any new species or kinds of creatures to be created; no other sort of souls will be created, than that which was at first: but yet God still creates individual souls, (My Father worketh hitherto and I work) of the same kind and nature with Adam's soul. And, (3.) For their detrusion into these bodies as a punishment of their sins in the former state; if we speak of sin in individuals, or particular persons, the scripture mentions none, either original or actual, defiling any soul in any other way but by its union with the body. Pre-existence therefore is but a dream.

But to me it is clear that the soul receives not its beginning by traduction or generation; for that which is generable, is also corruptible; but the spiritual, immortal soul (as it has been proved to be) is not subject to corruption. Nor is it imaginable how a soul should be produced out of matter, which is not endued with reason: or, how a bodily substance can impart that to another, which it has not in itself. If it be said, the soul of the child proceeds from the souls of the parents, that cannot be; for spiritual substances are impartible, and nothing can be discinded from them. "And it is absurd to think the soul of Adam should spring from one original, and the souls of his offspring from another, while both his and theirs are of one and the same nature and species." To all which let me add, That as the assertion of their creation is most reasonable, so it is most scriptural. It is reasonable to think and say, "That no active power can act beyond, or above the proper sphere of its activity and ability". But if the soul be elicited out of the power of matter, here would be an effect produced abundantly more noble and excellent than its cause. And as it is most reasonable, so it is most scriptural. To this purpose diverse testimonies of scripture are cited and produced by our divines, among which we may single out these four, which are of special remark and use; Heb. 12:9. "Furthermore, we had fathers of our flesh which corrected us, and we gave them reverence; shall we not much rather be in subjection to [the Father of spirits] and live?" Here God is called the Father of spirits, or of souls, and that in an emphatical antithesis, or contradistinction to our natural fathers, who are called the fathers of our flesh, or bodies only. The true scope and sense of this text, is, with great judgement and clearness, given us by that learned and judicious divine, Mr. Pemble, in these words; "[Nothing is more plain and emphatical than this antithesis; We receive our flesh and body from our parents, but our souls from God: if then we patiently bear the chastisements of our parents, who are the authors of the vilest part, and have the least right or power over us; with how much more equal a mind should we bear his chastisements, who has the supreme might to us, as he is the Father and only giver of that which is most excellent in us, viz. our souls or spirits?"] Here it appears evident, that our souls flow not to us in the material channel of fleshly generation or descent, as our bodies do, but immediately from God, their proper Father, in the way of creation. Yet he begets them not out of his own essence or substance, as Christ, his natural Son, is begotten, but, "ek me onton", out of nothing, that had been before, as Theodoret well expresseth it. Agreeable hereunto is that place also in Zech. 12:1. "The Lord which stretches forth the heavens, and layeth the foundations of the earth, and formeth the spirit of man within him:" "Were the forming of the spirit, or soul of man, is associated with these two other glorious effects of God's creating power, namely, the expansion of the heavens, and laying the foundations of the earth:" all three are here equally assumed by the Lord, as his remarkable and glorious works of creation. He that created the one, did as much create the other.

Now the two former we find frequently instanced in scripture, as the effects of his creating power, or works implying the Almighty power of God; and therefore are presented as strong props to our faith, when it is weak and staggering for want of visible matter of encouragement, Isa 40:22. and 42:5. Jer. 10:12. Job 9:8. Psal. 104:2. q.d. Are my people in captivity, and their faith nonplussed and at a loss, because there is nothing in sight that has a tendency to their deliverance, no prepared matter for their salvation? Why, let them consider who it was that created the heavens and the earth, yea, and their souls also, which are so perplexed with thoughts, out of nothing; the same God that did this, can also create deliverance for his people, though there be no pre-existent matter to work it out of.

Add to this that excellent place of Solomon, in Eccl. 12:7. "Then shall the dust return to the earth, as it was; and the spirit to God who gave it." There he shews us what becomes of man, and how each part, of which he consists, is bestowed, and disposed of after his dissolution by death, and thus he states it: The two constitutive parts of man are a soul and a body: these two parts have two distinct originals: the body, as to its material cause, is dust; the soul, in its nature, is a spirit, and as to its origin, it proceed from the Father of spirits; it is his own creature, in an immediate way. He gave it: he gave it the being, it has by creation, and gave it to us, i.e. to our bodies by inspiration. Now qualis Genesis, talis Analysis. When death dissolves the union which is betwixt them, each part returns to that from whence it came, dust to dust, and the spirit to God that gave it. The body is expressed by its material cause, dust; the soul only by its efficient cause, as the gift of God; because it had no material cause at all, nor was made out Of ally pre-existent matter, as the body was. And therefore Solomon here speaks of God, as if he had only to do with the soul, leaving the body to its material and instrumental causes, with which he concurs by a general influence. It is God, not man alone, or God by man, that has given us these bodies; But it is not man, but God alone, who has given us these souls. He therefore passes by the body, and speaks of the soul as the gift of God; because that part of man, and that only, flows immediately from God, and at death, returns to him that gave it. All these expressions, The Father of spirits, the former of the spirit of man, the giver of the spirit: how agreeable are they to each other, and all of them to the point under hand, that the soul flows from God by immediate creation? You see it has no principle out of which, according to the order of nature, it did arise, as the body had, and therefore it has no principle into which, according to the order of nature, it can be returned, as the body has; but returns to God, its efficient cause: if reconciled, to a Father, not only by creation, but adoption; if unreconciled, as a creature guilty of unnatural rebellion against the God that formed it, to be judged.

II. God created and infused it into the body, with an inherent inclination and affection to it. The nature of the soul and body is vastly different, there is no affinity or similitude betwixt them; but it is in this case as in that of marriage. Two persons of vastly different educations, constitutions, and inclinations, coming under God's ordinance, into the nearest relation to each other, find their affections knit and endeared by their relation to a degree beyond that which results from the union of blood: So it is here. Whence this affection arises, in what acts it is discovered, and for what reason implanted, will be at large discovered in a distinct branch of the following discourse, to which it is assigned. Mean while, I find my self concerned to vindicate what has been here asserted from the arguments which are urged against the immediate creation and infusion of the soul, and in the defence of the opinion of its traduction from the parents. To conceal, or dissemble these arguments and objections, would be but a betraying of the truth I have here asserted, and give occasion for some jealousy, that they are unanswerable. To come then to an issue; and first,

Objec. 1. It is urged, that it is manifest in itself, and generally yielded, that the souls of all other creatures come by generation, and therefore it is probable the human souls flow in the same channel also.

Solut. There is a specific difference betwixt rational souls, and the souls of all other creatures, and therefore no force at all in the consequence. A material form may rise out of matter, but a spiritual, rational being (as the soul of man is) cannot so rise, being much more noble and excellent than matter is.

What animal is there in the world, out of whose soul the acts of reason spring and flow, as they do out of human souls? Are they capable of inventing, (or which is much less) of learning the arts and sciences? Can they correct their senses, and demonstrate a star to be far greater than the whole earth, which to the eye seems no bigger than the rowel of a spur? Do they foreknow the positions and combination of the planets, and the eclipses of the sun and moon many years before they suffer them? And if they cannot perform these acts of reason, as it is sure they cannot, how much less can they know, fear, love, or delight in God, and long for the enjoyments of him! These things do plainly evince human souls to be of another species, and therefore of a higher original shall the souls of brutes. If all have one common nature and original, why are they not all capable of performing the same rational and religious acts?

Obj. 2. But though it should be granted, that the soul of the first man was by immediate creation and inspiration of God; yet it follows not, that the souls of all his posterity, must be so too. God might create him with a power of begetting other souls after his own image. The first tree was created with its seed in itself to propagate its kind, and so might the first man.

Sol. 1. Trees, animals, and such like, were not created immediately out of nothing, as the soul of man was; but the earth was the pre-existent matter out of which they were produced by the word of Gods blessing and power; but man's soul was immediately breathed into him by God, and had no pre-existent matter at all: And besides, all human souls being of one species, have therefore one and the same original: The soul of the poorest child is of equal dignity with the soul of Adam. And if we consult Job 33:4. we shall find Elihu giving us there the same account, and almost in the same words, of the original of his soul that Moses in my text gives us of the original of Adam's soul: "The Spirit of God has formed me, and the breath of the Almighty has given me life."

Sol. 2. But it is evident, souls spring not from the parent, as one plant, or an animal does from another; for they have their seed in themselves, apt and proper to produce their kind; but the seed of souls is not to be found in man: It is not to be found in his body; for then (as was said before) a spiritual and nobler essence must be produced out of a material and baser matter, (i.e.) the matter must give to the soul that which it has not in itself; nor is it to be found in his soul; for the soul being a pure, simple, and invisible being, can suffer nothing to be descinded from it, towards the production of another soul. A spirit, as the soul is, is substantia, simplex et impartibilis; an uncompounded, and indiscernible, or impartible being. Nor can it spring partly from the body, and partly from the soul, as from con-causes; for then it should be partly corporeal, and partly incorporeal, as its causes are. "So that there is no matter, seed, or principles of souls found in man; and to be sure (as Baronius strongly argues) he cannot produce soul without pre-existent matter; for that were to make him omnipotent, and assign a creating power to a creature." Besides, that which is generable, is also corruptible, as we see trees animals, &c. which are produced that way, to be; but the soul is not corruptible, as has in part been already proved, and more fully, in the following discourse. So that Adam's soul, and the souls of his posterity spring not from each other, but all from God by creation.

Obj. 3. If the soul be created and infused immediately by God, either it comes out of his hands pure, or impure; if pure, how comes it to be defiled and tainted with sin? If impure, how do we free God from being the author of sin?

Sol. If the question be, whether souls be pure or impure, as soon as they are united with their bodies? The answer is, they are impure, and tainted as soon as united: For the union constitutes a child of Adam, and consequently a sinful impure creature. But if it respect the condition and state in which God created them, I answer with Baronius. "They are created neither morally pure, nor impure; they receive neither purity nor impurity from him, but only their naked essence, and the natural powers and properties flowing there from." He inspires not any impurity in them; for he cannot be the author of sin, who is the revenger of it. Nor does he create them in their original purity end rectitude; for the sin of Adam lost that, and God justly withholds it from his posterity. Who wonders (says one) to see the children, the palaces and gardens of a traitor to droop and decay, and the arms of his house, and the badge of his nobility, to be defaced and reversed? That which is abused by men to the dishonour of God, may justly be destroyed (I add in this case, or with-held) by God to the detriment of man. Adam voluntarily and actually deprived himself, and meritoriously deprived all his posterity of that original righteousness and purity in which he was created. As an holy God, he cannot inspire ally impurity, and as a just and righteous God, he may, and does withhold, or create them void and destitute of that holiness, and righteousness which was once their yea, of happiness and glory.

Obj. 4. But how come they then to be defiled and tainted with original sin? It is confessed God did not make them impure, an the body cannot; for being matter, it cannot act upon a spirit; itself it is a dead lump, and cannot act at all.

Sol. What if this be one of those mysteries reserved for the world to come, about which we cannot in this state solve every difficulty that may be moved? Must we therefore deny its divine original? What if I cannot understand some mysteries, or answer some questions about the hypostatical union of the two natures, in the wonderful person of our Emmanuel, Must I therefore question whether he be

"Theantropos", God-man? We must remain ignorant of some things about our souls, till we come into the condition of the spirits of just men made perfect. Mean time, I think it much more our concernment to study how we may get sin out of our souls, than to puzzle our brains to find how it came into them.

But that the objector may not take this for an handsome slide, or go-by to this great objection, I return to it, in a few particulars.

(1.) What I think not original sin follows either part singly; it comes in neither by the soul alone, nor by the body alone, apart from the soul; but upon the union and conjunction of both in one person. It is the union of these two which constitutes a child of Adam, and as such only we are capable of being infected with his sin.

(2.) And whereas it is so confidently asserted in the objection, that sin cannot come into the soul by, or from the body, because it being matter, cannot act upon a spirit; I say, this is gratis dictum, easily spoken, but difficultly proved. Cannot the body act upon, or influence the soul? Pray then, how comes it to pass that so many souls become foolish, forgetful, injudicious, &c. by their union with ill disposed bodies? Nothing is more sensible, plain, and evident, than that there is a reciprocal communication betwixt the soul and body. The body doth as really (though we know not how) affect the soul with its dispositions, as the soul influences it with life and motion. The more excellent any form is, the more intimate is its union and conjunction with the matter. This soul of man has therefore a more intimate and perfect union with the body, than light has with the air, which is made, by some, to be the emblem and similitude to shadow forth this union. But the union betwixt them is too intimate to be conceived by the help of any such similitudes. That this infection is by way of physical agency, as a rusty scabbard infects and defiles a bright sword when sheathed therein, I will not confidently affirm as some do. It may be by way of natural concomitancy, as Estius will have it; or to speak, as Dr. Reynolds (modestly, and as becomes men that are conscious of darkness and weakness) by way of ineffable resultancy and emanation.

(3.) Upon the whole, original sin consists in two things, viz.

1. In the privation of that original rectitude which ought to be in us.

2. In that habitual concupiscence which carrieth nature to inordinate motions.

This privation and inordinate inclination, made up that original corruption, the rise whereof we are searching for: And to bring us as near as we can come, without a daring intrusion into unrevealed secrets, our solid divines proceed by these steps, in answering this objection.

(1.) If it be demanded how it comes to pass that an infant becomes guilty of Adam's sin; The answer is, because he is a child of Adam by natural generation.

(2.) But why is he deprived of that original rectitude in which Adam was created? They answer, because Adam lost it by his sin, and therefore could not transmit what he had lost to his posterity.

(3.) But how comes he to be inclined to that which is evil? Their answer is, because he wants that original rectitude: For whosoever wants original rectitude, naturally inclines to that which is evil. And so the propension of nature to that which is evil, seems to be by way of concomitancy with the defect or want of original righteousness.

And thus I have given some account of the nature and original of the soul of man, though alas! my dim eyes see but little of its excellency and glory. Yet, by what has been said, it appears the masterpiece of all God's work of creation, in this lower world.

But because I suspect the description I have given of it will be obscure and cloudy to vulgar readers, of a plain and low capacity, by reason of divers philosophical terms which have been forced to make use of; and reckoning myself a debtor to the weak and unlearned, as well as others, I will endeavour to strip this description of the soul, for their sakes, out of those artificial terms which darken it to them, and present it once more in the most plain and intelligible epitome I am capable to give it in; that so the weaker understanding may be able to form a true notion of the nature and original of the soul, in this manner.

The soul of mine is a true and real being; not a fancy, conceit, very nothing. It has a proper and true being in itself, whether I conceit it or not. Nor indeed can I conceive of it, but by it. It is not such a thing as whiteness is in snow, a mere accident, which depends upon the snow in which it is for the being it has, and must perish as soon as the snow is dissolved: My soul doth not so much depend upon my body, or any other fellow-creature for its being; but is as truly a substance as my body is, though not of so gross and material a kind and nature. My soul can, and will subsist and remain what it is, when my body is separated from it; but my body cannot subsist and remain what it now is, when my soul is separated from it: So that I find my soul to be the most substantial and noble part of me; it is not my body, but my soul which makes me a man. And if this depart, all the rest of me is but a dead log, a lump of inanimate clay, a heap of vile dust and corruption. From this independent substance it has in itself, and the dependence its properties and affections have upon it, I truly apprehend and call it a substance.

But yet, when I call it a substance, I must not conceive of it as a gross material, palpable substance, such as my body is, which I can see and feel: No, there are spiritual substances, as well as gross, visible, material substances. An angel is a spiritual substance, a real creature, and yet imperceptible by my sight or touch, such a substance is my soul. Spiritual substances are as real, and much more excellent than bodily substances are. I can neither see, hear, nor feel it, but I both see, hear, and feel by it.

My soul is also a vital substance. It is a principle of life to my body: It has a life in itself, and quickens my body therewith. My soul is the spring of all the actions and motions of life which I perform. It has been an error taken in from my childhood, that sense is performed in the outward organ, or members of my body; as touching in the hand, seeing in the eye, hearing in the ear, &c. in them, I say, and not only by them, as if nothing were required to make sense, but an object and an organ. No, no, it is not my eye that seeth, nor my ear that heareth, nor my hand that toucheth, but my soul, in and by them, performs all this. Let but an apoplex hinder the operations of my soul in the brain, and of how little use are my eyes, ears, hands, or feet to me? My life is originally in my soul, and secondarily by way of communication in my body. So that I find my soul to be a vital, as well as a spiritual substance.

And being both a vital and spiritual substance, I must needs conclude it to be an immortal substance. For in such a pure, spiritual nature as my soul is, there can be found no seeds or principles of death. Where there is no composition, there will he no dissolution. My body indeed having so many jarring humours, mixed elements, and contrary qualities in it, must needs fall and die at last: but my soul was formed for immortality, by the simplicity and spirituality of its nature. No sword can pierce it from without, nor opposition can destroy it from within; man cannot, and God will not.

And being an immortal spirit, fitted and framed to live for ever, I find that God has, answerably, endued and furnished it with an understanding, will, and affections, whereby it is capable of being wrought upon by the Spirit in the way of grace and sanctification in this world in order to the enjoyment of God, its chief happiness in the world to come.

By this its understanding, I am distinguished from, and advanced above all other creatures in this world. I can apprehend, distinguish, and judge of all other intelligible beings. By my understanding I discern truth from falsehood, good from evil; it shews me what is fit for me to choose, and what to refuse.

To this faculty or power of understanding, my thoughts and conscience do belong; the former to my speculative, the latter to my practical understanding. My thoughts are all formed in my mind or understanding in innumerable multitudes and variety. By it I can think of things present, or absent; visible, or invisible; of God, or myself; of this world, or the world to come.

To my understanding also belongs by conscience, a noble, divine, and awful power: By which I summon and judge myself, as at a solemn tribunal; bind and lose, condemn and acquit myself and actions, but still with an eye and respect to the judgement of God. Hence are my best comforts, and worst terrors.

This understanding of mine is the director and guide of my will, as the counsellor; and my will is as the prince: It freely chuseth and refuseth, as my understanding directs and suggests to it. The members of my body, and the passions of my soul, are under its dominion: The former are under its absolute command, the latter under its suasions and insinuations, though not absolutely, yet always with effect and success.

And both my understanding and will I find to have great influence upon my affections.

These passions and affections of my soul are of great use and dignity. I find them as manifold as there are considerations of good and evil. They are the strong and sensible motions of my soul, according to my apprehensions of good and evil. By them by soul is capable of union with the highest good. By love and delight I am capable of enjoying God, and resting in him as the centre of my soul. This noble understanding, thoughts, conscience, will, passions, and affections, are the principal faculties, acts, and powers of this my high and heaven-born soul. And being thus richly endowed and furnished,

I find it could never rise out of matter, or come into my body by way of generation; the souls of brutes, that rise that way, are destitute of understanding, reason, conscience, and such other excellent faculties and powers as I find in my own soul. They cannot know, or love, or delight in God, or set their affections on things spiritual, invisible, and eternal as my soul is capable to do; it was therefore created and infused immediately into this body of mine by the Father of spirits, and that with a strong inclination, and tender affection to my flesh, without which it would be remiss and careless in performing its several duties and offices to it, during the time of its abode therein.

Fearfully and wonderfully, therefore, am I made, and designed for nobler ends and uses, than for a few days to eat, and drink, and sleep, and talk, and die. My soul is of more value than ten thousand worlds. What shall a man give in exchange for his soul?

USE.

From the several parts and branches of this description of the soul, we may gather the choice fruits which naturally grow upon them, in the following inferences and deduction of truth and duty. For we may say of them all what the historian doth of Palestine, that there is nihil infructuosum, nihil sterile, no branch or shrub is barren, or unfruitful. Let us then search it branch by branch: and,

Inf. 1. From the substantial nature of the soul, which we have proved to be a being distinct from the body, and subsisting by itself, we are informed, That great is the difference betwixt the death of a man, and the death of all other creatures in the world. Their souls depend on, and perish with their bodies; but ours neither result from them, nor perish with them. My body is not a body, when my soul has forsaken it; but my soul will remain a soul when this body is crumbled into dust. Men may live like beasts, a mere sensual life; yea, in some sense, they may die like beasts, a stupid death; but in this there will be found a vast difference: Death kills both parts of the beasts, destroys the matter and form; it toucheth only one part of man; it destroyeth the body, and only dislodgeth the soul, but cannot destroy it.

In some things Solomon shews the agreement betwixt our death and theirs, Eccl. 3:19, 20, 21. "That which befalleth the sons of men, befalleth the beasts; even one thing befalleth them: as the one dieth, so dieth the other; all go to one place; all are of the dust, and all turn to dust again." We breathe the same common air they breathe; we feel the same puns of death they feel, our bodies are resolved into the same earth theirs are. Oh! but in this is the difference, The spirit of man goeth upward, and the spirit of a beast goeth downward to the earth. Their spirits go two ways at their dissolution; the one to the earth, and the other to God that gave it; as he speaks, chap. 12:7. Though our dissolution and expiration have some agreement, yet great is the odds in the consequences of death to the one and the other. They have no pleasures nor pains besides those they enjoy or feel now; but so have we, and those eternal, or unspeakable too. The soul of man, like the bird in the shell, is still growing or ripening in sin or grace, till at last the shell breaks by death, and the soul flies away to the piece it is prepared for, and where it must abide for ever. The body, which is but its shell, perisheth; but the soul lives when it is fallen away.

How doth this consideration expose and aggravate the folly and madness of this sensual world, who herd themselves with beasts though they have souls so near akin to angels! The princes and nobles of the world abhor to associate themselves with mechanics in their shops, or take a place among the sottish rabble upon an ale-bench; they know and keep their distance and decorum, as still carrying with them a sense of honour, and abhorring to act beneath it: But we equalise our high and noble souls in the manner of life with the beasts that perish. Our tables differ little from the crib At which they feed; or our houses from the stalls and stable, in which they lie down to rest, in respect of any divine worship or heavenly communication that is to be heard there. Happy had it been for such men (if so they live and die) that their souls had been of no higher extraction, or larger capacity, or longer duration than that of a beast: for then, as their comforts, so also their miseries had ended at death. And such they will one day wish they had been.

A separate soul immediately capable of blessedness.

Inf. 2. The soul of man being substance, and not depending in its being on the body or any other fellow-creature, There can be no reason, on the souls account, why its blessedness should be delayed: till the resurrection of the body.

It is a great mistake (and it is well it is so) that the soul is capable only of social glory, or a blessedness in partnership with the body: and that it can neither exert its own powers, nor enjoy its own happiness in the absence of the body. The opinion of a sleeping interval took its rise from this error (as it is usual for one mistake to beget another;) they conceived the soul to be so dependent on the body, at least in all its operations, that when death rends it from the body, it must needs be left in a swoon or sleep, unable to exert its proper powers, or enjoy that felicity which we ascribe to it in its state of separation.

But certainly its substantial nature being considered, it will be found, that what perfection soever the body receives from the soul, and how necessary soever its dependence upon it is, the soul receives not its perfection from the body, nor doth it necessarily depend on it, in its principal operations; but it can live and act out of a body as well as in it. Yea, I doubt not but it enjoys itself in a much more sweet and perfect liberty than ever it did, or could, while it was clogged and fettered with a body of flesh. "Doubtless, (says Tertullian) when it is separated, and as it were strained by death, it comes out of darkness into its own pure, perfect light, and quickly finds itself a substantial being, able to act freely in that light." Before the eyes of the dead body are closed, I doubt not, but the believing soul, with open eyes, beholdeth the face of Jesus Christ, Luke 23:43. Phil. 1:23. But this will also be further spoken to hereafter.

Inf. 3. The souls of men being created immediately out of no thing, and not seminally traduced; it follows, That all souls by nature are of equal value and dignity; one soul is not more excellent, honourable, or precious than another: but all by nature equally precious.

The soul of the poorest beggar that cries at the door for a crust, is, in its own nature, of equal dignity and value with the soul of the most glorious monarch that sits upon the throne. And this appears to be so,

1. Because all souls flow out of one and the same fountain, viz. the creating power of God. They were not made of better or worse, finer or coarser matter, but "ek me onton", out of nothing at all. The same Almighty Power was put forth to the forming of one, as of

another. All souls are mine, says he that created them, Ezek. 18:4. the soul of the child as well as of the father, the soul of the beggar as well as of the king; those that had no pre-existent matter, but received their beings from the same efficient cause, must needs be equal in their original nature and value. The bodies of men, which are formed out of matter, do greatly differ from one another; some are moulded (as we say) e meliori luto, out of better and finer clay; some are more exact, elegant, vigorous, and beautiful than others; but souls, having no matter of which they consist, are not so differenced.

2. All souls are created with a capacity of enjoying the infinite and blessed God. They need no other powers, faculties, or capacities than they are by nature endued with (if these be sanctified and devoted to God) to make them equally happy and blessed with them that are now before the throne of God in heaven, and with unspeakable delight and joy behold his blessed face. We pass through the fields, and take up an egg which lies under a clod, and see nothing in it but a little squalid matter; yea, but in that egg is seminally and potentially contained such a melodious lark as, it may be, at the same time we see mounting heavenward, and singing delicious notes above. So it is here, these poor despised souls, that are now lodged in crazy, despicable bodies on the earth, have, in their natures, a capacity for the same employments and enjoyments with those in heaven. They have no higher original than these have, and these have the same capacity and ability with them. They are beings improveable by grace, to the highest perfections attainable by any creature. If thou be never so mean, base, and despicable a creature in other respects, yet thou hast a soul, which has the same alliance to the Father of spirits, the same capacity to enjoy him in glory, that the most excellent and renowned saints ever had.

3. All souls are rated and valued in God's book, and account, at one and the same price; and therefore by nature are of equal worth and dignity. Under the law, the rich and the poor were to give the same ransom, Exod. 30:15. "The rich shall not give more, and the poor shall not give less than half a shekel." The redemption of souls, by the blood of Christ, costs one and the same price. The poorest and the most despised soul that believes in Jesus, is as much indebted to him for the ransom of his soul, as the greatest and most illustrious person in the world. Moses, Abraham, Paul, &c. did not cost Christ any thing more than poor Lazarus, or the meanest among all the saints did. "The righteousness of Christ is unto all, and upon all that believe, for there is no difference," Rom. 3:22.

But yet we must not understand this parity of human souls universally, or in all respects. Though being of one species or common nature, they are all equal, and those of them that are purchased by the blood of Christ are all purchased at one rate; yet there are divers other respects and considerations, wherein there are remarkable differences betwixt soul and soul. As, (1.) Some souls are much better lodged and accommodated in their bodies than others are, though none dwell at perfect rest and ease. God has lodged some souls in strong, vigorous, comely bodies; others in feeble, crazy, deformed, and uncomfortable ones. The historian says of Galba, Anima Galae male habitat; the soul of Galba dwelt in an ill body. And a much better man than Galba was as ill accommodated. John wishes in behalf of his beloved Gaius, that his body might but prosper as his soul did, Epistle iii. ver. 2. Timothy had his often infirmities. Indeed the world is full of instances and examples of this kind. If some souls had the advantages of such bodies as others have, who make little or very bad use of them; oh, what service would they do for God! (2.) There is a remarkable difference also betwixt soul, and soul, in respect of natural gifts and abilities of mind. Some have great advantages above others in this respect. The natural spirits and organs of the body being more brisk and apt, the soul is more vegete, vigorous, and able to exert itself in its functions and operations. How clear, nimble, and firm, are the apprehensions, fancies, and memories of some souls beyond others! What a prodigy of memory, fancy, end judgement, was father Paul the Venetian! and Suarez, of whom Strada says, "Such was the strength of his parts, that he had all St. Augustine's works (the most copious and various of all the fathers) as it were by heart, so that I have seen him, says he, readily pointing with the finger to any place or page he disputed of." Our Dr. Reynolds excelled this way, to the astonishment of all that knew him, so that he was a living library, a third university. But above all, the character given by Vives of Budaeus is amazing, That there was nothing written in Greek or Latin, which he had not turned over and examined; that both languages were alike to him, speaking either with more facility than he did the French, his mother tongue; and all by the penetrating force of his own natural parts, without a tutor; so that the France never brought forth a man of sharper wit, more piercing judgement, exact diligence, and greater learning, nor, in his time, Italy itself. Foelix et foecundum ingenium, quiod in se uo invenit, et doctorem, et discipulum! A happy and fruitful life, which in itself found both a master and a scholar! And yet Pasquier relates what is much more admirable of a young man, who came to Paris, in the 20th year of his age, and in the year 1445, shewed himself so excellent and exact in all the arts, sciences, and languages, that if a man of an ordinary good wit, and sound constitution, should live an hundred years, and during that time study incessantly, without eating, drinking, sleeping, or any recreation, he could hardly attain to that perfection. (3.) And yet a far greater difference is made between one soul and another, by the sanctifying work of the Spirit of God. This makes yet a greater disparity; for it alters and new-moulds the frame and temper of the soul, and restores the lost image of God to it; by reason whereof the righteous is truly said to be "more excellent than his neighbour," Prov. 12:26. This ennobles the soul, and stamps the highest dignity and glory upon it, that it is capable of in this world. It is true, it has naturally all excellency and perpetuity in it above other beings; as cedar has not only a beauty and fragrancy, but a soundness and durability far beyond other trees of the wood: but when it comes under the sanctification of the Spirit, then it is as cedar over-laid with gold. (4.) Lastly, a wonderful difference will be made betwixt one soul and another, by the judgement of God in the great day. Some will be blessed, and others cursed souls, Matt. 25:46. some received into glory, others shut out into everlasting misery; Matt. 8:11, 15. "Many shall come from the East, and West, and shall sit down with Abraham, and Isaac, and Jacob, in the kingdom of Heaven; but the children of the kingdom shall be cast out into outer darkness, there shall be weeping and gnashing of teeth." And that which will be the sting and aggravation of the difference which will then be made, will be this parity and equality in the nature and capacity of every soul; by reason whereof they that perish will find they were as naturally capable of blessedness, as those that enjoy it; and that it was their own inexcusable negligence and obstinacy that were there their ruin.

Inf. 4. If God be the immediate Creator, and former of the soul of man, Then sin must needs involve the most unnatural evil in it, as it is an horrid violation of the very law Of nature. No title can be so full, so absolute, as that which creation gives. How clear is this in the light of reason? If God created my soul, then my soul had once no being at all: that it had still remained nothing, had not the pleasure of its Creator chosen and called it into the being it has, out of the millions of mere possible beings: for as there are millions of possible beings, which yet are nothing; so there are millions of possible beings, which never shall be at all. So that since the pleasure and power of God were the only fountain of my being, he must needs be the rightful owner of it. What can be more his own, than that whose very being flowed merely from him, and which had never been at all, had he not called it out of nothing?

And seeing the same pleasure of God, which gave it a being, gave it also a reasonable being, capable of and fitted for moral government, by laws which other inferior natures are incapable of; it must needs follow that he is the supreme Governor, as well as the rightful owner of this soul.

Moreover, it is plain that he who gave my soul its being, and such a being, gave it also all the good it ever had, has, or shall have: and that it neither is, nor has any thing but what is purely from him: and therefore he must needs be my most bountiful benefactor, as well as absolute Owner, and supreme Governor. There is not a soul which he has created but stands bound to him, in all these ties and titles. Now for such a creature to turn rebelliously upon its absolute Owner, whose only, and wholly it is; upon its supreme Governor, to whom it owes entire and absolute obedience; upon its bountiful Benefactor, from whom it has received all, and every mercy it ever had, or has; to violate his laws, slight his sovereignty, despise his goodness, contemn his threatenings, pierce his very heart with grief, darken the glory of all his attributes, confederate with Satan his malicious enemy; and strike, as far as a creature can strike, at his very being (for in a sense, Omne peccatum est Deicidium, every sin strikes at the life and very existence of God): Blush, O heavens, at this, and be ye horribly afraid! O cursed sin, the evil of all evils, which no epithet can match; no name worse than its own can be invented, sinful sin. This is as if some venomous branch should drop poison upon the root that bears it. Love and gratitude to benefactors, is an indelible principle engraven by nature upon the hearts of all men. It teacheth children to love and honour their parents, who yet are but mere instruments of their being. O how just must their perdition be, who casting off the very bonds of nature, turn again with enmity against that God, in whom they both live, and move, and have their being! O think, and think again, on what a holy man once said; What a sad charge will this be against many a man at the great day, when God shall say, Hadst thou been made a dog, I never had had so much dishonour as I have had? It is pity God should not have honour from the meanest creature that ever he made, from every pile of grass in the field, or stone in the street; much more that he should not have glory from a soul more precious and excellent than all the other works of his hands. Surely it is better for us, our souls had still remained only in the number of possible beings, and had never had an actual existence in the second rank of beings, but a very little lower than the angels; than that we should be still dishonouring God by them. O that he should be put to levy his glory from us passively; that it should be with us as it was with Nebuchadnezzar, from whom God had more glory when he was driven out amongst the beasts of the field, than when he sat on the throne. In like manner, his glory will rise passively from us, when driven out among devils, and not actively and voluntarily, as from the saints.

Infer. 5. If God create and inspire the reasonable soul immediately, this should instruct and incite all Christian parents to pray earnestly for their children, not only when they are born into the world, but when they are at first conceived in the womb.

It is of great concernment both to us and our children, not only to receive them from the womb, with bodies perfectly and comely fashioned; but also with such souls inspired into them, whereby they may glorify God to all eternity. It is natural to parents to desire to have their children full and perfect in all their bodily members; and it would be a grievous affliction to see them come into the world defective, monstrous, and misshapen births; should a leg, an arm, an eye be wanting, such a defect would make their lives miserable, and the parents uncomfortable. But how few are concerned with what soul they are born into the world? "Good God, (says Musculus,) how few shall we find, who are equally solicitous to have such children as may live piously and honestly, as they are to leave them inheritances upon which they may live splendidly and bravely?" It pleaseth us to see our own image stamped upon their bodies; but, O! how few pray, even while they are in the womb, that their souls may, in due time, bear the image of the heavenly, and not animate and use the members of their bodies, as weapons of unrighteousness against the God that formed them?

Certainly, except they be quickened with such souls, as may in this world be united with Christ, better had it been for them that they had perished in the womb, while they were pure embryo's and had never come into the number and account of men and women; for such embryo's go for nothing in the world, having only rudiments and rough draughts of bodies, never animated and informed by a reasonable soul, Job 3:11, 12. But as soon as such a soul enters into them, though for never so little a time, it entails eternity upon them. We also know that as soon as ever God breathes, or infuses their souls into them, sin presently enters, and death by sin, and that by us, as the instruments of conveying it to them: which should have the efficacy of a mighty argument with us to lay our prayers and tears for mercy in the very foundation of that union.

Think on this particularly, you that are mothers of children, when you find the fruit of the womb quickened within you, that you then bear a creature within you of more value than all this visible world; a creature, upon whom, from that very moment, an eternity of happiness or misery is entailed; and therefore it concerns you to travail as in pain for their souls, before you feel the sorrows and pangs of travail for their bodies. O what a pity is it, that a part of yourselves should eternally perish! that so rare and excellent a creature as that you bear, should be cast away for ever, for want of a new creation super added to that it has already! O let your cries and prayers for them anticipate your kisses and embraces of them. If you be faithful and successful herein, then happy is the womb that bears them; if not, happy had it been for them, that the knees had prevented them, and the breasts they have sucked. O! ye cannot begin your suits for mercy too early for them, nor continue them too long, though your prayers measure all the time betwixt their conception and their death.

Inf. 6. Moreover, if God has created our souls vital substances to animate and act those bodies, How indispensably necessary is it that such a principle of spiritual life do quicken and govern that soul which quickens and governs our bodies and all the members of them? Otherwise, though in a natural sense, we have living souls, yet they are dead while they live.

The apostle, in 1 Cor. 15:45, 46. compares the animal life we live, by the union of our souls and bodies, with the spiritual life we live, by the union of our souls with Jesus Christ. And so it is written, (viz. in my text "The first man Adam was made a living soul, the last Adam was made a quickening Spirit." He opposes the animal to the spiritual life, and the two Adams, from whom they come; and shews, in both respects, the excellency of the spiritual above the animal life, not in point of priority, for that which is natural is before that which is spiritual, (and it must be so, because the natural soul is the recipient subject of the Spirit's quickening and sanctifying operations;) but in point of dignity and real excellency. To how little purpose, or rather to what a dismal and miserable purpose are we made living souls, except the Lord from heaven by His quickening power, make us spiritual and holy souls? The natural soul rules and uses the body as an artificer doth his tools: and except the Lord renew it by grace, Satan will rule that which rules thee, and so all thy members will be instruments of iniquity to fight against God. "The actions performed by our bodies, are justly reputed and reckoned by God to the soul," because the soul is the spring of all its motions, the fountain of its life and operations. What it doth by the body, its instrument, is as if it were done immediately by itself; for without the soul it can do nothing.

Inf. 7. Moreover, from the immaterial and spiritual nature of the soul, we are informed, That communion with God, and the enjoyment of him, are the true and proper intentions and purposes for which the soul of man as created.

Such a nature as this is not fitted to live upon gross, material, and perishing things as the body doth. The food of every creature is agreeable to its nature; one cannot subsist upon that which another doth: as we see among the several sorts of animals, what is food to one, is none to another. In the same plant is found a root which is food for swine, a stalk which is food for sheep, a flower which feeds the bee, a seed on which the bird lives: the sheep cannot live upon the root, as the swine do; nor the bird upon the flower as the bee doth: but every one feeds upon the different parts of the plant which are agreeable to its nature. So it is here, our bodies being of an earthly, material nature, can live upon things earthly and material, as most agreeable to them; they can relish and suck out the sweetness of these things; but the soul can find nothing in them suitable to its nature and appetite; it must have spiritual food, or perish. It were therefore too brutish and unworthy of a man that understood the nature of his own soul to cheer it up with the stores of earthly provision made for it, as he did, Luke 22:20. "I will say to my soul, Soul, thou hast much goods laid up for many years, take thine ease, eat, drink, and be merry." Alas! the soul can no more eat, drink, and be merry with carnal things, than the body can with spiritual and immaterial things: it cannot feed upon bread that perisheth, it can relish no more the best and daintiest fair of an earthly growth, than the white of an egg: but bring it to a reconciled God in Christ, to the covenant of grace, and the sweet promises of the gospel: set before it the joys, comforts, and earnests of the Spirit; and if it be a sanctified renewed soul, it can make a rich feast upon these. These make it a feast of fat things, full of marrow, as it is expressed, Isa.

FLAVEL

25:6. Spiritual things are proper food for spiritual and immaterial souls.

Inf. 8. The spiritual nature of the soul farther informs us, That no acceptable service can be performed to God, except the soul be employed and engaged therein.

The body has its part and share in God's worship as well as the soul; but its part is inconsiderable, in comparison, Prov. 23:26. "My son give me thy heart;" i.e. thy soul, thy spirit. The holy and religious acts of the soul are suitable to the nature of the object of worship: John 4:24. "God is a Spirit, and they that worship him, must worship him in spirit and in truth. Spirits only can have communion with that great Spirit. They were made spirits for that very end, that they might be capable of converse with the Father of spirits, "They that worship him must worship him in spirit and in truth;" that is, with inward love, fear, delight, and desires of soul, that is, to worship him in our spirits; and in truth, i.e. according to the rule of his word which prescribes our duty. Spirit respects the inward power; truth the outward form. The former strikes at hypocrisy, the latter at superstition and idolatry: the one opposes the inventions of our heads; the other the looseness and formality of our hearts.

No doubt but the service of the body is due to God, and expected by him: for both the souls and bodies of his people are bought with a price, and therefore he expects we glorify him with our souls and bodies which are his: but the service of the body is not accepted of him otherwise than it is animated and enlivened by an obedient soul, and both sprinkled with the blood of Christ. Separate from these, bodily exercise profits nothing, 1 Tim. 4:8. What pleasure can God take in the fruits and evidences of men's hypocrisy? Ezek. 33:31.

Holy Paul appeals to God in this matter; Rom. 1:9. "God is my witness (says he) whom I serve with my spirit;- q.d. I serve God in my spirit, and he knows that I do so. I dare appeal to him who searches my heart, that it is not idle and unconcerned in his service. The Lord humble us, the best of us, for our careless, dead, gadding, and vain spirits, even when we are engaged in his solemn services. O that we were once so spiritual, to follow every excursion from his service with a groan, and retract every wandering thought with a deep sigh! Alas, a cold and wandering spirit in duty is the disease of most men, and the very temper and constitution of unsanctified ones. It is a weighty and excellent expression of the Jews, in their Euchologium or prayer-book,

"Where withal shall I come before his face, unless it be with my spirit? For man has nothing more precious to present to God than his soul." Indeed it is the best man has: thy heart is thy totum posse: it is all that thou art able to present to him. If thou cast thy soul into thy duty, thou dost as the poor widow did, cast in all that thou hast: and in such an offering the great God takes more pleasure than in all the external, costly, pompous ceremonies, adorned temples, and external devotions in the world. It is a remarkable and astonishing expression of his own in this case, Isa. 66:1,2. "Thus says the Lord, The heaven is my throne, and the earth is my footstool: Where is the house that ye built me? and where is the place of my rest? For all these things have mine hands made, and all these things have been, says the Lord; but unto this man will I look, even to him that is poor, and of a contrite spirit, and trembleth at my word;" q.d. Think not to please me with magnificent temples, and adorned altars; if I had pleasure in such things, heaven is a more glorious throne than any you can build me; and yet I have more delight in a poor contrite spirit, that trembles with an holy awe and reverence at my word, than I have in heaven or earth, or all the works of my hands in either. Oh! if there had been more trembling at his word, there had not been such trembling as now there is, under fears of the loss and removal of it. Some can superstitiously reverence and kiss the sacred dust of the sanctuary, as they call it, and express a great deal of zeal for the externals of religion, but little consider how small the interest of these things is in religion, and how little God looks at, or regards them.

Inf. 9. How much are the spirits of men sunk by sin, below the dignity and excellency of their nature?

Our souls are spirits by nature, yet have they naturally no delight in things spiritual: they decline that which is homogeneal and suitable to spirits, and relish nothing but what is carnal and unsuitable to them. How are its affections inverted and misplaced by sin! That noble, spiritual, heaven-born creature the soul, whose element and centre God alone should be, is now fallen into a deep oblivion both of God and itself, and wholly spends its strength in the pursuit of sensual and earthly enjoyments, and becomes a mere drudge and slave to the body. Carnal things now measure out and govern its delights and hopes, its fears and sorrows. O! how unseemly is it to behold such a high-born spirit lacqueying up and down the world in the service of the perishing flesh. "Their heart (says the prophet) goeth after their covetousness, Ezek. 33:31. as a servant at the beck or nod of his master.

O how many are there to be found in every place who melt down the precious affections and strength of their souls, in sensitive brutish pleasures and delights? Jam. 5:6. "Ye have lived in pleasures upon earth," as the fish in the waters, or rather as the eel in the mud; never once lifting up a thought or desire to the spiritual and eternal pleasures that are at God's right hand.

Our creation did not set us so low; we are made capable of better and higher things.

God did not inspire such a noble, excellent, spiritual soul unto us, merely to salt our bodies, or carry them up and down this world for a few years, to gaze at the vanities of it. It was a great saying of an Heathen, I am greater, and born to greater things, "than that I should be a slave to my body." We have a spirit about us, that might better understand its original, and know it is not so base a being, as its daily employments speak it to be. The Lord raise our apprehensions to a due value of the dignity of our own souls, that we may turn from these sordid employments with a generous disdain, and set our affections on what is agreeable to, and worthy of an high born spirit.

Inf. 10. Is the soul of man a vital, spiritual, and immortal substance? Then it is no wonder, that we find the resentments and impressions of the world to come, naturally engraven upon the souls of men all the world over. These impressions and sentiments of another life after this, do as naturally and necessarily spring out of an immortal nature, as branches spring out of the body of a tree, or feathers out of the body of a bird. So fairly and firmly are the characters and impressions of the life to come sealed upon the immortal spirits of all men, that no man can offer violence to this truth, but he must also do violence to his own soul, and unman himself by the denial of it. Who feels not a cheeriness to spring from his absolving, and an horror from his accusing conscience? neither of which could arise from any other principle than this. We are beings conscious to ourselves of a future state, and that our souls do not vanish when our breath doth: that we cease not to be when we cease to breathe.

And this is common to the most barbarous and savage Heathens: "They shew (says the apostle) the work of the law written in their hearts, their consciences also bearing them witness, and their thoughts in the meantime accusing, or else excusing one another." By the work of the law, understand the sum and substance of the ten commandments, comprising the duties to be done, and the sins to be avoided. This work of the law is said to be written upon the hearts of the Gentiles, who had no external written law; upon their hearts it was written, though many of them gave themselves over to all uncleanness; and they shewed or gave evidence and proof, that there was such a law written upon their hearts. They shewed it two ways: (1.) Some of them shewed it in their temperance, righteousness, and moral honesty, wherein they excelled many of us, who have far greater advantages and obligations. (2.) In the efficacy of their consciences; which, as it cleared and comforted them for things well done: so it witnessed against them, yea, judged and condemned them for things ill done. And these evidences of a law written on the heart are to be found, wherever men are to be found. Their ignorance and barbarity cannot stifle these sentiments and impressions of a future state, and a just tribunal to which all must come. And the universality of it plainly evinces, that it springs not out of education, but the very nature of an immortal soul.

Let none say that these universal impressions are but the effects of an universal tradition, which have been, time out of mind, spread among the nations of the world: for as no such universal tradition can be proved; so if it could, the very propension that is found in the minds of all men living, to embrace and close with the proposals of a life to come, will evince the agreeableness of them to the nature of an immortal soul. Yea, the natural closing of the soul with these proposals, will amount to an evidence of the reality and existence of those invisible things. For as the natural senses and their organs prove that there are colours, sounds, savours, and juices; as well as, or rather because there are eyes, ears, &c. naturally fitted to close with; and receive them; so it is here, if the soul naturally looks beyond the line of time, to things eternal, and cannot bound and confine its thoughts and expectations within the too narrow limits of present things, surely there is such a future state, as well as souls made apprehensive of it, and propense to close with the discoveries thereof. So natural are the notions of future state to the souls of men, that those who have set themselves designedly to banish them, and struggled hard to suppress them, as things irksome and grievous to them, giving interruption to their sensual lusts and pleasures; yet still these apprehensions have returned upon them, and gotten a just victory over all their objections and prejudices; they follow them wheresoever they go; they can no more flee from them than from themselves; whereby they evidence themselves to be natural and indelible things.

Inf. 11. Has God endued the soul of man with understanding, will, and affections, whereby it is made capable of knowing, loving, and enjoying God? It is then no wonder to find the malice and envy of Satan engaged against man more than any other creature, and against the soul of man, rather than any thing else in man.

It grates that Spirit of envy to see the soul of man adorning and preparing, by sanctification, to fill that place in glory from which he fell irrecoverably. It cut Haman to the very heart, to see the honour that was done to Mordecai; much more doth it grate and gall Satan, to see what Jesus Christ has purchased and designed for the souls of men. Other creatures being naturally incapable of this happiness, do therefore escape his fury; but men shall be sure to feel it as far as he can reach them; 1 Pet. 5:8. "Your adversary the devil goeth about like a roaring lion, seeking whom he may devour." He walks to and fro; that speaks his diligence; seeking whom he may devour; that speaks his design; his restlessness in doing mischief is all the rest and relief he has in his own torments. It is a mark of pure and perfect malice to endeavour to destroy, though he knows he shall never be successful in his attempts. We read of many bodies possessed by him; but he never takes up his quarters in the body of any but with design to do mischief to the soul. No room but the best in the house will satisfy him; no blood so sweet to him as soul-blood. If he raise prosecution against the bodies of men, it is to destroy their souls: holiness is what he hates, and happiness is the object of his envy: the soul being the subject of both, is therefore pursued by him as his prey.

Inf. 12. Upon the consideration both of its excellent nature and divine original, it follows, That the corruption and defacing of such an excellent creature by sin deserves to be lamented and greatly bewailed; and the recovery of it by sanctification to he studied and diligently prosecuted, as the great concern of all men.

What a beautiful and blessed creature was the soul of man at first, while it stood in its integrity? His mind was bright, clear, and apprehensive of the law and will of God; his will cheerfully complied therewith; his sensitive appetite and inferior powers stood in an obedient subordination. God made man upright, Eccles. 7:29. "yashar" straight, and equal, bending to neither extreme. The law of God was fairly engraven upon the table of his heart. Principles of holiness and righteousness were inlaid in the frame of his mind, fitting him for an exact and punctual discharge of his duties both to God and man. This was the soundness of his constitution, the healthful temper of his inner-man, whereby it became the very region of light, peace, purity, and pleasure. For think how serene, lightsome, and placid the state of the soul must be, in which there was no obliquity, not a jar with the Divine will; but joy and peace continually transfused through all its faculties!

But sin has defaced its beauty, razed out the Divine image which was its glory, and stamped the image of Satan upon it; turned all its noble powers and faculties against the author and fountain of its being. Surely if all the posterity of Adam, from the beginning to the end of the world, should do nothing else but weep and sigh for the sin and misery of the fall, it could not be sufficiently deplored: Other sins, like single bullets, kill particular persons, but Adam's sin, like a chain-shot, mowed down all mankind at once. It murdered himself actually, and his posterity virtually, and Christ himself occasionally. Oh! what a black train of doleful consequents attend this sin! It has darkened the bright eye of the soul's understanding, 1 Cor. 2:14. made its complying and obedient will stubborn and rebellious, Job 5:40. rendered his tender heart obdurate and senseless, Ezek. 36:26. filled its serene and peaceful conscience with guilt and terror, Tit. 1:15. The considerations of these things is very humbling, and should cause those that glory in their high and illustrious descents, to wrap their silver star in cypress, and cover all their glory with a mourning veil. But this is but one part of their duty.

How should this consideration provoke us to apply ourselves with the most serious diligence to recover our lost beauty and dignity in the way of sanctification! This is the great and most proper use of the fall, as Musculus excellently speaks; — ut gratiam Christi eo subnixiusa ambimus, to inflame our desires the more vehemently after grace.

Sanctification restores the beauty of the soul, which sin defaced, Eph. 4:25. Col. 3:10. Yea, it restores it with this advantage, that it shall never be lost again; holiness is the beauty of God impressed upon the soul, and the impression is everlasting. Other beauty is but a fading flower: Time will plough deep furrows upon the fairest faces, but this will be fresh to eternity.

FLAVEL

All moral virtues, homilitical qualities, which adorn and beautify nature, and make it attractive and lovely in the eyes of men, are but separable accidents, which death discinds and crops off like a sweet flower from the stalk, Job 4:21. "Does not their excellency that is in them go away?" But sanctification is inseparable, and will ascend with the soul into heaven. Oh! that God would set the glass of the law before us, that we may see what defiled souls we have by nature, that we might come by faith to Jesus Christ, who cometh to us by water and by blood, 1 John 5:6.

Inf. 13. To conclude. Upon the consideration of the whole matter before us, if this excellent creature, the soul, receive both its being and excellencies from God; Then he that formed it must needs have the full, and only right to possess and use it, and is therefore most injuriously kept out of the possession of it by unsanctified and disobedient persons.

The soul of man is a building of God; He has laid out the treasures of his wisdom, power, and goodness in this noble structure, he built it for an habitation for himself to dwell in; and indeed such noble rooms as the understanding, will, and affections, are too good for any other to inhabit. But sin has set open the gates of this hallowed temple, and let in the abomination which maketh desolate. All the doors of the soul are barred and chained up against Christ, by ignorance and infidelity; he seeks for admission into the soul which he made, but findeth none. A forcible entry he will not make; but expects when the will shall bring him the keys of the soul, as to its rightful owner. So he expresseth himself to us in Lev. 3:20. "Behold I stand at the door and knock: If any man hear my voice, and open the door, I will come in to him, and sup with him, and he with me." His standing at the door, denotes his earnest desire and patient waiting, in the use of all those means that are introductive of Jesus Christ into the souls of men. His knocking signifies the various essays he makes by his ordinances and providences externally, and the convictions and persuasions of his Spirit, and the consciences of sinners internally: Every call of the word, and every conviction of conscience is a call, a knock from heaven, at the door of the soul, for the admission of Christ into it. By the soul's hearing his voice, and opening the door, understand its approbation, and consent to the motion and offer of God. By Christ's coming in, is meant his uniting that soul unto himself that opens to him. And as his coming in denotes union, so his supping with the soul, and the soul with him denotes his sweet communion; imperfect here, complete and full in heaven.

O the admirable condescension of God to poor sinners! The God that formed you with a word, and can as easily ruin you with a frown, yet waits at the gates of your souls for admission into them. There be many souls within the sound of this complaint, that have kept God out of his own right all their days. They have shut out Jesus Christ, and delivered up their souls to Satan: If he but knock by a slight temptation, the door is presently opened; but Jesus Christ may wait in vain upon them from sabbath to sabbath, and from year to year: But the longest day of his patience has an end; and there is a refusal of grace, after which no more tenders of mercy shall ever be made.

What say you, Souls? Will you at last open the door to Jesus Christ, or will you still exclude him? If you will open to him, he will not come empty-handed, he will bring a feast with him, such a feast as you never tasted any thing like it in your lives: But, if you will not open to him, then I call heaven and earth to witness against you this day, that you have once barred the doors of your soul against him, whose pleasure and power gave them their very beings; against him who is their sovereign Lord, and rightful Owner. And consequently this act of yours must stop your mouths, and deprive you of all pleas and apologies when you shall knock here after at the door of mercy, and God shall ever shut it up against you, according to his just, but dreadful threatenings, Matt. 7:22. Prov. 1:24,25. And thus much of the divine original, and excellent nature of the soul of man.

Having taken a view of this excellent creature, the soul, in opening the former proposition: we come next to the consideration of its union with the body, in this second proposition.

Doct. 2: That the souls and bodies of men are knit together, by the feeble band of the breath in their nostrils.

"There is (says a learned man) no greater mystery in nature, than the union betwixt the soul and body; that a mind and spirit should be so tied and linked with a clod of clay, that while that remains in a due temper, it cannot by any art or power free itself. It can by an act of the will move an hand, or a foot, or the whole body, but cannot move from it one inch. If it move hither, or thither, or by a leap upward do ascend a little, the body still follows it: it cannot shake or throw it off. We cannot take ourselves out; by any allowable means we cannot; nor by any at all (that are at least, within mere human power) as long as the temperament lasts. While that remains, we cannot go; if that fail, we cannot stay; though there be so many open avenues, (could we suppose any material bounds to hem in, or exclude a spirit) we cannot go out or in at pleasure. A wonderful thing! and I wonder we no more wonder at our own make and frames in this respect. - What, so much a-kin are a mind and a piece of earth, a clod and a thought, that they should be thus affixed to one another?"

My design here is to shew by what ligament, tie, or bond, it has pleased the great and wise Creator, to affix and link these so different parts of man together: And this Moses in the text tells us, is no other but the breath of his nostrils.

The breath and soul of man are two distinct things. His breath is not his soul, nor his soul his breath, but the nexus or bond that couples and unites his soul and body in a personal union. The body has no life in itself, but its life results from its union with the soul, James 2:26. This union is maintained by the breath of our nostrils, which upon that account is here called the breath of life. Breath is an act of life, proceeding from the soul's union with its body, and ending with the dissolution of it. Life is continued by its respiration, and ended by its expiration. While we live, and while breath is in our bodies, are terms synonymous.

That little quantity of air, which we thus breathe in and out at our nostrils, is more to us, than all the three regions of air, which fill up the vast space between earth and heaven. It is, in a sense, our life.

For this use and office of respiration, the lungs were formed and placed where they are, not without the most wise counsel and direction of God. They are that organ in the body, which, by the help of that artery celled arteria trachea, leading to them as channel, for the passage of air from the mouth and nostrils, the air is transmitted to, and ventilated by them for the refreshment of the heart, and exhaling the fumes thereof.

The heart has continual need of such a vent and refreshment; and therefore the lungs, like a pair of bellows, must be kept continually going. No longer than breath is going, is the heart a dying; that which stops the one, suffocates the other.

And here we may, with admiration, contemplate the wonders by which our lives are continued. These lungs are the most frail and tender part of the body, and kept in continual motion and agitation; yet are made serviceable for seventy or eighty years together, which is the wonder of Providence. Were a piece of brass, or iron or steel kept in continual and incessant use, it would not endure half the time. In a word, the heart, that noble part of the body, is the shop wherein the spirits are laboured and prepared, which therefore is in continual motion and heat; and so needs continual cooling and refreshing. We can live no longer than it labours, it can labour no longer than it is refreshed and cooled by respiration.

God has therefore prepared the lungs for this service; which being of a thin, porous, and spungy substance, can easily be dilated and contracted. By dilating themselves, they attract and suck in the air into themselves; first duly to prepare and temper it, and then communicate it to the heart for its refreshment; which being quickly heated in the heart, is again breathed out by the lungs, by contracting themselves again. This double motion of inspiration and expiration, we call respiration; and this respiration is the bond that holds our souls and bodies together.

And indeed, this is but a feeble bond, a very slender and weak thread, which holds our souls and bodies in union. What more volatile, evanid and uncertain than a puff of breath? The nostrils are the outer door of the body, our breath is continually in our nostrils; and how soon may that depart, which is day and night at the door, as if it were still taking leave of us? Our breath is always going; and what is still going, will be gone at last. How small a difference is there betwixt respiration and expiration, a breathing and a breathless lump of clay? Breath cannot continue long, and life cannot stay a moment behind it, Psal. 104:29. "Thou takest away their breath, they die, and return to their dusts. Life is breath given, and death is breath taken away. The breath of man is like a written sentence, in which there are divers commas, or short pauses, after which speedily follows a full stop, and there is an end of it.

Some conceive Solomon points at the continual motion of the lungs, in that figurative and elegant description of the death of man, Eccles. 12:6. "Or ever the silver cord be loosed, or the golden bowl be broken, or the pitcher be broken at the fountain, or the wheel be broken at the cistern." The double motion of the lungs he seems here to compare to the double motion of the buckets in a well; the turn of the wheel sends one down, and draws the other up. But as we use to say proverbially, The bucket or pitcher that goes so often to the cistern or well, is broken at last: So we must say of these, they will fail at last. One sitting by the bed-side of a dying person, sighed out this compassionate expression, Ah! quid sumus? His sick friend hearing it, replied Pulvis umbra, fumus, dust, a shadow, a puff of wind. The wind without us is fickle and inconstant to a proverb, and so is that within us too. Many grudge at the shortness of life; but considering the feebleness of this bond, we have more cause to wonder at the slowness of death. For let us seriously consider the frailty of our breath, on a double account, viz.

    1. In respect of our breathing instruments.
    2. Or of breath-stopping accidents.

    1. Great is the frailty of our breathing instruments. What is flesh but weakness? even the most solid and substantial; it is as fading grass, Isa. 40:6 "But our lungs are the most lax, spungy, and tender of all flesh, if that which is so airy, light, and spumous, deserves the name of flesh." And as it is the most frail of all flesh, so it is in continual motion, labouring night and day without rest or intermission; and that which wants alternate rest cannot be durable. We see motion wears out the wheels of the watch, though made of brass; but our strength (as Job speaks) is not the strength of stones; nor our bones (the most solid, much less our lungs the most frail and feeble parts) of brass. Beside,

    2. There are a multitude of breath-stopping accidents, which may, and daily do bent the last breath out of men's nostrils, before any decay of nature cause it to expire.

    Many mortal diseases are incident to these frail and tender parts. Phtysics, internations, ulcers, easily bar the passage of our breath there; yea, and slighter accidents, which immediately touch not that part, are sufficient to stop our breath, and dislodge our souls. A fly, a gnat, the stone of a raisin, a crumb of bread, have often done it. There is not a pore in the body but is a door large enough to let in death, nor a creature so despicably small but is strong enough (if God commission it) to serve a writ of ejection upon the soul: The multitudes of diseases are so many lighted candles put to this slender thread of our breath, besides the infinite diversity of external accidents by which multitudes daily perish. So that there are as great and astonishing wonders in our preservation as in our creation.

Inf. 1. How admirable then is the mystery of providence in the daily continuation of the breath of our nostrils?

That our breath is yet in our nostrils, is only from hence, that he who breathed it into them at first is our life, and the length of our days, as it is Deut. 30:20. It is because our breath is in his hand, Dan. 5:23. not in our own, nor in our enemies' hands. Till he take it away, none shall be able to do it; Psal. 104:29. "Thou takest away their breath, they die, and return to their dust.

It is neither food nor physic, but God in and by them, that "holdeth our souls in life", Psal. 66:9. We hang every moment of our life over the grave and the gulph of eternity, by this slender thread of our breath: But it cannot break, how feeble so ever it be, till the time appointed be fully come. If it be not extinguished and suffocated; as others daily are, it is because he puts none of these diseases upon us, as it is Exod. 15:26. or if he do, yet he is Jehovah Rophe, the Lord that healeth us, as it follows in that text.

We live in the midst of cruel enemies, yea, "among them that breathe out cruelty," as the psalmist complaineth, Psal. 27:12. Such breath would quickly suffocate ours, did not he, in whose hand ours is, wonderfully prevent it. O what cause have we to employ and spend that breath in his praise, who works so many daily wonders to secure it!

Inf. 2. Is it but a puff of feeble breath which holds our souls and bodies in union? Then every man is deeply concerned to make all haste, to take all possible care and pains to secure a better and, more durable habitation for his soul in heaven, while yet it sojourns in this frail tabernacle of the body.

The time is at hand, when all these comely and active bodies shall be so many breathless carcases, no more capable of any use or service for our souls than the seats you sit on, or the dead bodies that lie under your feet. Your breath is yet in your nostrils, and all the means and seasons of salvation will expire with it; and then it will be as impossible for the best minister in the world to help your souls, as for the ablest Physician to recover your bodies. As physic comes too late for the one, so counsels and persuasions for the other.

FLAVEL

Three things are worth thinking on this matter.

1. That you are not without the hopes and possibilities of salvation, while the breath of life is in your nostrils. A mercy, (how lightly soever you value it) that would ravish with joy those miserable souls that have already shot the gulf of eternity, and turn the shrieks and groans of the damned unto joyful shouts and acclamations of praise. Poor wretch, consider what thou readest; that thy soul is not yet in Christ, is thy greatest misery; but that yet it may be in Christ, is an unspeakable mercy; though thy salvation be not yet secured, yet what a mercy is it that it is not desperate?

2. When this uncertain breath is once expired, the last hope of every unregenerate person is gone for ever: It is as impossible to recover hope as it is to recover your departed breath, or recall the day that is past. When the breath is gone, the compositum is dissolved; we cease to be what we now are, and our life is as water spilt on the ground which shall not be gathered up till the resurrection. Our life is carried like a precious liquor in a brittle glass, which death breaks to pieces. The spirit is immediately presented to God, and fixed in its unalterable state, Heb. 9:27. All means of salvation now cease for ever; no ambassadors of peace are sent to the dead; no more calls or strivings of the spirit: no more space for repentance. O! what an inconceivable weight has God hanged on a puff of breath!

3. And since matters stand thus, it is to be admired what shift men make to quiet themselves in so dangerous a state as most souls live in; quiet and unconcerned, and yet but one puff of breath betwixt them and hell! O the stupefying and besotting nature of sin! O the efficacy and power of spiritual delusions! Are our lives such a throng and hurry of business that we have no time to go alone and think where we are, and where we shortly must be? What shall I say? If bodily concerns be so weighty, and the matters of eternity such trifles; if meat and drink, and trade and children be such great things, and Christ, and the soul, and heaven, hell, and the world to come such little things in your eyes, you will not be long in that opinion I dare assure you.

Inf. 3. Is the tie so weak betwixt our souls and bodies? How close and near then do all our souls confine and border upon eternity?

There is no more than a puff of breath, a blast of wind betwixt this world and that to come. A very short step betwixt time and eternity: There is a breath which will be our last breath: respiration must, and will terminate in expiration: The dead are the inhabitants, and the living are borderers upon the invisible world. This consideration deserves a dwelling place in the hearts of all men whether,

    I. Regenerate, or
    II. Unregenerate.

    I. Regenerate souls should ponder this with pleasure. O it is transporting to think how small a matter is betwixt them and their complete salvation. No sooner is your breath gone, but the full desire of your hearts is come; every breath you draw, draws you a degree nearer to your perfect happiness; Rom. 13:11. "Now is your salvation nearer than when ye believed;" therefore, both your cheerfulness and diligence should be greater than when you were in the infancy of your faith. You have run through a considerable part of your Christian course and race, and are now come nearer the goal and prize of eternal life. O despond not, loiter not now at last, who were so fervent and zealous in the beginning.

    It is transporting to think how near you approach the region of light and joy. O that you would distinctly consider,

    1. Where you lately were.
    2. Where now you are.
    3. Where shortly you shall be.

    1. You that are now so near salvation, were lately very near unto damnation, there was but a puff of breath betwixt you and hell. How many nights did you sleep securely in the state of nature and unregeneracy? How quietly did you rest upon the brink of hell, not once imagining the danger you were in? Had any of those sicknesses you then suffered, been suffered by God, like a candle, to burn asunder this slender thread of life which was so near them, you had been as miserable, and as hopeless as those that now are roaring in the lowest hell. I have heard of one that rid over a dangerous bridge in the night, who, upon the review of that place, fell into a swoon, when he was sensible of that danger which the darkness of the night hid from him. O reader, shall not an escape from hell affect thee as much as such an escape would do?

    2. It is no less marvellous to consider where you now are; you that were afar off are now made nigh, Eph. 2:13. You that were not beloved, are now beloved, Rom. 9:25. You were in the state of death

and condemnation. You are now passed from death to life by your free justification, 1 John 3:14. Your union with Christ has set you free from condemnation, Rom. 8:1. Die you must though Christ be in you, but there is no hazard or hurt in your death. The stopping of your breath can put no stop to your happiness, it will hasten not hinder it: If the pale horse come to you, heaven, not hell, will now follow him; your sins are pardoned, the covenant of your salvation sealed. Death is disarmed of its fatal sting; and what then should hinder you from a like triumph, even upon your death-bed with that, 1 Cor. 15:55. "O death, where is thy sting? O grave, where is thy victory?"

3. And yet you have more room for joy, while you consider where you must, and shall shortly be. You are now in Christ, but in a few days you shall be with Christ as well as in him; it is well now, but it will be better ere long. Your sin is now fully pardoned, but not fully purged out of your souls. Your persons are freed from guilt, but your hearts are not either freed from filth or grief: But in a little time you shall be absolutely and eternally freed from both. Your present condition is in heaven, compared with your former, and your future state will be in heaven indeed, compared with your present. "The path of the just is as the shining light, which shineth more and more unto the perfect day," Prov. 4:18.

II. But on the other side, what meditation can be more startling and amazing to all the unregenerate and christless world? Ponder it, thou poor christless and unsanctified soul. Get thee out of the noise and clamour of this world, which make such a continual din in thine ears, and consider how thou hangest over the mouth of hell itself, by the feeble thread which is spun every moment out of thy nostrils; as soon as that gives way, thou art gone for ever. What shift do you make to quiet your fears, and eat, drink, and labour with any pleasure? It is storied of Dionysius the tyrant, that when Damocles would have flattered him into a conceit of the perfection of his happiness, as he was an absolute sovereign prince, and could do what he pleased with others, as his vassals; Dionysius, to confute his fancy, caused him to be placed at a table richly furnished, and attended with the most curious music, but just over his head hanged a sharp and heavy sword by one single hair; which when Damocles saw, no meat would go down with him, but he earnestly begged for a discharge from that place. This is the lively emblem of thy condition, thou unregenerate man.

There are three things in thy state, sadly opposed to the former state last described.

1. The state you were born in, was bad.
2. The state you are now in, is worse.
3. The state you shall shortly be in, if you thus continue, will be unspeakably the worst of all.

I. The state you were born in was a sad state; you were born in sin, Psal. 51:5, and under wrath, Eph. 2:3. The womb of nature cast you forth into this world, defiled and condemned creatures.

2. The state you are in now is much worse than that you were born in; for what have you been doing ever since you were born, but treasuring up wrath against the day of wrath? Rom. 2:5. For every sand of time which runs out of the glass of God's patience towards you, a drop of wrath has been running into the vials of his indignation against you. Oh! what a treasure of sin and wrath then, is laid up in so many years as you have lived in sin! Every sin committed, every mercy abused, every call of God neglected and slighted, adds still more and more to this treasure.

3. It will be much worse shortly than it is now, except preventing, renewing grace step in betwixt you and that wrath, into which you are hastening so fast. It is sad to be under the sentence of condemnation, but unspeakably worse to be under the execution of that sentence. To be a christless man is lamentable, but to be a hopeless man is more lamentable. For though you be now without Christ, yet while the breath of life is in your nostrils, you are not absolutely without hope. But when once that breath is gone, all the world cannot save or help you. Your last breath and your last hope expire together. Though you be under God's damning sentence, yet that sentence, through the riches of forbearance, is not executed; but as soon as you die, all that wrath which hanged over your heads so many years, in the black clouds of God's threatenings, will pour down in a furious storm upon you, which will never break up while God is God. O! think, and think again, and let your thoughts think close to this sad and solemn subject, there is but a breath betwixt you and hell.

Inf. 4. Doth God maintain your life by breath? Let not that breath destroy your life, which God gave to preserve it.

No man can live without breath; and yet some might live longer than they do, if their breath were better employed. "Some men's throats have been cut by their own tongues," as the Arabian proverb intimates. Life and death (says Solomon) are in the power of the tongue. Critics observe, that a word and a plague grow upon the same root in the Hebrew tongue. It is certain, that some men's breath has been baneful poison both to themselves and others. It was a word that cut off the life of Adonijah, 1 Kings 2:23. and thousands since his day have died upon the point of the same weapon. It is therefore wholesome advice that is given us, Psal. 34:12. "What man is he that desireth life, and loveth many days, that he may see good; keep thy tongue from evil, and thy lips from speaking guile."

And the more evil the times are, the stricter guard we should keep upon our lips. "It is an evil time, the prudent will keep silence," Amos 5:18. When wicked men watch to make a man an offender for a word, as it is, Isa 29:20,21. it behoves us to be upon our watch, that we offend not with our lips. It is good to keep, what is not safe to trust. David was a deaf and dumb man, when in the company of wicked men, Psal. 38:13. he thought silence to be his prudence. It is better they should call you fools, than find you so.

Inf. 5. Employ not that breath to the dishonour of God, which was first given, and is still graciously maintained by him for your comfort and good.

It were better you had never breathed at all, than to spend your breath in profane oaths, or foolish and idle chat, whereby at once, you wound the name of God, draw guilt upon your own souls, and help on the ruin of others. That is a startling text, Matt. 12:36. "But I say unto you, that every idle word that men shall speak, they shall give an account thereof in the day of judgement."

To give an account, is here, by a metalepsis of the antecedent for the consequent, put for punishment in hell-fire, without an intervening change of heart, and sprinkling of the blood of Jesus.

And there is more evil in this abuse of our breath, than we can easily discern, especially upon two accounts; (1.) Because it is a sin most frequently committed, and seldom repented of. The intercourse betwixt the heart and tongue is quick, and the sense of the evil as easily and quickly passeth away. (2.) Because the poisonous and malignant influence thereof abides and continues long after: our words may do mischief to others, not only a long time after they are spoken, but a long time after the tongue that spake them is turned to dust. How many years may a foolish or filthy word, a profane scoff, an atheistical expression, stick in the minds of them that heard them, after the speaker's death. A word spoken is physically transient, and passed away with the breath that delivered it; but morally, it is permanent: For as to its moral efficacy, no more is required, but its objective existence in the minds and thoughts of them that once heard it: And, upon that very ground, Suarez argues for a general judgement, after men at death have passed their particular judgement; because (says he) long after that, abundance of good and evil will be done in this world by the dead, in the persons of others that over-live them. For look, as it was said of Abel, that being dead, he yet speaketh; so it may be said of Julian, Porphyry, and multitudes of scoffing Atheists, that being dead, they yet speak. Oh, therefore, get a sanctified heart to season your breath, that it may minister grace to the hearers.

Inf. 6. Let your breath promote the spiritual life of others, as well as maintain the natural life in yourselves.

Though the maintaining of your natural life be one end why God gave you breath, yet it is not the only, or principal end of it. Your breath must be food to others, as well as life to you; Prov. 10:21. "The lips of the righteous feed many." It will be comfortable to resign that breath to God at death, which has been instrumental to his glory in this life. It was no low encomium Christ gave of the church, when he said, Cant. 4:11. "Thy lips, O my spouse, drop as the honeycomb, honey and milk are under thy tongue." Sweet, wholesome, and pleasant words drop from her lips. They drop (says Christ) as the honey-comb. Some drops ever and anon fall actually, and others hang, at the same time, prepared and ready to fall. Such a prepared and habitual disposition should every Christian continually have. Your words may stick upon men's hearts to their edification and salvation, when you are in your graves. Your tongues may now sow that precious seed, which may spring up to the praise of God, though you may not live to reap the comfort of it in this world, John 4:36,37. It is a rich expense of your breath, to bring but one soul to God, and yet God has used the breath of one, as his instrument, to save, edify, and comfort the souls of thousands, Prov. 11:30. "The fruit of the righteous is a tree of life, and he that winneth souls is wise." The good Lord make all his people wise in this.

Surely, whether we consider the invaluable worth and preciousness of souls, the benefits you have had from the breath of others yourselves, the innate property of grace, wherever it is, to diffuse and communicate itself, how short a time you have to breathe, and how comfortable it will be, when you breathe your last, to remember how it has been employed for God; all this should open your lips to counsel, reprove, and comfort others, as often as opportunity is ministered.

Did Christ spend his blood for our souls, and shall not we spend our breath for them! Oh! let our lips dispense knowledge. If you will not spend your breath for God, how will you spend your blood for him? If you will not speak for him, I doubt you will not die for him. Away with a sullen reservedness, away with unprofitable chat; all subjects of discourse are not fit for a Christian's lips. It is a grave admonition God once gave his people by the pen of a faithful minister. "You may rue (says he) the opportunities you have lost. Here lay a poor wretch with one foot in hell; would he not have started back, if he had had light to discover his danger? Well, you are now together, something you must say; the same breath would serve for a compassionate admonition, as for a complacent impertinency, which will redound to the advantage of neither. You part, the man dies, and in the midst of hell cries out against you, one word of yours might have saved me; you had me in your reach, you might have told me my danger; you forebore, I hardened; the Lord reward your negligence."

Inf. 7. If breath be the tie betwixt soul and body, How are we concerned to improve, and draw forth the precious breath of ministers and Christians, while it is yet in their nostrils.

The breath of many ministers is judicially stopt already, their breath serves to little other use than to preserve their own lives; it will be stops ere long by death, and then those excellent treasures of gifts and graces, wherewith they are richly furnished, will be gone out of your reach, never to be further useful to your souls. You should do by them therefore (as one aptly speaks) as scholars do by some choice book they have borrowed, and must return in a few days to the owner: They diligently read it night and day, and carefully transcribe the most useful and excellent notes they can find in it, that they may make them their own, when the book is called out of their hands.

But alas! we rather divert, than draw forth these excellencies that are in them. You may yet converse with them, and greatly benefit yourselves by these converses; but (as one speaks) by the stream of your impertinent talk, that season is neglected. Afterwards You see your lack of knowledge, but then the instrument is removed. How must it gall an awakened Jew, to think what discourse he had with Jesus Christ! Is it lawful to give tribute to Caesar? Why do not thy disciples fast? Oh! had I nothing else to enquire of the Lord Jesus? Would it not have been here pertinent to have asked, What shall I do to be saved? But he is gone, and I dead in my sins. How many persons have we sent away, that had a word of wisdom in their hearts, having only learnt from them what a clock it is, what weather, or what news; forgetting to ask our own hearts, what is all this to us? and to enquire of them things worthy of their wisdom and experience. "Wherefore is there a price in the hand of a fool, seeing he has no heart to it?" Prov. 17:16. The expense of one minute's breath in season, may, if God concur with it, be to you the ground of breathing forth praises to God to all eternity.

Inf. 8. Are soul and body tacked together by so frail a thing as a puff of breath? How vain and groundless then are all those pleasures men take in their carnal projects and designs in this world?

We lay the plot and design of our future earthly felicity in our own thoughts; we mould and contrive a design for a long and pleasant life. The model for raising an estate is already formed in our thoughts, and we have not patience to defer our pleasure till the accomplishment of it, but presently draw a train of pleasing consequents from this chimera, and our thoughts can stoop to nothing less than sitting down all the remainder of our days in the very lap of delight and pleasure; forgetting that our breath is all the while in our nostrils, and may expire the next moment: and if it do, the structure of all our expectations and projects comes to nothing in the same moment. "His breath goeth forth, he returneth to his dust: And in that very day his thoughts perish," Psal. 146:4. The whole frame of his thoughts fall instantly abroad, by drawing out this one pin, his breath. It is good with all our earthly designs to mingle the serious thoughts of the dominion of providence, and our own frailty; James 4:15. "If the Lord will, and we live."

It is become a common observation, that as soon as men have accomplished their earthly designs, and begin to hug and bless themselves in their own acquisitions, a sudden and unexpected period is put to their lives and pleasures, as you may see Luke 12:19,20; Dan. 4:30.

Oh then drive moderately; you will be at the end of all these things sooner than you imagine. We need not victual a ship to cross the channel, as they do that are bound to the Indies. "What is your life? It is even a vapour which appeareth for a little while, and then vanisheth away," James 4:14. In one moment the projects of many years are overturned for ever.

Inf. 9. Is it but a puff of breath that holds men in life? The build not too much hope and confidence upon any man.

Build not too high upon so feeble a foundation. "Cease ye from man (says the prophet) whose breath is ill his nostrils; for wherein is he to be accounted of?? Isa. 2:22. There are two things that should deter us from dependence upon any man, viz. his falseness and his frailty. Grace in a great measure may cure the first, but not the last. The best of men must die, as well as the worst, Rom. 8:10. it is a vanity therefore to rely upon any man. It was the saying of a philosopher when he heard how merchants lost great estates at sea in a moment,— Non amo felicitatem e funibus pendentem; - I love not that happiness (says he) which hangs upon a rope. But all the happiness of many men hangs upon a far weaker thing than a rope, even the perishing breath of a creature.

Let not parents raise their hopes too high, or lean too hard upon their children. Say not of thy child, as Lamech did of Noah, "This son shall comfort us," Gen. 5:29. The world is full of the lamentings and bitter cries of disappointed parents. Let not the wife depend too much on her husband, as if her earthly comforts were secured in him against all danger. God is often provoked to stop our friend's breath, that thereby he may stop our way to sin, 1 Tim. 5:5. The trust and dependence of a soul are too weighty to be hanged upon such a weak and rotten pin as the breath of a creature.

Inf. 10. To conclude; if this frail breath be all that differenceth the living from the dead, then fear not man whose breath is in his nostrils. There is as little ground for our fear of man, as there is for our trust in man. As death, in a moment, can make the best man useless, and put him out of a capacity to do us any good; so it can in a moment make the worst man harmless, and put him out of capacity to do us any injury. Indeed, if the breath of our enemies were in their power, and ours at their mercy, there would be just cause to tremble at them; but they are neither masters of their own, nor ours. "Who art thou that thou shouldest be afraid of a man that shall die?" said God to Jacob, Isa

51:12. The breath of the mightiest is no better secured than of the meanest, nor never in more danger to be stopt than when they breathe out threatenings against the upright.

Julian's breath was soon stopt after he threatened to root out the Galileans. Queen Mary resigned her breath at the very time when she had filled the prisons with many of Christ's sheep, and designed them for the slaughter. Read Isa 17:12. and see what mush rooms we are afraid of. The best way to continue your relations and friends to your comfort, is to give God and not them your dependence; and the best way to secure yourselves against the rage of enemies, is to give God your fear, and not them. And thus much of the nature of the soul, and its tie with the body.

Rev. 6:9,10,11

And when he had opened the fifth seal, I saw under the altar the souls of them that were slain for the word of God, and for the testimony which they held:

And they cried with a loud voice, saying, How long, O Lord, holy and true, dost thou not judge and avenge our blood on them that dwell on the earth?

And white robes were given unto every one of them; and it was said unto them, that they should rest yet for a little season, until their fellowservants also and their brethren, that should be killed as they were, should be fulfilled.

Having from the former text, spoken of the nature of the soul, and the tie betwixt it and the body, I shall, from this scripture, evince the immortality of the soul, which is a chief part of its excellency and glory; and in this scripture it has a firm foundation.

This book of the Revelation completes and seals up the whole sacred canon, Rev. 22:18. It also comprehends all the great and signal events of providence, relating either to the Christian church, or to its antichristian enemies in the several periods of time, to the end of the world; chap. 1:19. All which the Spirit of God discovers to us in the opening of the seven seals, the sounding of the seven trumpets, and the pouring out of the seven vials.

The first five seals express the state of the church under the bloody, persecuting, Heathen emperors.

SEAL 1

The first seal opened, ver. 2. gives the church a very encouraging and comfortable prospect of the victories, successes, and triumphs of Christ, notwithstanding the rage, subtlety, and power of all its enemies. He shall ride on conquering, and to conquer, and his arrows shall be sharp in the hearts of his enemies, whereby the people shall fall under him. And this cheering prospect was no more than was needful: For,

SEAL 2

The second seal opened, ver. 3, 4. represents the first bloody persecution of the church under Nero, whom Tertullian calls Dedicator damnationis nostrae: he that first condemned Christians to the slaughter. And the persecution under him is set forth by the type of a red horse, and a great sword in the hand of him that rode thereon. His cruelty is by Paul compared to the mouth of a lion, 2 Tim. 4:17. Paul, Peter, Bartholomeus, Barnabas, Mark, are all said to die by his cruel hand; and so fierce was his rage against the Christians, that at that time, as Eusebius says, "a man might see cities lie full of dead bodies, the old and young, men and women, cast out naked, without any reverence of persons or sex, in the open street." And when the day failed. Christians (says Tacitus) were burnt in the night, instead of torches, to give them light in the streets.

SEAL 3

The third seal opened, ver. 5, 6. sets forth the calamities which should befal the church by famine; yet not so much a literal as a figurative famine, as a grave and learned commentator expounds it, like that mentioned, Amos 8:11,12. which fell out under Maximinus and Trajan; the former directing the persecution, especially against ministers, in which many bright lamps were extinguished; the latter expressly condemning all Christian meetings and assemblies by a law. The type by which this persecution was set forth, is a black horse. A gloomy and dismal day it was indeed to the poor saints, when they eat the bread of their souls, as it were, by weight; for he that sat on him had a pair of balances in his hand. Then did John hear this sad voice, "A measure of wheat for a penny, and three measures of barley for a penny." The quantity was but the ordinary allowance to keep a man alive for a day, and a Roman penny was the ordinary wages given for a day's work to a labourer. The meaning is, that in those days, all the spiritual food men should get to keep their souls alive from day to day, with all their travail and labour, should be but sufficient for that end.

FLAVEL

SEAL 4

The fourth seal opened, ver. 7, 8. represents a much more sad and doleful state of the church; for under it are found all the former sufferings, with some new kinds of trouble super-added. Under this seal, Death rides upon the pale horse, and Hell, or the Grave, follows him. It is conceived to point at the persecution under Dioclesian, when the church was mowed down as a meadow.

SEAL 5

The fifth seal is opened in my text, under which the Lord Jesus represents to his servant John, the state and condition of those precious souls which had been torn and separated from their bodies, by the bloody hands of tyrants, for his name's sake, under all the former persecutions. The design whereof is, to support and encourage all that are to come in the same bloody path. I saw under the altar, &c. In which we have an account,

1. Of what John saw.
2. Of what he heard.

1. We have an account of what he saw; "I saw the souls of them that were slain for the word of God, and for the testimony which they held."

Souls, in this place, are not put for blood, or the dead carcasses of the saints who were slain, as some have groundlessly imagined; but are to be understood properly and strictly, for those spiritual and immortal substances, which once had a vital union with their bodies, but were now separated from them by a violent death; yet still retained a love and inclination to them, even in a state of separation; and therefore here brought in complaining of the shedding of their blood, and destruction of their bodies.

These souls (even of all that died for Christ, from Abel to that time, John saw, that is, in spirit; for these immaterial substances are not perceptible by the gross external senses. He had the privilege and favour of a spiritual representation of them, being therein extraordinarily assisted, as Paul was when his soul was wrapt into the third heaven, and heard things unutterable, 2 Cor. 12:2. God gave him a transient visible representation of those holy souls, and that under the altar: he means not any material altar, as that at Jerusalem was; but as the holy place figured heaven, so the altar figured Jesus Christ, Heb. 13:10.

A TREATISE OF THE SOUL OF MAN

And most aptly Christ is represented to John in this figure, and souls of the martyrs at the foot or basis of this altar; thereby to inform us,

(1.) That however men look upon the death of those persons, and though they kill their names by slanders, as well as their persons by the sword, yet, in God's account, they die as sacrifices, and their blood is no other than a drink-offering poured out to God, which He highly prizeth, and graciously accepteth. Suitable whereunto Paul's expression is, Phil. 2:17.

(2.) That the value and acceptation their death and blood-shed have with God, are through Christ, and upon his account; for it is the altar which sanctifieth the gift, Matt. 13:19. And,

(3.) It informs us, that these holy souls, now in a state of separation from their bodies, were very near to Jesus Christ in heaven. They lay, as it were, at his foot.

Once more, they are here described to us by the cause of their sufferings and death in this world; and that was, "for the word of God, and for the testimony which they held;" i.e. They died in defence of the truths, or will of God revealed in his word, against the corruptions, oppositions, and innovations of men. As one of the Martyrs, that held up the Bible at the stake, said, This is it that brought me hither. They died not as malefactors, but as witnesses. They gave a threefold testimony to the truth; a lip testimony, a life testimony, and a blood testimony; while the hypocrite gives but one, and many Christians but two. Thus we have an account what John saw.

2. Next he tells us what he heard: and that was,

(1.) A vehement cry from those souls to God.

(2.) A gracious answer from God to them.

(1.) The cry which they uttered with a loud voice was this, "How long, O Lord, holy and true, dost thou not avenge our blood on them that dwell on the earth?" A cry like that from the blood of Abel. Yet let it be remembered,

1. This cry does not imply these holy souls to be in a restless state, or to want true satisfaction and repose out of the body; nor yet,

2. That they carried with them to heaven any malevolent or revengeful disposition: that which is principally signified by this cry,

is their vehement desire after the abolition of the kingdom of Satan, and the completion and consummation of Christ's kingdom in this world; that those his enemies, which oppose his kingdom, by slaying his saints, may be made his footstool: which is the same thing Christ waits for in glory, Heb. 10:13.

(2.) Here we find God's gracious answer to the cry of these souls, in which he speaks satisfaction to them two ways:

1. By somewhat given them for present.
2. By somewhat promised them hereafter.

1. That which he gives them in hand; "White robes were given to every one of them." It is generally agreed, that these white robes given them, denote heavenly glory, the same which is promised to all sincere and faithful ones, who preserve themselves pure from the corruptions and defilements of the world, Lev. 3:4. And it is as much as if God should have said to them, Although the time be not come to satisfy your desires, in the final ruin and overthrow of Satan's tyrannical kingdom in the world, and Christ's consummate conquest of all his enemies, yet it shall be well with you in the mean time: you shall walk with me in white, and enjoy your glory in heaven.

2. And this is not all; but the very things they cry for shall be given them also after a little season; q.d. wait but a little while, till the rest that are to follow, in the same suffering path, be got through the red sea of martyrdom, as you are, and then you shall see the foot of Christ upon the necks of all his enemies, and justice shall fully avenge the precious, innocent blood of all the saints which in all ages has been shed for my sake; from the blood of Abel, to the last that shall ever suffer for righteousness sake in the world. From all which, this conclusion is most fair and obvious.

Doct. That the souls of men perish not with their bodies, but do certainly over-live them, and subsist in a state of separation from them. Matt. 10:28. "Fear not them that kill the body, but are not able to kill the soul."

The bodies of these Martyrs of Jesus were destroyed by divers sorts of torments, but their souls were out of the reach of all these cruel engines; they were in safety under the altar, and in glory clothed with their white robes, when their bodies they lately inhabited on earth, were turned to ashes, or torn to pieces by wild beasts.

The point I am to discourse from this scripture, is the immortality of the soul. For the better understanding whereof, let it be noted that there is a twofold immortality.

I. Simple, and absolute in its own nature.
II. Derived, dependent, and from the pleasure of God.

In the former sense, God only has immortality, as the apostle speaks, 1 Tim. 6:16. Our souls have it as a gift from him. He that created our souls out of nothing, can, if he please, reduce them to nothing again; but he has bestowed immortality upon them, and produced them in a nature suitable to that his appointment, fitted for an everlasting life. So that though God by his absolute power can, yet he never will annihilate them, but they shall, and must live for ever in endless blessedness or misery; death may destroy these mortal bodies, but it cannot destroy our souls. And the certainty of this assertion is grounded upon these reasons, and will be cleared by these following arguments.

Argument 1

The first argument for proof of the soul's immortality, may be taken from the simplicity, spirituality, and uncompoundedness of its nature; it is a pure, simple, unmixed being. Death is the dissolution of things compounded; where therefore no composition ar mixture is found, no death or dissolution can follow.

Death is the great divider, but it is of things that are divisible. The more simple, pure, and refined any material thing is, by so much the more permanent and durable it is found to be. The nearer it approaches to the nature of spirits, the farther it is removed from the power of death: but that which is not material, or mixed at all, is wholly exempt from the stroke and power of death. It is from the contrarient qualities, and jarring humours, in mixed bodies, that they come under the law and power of dissolution. Matter and mixture, are the doors at which death enters naturally upon the creatures.

But the soul of man is a simple, spiritual, immaterial, and unmixed being, not compounded of matter and form, as other creatures are, but void of matter, and altogether spiritual, as may appear in the vast capacity of its understanding faculty, which cannot be straitened by receiving multitudes of truths into it. It need not empty itself of what it had received before, to make way for more truth; nor doth it find itself clogged or burdened by the greatest multitudes or varieties of truths; but the more it knows, the more it still desires to know. Its capacity and appetite are found to enlarge themselves according to the increase of knowledge. So that to speak, as the matter is, If the knowledge of all arts, sciences, and mysteries of nature, could be gathered into the mind of one man, yet that mind could thirst, and even burn with desire after more knowledge, and find more room for it than it did when it first sipt, and relished the sweetness of truth. Knowledge, as knowledge, never burdens or cloys the mind; but like fire increases and enlarges, as it finds more matter to work upon. Now this could never be, if the soul were a material being. Take the largest vessel, and you shall find the more you pour into it, the less room is still left for more; and when it is fun, you cannot pour in one drop more, except you let out what was in it before. But the soul is no such vessel, it can retain all it had, and be still receptive of more; so that nothing can fill it, and satisfy it, but that which is infinite and perfect.

The natural appetite after food is sometimes sharp and eager, but then there is a stint and measure beyond which it craves not; but the appetite of the mind is more eager and unlimited; it never says till it come to rest in God, it is enough, because the faculty which produceth it, is more active, spiritual, and immaterial. All matter has its limits, bounds, and just measures, beyond which it cannot be extended. But the soul is boundless, and its appetition infinite; it rests not, but in the spiritual and infinite Being, God alone being its adequated object, and able to satisfy its desires; which plainly proves it to be a spiritual, immaterial, and simple being. And being so, two things necessarily follow there from.

1. That it is void of any principle of corruption in itself.
2. That it is not liable to any stroke of death, by any adverse power without itself

1. It cannot be liable to death, from any seeds or principles of corruption within itself, for where there is no composition, there is no dissolution: the spirituality and simplicity of the soul admit of no corruption.

2. Nor is it liable to death by any adverse power without itself; no sword can touch it, no instrument of death can reach it: it is above the reach of all adversaries, Matt. 10:28. "Fear not them that kill the body, but cannot kill the soul." The bounds and limits of creature-power are here fixed by Jesus Christ, beyond which they cannot go. They can wound, torment, and destroy the body, when God permits

them: but the soul is out of their reach; A sword can no more hurt or wound it, than it can wound or hurt the light; and consequently it is, and must needs be of an immortal nature.

Object. But there seems to be a decay upon our souls in our old age, and decays argue and imply corruption, and are so many steps and tendencies towards the death and dissolution thereof. The experience of the whole world shows us how the apprehensions, judgements, wit, and memory of old men fail, even to that degree that they become children again in respect of the abilities of their minds: their souls only serving, as it were, to salt their bodies, and keep them from putrefaction for a few days longer.

Sol. It is a great mistake; there is not the least decay upon the soul; no time makes any change upon the essence of the soul: all the alteration that is made, is upon the organs and instruments of the body, which decay in time, and become unapt and unserviceable to the soul.

The soul, like an expert, skilful musician, is as able as ever it was, but the body, its instrument, is out of tune: and the ablest artist can make no pleasing melody upon an instrument whose strings are broken, or so relaxed that they cannot be screwed up to their due height.

Let Hippocrates, the prince of physicians, decide this matter for us. "The soul (says he) cannot be changed or altered as to its essence, by the access of meat or drink, or any other thing whatsoever; but all the alterations that are made, must be referred either to the spirits with which it mixeth itself, or to the vessels and organs through which it streameth." So that this roves not its corruptibility: and being neither corruptible in itself nor vulnerable by any creature without itself; seeing man cannot, and God will not destroy it, the conclusion is strongly inferred, That therefore it is immortal.

Argument 2

The immortality of the souls of men may be concluded-from the promises of everlasting blessedness, and the threatenings of everlasting miseries, respectively made in the scriptures of truth, to the godly and ungodly after this life; which promises and threatenings had been altogether vain and delusory, if our souls perish with our bodies.

1. God has made many everlasting promises of blessedness, yea, he has established an everlasting covenant betwixt himself and the

souls of the righteous, promising to be their God for ever, and to bestow endless blessedness upon them in the world to come. Such a promise is that, John 8:28. "I give unto them eternal life, and they shall never perish." And John 4:14. "Whosoever drinketh of the water that I shall give him shall never thirst: but the water that I shall give him, shall be in him a well of water springing up into everlasting life." And again, John 11:26. "Whosoever liveth and believeth in me, shall never die." And once more, Rom. 2:7. "To them who by patient continuance in well doing, seek for glory and honour, and immortality, eternal life;" with multitudes more of like nature.

Now if these be no vain and delusory promises, (as to be sure they are not, being the words of a true and faithful God) then those souls to whom they are made, must live for ever; for if the subject of the promises fail, consequently the performance of the promises must fail too. For how shall they be made good, when those to whom they are made, are perished?

Let it not be objected here, That the bodies of believers are concerned in the promises as well as their souls, and yet their bodies perish notwithstanding.

For we say, though their bodies die, yet they shall live again, and enjoy the fruit of the promises in eternal glory; and while their bodies lie in the grave, their souls are with God, enjoying the covenant and blessedness in heaven, Rom. 8:10,11. and so the covenant-bond is not loosed betwixt them and God by death, which it must needs be, in case the soul perish when the body doth. And upon this hypothesis, that argument of Christ is built, Matt. 22:32. proving the resurrection from the covenant God made with Abraham, Isaac, and Jacob; "I am the God of Abraham, and the God of Isaac, and the God of Jacob: God is not the God of the dead, but of the living," q.d. If Abraham, Isaac, and Jacob be perished in soul as well as in body, how then is God their God; what is become of the promise and covenant-relation? for if one correlate fail, the relation necessarily fails with it. If God be their God, then certainly they are in being; "for God is not the God of the dead," i.e. of those that are utterly perished. Therefore it must needs be, that though their bodies be naturally dead, yet their souls still live; and their bodies must live again at the resurrection by virtue of the same promise.

On the contrary, many threatenings of eternal misery, after this life, are found in the scriptures of truth, against ungodly end wicked persons. Such is that in 2 Thess. 1:7,8,9. "The Lord Jesus shall be revealed from heaven in flaming fire, to render vengeance on them that know not God, and that obey not the gospel of our Lord Jesus Christ, who shall be punished with everlasting destruction, from the presence of the Lord, and the glory of His power." And speaking of the torments of the damned; Christ thus expresseth the misery of such wretched souls in hell, Mark 9:44. "Where their worm dieth not, and the fire is not quenched." But how shall the wicked be punished with everlasting destruction, if their souls have not an everlasting duration? or how can it be said, Their worm (viz. the remorse and anguish of their conscience) dieth not, if their souls die? Punishment can endure no longer than its subject endureth. If the being of the soul cease, its pains and punishments must have an end.

You see then, there are everlasting promises and threatenings to be fulfilled, both upon the godly and ungodly, "He that believeth on the Son has everlasting life, and he that believeth not the Son, shall not see life, but the wrath of God abideth on him, John 3:16. The believer shall never see spiritual death, viz. the separation of his soul from God; and the unbeliever shall never see life, viz. the blessed fruition of God; but the wrath of God shall abide on him. If wrath must abide on him, he must abide also as the wretched subject thereof, which is another argument of the immortality of souls.

Argument 3

The immortality of the soul is a truth asserted and attested by the universal consent of all nations and ages of the world. "We give much (said Seneca) to the presumption of all men," and that justly; for it would be hard to think that an error should obtain the general consent of mankind, or that God would suffer all the world, in all ages of it, to bow down under an universal deception.

This doctrine sticks close to the nature of man; it springs up easily, and without force from his conscience. It has been allowed as an unquestionable thing, not only among Christians who have the oracles of God to teach and confirm this doctrine, but among Heathens also, who had no other light but that of nature to guide them into the knowledge and belief of it. Learned Zanchius cites out of Cicero an excellent passage to this purpose. "In every thing says he, the consent of all nations is to be accounted the law of nature; and therefore, with all good men, it should be instead of a thousand demonstrations; and to resist it, (as he there adds) what is it, but to resist the voice of God?"

and how much more, when, with his consent, the word of God doth also consent? As for the consent of nations, in this point, the learned author last mentioned, has industriously gathered many great and famous testimonies from the ancient Chaldeans, Grecians, Pythagoreans, Stoics, Platonists, &c. which evidently shew they made no doubt of the immortality of their souls. How plain is that of Phocylides? Psuche de athanatos kai ageros zei dia pantos. Speaking of the soul, in opposition to the body, which must be resolved into dust, he says, "But for the soul, that is immortal, and never grows old, but lives for ever." And Tresmegistus, the famous and celebrated Philosopher, gives this account of man, "That he consists of two parts, being mortal in respect of his body, but immortal in respect of his soul, which is the best and principal part." Plato not only asserts the immortality of the souls of men, but disputes for it: and among other arguments, he urges this; "That if it were not so, wicked men would certainly have the advantage of righteous and good men, who, after they have committed all manner of evils, should suffer none." But what speak I of philosophers? the most barbarous nations in the world constantly believe it. The Turks acknowledge it in their Alcoran; and though they grossly mistake the nature of heaven, in fancying it to be a paradise of sensual pleasures, as well as the way thither, by their impostor Mahomet; yet it is plain they believe the soul's immortality, and that it lives in pain or pleasure after this life.

The very savage and illiterate Indians are so fully persuaded of the souls immortality, that wives cast themselves cheerfully into the flames to attend the souls of their husbands; and subjects, to attend the souls of their kings into the other world.

Two things are objected against this argument.

1. That some particular persons have denied this doctrine, as Epicurus, &c. and by argument maintained the contrary.

To which I answer, That though they have done so, yet (1.) This no way shakes the argument from the consent of nations, because some few persons have denied it: we truly say, the earth is spherical, though there be many hills and risings in it. If Democritus put out his own eyes, must we therefore say all the world is blind?

(2.) It is worth thinking on, whether they that have questioned the immortality of the soul, have not rather made it the matter of their option and desire, than of their faith and persuasion. We distinguish

Atheists into three classes, such as are so in practice, in desire, or in judgement; but of the former sorts there may be found multitudes, to one that is so in his settled judgement. If you think it strange that any man should wish his soul to be mortal, Hierocles gives us the reason of it: "A wicked man (says he) is afraid of his Judge; and therefore wishes his soul and body may perish together by death, rather than it should come to God's tribunal."

Object. 2. Nor can the strength of the argument be eluded, by saying, "All this may be but an universal tradition, one nation receiving it from another.

Sol. For as this is neither true in itself, nor possible to be made good; so if it were, it would not invalidate the argument: for if it were not a truth agreeable to the sight of nature, and so easily received by all men upon the proposal of it, it were impossible that all the nations in the world should embrace it so readily, and hold it so tenaciously as they do.

Argument 4

The immortality of the soul may be evinced from the everlasting habits which are subjected, and inherent in it. If these habits abide for ever, certainly so must the souls in which they are planted.

The souls of good men are the good ground, in which the seed of grace is sown by the Spirit, Matt. 13:28. i.e. the subjects in which gracious properties and affections do inhere and dwell, (which is the formal notion of a substance) and these implanted graces are everlasting things. So John 4:14. "It shall be in him a well of water, springing up into everlasting life," i.e. the graces of the Spirit shall be in believers, permanent habits, fixed principles, which shall never decay. And therefore that seed of grace, which is cast into their souls at their regeneration, is in 1 Pet. 1:23. called "incorruptible seed, which liveth and abideth for ever:" and it is incorruptible, not only considered abstractly, in its own simple nature, but concretely, as it is in the sanctified soul, its subject: for it is said, 1 John 3:9. "The seed of God remaineth in him." It abideth for ever in the soul. If then these two things be clear unto us, viz.

1. That the habits of grace be everlasting;

2. That they are inseparable from sanctified souls;

It must needs follow, That the soul, their subject, is so too, an everlasting and immortal soul. And how plainly do both these propositions lie before us in the scriptures? As {or the immortal and indeterminable nature of saving grace, it is plain to him that considers, not only what the forecited scriptures speak about it, calling it incorruptible seed, a well of water springing up into everlasting life; but add to these, what is said of these divine qualities in 2 Pet. 1:4. where they are called the divine nature; and Eph. 4:18. the life of God, noting the perpetuity of these principles in believers, as well as their resemblance of God in holiness, who are endowed with them.

I know it is a great question among divines, An gratia in renatis sit natura et essentia sua interminabilis? Whether these principles of grace in the regenerate be everlasting and interminable in their own nature and essence? For my own part, I think that God only is naturally, essentially, and absolutely interminable and immortal. But these gracious habits, planted by him in the soul, are so by virtue of God's appointment, promise, and covenant. And sure it is, that by reason hereof they are interminate, which is enough for my purpose, if they be not essentially interminable. Though grace be but a creature, and therefore has a posse mori, yet it is a creature begotten by the Word and Spirit of God, which live and abide for ever, and a creature within the promise and covenant of God, by reason whereof it can never actually die.

And then as for the inseparableness of these graces from the souls in whom they are planted, how clear is this from John 2:27. where sanctifying grace is compared to an unction, and this unction is said to abide in them? And 1 John 3:9. it is called the seed of God, which remaineth in the soul. All our natural and moral excellencies and endowments go away when we die; Job 4:21. "Does not their excellency that is in them go away?" Men may outlive their acquired gifts, but not their supernatural graces. These stick by the soul, as Ruth to Naomi, and where it goes they go too: so that when the soul is dislodged by death, all its graces ascend up with it into glory; it carries away all its faith, love, delight in God, all its comfortable experiences, and fruits of communion with God, along with it to heaven. For death is so far from divesting the soul of its graces, that it perfects in a moment all that was defective in them; 1 Cor. 13:10. "When that which is perfect shall come, then that which is in part shall be done away," as the twilight is done away when the sun is up, and at its zenith. So then, grace never dieth, and this never-dying grace is inseparable from its subject; by which it is plain to him that considers, that as graces, so souls, abide for ever.

Object. But this only proves the immortality of regenerate souls.

Sol. It does so. But then consider, as there be gracious habits in the regenerate that never die, so there are vicious habits in the unregenerate that can never be separated from them in the world to come. Hence, John 8:24. they are said to "die in their sins," and Job 20:11. "Their iniquities lie down with them in the dust," and Ezek. 24:13 "They shall never be purged." Remarkable is that place, Rev. 22:11. "Let him that is filthy be filthy still." And if guilt sticks so fast, and sin be so deeply engraven in impenitent souls, they also must remain for ever, to bear the punishment of them.

Argument 5

The immortality of the soul of man may be evinced from the duty of man above all other creatures, (angels only excepted) and his dominion over them all.

In this, the scriptures are clear, that man is the master-piece of all God's other works; Psal. 8:5,6. "For thou hast made him a little lower than the angels, and hast crowned him with glory and honour. Thou hast made him to have dominion over the works of thy hand, thou hast put all things under his feet." Other creatures were made for his service, and he is crowned king over them all. One man is of more worth than all the inferior creatures.

But wherein is his dignity and excellency above all other creatures, if not in respect of the capacity and immortality of his soul? Sure it can be found nowhere else; for as to the body, many of the creatures excel man in the perfections of sense, greatness of strength, agility of members, &c.

Nos aper auditu praecellit, aranea tactu,

Vultur odorat, lynx visu, simia gustu.

And for beauty, Solomon in all his glory was not arrayed like one of the lilies of the field. The beasts and fowls enjoy more pleasure, and live divested of all those cares and cumbers which perplex and wear out the lives of men. It cannot be in respect of bodily perfections and pleasures, that man excels other creatures.

If you say, He excels them all in respect of that noble endowment of reason, which is peculiar to man, and his singular excellency above them all.

It is true, this is his glory: but if you deprive the reasonable soul of immortality, you despoil it of all, both of its glory and comfort, and put the reasonable into a worse condition than the unreasonable and brutish creatures. For if the soul may die with the body, and man perish as the beast, happier is the life of the beast, which is perplexed with no cares nor fears about futurities: our reason serves to little other purpose but to be an engine of torture, a mere rack to our souls.

Certainly, the privilege of man doth not consist in reason, as abstracted from immortality. But in this, it properly consists, that he enjoys not only a reasonable, but also rejoiceth in an immortal soul, which shall over-live the world, and subsist separate from the body, and abide for ever, when all other souls, being but a material form, perish with that matter on which they depend. This is the proper dignity of man, above the beast that perisheth; and to deprive him of immortality, and leave him his reason, is but to leave him a more miserable and wretched creature than any that God has put under his feet. For man is a prospecting creature, and raiseth up to himself vast hopes and fears from the world to come: by these he is restrained from the sensual pleasures, which other creatures freely enjoy, and exercised with ten thousand cares, which they are unacquainted with; and to fail at last of all his hopes and expectations of happiness, in the world to come, is to fall many degrees lower than the lowest creature shall fall; even so much lower as his expectations and hopes had lifted him higher.

Argument 6.

The souls of men must be immortal, or else the desires of immortality are planted in their souls in vain.

That there are desires of immortality found in the hearts of all men, is a truth too evident to be denied or doubted. Man cannot bound and terminate his desires within the narrow limits of this world and the time that measures it. Nothing that can be measured by time is commensurate to the desires of man's soul. No motto better suits it than this, Non est mortale quod opto; I seek for that which will not die, Rom. 2:7. And his great relief against death lies in this, Non omnis mortar: That he shall not totally perish. Yea, we find in all men, even in those that seem to be most drowned and lost in the love and delights of this present world, a natural desire to continue their names and memories to posterity after death. Hence it is said, Psal. 49:11. "Their inward thought is, that their houses shall continue for ever, and their dwelling places to all generations; they call their lands after their own names."

And hence is the desire of children, which is, as one says, nodosa aeternitas, a knotty eternity; when our thread is spun out and cut off, their thread is knit to it; and so we dream of a continued succession in our name and family.

Absalom had no children to continue his memory; to supply which defect, he reared up a pillar, 2 Sam. 18:18. Now it cannot be imagined that God should plant the desire of immortality in those souls, that are incapable of it; nor yet can we give a rational account how these apprehensions of immortality should come into the souls of men, except they themselves be of an immortal nature. For, either these notions and apprehensions of immortality are impressed upon our souls by God, or do naturally spring out of the souls of men. If God impress them, those impressions are made in vain, if there be no such thing as immortality to be enjoyed; and if they spring and rise naturally out of our souls, that is a sufficient evidence of their immortality. For we can no more conceive, and form to ourselves, ideas and notions of immortality, if our souls be mortal, than the brutes which are void of reason, can form to themselves notions and conceptions of rationality. So then the very apprehensions and desires that are found in men's hearts of immortality, do plainly speak them to be of an immortal nature.

Argument 7.

Moreover, the account given us in the scripture of the return of several souls into their own bodies again after death, and real separation from them, shews us that the soul subsists and lives in a separate state after death, and perisheth not by the stroke of death: For if it were annihilated or destroyed by death, the same soul could never be restored again to the same body. A dead body may indeed be acted by an assisting form, which may move and carry it from place to place; so the devil has acted the dead bodies of many; but they cannot be said to live again by their own souls, after a real separation by death, unless those souls over-lived the bodies they forsook at death, and had their abode in another place and state. You have divers unquestionable examples of the soul's return into the body recorded in scripture: As that of the Shunamite's son, 2 Kings 4:18,19,20,32,33,34,35,36,37. That of the ruler's daughter, Matt. 9:18,23,24,25. That of the widow's son, Luke 7:12,13,14,15. And that of Lazarus, John 11:39,40,41,42,43,44, 45. "These are no other but the very same souls, their own souls which returned to them again; which, as Chrysostom well observes, is a great proof of their immortality against them that think the soul is annihilated after the death of the body.

It is true, the scripture gives us no account of any sense or apprehension they retained after their re-union of the place or state they were in during their separation. There seemed to be a perfect amnesia, forgetfulness of all that they saw or felt in the state of separation. And indeed it was necessary it should be so, that our faith might be built rather upon the sure promises of God, than such reports and narratives of them that come to us from the dead, Luke 16:81. And if we believe not the word, neither would we believe if one came from the dead.

Argument 8

Moreover, Eighthly, The supposition of the soul's perishing with the body, is subversive of the Christian religion in the principal doctrines and duties thereof:take away the immortality of the soul, and all religion falls to the ground. I will instance in

1. The doctrines of religion.

2. The duties of religion.

First, It overthrows the main principles and doctrines of the Christian religion, upon which both our faith and comfort is founded and consequently it undoes and ruins us as to all solid hope and true joy. The doctrines or principles it overthrows, are, among many other, such as follow.

1. It nullifies and makes void the great design and end of God's eternal election. The scriptures tells us, That from all eternity God has chosen a certain number in Christ Jesus, to eternal life, and to the means by which they shall attain it, out of his mere good pleasure, and for the praise of his grace. This was (1.) An eternal act of God, Eph. 1:4. Long before we had our being, Rom. 9:11. (2.) This choice of God, or his purpose to save some, is immutable, 2 Tim. 2:19. James 1:17. (3.) This choice he made in Christ, Eph. 1:4. Not that Christ is the cause of God's choosing us: For we were not elected because we

were, but that we might be in Christ. Christ was ordained to be the Medium of the execution of this decree. And all the mercies which were purposed and ordained for us, were to be purchased by the blood of Christ. He was not the cause of the decree, but the purchaser of the mercies decreed for us. (4.) This choice was of a certain number of persons who are all known to God, 2 Tim. 2:19. and all given to Christ in the covenant of redemption, John 17:2,6. So that no elect person can be a reprobate, no reprobate an elect person. (5.) This number was chosen to salvation, 1 Thess. 5:9. No less did God design for them that glory and happiness, and that for ever. (6.) The same persons that are appointed to salvation as the end, are also appointed to sanctification as the way and means by which they shall attain that end, 1 Pet. 1:1,2. 2 Thess. 2:13,14. (7.) The impulsive cause of this choice was the mere good pleasure of his will, 2 Tim. 1:9. Rom. 9:15,16. Eph. 1:9. (8.) The end of all this is the praise of his glorious grace, Eph. 1:5,6. to make a glorious manifestation of the riches of his grace for ever. This is the account the scripture gives us of God's eternal choice.

But if our souls be mortal, and perish with our bodies, all this is a mistake, and we are imposed upon, and our understandings are abused by this doctrine: For to what purpose are all these decrees and contrivances of God from everlasting, if our souls perish with our bodies? Certainly, if it be so, he loses all the thoughts and counsels of his heart about us; and that counsel of his will, which is so much celebrated in the scriptures, and admired by his people, comes to nought. For this is evident to every man's consideration, that if the soul (which is the object about which all those counsels and thoughts of God were employed and laid out) fail in its being, all those thoughts and counsels that have been employed about it, and spent on it, must necessarily fail and come to nothing with it. The thoughts of his heart cannot stand fast, as it is said, Psal. 33:11. if the soul slide, about which they are conversant. In that day the elect soul perisheth, the eternal consultations and purposes of God's heart perish with it. Keckerman tells us, that "Albertus Magnus, with abundance of art, and the study of thirty years, made a vocal statue in the form of a man. It was a rare contrivance, and much admired; the cunning Artist had so framed it, that by wheels and other machines placed within it, it could pronounce words articulately." Aquinas being surprised to hear the statue speak, was affrighted at it, and brake it all to pieces; upon which Albertus told him he had at one blow destroyed the work of thirty years. Such a blow would the death of the soul give to the counsels and thoughts, not of man, but of God, not of thirty years, but from everlasting.

If the souls of men perish at death, either God never did appoint any souls to salvation, as the scriptures testify he did, 1 Thess. 5:9. or else the foundation of God stands not sure, as his word tells us it doth, 2 Tim. 2:19. So then this supposition overturns the eternal decrees and counsels of God, which is the first thing.

2. It overthrows the covenant of redemption betwixt the Father and the Son before this world was made. There was a federal transaction betwixt the Father and the Son from eternity, about our salvation, 2 Tim. 1:9. Zech. 6:13. In that covenant Christ engaged to redeem the elect by his blood; and the Father promised him a reward of those his sufferings, Isa 53:12. Accordingly he has poured out his soul to death for them, finished the work, John 17:4. and is now in heaven, expecting the full reward and fruits of his sufferings, which consist not in his own personal glory, which he there enjoys, but in the completeness and fulness of his mystical body, John 17:24.

But certainly, if our souls perish with our bodies, Christ would be greatly disappointed: Nor can that promise be ever made good to him; Isa. 53:11. "He shall see of the travail of his soul and be satisfied." He has done his work, but where is his reward? See how this supposition strikes at the justice of God, and wounds his faithfulness in his covenant with his Son. He has as much comfort and reward from the travail of his soul, as a mother that is delivered after many sharp pangs of a child that dies almost as soon as born.

5. It overthrows the doctrines of Christ's incarnation, death, resurrection, ascension and intercession in heaven for us. And these are the main pillars both of our faith and comfort. Take away these, and take away our lives too, for these are the springs of all joy and comfort to the people of God, Rom. 8:34.

His incarnation was necessary to capacitate him for his mediatorial work: It was not only a part of it, but such a part, without which he could discharge no other part of it. This was the wonder of men and angels, 1 Tim. 3:16. A God incarnate is the world's wonder; no condescension like this, Phil. 2:6,7.

The death of Christ has the nature and respect of a ransom, or equivalent price laid down to the justice of God for our redemption,

Matt. 20:28. Acts 20:28. It brought our souls from under the curse, and purchased for them everlasting blessedness, Gal. 4:4,5.

The resurrection of Christ from the dead has the nature both of a testimony of his finishing the work of our redemption, and the Father's full satisfaction therein, John 6:10. and of a principle of our resurrection to eternal life, 1 Cor. 15:20.

The ascension of Christ into heaven was in the capacity and relation of a forerunner, Heb. 6:20. It was to prepare places for the redeemed, who were to come after him to glory in their several generations, John 14:2,3.

The intercession of Christ in heaven, is for the security of our purchased inheritance to us, and to prevent any new breaches which might be made by our sins, whereby it might be forfeited, and we divested of it again, 1 John 2:1,2.

All these jointly make up the foundation of our faith and hope of glory: But if our souls perish, or be annihilated at death, our faith, hope, and comforts, are all delusions, vain dreams, which do but amuse our fond imaginations. For,

(1.) It was not worth so great a stoop and abasement of the blessed God, as he submitted to in his incarnation, when he appeared in flesh, yea, in the likeness of sinful flesh, Rom. 8:8. and made himself of no reputation, Phil. 2:7. An act that is, and ever will be admired by men and angels: I say, it was not worth so great a miracle as this, to procure for us the vanishing comfort of a few years, and that short lived comfort no other than a deluding dream, or mocking phantasm: For seeing it consists in hope and expectation from the world to come, as the scriptures every where speak, 1 Thess. 5:8. and 2 Cor. 3:12. Rom. 5:8,4,5. if there be no such enjoyments for us there (as most certainly there are not, if our souls perish) it is but a vanity, a thing of nought, that was the errand upon which the Son of God came from the Father's bosom, to procure for us.

(2.) And for what, think you, was the blood of God upon the cross? What was so vast and inconceivable a treasure expended to purchase? What! the flattering and vain hopes of a few years, of which we may say, as it was said of the Roman consulship, unius anni volaticum gaudium; the fugitive joy of a year: Yea, not only short lived and vain hopes in themselves, but such for the sake whereof we abridge ourselves of the pleasures and desires of the flesh, 1 John 3:3, and submit ourselves to the greatest sufferings in the world, Rom. 8:18. For the hope of Israel am I bound with this chain, &c. Acts 28:20. Was this the purchase of his blood? Was this it for which he sweat, and groaned, and bled, and died? Was that precious blood no more worth than such a trifle as this?

(3.) To what purpose did Christ rise again from the dead? Was it not to be the first-fruits of them that sleep? Did he not rise as the common head of believers, to give us assurance we shall not perish, and be utterly lost in the grave? Col. 1:18. But if our souls perish at death, there can be no resurrection; and if none, then Christ died and rose in vain, we are yet in our sins, and all those absurdities are unavoidable, with which the apostle loads this supposition, 1 Cor. 15:13, &c.

(4.) And to as little purpose was his triumphant ascension into heaven, if we can have no benefit by it. The professed end of his ascension was "to prepare a place for us," John 14:2. But to what purpose are those mansions in the heavens prepared, if the inhabitants for whom they are prepared be utterly lost? And why is he called the forerunner, if there be none to follow him? as surely there are not, if our souls perish with our bodies. Those heavenly mansions, that city prepared by God, must stand void for ever if this be so.

(5.) To conclude; in vain is the intercession of Christ in heaven for us, if this be so. They that shall never come thither, have no business there to be transacted by their advocate for them. So that the whole doctrine of redemption by Christ is utterly subverted by this one supposition.

4. As it subverts the doctrine of redemption by Christ, and all the hopes and comforts we build thereon, so it utterly destroys all the works of the spirit, upon the hearts of believers, and makes them vanish into nothing.

There are divers acts and offices of the Spirit of God about, and upon our souls; I will only single out three, via. his sanctifying, sealing and comforting work: all things of great weight with believers.

(1.) His sanctifying work, whereby he alters the frames and tempers of our souls, 2 Cor. 5:17. "Old things are passed away, behold all things are become new."

The declared and direct end of this work of the Spirit upon our souls, is to attemper and dispose them for heaven, Col. 1:12. For seeing "nothing that is unclean can enter into the holy place," Rev. 21:27. "and without holiness no man shall see the Lord," Heb. 12:14. it is necessary that all those that have this hope in them, should expect to be partakers of their hopes in the way of purification, 1 John 3:3. And this is the ground upon which the people of God do mortify their lusts, and take so much pains with their own hearts, Matt. 18:8. counting it better (as their Lord tells them) "to enter into life halt and maimed, than having two eyes or hands to be cast into hell." But to what purpose is all this self-denial, all these heart searchings, heart humblings, cries, and tears, upon the account of sin, and for an heart suited to the will of God, if there be no such life to be enjoyed with God, after this animal is finished;

Object. If you say there is a present advantage resulting to us in this world, from our abstinence and self-denial; we have the truer and longer enjoyment of our comforts on earth by it; debauchery and licentiousness do not only flatten the appetite, and debase and alloy the comforts of this world, but cut short our lives by the exorbitances and abuses of them.

Solut. Though there be a truth in this worth our acting, yet (1.) morality could have done all this without sanctification; there was no need for the pouring out of the Spirit, for so low an use and purpose as this. (2.) And therefore as the wisdom of God would be censured and impeached, in sending his Spirit for an end which could as well be attained without it; so the veracity of God must needs be affronted by it, who, as you heard before, has declared our salvation to be the end of our sanctification.

(2.) His sealing, witnessing, and assuring work. We have a full account in the scriptures, of these offices and works of the Spirit, and some spiritual sense and feeling of them upon our own hearts, which are two good assurances that there are such things as his bearing witness with our spirit, Rom. 8:16. "his sealing us to the day of redemption," Eph. 4:80. "his earnest given into our hearts," 2 Cor. 1:22. All which acts and works of the Spirit have a direct and clear aspect upon the life to come, and the happiness of our souls in the full enjoyment of God to eternity; for it is to that life we are now sealed, and of the full sum of that glory, that these are the pledges and earnests. But if our souls perish by death, these witnesses of the Spirit are delusions, and his earnests are given us but in jest.

(3.) His comforting work is a sweet fruit and effect sensibly felt and tasted by believers in this world. He is from this office stiled the Comforter, John 16:7. signanter, et eminenter. He so comforts as none other doth, or can. And what is the matter of his comforts, but the blessedness to come, the joys of the coming world? John 16:13. Eye has not seen, &c.

Upon the account of these unseen things, he enableth believers to glory in tribulation, Rom. 5:4. to despise present things, whether the smiles or the frowns of the world, Heb. 11:24. and ver. 26. But if the being of our souls fail at death, these are but the fantastic joys of men in a dream, and the experiences of all God's people are found but so many fond conceits, and gross mistakes.

5. This supposition overthrows the doctrine of the resurrection, which is the consolation of Christians. We believe, according to the scripture, that after death has divorced our souls and bodies for a time, they shall meet again, and be re-united, and that the joy at their re-union will be to all that are in Christ, greater than the sorrows they felt at parting. This seems not incredible to us, whatever natural improbabilities and carnal reasons may be against it, Acts 26:8. and that because the Almighty Power, which is able to subdue all things to himself, undertakes this task, Phil 3:21.

We believe this very same numerical body shall rise again, Job 21:27. by the return of the same soul into it, which now dwelleth in it; and that we shall be the same persons that now we are: the remunerative justice of God requiring it to be so.

We believe the souls of the righteous shall be much better accommodated, and have a more comfortable habitation in their bodies than now they have, 1 Cor. 15:42,43. seeing they shall be made like unto Christ's glorious body, Phil. 3:22. And that then we shall live after the manner of angels, Luke 20:36. without the necessities of this animal life. These are the things we look for according to promise; and this expectation is our great relief against (1.) The fears of death, 1 Cor 15:55. (2.) Against the death of our friends and relations, 1 Thess. 4:14. (3.) Against all the pressures and afflictions of this life, Job 19:25,26,27.

But if the being of our souls fall at death, all hopes and comforts from the resurrection fail with it; for it is not imaginable that the body should rise till it be revived, nor how it should be revived, but by the re-union of the soul with it: and if it be not the same soul that now inhabits it, we cannot be the same persons in the resurrection we are now; and consequently, this supposition subverts not only the doctrine of the resurrection, but,

6. It overthrows also the faith of the judgement to come. For if the soul perish, the body cannot rise; or if it rise by a new-created soul, the person raised is another, and not the same that lived and died in this world; and consequently the rewards and punishments to be bestowed and awarded to all men in that day cannot be just and equal: for we believe, according to the scriptures, that,

(1.) The actions which men perform in this life, are not transient, but are filed to their account in the world to come: Gal. 6:7. here we sow, and there we reap. Actions done in this world are two ways considerable, viz. physically, or morally; in the first consideration they are transient, in the last permanent and everlasting. A word is spoken, or an act done in a moment, but though it be past and gone, and perhaps by us quite forgotten, God registers it in his book, in order to the day of account.

(2.) We believe that God has appointed a day in which all men shall appear before his judgement-seat, to give an account of all they have done in the body, whether it be good or evil, 2 Cor. 5:10.

(3.) And that in order hereunto, the very same Persons shall be restored by the resurrection, and appear before God, the very same bodies and souls, which did good or evil in this world: Shall not the Judge of all the earth do right? Justice requires that the rewards and punishments be then distributed to the same persons that did good or evil in this world: which strongly infers the immortality of the soul, and that it certainly overlives the body, and must come back from the respective places of their abode, to be again united to them, in order to their great account.

By all which you see the clearest proof of the soul's immortality, and how the contrary supposition overthrows our faith, duties, and comforts. Yet notwithstanding all this, how apt are we to suspect this doctrine, and remain still dissatisfied and doubting about it, when all is said? Which comes to pass partly from the subtlety of Satan, who knows he can never persuade men to live the life of beasts, till he first persuade them to think they shall die as the beasts do. (2.) And partly from the influence of sense and reason upon us, whereby we do too much suffer ourselves to be swayed and imposed upon in matters of the greatest moment in religion. For these being proper arbiters and judges in other matters within their sphere, they are arrogant, and we easy enough to admit them to be arbiters also in things that are quite above them. Hence come such plausible objections as these:

Object. 1. The soul seems to vanish and die, when it leaves the body: for when it has struggled as long as it can to keep its possession in the body, and, at last, is forced to depart, we can perceive nothing but a puff of breath, which immediately vanishes into air, and is lost.

Solut. We cannot perceive, therefore it is nothing but what we do and can perceive, viz. a puff of vanishing breath. By this argument the being of the soul in the body is as questionable as after its departure out of the body; for we cannot discern it by sight in the body: yea, by this argument we may as well deny the existence of God and angels as of the soul; for it is a spiritual and invisible being as they are; our gross senses are incapable of discerning spirits, which are immaterial and invisible substances.

Object. 2. But you allow the soul to have a rise and beginning, it is not eternal a parte ante; and it is certain, whatever had a beginning, must have an end.

Solut. Every thing which had a beginning may have an end, and what once was nothing, may by the power that created it, be reduced to nothing again. But though we allow it may be so, by the absolute power of God, we deny the consequence, that therefore it shall, and must be so. Angels had a beginning, but shall never have an end. And indeed, their immortality, as well as ours, flows not so much from the nature of either as from the will and pleasure of God, who has appointed them to be so. He can, but never will, annihilate them.

Object. 3. But the soul depends upon matter in all its operations, nothing is in the understanding which was not first in the senses; it useth the natural spirits, as its servants and tools in all its operations, and therefore how can it either subsist or act in a state of separation?

Sol. 1. The hypothesis is not only uncertain, but certainly false. There are acts performed by the soul, even while it is in the body, wherein it makes no use at all of the body. Such are the acts of self-intuition and self-reflection: and what will you say of its acts, in raptures and extasies, such as that of Paul, 2 Cor. 12:2. and John, Rev. 21:10. what use did their souls make of the bodily senses or natural spirits then?

Solut. 2. And though in its ordinary actions in this life, it does use the body as its tool or instrument in working, does it thence follow that it can neither subsist or act separate from them in the other world? While a man is on horseback in his journey, he useth the help and service of his horse, and is moved according to the motion of his horse; but does it thence follow, he cannot stand nor walk alone, when dismounted at his journey's end? We know angels both live and act, without the ministry of bodies, and our souls are spiritual substances as well as they.

Object. 4. But many scriptures seem to favour the total cessation of the soul's actions, if not of its being also, after separation, as that in 2 Sam. 14:14. We must needs die, and are as water spilt upon the ground which cannot be gathered up, and Psal. 88:10,11,12. with Isa. 38:18,19. The dead cannot praise thee.

Solut. These words of the woman of Tekoah, are not to be understood absolutely, but respectively: and the meaning is, that the soul is in the body as some precious liquor in a brittle glass, which being broken by death, the soul is irrecoverably gone as the water spilt on the ground, which by no human power or art of man can be recovered again. All the means in the world cannot fetch it back into the body again. She speaks not of the resurrection, or what shall be done in the world to come, by the Almighty power of God, but of what is impossible to be done in this world by all the skill and power of man.

And for the expressions of Heman and Hezekiah, they only respect and relate unto those services their souls were now employed about for the praise of God, with respect to the conversion or edification of others, as Psal. 30:8,9. or at most, to that mediate service and worship which they give God, in and by their attendance upon his ordinances in this world, and not of that immediate service and praise that is performed and given him in heaven by the spirits of just men made perfect; such was the sweetness they had found in these ordinances and duties, that they express themselves as loth to leave them.

FLAVEL

The same answer solves also the objections grounded upon other mistaken scriptures, as that of Psal. 78:39. where man is called a wind that passeth away and cometh not again. It is only expressive of the frailty and vanity of the present animal life we live in this world, to which we shall return no more after death; it denies not life to departed souls, but affirms the end of this animal life at death: the life we live in the other world is of a different nature.

Inf. 1. Is the soul immortal? Then it is impossible for souls to find full rest and contentment in any enjoyments on this side heaven. All temporary things are inadequate, and therefore unsatisfying to our souls. What gives the soul rest and satisfaction, must be as durable as the soul is; for if we could possibly find in this world a condition and state of things most agreeable in all other respects to our desires and wishes, yet if the soul be conscious to itself, that it shall, and must overlive and leave them all behind it, it can never reach true contentment in the greatest affluence and confluence of them. Man being an immortal, is therefore a prospecting creature, and can never be satisfied with this, that it is well with him at present, except he can be satisfied that it shall be so for ever. The thoughts of leaving our delightful and pleasant enjoyments embitters them all to us while we have them. All outward things are fluxu continuo, passing away as the waters, 1 Cor. 7:31. Riches are uncertain, 1 Tim. 6:17. "They fly away as an eagle towards heaven, and with wings of their own making," Prov. 23:5. i.e. As the feathers that enable a bird to fly from us, grow out of its own substance, so does that vanity that carries away an earthly enjoyments. This alone will spoil all contentment.

Inf. 2. Then see the ground and reason of Satan's envy and enmity against the soul, and his restless designs and, endeavours to destroy it. It grates that spirit of envy, to find himself, who is by nature immortal, sunk everlastingly and irrecoverably into misery, and the souls of men appointed to fill up those vacant places in heaven from which the angels fell. No creature but man is envieth by Satan, and the soul of man much more than his body: it is true, he afflicts the bodies of men when God permits him, but he ever aims at the soul when he wounds the body, Heb. 10:37. This roaring lion is continually going about, "seeking whom he may devour," Pet. 5:8. It is the precious soul he hunts after; that is the Morsus diaboli, the bit he gapes for, as the wolf tears the fleece to come at the flesh. All the pleasure those miserable creatures find, is from the success of their temptations upon the souls of men. It is a kind of delight to them to plunge souls into the same condemnation and misery with themselves. This is the trade they have been driving ever since their fall. By destroying souls he at once exercises his revenge against God, and his envy against man, which is all the relief his miserable condition allows him.

Inf. 3. Do the souls of men out-live their bodies? Then it is the height of madness and spiritual infatuation, to destroy the soul for the body's sake; to cast away an immortal soul for the gratification of perishing flesh; to ruin the precious soul for ever, for the pleasures of sin which are but for a moment; yet this is the madness of millions of men. They will drown their own souls in everlasting perdition, to procure necessary things for the body, 1 Tim. 6:9. "They that will be rich," &c. Every cheat and circumvention in dealing, every lie, every act of oppression, is a wound given the immortal soul, for the procuring some accommodations to the body.

O what soul-undoing bargains do some make with the devil! Some sell their souls out-right for the gratification of their lusts, 1 Kings 21:20. Many pawn their souls to Satan in a conditional bargain; so do all that venture upon sin, upon a presumption of pardon and repentance. The devil is a great trader for souls, he has all sorts of commodities to suit all men's humours that will deal with him. He has profits for the covetous, honours for the ambitious, pleasures for the voluptuous: but a soul is the price at which he sells them; only he will be content to sell at a day, and not require present pay: so that it be paid on a death bed, in a dying hour, he is satisfied. But oh! what an undoing bargain do sinners make, to part with a treasure for a trifle! Matt. 16:26. the precious soul for ever, "for the pleasures of sin, which are but for a season! Heb. 11:25. We are charmed with the present pleasure and sweetness there is in sin; but how bitter will the after-fruits thereof be! — See the texts in the margin. (Prov 20:17; Prov 23:31,32; Job 20:12,13; James 1:15). You will say hereafter as Jonathan did, 1 Sam. 14:31. "I tasted but a little honey, and I must die."

Inf. 4. Then the exposing of the body to danger, yea, to certain destruction, for the preservation of the soul, is the dictate of spiritual wisdom, and that which every Christian is bound to choose and practise, when both interests come in full opposition, Heb. 11:35. Dan. 3:28. Rev. 12:11. No promises of preferment, no threats of torments, have been able to prevail with the people of God to give the least wound, or do the least wrong to their own souls. When Secundus was commanded to deliver his bible, he answered, Christian sum, non traditor: I am a Christian, I will not deliver it: then they desired him to deliver aliquam ecvolam, a chip, a straw, any thing that came to his hand in lieu of it: he refused to redeem his life by delivering the least trifle on that account to save it.

That is a great word of our Lord's, Luke 9:24. "He that will save his life, shall lose it: and he that loseth it for my sake shall find it." Christians, this is your duty and wisdom, and must be your resolution and practice in the day of temptation, to yield your bodies to preserve your souls, as we offer our arm to defend the head. Oh! better thy body had never been given thee, than that it should be a snare to thy soul, and the instrument of casting it away for ever. Oh! how dear are some persons like to pay for their tenderness and indulgence to the flesh, when the hour of temptation shall come! mortify your irregular affections to the body, and never hazard your precious immortal souls for their sakes. It is the character of an hypocrite to choose sin rather than affliction, Job 36:21. But if ever thou hast been in the deeps of spiritual troubles for sin, if God have opened thine eyes to see the evil of sin, the immense weight and value of thy soul, and of eternity, "Thou wilt not count thy life dear to thee, to finish thy course with joy," Acts 20:24.

Inf. 5. If the soul be an immortal being, that shall have no end, Then it is the great concern of all men to strive to the utmost for the salvation of their souls, whatever become of all lesser temporary interests in this world, Luke 13:24. There is a gate, i.e. an introductive means of life and salvation; This gate is strait, i.e. there are a world of difficulties to be encountered in the way of salvation: but he that values and loves his never-dying soul, must, and will be diligent and constant in the use of all those means that have a tendency to salvation, be they never so difficult or unpleasant to flesh and blood. There be difficulties from within ourselves, such as mortification, self-denial, contempt of the world, parting with all at the call of Christ; and difficulties from without, the reproaches, persecutions, and sufferings for Christ, which would not be so great as they are, were it not for our unmortified lusts within; but be they what they will, we are bound to strive through them all, for the salvation of our precious and immortal souls.

(1.) For it is the greatest concernment of the soul, yea, of our own souls; we are bound to do much for the saving of another's soul, 2

Tim. 4:10. much more for our own; this is our darling, Psal. 22. our only one.

(2.) Others have done and suffered much for the saving of their souls; and are not ours, or ought they not to be, as dear to us, as the souls of any others have been to them? Matt. 21:32.

(3.) The utmost diligence is little enough to save them. Do all that you can do, and suffer all that you can suffer, and deny yourselves as deeply as ever any did, yet you shall find all this little enough to secure them, 1 Pet. 4:18. The righteous themselves are scarcely saved, 1 Cor. 9:24.

(4.) The time to strive for salvation is very short and uncertain, Luke 13:25. John 12:35. It will be to no purpose, when the seasons and opportunities of salvation are once over. There is no striving in hell, a death-pang of despair has seized them, hope is extinguished, and endeavours fail.

(5.) Does not reason dictate and direct you to do now, while you are in the way, as you will wish you had done, and repent with rage, and self-indignation, because you did it not, when you come to the end, and behold the final issues of things? Suppose but thyself now either, (1.) Upon a death-bed launching into eternity; (2.) Or at the bar of Christ; (3.) Or in view of heaven; (4.) Or in the sight and hearing of the damned: what think you? will not you then wish, Oh! that I had spent every moment in the world that could possibly be redeemed from the pure necessities of life, in prayer, in hearing, in striving for salvation? >From a prospect of this it was, that one spent many hours daily on his knees to the macerating of his body; and being admonished of the danger of health, and advised to relax, he answered, I must die, I must die.

Objection 1. Do not say, you have many incumbrances, and other employments in the world: for (1.) "One thing is necessary," Luke 10:42. Those are conveniences, but this is of absolute necessity. (2.) They will strive the better for this, Matt. 6:33. "Seek this, and they shall be added." (3.) Do but redeem the time that can be redeemed to this purpose; let not so much precious time run waste as daily does.

Objection 2. Say not, no man can save his soul by his own striving, and therefore it is to little purpose; for "it is not of him that willeth, nor of him that runneth, but of God that sheweth mercy," Rom. 9:16.

True, this in itself cannot save you; but what then? must we oppose those things which God has subordinated? Bring this home to your natural or civil actions, eating, drinking, ploughing, or sowing, and see how the consequence will look.

Objection 3. Say not, it is a mercenary doctrine, and disparages free grace; for, are not all the enjoyments and comforts of this life confessedly from free grace, though God has dispensed them to you in the way of your diligence and industry.

Objection 4. To conclude, Say not, the difficulties of salvation are insuperable; it is so hard to watch every motion of the heart, to deny every lust, to resist a suitable temptation, to suffer the loss of all for Christ, that there is no hope of over-coming them.

For (1.) God can, and does make difficult things easy to his people, who work in the strength of Christ, Phil. 4:13. (2.) These same difficulties are before all others that are before you, yet it discourageth not them, Phil. 3:11. Others strive to the uttermost. There are extremes found in this matter: some work for salvation, as an hireling for his wages, so the Papists; these disparage grace, and cry up works. Others cry down obedience as legal, as the Antinomians, and cry up grace to the disparagement of duties. Avoid both these, and see that you strive: But (1.) Think not heaven to be the price of your striving, Rom. 4:3. (2.) Strive, but not for a spurt; let this care and diligence run throughout your lives; while you are living, be you still striving: your souls are worth it, and infinitely more than all this amounts to.

Inf. 6. Does the soul out-live the body, and abide for ever? Then it is a great evil and folly to be excessively careful: for the mortal body, and neglective of the mortal inhabitant. In a too much indulged body, there ever dwells a too much neglected soul.

The body is but a vile thing, Phil 3:21. the soul more valuable than the whole world, Matt. 16:26. To spend time, care, and pains for a vile body, while little or no regard is had to the precious mortal soul, is an unwarrantable folly and madness. To have a clear and washed body, and a soul all filth, (as one speaks) a body neatly clothed and dressed, with a soul all naked and unready: a body fed, and a soul starved; a body full of the creature, and a soul empty of Christ, these are poor souls indeed. We smile at little children, who in a kind of laborious idleness take a great deal of pains to make and trim their babies, or build their little houses of sticks and straws: And what are they but children of a bigger size, that keep such ado about the body, a house of clay, a weak pile, that must perish in a few days. It is admirable, and very convictive of most Christians, what we read in a Heathen. "I confess (says Seneca) there is a love to the body implanted in us all; we have the tutelage and charge of it; we may be kind and indulgent to it, but must not serve it; but he that serves it, is a servant to many cares, fears, and passions. Let us have a diligent care of it, yet so as when reason requires, when our dignity or faith require it, we commit it to the fire."

It is true, the body is beloved of the soul, and God requires that it moderately care for the necessities and conveniences of it; but to be fond, indulgent, and constantly solicitous about it, is both the sin and snare of the soul. One of the fathers being invited to dine with a lady, and waiting some hours till she was dressed, and fit to come down; when he saw her, he fell a weeping; and being demanded why he wept, Oh! said he, I am troubled that you should spend so many hours this morning in pinning and trimming your body when I have not spent half the time in praying, repenting and caring for my own soul. Two things a master commits to his servant's care, (says one) the child, and the child's clothes: It will be but a poor excuse for the servant to say, at his master's return, Sir, here are all the child's clothes neat and clean, but the child is lost. Much so will be the account that many will give to God of their souls and bodies, at the great day, Lord, here is my body, I was very careful for it, I neglected nothing that belonged to its content and welfare: But for my soul, that is lost and cast away for ever, I took little care and thought about it. It is remarkable what the apostle says, Rom. 8:12. We owe nothing to the flesh, we are not in its debt, we have given it all, more than all that belongs to it: But we owe many an hour, many a care, many a deep thought to our souls, which we have defrauded it of for the vile body's sake. You have robbed your souls to pay your flesh. This is madness.

Inf. 7. How great a blessing is the gospel which brings life and immortality to light, the most desirable mercies to immortal souls! This is the great benefit we receive by it, as the apostle speaks, 2 Tim. 1:10. "Christ has abolished death, and brought life and immortality to light by the gospel." Life and immortality by a "en dia duoin", is put for immortal life, the thing which all immortal souls desire and long

FLAVEL

for. These desires are found in souls that enjoy not the gospel light; for, as I said before, they naturally spring out of the very nature of all immortal souls: But how and where it is to be obtained, that is a secret for which we are entirely beholden to the gospel discovery. It lay hid in the womb of God's purpose, till by the light of gospel-revelation it was made manifest. But now all men may see what are the gracious thoughts and purposes of God concerning men, and what that is he has designed for their immortal souls, even an immortal life; and this life is to be obtained by Christ, than which no tidings can be more welcome, sweet, or acceptable to us.

O therefore study the gospel. "This is life eternal, to know Thee, the only true God, and Jesus Christ whom thou hast sent," John 17:8. And see that you prize the gospel above all earthly treasure. It is a faithful saying, and worthy of all acceptation. You have two inestimable benefits and blessings by it. (1.) It manifests and reveals eternal life to you, which you could never have come to the knowledge of any other way; those that are without it are groping or feeling after God in the dark, Acts 17:27. Poor souls are conscious to themselves, that there is a just and terrible God, and that their sins offend and provoke him; but how to atone the offended Deity they know not, Micah 6:6,7. But the way of reconciliation and life is clearly discovered to us by the gospel. (2.) As it manifests and reveals eternal life to us, so it frames and moulds our hearts, as God's sanctifying instrument for the enjoyment of it. It is not only the instrument of revelation, but of salvation; the word of life, as well as the word of light, Phil. 2:16. It can open your hearts, as well as your eyes, and is therefore to be entertained as that which is in the first rank of blessings, a peerless and inestimable blessing.

Inf. 8. If our souls be immortal, certainly our enemies are not so formidable as we are apt, by our sinful fears, to represent these. They may, when God permits them, destroy your bodies, they cannot touch or destroy your souls, Matt. 10:28. As to your bodies, no enemy can touch them till there be leave and permission given them by God, Job 1:10. The bodies of the saints, as well as their souls, are within the line or hedge of Divine Providence: They are securely fenced, sometimes mediately by the ministry of angels, Psal. 34:7. and sometimes immediately by his own hand and power, Zech. 2:5. As to their souls, whatever power enemies may have upon them, (when Divine permission opens a gap in the hedge of providence for them) yet they cannot reach their souls to hurt them, or destroy them, but by their own consent. They can destroy our perishing flesh, it is obnoxious to their malice and rage; they cannot reach home to the soul: No sword can cut asunder the band of union between them and Christ: they would be dreadful enemies indeed if they could do so. Why then do we tremble and fear at this rate, as if soul and body were at their mercy, and in their power and hand? The souls of those martyrs were in safety under the altar in heaven, they were clothed with white robes, when their bodies were given to be meat to the fowls of heaven, and the beasts of the earth. The devil drives but a poor trade by the persecution of the saints; he tears the nest, but the bird escapes; he cracks the shell, but loseth the kernal. Two things make a powerful defensative against our fears: (1.) That all our enemies are in the hand of Providence. (2.) That all providences are steered by that promise, Rom. 8:28.

Inf. 9. If souls be immortal, Then there must needs be a vast difference betwixt the aspects and influences of death upon the godly and ungodly.

Oh! if souls would but seriously consider what an alteration death will make upon their condition, for evil or for good, how useful would such meditations be to them! (1.) They must be disseized and turned out of these houses of clay, and live in a state of separation from them; of this there is an inevitable necessity, Eccl. 8:8. It is in vain to say, I am not ready; ready or unready, they must depart when their lease is out. It is as vain to say, I am not willing; for willing or unwilling, they must be gone; there is no hanging back, and begging, Lord, let death take another at this time, and spare me; for no man dies by a proxy. (2.) The time of our soul's departure is at hand, 2 Pet. 1, 13, 14. Job 16:22. The most firm and well built body can stand but a few days; but our ruinous tabernacles give our souls warning, that the days of their departure is at hand. The lamp of life is almost burnt down, the glass of time is almost run; yet a few, a very few days and nights more, and then time, nights and days shall be no more. (3.) When that most certain and near-approaching time is come, wonderful alterations will be made on the state of all souls, godly, and ungodly.

(1.) A marvellous alteration will then be made on the souls of the godly. For, (1.) No sooner is the dividing stroke given by death, and the parting pull over, but they shall find themselves in the arms of angels, mounting them through the upper regions in a few moments, far above all the aspectable heavens, Luke 16:22. The airy region is, indeed, the place where devils inhabit, and have their hauntsand walks;

but angels are the saints convoy through Satan's territories. They pass from the arms of mourning friends, into the welcome arms of officious and benevolent angels. (2.) From the sight and converses of men, to the sight of God, Christ, and the general assembly of blessed and sinless spirits. The soul takes its leave of all men et death, Isa. 38:11. Farewell vain world, with all the mixed and imperfect comforts of it, and welcome the more sweet suitable, and satisfying company of Father, Son, and Spirit, holy angels, and perfected saints, Heb. 12:23. "The spirits of just men made perfect." (3.) From the bondage of corruption to perfect liberty and everlasting freedom; so much is implied, Heb. 12:28. "The spirits of just men made perfect." (4.) From all fears, doubtings, and questionings of our conditions, and anxious debates of our title to Christ, to the clearest, fullest, and most satisfying assurance; for what a man sees, how can he doubt of it? (5.) From all burdens of affliction, inward and outward, under which we have groaned all our days, to everlasting rest and ease, 2 Cor. 5:1,2,3. Oh what a blessed change to the righteous must this be!

(2.) A marvellous change will also be then made upon the souls of the ungodly, who shall then part from (1.) All their comforts and pleasant enjoyments in the world; for here they had their consolation; Luke 16:25. here was all their portion, Psal. 17:14. and, in a moment, find themselves arrested and seized by Satan, as God's gaoler, hurrying them away to the prison of hell, 1 Pet. 3:19. "there to be reserved to the judgement of the great day," Jude 6. (2.) From under the means of grace, life, and salvation, to a state perfectly void of all means, instruments, and opportunities of salvation, John 9:4. Eccl. 9:10. never to hear the joyful sound of preaching or praying any more; never to hear the wooing voice of the blessed bridegroom, saying, Come unto me, come unto me, any more. (3.) From all their vain, ungrounded, presumptuous hopes of heaven, into absolute and final desperation of mercy. The very sinews and nerves of hope are cut by death, Prov. 14:152. "The wicked is driven away in his wickedness, but the righteous has hope in his death." These are the great and astonishing alterations that will be made upon our souls, after they part with the bodies which they now inhabit. Oh that we, who cannot but be conscious to ourselves that we must over-live our bodies, were more thoughtful of the condition they must enter into, after that separation which is at hand.

Inf. 10. If our souls be immortal, then death is neither to he scared by them in heaven, nor hoped for them in hell. The being of souls never fails, whether they be in a state of blessedness or of misery. "In glory they are ever with the Lord," 1 Thes. 4:17. There shall be no death there, Rev. 21:4. And in hell, though they shall wish for death, yet death shall flee from them. Though there be no fears of annihilation in heaven, yet there be many wishes for it in hell, but to no purpose; there never will be an end put, either to their being, or to their torments. In this respect no other creatures are capable of the emery that wicked men are capable of: When they die, there is the end of all their misery; but it is not so with men. Better therefore had it been for them, if God had created them in the basest and lowest order and rank of creatures; a dog, a toad, a worm, is better than a man in endless misery, ever dying, and never dead. And so much of the soul's immortality.

Eph. 5:29

For no man ever yet hated his own flesh; but nourisheth and cherisheth it, even as the Lord the church.

Having given some account of the nature and immortality of the soul, we next come, from this text, to discourse of its love and inclination to the body, with which it is united. The scope of the apostle is, to press Christians to the exact discharge of those relative duties they owe to each other; particularly, he here urgeth the mutual duties of husbands and wives, ver. 22. wives to an obedient subjection, husbands to a tender love of their wives. This exhortation he enforceth from the intimate union, which, by the ordinance of God, is betwixt them, they being now one flesh. And this union he illustrates by comparing It with,

1. The mystical union of Christ and the church.

2. The natural union of the soul and body.

And from both these, as excellent examples and patterns, he, with great strength of argument, urgeth the duty of love: ver. 28. "So ought men to love their wives as their own bodies; he that loveth his wife, loveth himself." Self love is naturally implanted in all men, and it is the rule by which we measure out and dispense our love to others. "Thou shalt love thy neighbour as thyself.

This self love he opens in this place, by,

(1.) The universality of it.

(2.) The effects that evidence it.

1. The universality of it. No man ever yet hated his own flesh. By flesh, understand the body by an usual metonymy of a part for the whole, called flesh. By hating it, understand a simple hatred, or hatred

itself. It is usual for men to hate the deformities and diseases of their own bodies, and upon that account to deal with the members of their own bodies as if they hated them; hence it is, they willingly stretch forth a gangrened leg or arm to be cut off for the preservation of the rest: but this is not a simple hatred of a man's self, but rather an argument of the strength of the soul's love to the body, that it will be content to endure so much pain kind anguish for its sake. And if the soul be at any time weary of, and willing to part, not with a single member only, but with the whole body, and loaths its union with it any longer, yet it hates it and loaths it not simply in, and for itself, but because it is so filled with diseases all over, and loads the soul daily with so much grief, that how well soever the soul loves it in itself, yet upon such sad terms and conditions it would not be tied to it. This was Job's case, Job 10:1. "My soul is weary of my life;" yet not simply of his life, but of such a life of pain and trouble. Except it be in such respects and cases, no man, says he, ever yet hated his own flesh, i.e. no man in his right mind, and in the exercise of his reason and sense; for we must expect distracted and delirious men, who know not what they do, as also men under the terrors of conscience, when God suffers it to rage in extremity, as Spira and others, who would have been glad with their own hands to have cut the thread that tied their miserable souls to their bodies, supposing that way, and by that change, to find some relief. Either of these cases forces men to act beside the stated rule of nature and reason.

 2. This love of the soul to the body is further discovered by the effects which evidence it, viz. its nourishing and cherishing the body, "ektrefei kai talpei". These two comprise the necessaries for the body, viz. food and raiment. The first signifies to nourish with proper food; the latter to warm by clothing, as the word "talpein" is rendered, James 2:16. to which the Hebrew word "yitchamam" answers, Job 31:20. The care and provision of these things for the body evidences the soul's love to it.

 Doct. That the souls of men are strongly inclined, and tenderly affected towards the bodies in which they now dwell.

 The soul's love to the body, is so strong, natural, and inseparable, that it is made the rule and measure by which we dispense and proportion our love to others, Matt. 19:19. Thou shall love thy neighbour as thyself: And the apostle, Gal. 5:14. tells us, That the whole law, i.e. the second table of the law, is fulfilled, or summoned up in this precept, Thou shalt lope thy neighbour as thyself. The meaning is not, that all and every one who is our neighbour, must be equally near to us as our own bodies; but it intends, (1.) The sincerity of our love to others, which must be without dissimulation, for we dissemble not in selflove. (2.) That we be as careful to avoid injuring others, as we would ourselves, Matt. 7:12. To do by others, or measure to them, as we would have done or measured unto us: for which rule, Severus, the Heathen emperor, honoured Christ and Christianity, and caused it to be written in capital letters of gold. (3.) That we take direction from this principle of self-love, to measure out our care, love, and respect to others, according to the different degrees of nearness in which we stand to them. As, (1.) The wife of our bosom, to whom, by this Rule, is due our first care and love as in the text. (2.) Our children and family, 1 Tim. 5:8. (3.) To all in general, whether we have any bond of natural relation upon them or no; but especially those to whom we are spiritually related, as Gal. 6:10. And indeed, as every Christian has a right to our love and care above other men, so in some cases, we are to exceed this rule of self-love, by a transcendent act of self-denial for them, 1 John 3:16. And Paul went higher than that, in a glorious excess of charity to the community or body of God's people, preferring their salvation not only to his own body, but to his soul also, Rom. 9:3. But to these extraordinary cases we are seldom called; and if we be, the gospel furnisheth us with an higher rule than self-love, John 13:34. But by this principle of self love, in all ordinary cases, we must proportion and dispense our love to all others; by which you see what a deep-rooted and fixed principle in nature self-love is, how universal and permanent alone this is, which else were not fit to be made the measure of our love to all others.

Two things well deserve our consideration in the doctrinal part of this point.

First, Wherein the soul evidenceth its love to the body.

Secondly, What are the grounds and fundamental causes or reasons of its love to it; and then apply it.

First, Wherein the soul evidenceth its love to the body, and that it does in divers respects.

1. In its cares for the things needful to the body, as the text speaks, in nourishing and cherishing it, i.e. taking care for food and raiment for it. This care is universal, it is implanted in the most savage

and barbarous people; and is generally so excessive and exorbitant, that though it never needs a spur, yet most times, and with most men, it does need a curb; and therefore Christ, in Matt. 6:32. shews how those cares torture and distract the nations of the world, warns them against the like excesses, and propounds a rule to them for the allay and mitigation of them, ver. 25, 26, 27. So does the apostle also, 1 Cor. 7:29,30,31. To speak as the matter is, most souls are over heated with their cares, and eager pursuits after the concerns of the body. They pant after the dust of the earth. They pierce themselves through with many sorrows, 1 Tim. 6:10. They are cumbered like Martha with much serving. It is a perfect drudge and slave to the body, bestowing all its time, strength, and studies about the body; for one soul that puts the question to itself, "What shall I do to be saved?" a thousand are to be found that mind nothing more but "What shall I eat, what shall I drink, and wherewithal shall I and mine be clothed?" I do not say, that these are proofs of the soul's regular love to the body; no, they differ from it, as a fever does from natural heat. This is a coating fondness upon the body. He truly loves his body, that moderately and ordinately cares for what is necessary for it, and can keep it under, 1 Cor. 9:27. and deny its whining appetite, when indulgence is prejudicial to the soul, or warm its lusts. Believers themselves find it hard to keep the golden bridle of moderation upon their affections in this matter. It is not every man that has attained Agur's cool temper, Prov. 30:8. that can slack his pace and drive moderately where the interests of the body are concerned: the best souls are too warm, the generality in raging heats, which distract their minds, as that word, Matt. 6:25 "me merimnate" signifies. If the body were not exceeding dear to the soul, It would never torture itself, day and night, with such anxious cares about it.

2. The soul discovers its esteem and value for the body in all the fears it has about it. Did not the soul love it exceedingly, it would never be affrighted for it, and on its account, so much and so often as it is. What a panic fear do the dangers of the body cast the soul into? Isa. 7:2. When the body is in danger, the soul is in distraction, the soul is in fears and tremblings about it: these fears flow from the souls tender love and affection to the body; if it did not love it so intensely, it would never afflict and torment itself at that rate it does about it: Satan, the professed enemy of our souls, being thoroughly acquainted with those fears which flow from the fountain of love to the body, politicly improves them in the way of temptation to the utter ruin of some, and the great hazard of other's souls; he edges and sharpens his

temptations upon us this way; he puts our bodies into danger, that he may thereby endanger our souls; he reckons, if he can but draw the body into danger, fear will quickly drive the soul into temptation; it is not so much from Satan's malice or hatred of our bodies, that he stirs up persecutions against us: but he knows the tie of affection is so strong betwixt these friends, that love will draw, and fear will drive the soul into many and great hazards of its own happiness, to free the body out of those dangers. Prov. 29:25. "The fear of man brings a snare:" and Heb. 11:37. "Tortured and tempted."

Upon this ground also it is, that this life becomes a life of temptation to all men, and there is no freedom from that danger, till we be freed from the body, and set at liberty by death. Separated souls are the only free souls. They that carry no flesh about them, need carry no fears of temptation within them. It is the body which catches the sparks of temptation.

3. The soul manifests its dear love and affection to the body, by its sympathy, end compassionate feeling of all its burdens: whatever touches the body, by way of injury, affects the soul also by way of sympathy. The soul and body are as strings of two musical instruments set exactly at one height; if one be touched, the other trembles. They laugh and cry, are sick and well together. This is a wonderful mystery, and a rare secret (as a learned man observes) how the soul comes to sympathise with the body, and to have not only a knowledge, but as it were a feeling of its necessities and infirmities; how this fleshly lump comes to affect, and make its deep impressions upon a creature of so different a nature from it, as the soul or spirit is. But that it does so, though we know not how, is plain and sensible to any man. If any member of the body, though but the lowest and meanest, be in pain and misery, the soul is presently affected with it, and commands the eyes to watch, yea, to weep, the hands to bind it up with all tenderness, and defend it from the least injurious touch; the lips to complain of its misery, and beg pity and help from others for it. If the body be in danger, how are the faculties of the soul, understanding, memory, invention, &c. employed with utmost strength and concernment for its deliverance! This is a real and unexceptionable evidence of its dear and tender love to the body. As those that belong to one mystical body show their sincere love this way, 1 Cor. 12:25,26 so the soul.

4. The soul manifesteth its love to the body, by its fears of death, and extreme aversion to a separation from it. On this account

death is called in Job 18:14. "The king of terrors, or the black prince, or the prince of clouds and darkness, as some translate that place: We read it, "The king of terrors, meaning, that the terrors at death are such terrors as subdue and keep down all other terrors under them, as a prince does his subjects. Other terrors compared with those that the soul conceives and conflicts with at parting, are no more than a cut finger, to the laying one's head on the block. Oh! the soul and body are strongly twisted and knit together in dear bands of intimate union and affection, and these bands cannot be broken without much struggling: Oh! it is a hard thing for the soul to bid the body farewell, it is a bitter parting, a doleful separation: Nothing is heard in that hour but the most deep and emphatical groans; I say emphatical groans, the deep sense and meaning of which the living are but little acquainted with: For no man living has yet felt the sorrows of a parting pull; whatsoever other sorrows he has felt in the body, yet they must be supposed to be far short of these.

The sorrows of death are in scripture set forth unto us, by the bearing throes of a travailing woman, Acts 2:24. "odinas tou tanatou", and what those mean, many can tell. The soul is in labour, it will not let go its hold of the body, but by constraint: Death is a close siege, and when the soul is beaten out of its body, it disputes the passage with death, as soldiers use to do with an enemy that enters by storm, and fights and strives to the last. It is also compared to a battle or sharp fight, Eccl. 8:8. that war. That war with an emphasis. No conflict so sharp, each labour to the utmost to drive the other from the ground they stand on, and win the field. And though grace much over-powers nature in this matter, and reconciles it to death, and makes it desire to be dissolved, yet saints wholly put not off this reluctation of nature, 2 Cor. 5:2. Not that we would be unclothed; as it is with one willing to wade over a brook to his father's house, puts his foot into the water, and feels it cold, starts back, and is loth to venture in; Not that we would be unclothed. And if it be so with sanctified souls, how is it, think you, with others? Mark the scripture language, Job 27:8 God taketh away their souls, says our translation; but the root is, "kashal", extrahere, and signifies to pull out by plain force and violence. A graceless soul dieth not by consent, but force. Thus Adrian bewailed his departure, O Animula, vagula, blandula, heu, quo vadis! Yea, though the soul have never so long a time been in the body, though it should live as long as the Antediluvian fathers did, for many hundred years, yet still it would be loth to part; yea, though it endure abundance of misery in the body, and have little rest or comfort, but time spent in griefs and fears, yet for all that it is loth to part with it. All this shews a strong inclination and affection to it.

5. Its desire of re-union continuing still with it, in its state of separation, speaks its love to the body. As the soul parted with it in grief and sorrow, so it still retains, even in glory, an inclination to re-union, and waits for a day of re-espousals: and to that sense some searching and judicious men understand those words of Job, chap. 14:14. "If a man die, shall he live again?" viz. by a resurrection: if so, then all the days of my appointed separation, my soul in heaven shall wait till that change come. And to the same sense is that cry of separated souls, Rev. 6:9,10,11. "How long, O Lord, how long?" i.e. to the consummation of all things. when judgement shall be executed on them that killed our bodies, and our bodies so long absent restored to us again? In that day of resurrection, the souls of the saints come willingly from heaven itself; to repossess their bodies, and bring them to a partnership with them in their glory: for it is with the soul in heaven as it is with an husband who is richly entertained, feasted, and lodged abroad, but his dear wife is solitary and comfortless; it abates the completeness of his joy. Therefore we say, the saints joy is not consummate till that day.

There is an exercise for faith, hope, and desire, on this account in heaven.

The union of soul and body is natural, their separation is not so: many benefits will redound to both by a re-union, and the resurrection of the body is provided by God, as the grand relief against those prejudices and losses the bodies of the saints sustain by separation. I say not that the propension or inclination of the soul to re-union with its body, is accompanied with any perturbation or anxiety, in its state of separation; for it enjoys God, and in him a placid rest; and as the body, so the soul rests in hope, it is such a hope as disturbs not the rest of either; yet when the time is come for the soul to be re-espoused, it is highly gratified by that second marriage, glad it is to see its old dear companion, as two friends after a long separation. And so much of the evidence of the soul's love to the body.

Secondly, Next we are to enquire into the grounds and reasons of its love and inclination to the body. And,

A TREATISE OF THE SOUL OF MAN

1. The fundamental ground and reason thereof will be found in their natural union with each other. There my text lays it: "No man ever yet hated his [own] flesh." Mark, the body is the soul's own; they are strictly married and related to each other: the soul has a property in its body, these two make up, or constitute one person. True, they are not essentially one, they have far different natures, but they are personally one; and though the soul be what it was, after Its separation, yet to make a man the who he was, i.e. the same complete and perfect person, they must be re-united. Hence springs its love to the body. Every man loves his own, John 17:19. All the world is in love with its own, and hence it cares to provide for its welfare; 1 Tim. 5:8. "If any man provide not for his own, he is worse than an infidel." For nature teacheth all men to do so. Why are children dearer to parents than to all others, but because they are their own? Job 19:17. But our wives, our children, our goods are not so much our own as our bodies are; this is the nearest of all natural unions.

In this propriety and relation are involved the reasons and motives of our love to, and care over the body, which is no more than what is necessary to their preservation. For, were it not for this propriety and relation, no man would be at any more cost or pains for his own body, than for that of a stranger. It is propriety which naturally draws love, care, and tenderness along with it; and these are ordered by the wisdom of providence, for the conservation of the body, which would quickly perish without it.

2. The body is the soul's ancient acquaintance and intimate friend, with whom it has assiduously and familiarly conversed from its beginning. They have been partners in each others comforts and sorrows. They may say to each other, as Miconius did to his colleague, with whom he had spent twenty years in the government of the Thuringian church: Currimus, certavimus, laboravimus, pugnavimus, vicimus, et viximus conjunctissime. We have run, striven, laboured, fought, overcome, and lived most intimately and lovingly together. Consuetude, and daily conversation, begets and conciliates friendship and love betwixt creatures of contrary natures: Let a lamb be brought up with a lion, and the lion will express a tenderness towards it, much more the soul to its own body.

8. The body is the soul's house and beloved habitation, where it was born, and has lived ever since it had a being, and in which it has enjoyed all its comforts, natural and supernatural, which cannot but

strengthen the soul's engagement to it. Upon this account the apostle calls it the soul's home, 2 Cor. 5:6. "While we are at home in the body." It is true, this house is not so comfortable an habitation, that it should be much desired by many souls; we may say of many gracious souls, that they pay a dear rent for the house they dwell in: or as it was said of Galba, Anima Galbae male habitat, their souls are but ill accommodated; but yet it is their home, and therefore beloved by them.

4. The body is the soul's instrument by which it does its work and business in the world, both natural and religious, Rom. 6:13. Through the bodily senses it takes in all the natural comforts of this world, and by the bodily members it performs all its duties and services. When these are broken and laid aside by death, the soul knows it can work no more in that way it now does, John 9:4. Eccl. 9:10. Natural men love their bodies for the natural pleasures they are instrumental to convey to their souls; and spiritual men, for the use and service they are of to their own and other souls, Phil. 1:23.

5. The body is the soul's partner in the benefit of Christ's purchase. It was bought with the same price, 1 Cor. 6:20. sanctified by the same Spirit, 1 Thess. 5:28. interested in the same promise, Matt. 22:82. and designed for the same glory, 1 Thess. 4:16,17. So that we may say of it as it was said of Augustine and his friend Alippius, they are sanguine Christi conglutinati, glued together by the blood of Christ. And thus of the grounds and reasons of its love.

Inf. 1. Is it so? Learn hence the mighty strength and prevalence of divine love, which, overpowering all natural affections, does not only enable the soul, of men to take their separation from the body patiently, but to long for it ardently, Phil. 1:23. While some need patience to die, others need it as much to live, 2 Thes. 3:5. It is said, Rev. 12:11. "They loved not their lives. And, indeed, on these terms they first closed with Christ, Luke 12:26. "to hate their lives for his sake," (i.e.) to love them in so remiss a degree, that whenever they shall come in competition with Christ, to regard them no more than the things we hate.

The love of Christ is to be the supreme love, and all others to be subordinate to it, or quenched by it. It is not its own comfort in the body, it principally and ultimately designs and aims at, but Christ's glory; and if this may be furthered by the death of the body, its death thereupon becomes as eligible to the soul as its life, Phil. 1:20. Oh! this is an high pitch of grace, a great attainment to say as one did, vivere renuo, ut Christo vivam; I refuse life, to be with Christ: Or another, when he was asked whether he was willing to die? answered, illius est nolle mori, qui nolit ire ad Christum; let him be loth to die, that is loth to go to Christ. So 2 Cor. 5:8. "We are willing rather to be absent from the body, and present with the Lord."

It is not every Christian that can arrive to this degree of love, though they love Christ sincerely, yet they shrink from death cowardly, and are loth to be gone. There are two sorts of grounds upon which Christians may be loth to be unbodied;

1. Sinful.

2. Allowable.

1. The sinful and unjustifiable grounds are such as these, viz. (1.) Guilt upon the conscience, which will damp and discourage the soul, and make it loth to die. It arms death with terror, "the sting of death is sin." (2.) Unmortified affections to the world, I mean in such a degree as is necessary to sweeten death, and make a man a volunteer in that sharp engagement with that last and dreadful enemy. It is with our hearts as with fuel; if green, and full of sap, it will not burn; but if that be dried up, it catches presently. Mortification is the drying up of carnal affections to the creature, which is that which resists death, as green wood does the fire. (3.) The weakness and cloudiness of faith. You need faith to die by, as well as live by. Heb. 11:13. All these died in faith. The less strength there is in faith, the more in death. A strong believer welcomes the messengers of death, when a weak one, unless extraordinarily assisted, trembles at them.

2. There are grounds on which we may desire a longer continuance in the body, warrantably and allowably: As (1.) to do him yet more service in our bodies, before we lay them down. Thus the saints have pleaded for longer life, Psal. 30:9. Psal. 88:11,12,13. and Isa. 38:18,19. (2.) To see the clouds of God's anger dispelled, whether public or personal, and a clear light break out e'er we die; Psal. 27:13. (3.) They may desire, with submission, to out-live the days of persecution, and not to be delivered into the hands of cruel men, but come to their graves in peace, Psal. 31:15. and 2 Thess. 3:2. that they may be delivered from absurd men.

3. But though some Christians shun death upon a sinful account, and others upon a justifiable one; yet others there be, who

seeing their title clear, their work done, and relishing the joys of heaven, in the prelibations of faith, are willing to be unclothed, and to be with Christ. Their love to Christ has extinguished in them the love of life; and they can say with Paul, Acts 21:18. I am ready. Ignatius longed to come to those beasts that were to devour him; and so many of the primitive Christians: Christ was so dear, that their lives were cheap, and low prized things for this enjoyment. And here indeed is the glory and triumph of a Christian's faith and love to Christ: For (1.) It enables him to part cheerfully with what he sees and feels, for what his eyes never yet saw, 1 Pet. 1:8. "Whom having not seen, ye love." (2.) To part with what is dearest on earth, and lies nearest the heart of all he enjoys for Christ's sake. (3.) To reconcile his heart to what is most abhorrent and formidable to nature. (4.) To endure the greatest of pains and torments to be with him. (5.) To cast himself into the vast ocean of eternity, the most amazing change, to be with Christ, O the glorious conquests of love!

Inf. 2. Then the apostasy of unregenerate professors in times of imminent danger, is not to be wondered at. They will, and must warp from Christ, when their lives are in hazard for him. The love of the body will certainly prevail over their love to Christ and religion. Amor meus pondus meum. Self-love will now draw. Love is the weight of the soul, which inclines and determines it, in the competition of interests' and the predominant interest always carries it. Every unregenerate professor loves his own life more than Christ, prefers his body before his soul; such an one may, upon divers accounts, as education, example, slight convictions of conscience, or ostentation of gifts, fall into a profession of religion, and continue a long time in that profession, before he visibly recede from Christ; hope of the resurrection of the interest of religion in the world; shame of retracting his profession; applause of his zeal and constancy in higher trials, the peace of his own conscience, and many such motives, may prevail with a carnal professor to endure a while: but, when dangers of life come to an height, they are gone, Matt. 24:8,9,10. And therefore, our Lord tells us, that they "who hate not their lives, cannot be his disciples," Luke 12:26. Now will they lose their lives by saving them, Matt. 16:25. and the reasons are plain and forcible: For,

1. Now is the proper season for the predominant love to be discovered, it can be hid no longer: and the love of life is the predominant love in all such persons; for do but compare it with their love to Christ, and it will easily be found so. They love their lives truly and

really, they love Christ but feignedly and pretendedly; and the real will, and must prevail over the feigned love. They love their lives fervently and intensely, they love Christ but coldly and remissly: And the fervent love will prevail over the remiss-love. Their love to their bodies has a root in themselves, their love to Christ has no root in themselves, Matt. 13:21. And that which has a root must needs out-last and out-live that which has none.

2. Because when life is in hazard, conscience will work in them by way of discouragement; it will hint the danger of their eternal state to them, and tell them they may cast away their souls for ever in a bravado; for though the cause they are called to suffer for be good, yet their condition is bad; and if the condition be not good as well as the cause, a man is lost for ever, though he suffer for it, 1 Cor. 13:3. Conscience, which encourages and supports the upright, will discourage and daunt the hypocrite, and tell him, he is not on the same terms in sufferings that other men are.

8. Because then all the springs by which their profession was fed and maintained, fail and dry up. Now the wind that was in their backs is come about, and blows a storm in their faces; there are no preferments nor honours now to be had from religion. These men's sufferings are a perfect surprise to them, for they never counted the cost, Luke 14:28. Now they must stand alone, and resist unto blood, and sacrifice all visibles for invisibles; and this they can never do.

O therefore, professors, look to your hearts, try their predominant love; compare your love to Christ with that to your lives. Now the like question will be put to you, that once was put to Peter, John 21:15. "Lovest thou me more than these?" What say you to this? You think now you do, but alas your love is not yet brought to the fire to be tried: you think you hate sin, but will you be able to strive unto blood against sin? Heb. 12:4. Will you choose suffering rather than sin? Job 26:21. O try your love to Christ, before God bring it to the trial. Sure I am, the love of life will make you warp in the hour of temptation; except,

1. You sat down and counted the cost of religion beforehand: if you set out in procession only for a walk, not for a journey? If you go to sea for recreation, not for a voyage; if you be mounted among other processors, only to take the air, and not to engage an enemy in sharp and bloody encounters, you are gone.

2. Except you live by faith, and not by sense, 2 Cor. 4:18. "While we look not at the things that are seen." You must balance present sufferings with future glory. You must go by that account and reckoning, Rom. 8:18. or you are gone. "Now the just shall live by faith;" and if faith do not support, your fears will certainly sink you.

3. Except you be sincere and plain-hearted in religion, driving no design in it but to save your souls, you may see your lot in that example, 2 Tim. 4:10. "Demas has forsaken me." O take heed of a cunning, deceitful, double heart in religion; be plain, be open, care not if your ends lie open to the eyes of all the world.

4. Except you experience the power of religion in your own souls, as well as wear the name of it. O my brethren, it is not a name to live that will do you service now. Many ships are gone down to the bottom, for all the brave names of the Success, the Prosperous, the Happy Return, and so will you. There is a knowing of ourselves by taste and real experience, Heb. 10:34. which does a soul more service in a suffering hour, than all the splendid names and titles in the world.

5. Except you make it your daily work to crucify the flesh, deny self for Christ, in all the forms and interests of it. He that cannot deny himself, will deny Jesus Christ, Matt. 16:24. "Let him deny himself, take up his cross, and follow me," else he cannot be my disciple. Ponder these things in your hearts, while yet God delays the trial.

Inf. 8. If the souls of men be naturally so strongly inclined and affected towards the body; Then hence you may plainly see the wisdom of God in all the afflictions and burdens he lays upon his people in this world, and find that all is but enough to wean off their souls from their bodies, and make them willing to part with them.

The life of the saints in this world, is generally a burdened and a groaning life; 2 Cor. 5:2. "In this tabernacle we groan, being burdened." Here the saints feel, (1.) A burden of sin, Rom. 7:24. this is a dead and a sinking weight. (2.) A burden of affliction; of this all are partakers, Heb. 12. though not all in an equal degree, or in the same kind, yet all have their burdens equal to, and even beyond their own strength to support it; 2 Cor. 1:8. "pressed above measure." (3.) A burden of inward troubles for sin, and outward troubles in the flesh both together, so had Job, Heman, David, and many of the saints.

Certainly this befals them not, (1.) Casually, Job 5:6. "It rises not out of the dust:" (2.) Nor because God loves and regards them not, for they are fruits of his love; Heb. 12:6. "Whom he loveth he correcteth:" (3.) Nor because he takes pleasure in their groans; Lam. 3:34. "To tread under his feet the prisoners of the earth, - the Lord has no pleasure:" it is not for his own pleasure, but his children's profit, Heb. 12:10. And among the profits that result from these burdens, this is not the least, to make you less fond of the body than you would else be, and more willing to be gone to your everlasting rest. And certainly all the diseases and pains we endure in the body, whether they be upon inward or outward accounts, by passion or compassion from God or men, will be found but enough to wean us, and loose off our hearts from the fond love of life. Afflictions are bitter things to our taste, Ruth 1:20. so bitter, that Naomi thought a name of a contrary signification fitter for her afflicted condition: call me Marah, i.e. bitter, not Naomi, pleasant, beautiful. And the church, Lam. 3:9. calls them wormwood and gall.

The great design of God in afflicting them, is the same that a tender mother projects in putting wormwood to her breast when she would wean the child.

It has been observed by some discreet and grave ministers, that before their removal from one place to another, God has permitted and ordered some weaning providence to befal them;. either denying wonted success to their labour, or alienating and cooling the affections of their people towards them, which not only makes the manner of their departure more easy, but the grounds of it more clear. Much so it falls out in our natural death, the comfort of the world is imbittered to us before we leave it; the longer we live in it, the less we shall like it. We over-live most of our comforts which engaged our hearts to it, that we may more freely take our leave of it. It were good for Christians to observe the voice of such providences as these, and answer the designs of them in a greater willingness to die.

1. Is thy body which was once hale and vigorous, now become a crazy, sickly, pained body to thee, neither useful to God, nor comfortable to thee? a tabernacle to groan and sigh in; and little hopes it will be recovered to a better temper; God has ordained this to make thee willing to be divorced from it: the less desirable life is, the less formidable death will be.

2. Is thy estate decayed and blasted by providence, so that thy life which was once full of creature comforts, is now filled with cares and anxieties? O it is a weaning providence to thee, and bespeaks thee the more cheerfully to bid the world farewell. The less comfort it gives you, the less it shall entangle and engage you. We little know with what aching hearts, and pensive breasts, many of God's people walk up and down, though for religion, or reputation sake, they put a good face upon it; but by these things, God is bespeaking and preparing them for a better state.

3. Is an husband, a wife, or dear children dead, and with them the comfort of life laid in the dust? why this the Lord sees necessary to do to persuade you to come after willingly? It is the cutting asunder thy roots in the earth, that thou mayest fall the more easily. O how many strokes must God give at our names, estates, relations, and health, before we will give way to the last stroke of death that fells us to the ground?

4. Do the times frown upon religion? Do all things seem to threaten stormy times at hand? Are desirable assemblies scattered? nothing but sorrows and sufferings to be expected in this world? by these things God will imbitter the earth, and sweeten heaven to his people.

5. Is the beauty and sweetness of Christian society defaced and decayed? Is that communion which was wont to be pithy, substantial, spiritual, and edifying, become either frothy or contentious, so that thy soul has no pleasure in it? this also is a weaning providence to our souls: Strigelius desired to die that he might be freed ab implacabilibus theologorum odiis, from the wranglings and contentions that were in his time. Our fond affection to the body requires all this and much more to wean and mortify them.

Inf. 4. How comfortable is the doctrine of the resurrection to believers, which assures them of receiving their bodies again, though they part with them for a time!

Believers must die as well as others; their union with Christ privileges them not from a separation from their bodies, Rom. 8:10. Heb. 9:27. But yet they have special grounds of consolation against this doleful separation above all others. For,

1. Though they part with them, yet they part in hopes of receiving them again, 1 Thes. 4:13,14. They take not a final leave of them when they die. Husbandmen cast their seed-corn into the earth cheerfully and willingly, because they part with it in hope; so should we, when we commit our bodies to the earth at death.

2. Though death separates these dear friends from each other, yet it cannot separate either the one or other from Christ, Luke 20:37,38. "I am the God of Abraham," &c. Your very dust is the Lord's, and the grave rots not the bond of the covenant.

3. The very same body we lay down at death, we shall assume again at the resurrection; not only the same specifical, but the same numerical body; Job 19:25,26. "With these eyes shall I see God."

4. The unbodied soul shall not find the want of its body, so as to afflict or disquiet it; nor the body the want of its soul; but the one shall be at rest in heaven, and the other sweetly asleep in the grave; and all that long interval shall slide away without any afflicting sense of each others absence. The time will be long, Job 14:12. but if it were longer, it cannot be afflicting, considering how the soul is clothed immediately, 2 Cor. 5:1,2. and how the body sleeps sweetly in Jesus, 1 Thes. 4:14.

5. When the day of their re-espousals is come, the soul will find the body so transformed and improved, that it shall never receive prejudice from it any more, but a singular addition to its happiness and glory. Now it clogs us: Matt. 26:41. "The spirit indeed is willing, but the flesh is weak." It encumbers us with cares to provide for it, and eats up time and thoughts; but then it will be a spiritual body, 1 Cor. 15:43. like to the angels for manner of subsistence, Luke 20:35,36. 1 Cor. 6:13. and, which is the highest step of glory, like unto Christ's glorious body, Phil. 3:21. Well therefore might the father say, Resurrectio mortuorem est consolatio Christianorum; the resurrection of the dead is the consolation of Christians.

Use second, of reproof.

In the next place, let me press you to regulate your love to your bodies, by the rules of religion and right reason. I must press you to love them, though nature itself teacheth you so to do; but I press you to love them as Christians, as men that understand the right use and improvement of their bodies. There are two sorts of errors in our love to the body, one in defect, the other in excess; both come fitly here to be censured and healed.

First, Some offend in the defect of love to their own bodies, who use them as if they had no love for them, whose souls act as if they were enemies to their own bodies; they do not formally and directly hate them, but consequentially and eventually they may be said to hate them, and that,

(1.) By defiling them with filthy lusts; so the apostle speaks, 1 Cor. 6:18. "Every sin that a man does, is without the body, but he that committeth adultery sinneth against his own body:" In other sins it is the instrument, but here it is both instrument and object; not only God, but your own bodies are abused and wronged by it. The body may be considered two ways, Either,

1. As our vessel; or

2. As the Spirit's temple.

1. As our vessel or instrument for natural and spiritual uses and services: and on that account we should not injure or defile it, 1 Thess. 4:4,5. but possess it in sanctification and honour. The lusts of uncleanness, gluttony, and drunkenness, quench the vigour, wast the beauty, and destroy the health and honour of the body; and so render it both naturally and morally unfit for the service and use of the soul.

2. And the injury is yet greater, if we consider it as the Spirit's temple. On this ground the apostle strongly convinceth and dissuadeth Christians from these abuses of the body, 1 Cor. 6:15,16. He argues from the dignity God will put upon our bodies by the resurrection, ver. 13,14. They are to be transformed, and made like unto Christ's glorious body; and from the honour he has already put upon the bodies of the saints in their union with Christ, ver. 15,16. They, as well as the soul, are ingrafted into him, and joined with him; they are his temples, to be dedicated, hallowed, and consecrated to his service. O let them not be made a sink for lusts, or mere strangers for meat and drink.

(2.) By macerating them with covetous lusts, denying them their due comforts and refreshments, and unmercifully burdening them with labours and sorrows about things that perish. (1.) Some deny their bodies due comforts and refreshments, which the natural and positive laws of God both allow and command. Their souls are cruel stepmothers to their bodies, and keep them too short; not out of a prudent and Christian design to starve their lusts, but to advance their estates. Of this Solomon speaks, Eccl. 6:22. "There is an evil which I have seen under the sun, and it is common among men; A man to whom God has given riches, wealth and honour, so that he wanteth nothing for his soul of all that he desireth; yet God giveth him not power to eat thereof, but a stranger eateth it. This is vanity, and it is an evil disease." Tenacity is a disease of the soul, like that of a dyscrasy in the stomach, which so indisposeth it that it cannot receive with any appetite or delight the best refreshments at a plentiful table. (2.) And others there are that wrong and abuse their own bodies, by laying unreasonable and unmerciful loads upon them, especially loads of grief and sorrow, wasting and weakening them beyond all rules of reason or religion. If a friend or relation die, they have less mercy on their own bodies than a conscientious man has on the horse he rides. Cares and sorrows are as deadly to the body as a sword, 1 Tim. 6:10. Intense and immoderate griefs about worldly losses and crosses have slain their ten thousands; and, which is strange, the soul seems to take a certain kind of pleasure in loading and tormenting the body. There is a real truth in that strange expression of Seneca, "Sorrow itself has a certain kind of pleasure attending it."

The souls of some mourners do willingly excite and provoke their own grief, when they begin to abate, which is like the whetting of the knife that grows dull, to make it cut the deeper into the body. Thus, as Seneca observes, "some parents that have lost their beloved children, willingly call to mind their pleasant sayings, and pretty actions to find a kind of pleasure in a fresh shower of tears for them;" when, poor hearts! sorrow has so broken them already, that they need consolations under their present sorrows, rather than irritations of new ones. And the soul's unmercifulness to the body, is in such causes farther discovered by its obstinate refusal of all that is comforting and relieving. So it is said of Rachel, Jer. 31:15. "Rachel weeping for her children, would not be comforted, because they were not." So the Israelites hearkened not unto Moses, because of the anguish of spirit, and the cruel bondage, Exod. 6:9. Thus we studiously rake together and exasperate whatsoever is piercing, wounding, and overwhelming; and shut our ears to all that is relieving and supporting, which is cruelty to our own bodies, and that which has so far broken the health and strength of some bodies, that they are never like to be useful instruments to the soul any more in this world; such deep and desperate wounds have their own souls given them by immoderate grief, as will never be perfectly healed, but by the resurrection. Of those wounds the body may say, as it is Zech. 13:6. These are the wounds "with which I was wounded in the house (or by the hand) of my friend;" thus my own soul has dealt cruelly and unmercifully with me.

Secondly, Others offend in the excess and extravagancy of their love to the body, and these are a hundred to one in number compared with those that sin in defect of love. My friends, upon a due search, it will be found, that the love of our souls generally degenerates into fondness and folly: there is but little well-tempered and ordinary love found among men. We make fondlings, yea, we make idols of our bodies; we rob God, yea, our own souls, to give to the body. It is not a natural and kindly heat of love, but a mere feverish heat, which preys upon the very spirits of religion, which is found with many of us. The feverish distemper may be discovered, by the beating of our pulse, in three or four particulars.

(1.) This appears by our sinful indulgence to our whining appetites. We give the flesh whatsoever it craves, and can deny it nothing it desires; pampering the body, to the great injury and hazard of the soul. Some have their conversation in the lusts of the flesh, as it is, Eph. 2:3. trading only in those things that please and pamper the flesh, "They sow to the flesh," Gal. 6:8. i.e. all their studies and labours are but the sowing of the seeds of pleasure to the flesh. Not a handful of spiritual seed sown in prayer for the soul all the day long: what the body craves, the obsequious soul like a slave, is at its beck to give it; Tit. 3:3. "Serving divers lusts and pleasures;" attending to every knock and call, to fulfil the desires of the flesh. O how little do these men understand the life of religion, or the great design of Christianity! which consists in mortifying, and not pampering and gratifying the body, Rom. 14:13,14. And according to that rule, all serious Christians order their bodies, giving them what is needful to keep them serviceable and useful to the soul, but not gratifying their irregular desires; giving what their wants, not what their wantonness calls for. So Paul, 1 Cor. 9:27. "I beat it down, and keep it under;" he understood it as his servant, not his master. He knew that Hagar would quickly perk up, and domineer over Sarah, expect more attendance than the soul, except it were kept under: these two verbs, "hupopiadzo" and "doulagogo", are very emphatical; the former signifies to make it black and blue with buffeting, the other to bring it under by checks and rebukes, as masters that understand their place and authority use to do with insolent and wanton servants.

It was a rare expression of a Heathen, Major sum, et ad majora natus, quam ut corporis mei sim mancipium; I am greater, and born to greater things, than that I should be a slave to my body. And it was the saying of a pious divine, when he felt the flesh rebellious and wanton, Ego faciam, aselle, ut ne calcitres; I will make thee, thou ass, that thou shalt not kick. I know the superstitious Papists place much of religion in these external things, but though they abuse them to an ill purpose, there is a necessary and lawful use of these abridgements and restraints upon the body; and it will be impossible to mortify and starve our lusts without a due rigour and severity to our flesh. But how little are many acquainted with these things? They deal with their bodies as David with Adonijah, of whom it is said, 1 Kings 1:6. His father had not displeased him at any time, in saying, Why hast thou done so? And just so our flesh requites us, by its rebellions and treasons against the soul; it seeks the life of the soul, which seeks nothing more than its content and pleasure; this is not ordinate love, but fondness and folly, and what we shall bitterly repent for at last.

(2.) It appears by our sparing and favouring of them, in the necessary uses and services we have for them in religion. Many will rather starve their soul, than work and exercise their bodies, or disturb their sluggish rest: thus the idle excuses and pretences of endangering our health, oftentimes put by the duties of religion, or, at least, lose the fittest and properest seasons for them: we are laying upon our beds, when we should be wrestling upon our knees: the world is suffered to get the start of religion in the morning, and so religion is never able to overtake it all the day long. This was none of David's courses, he prevented the dawning of the morning, and cried, Psal. 119:147. and Psal. 5:3. "My voice shalt thou hear in the morning, O Lord, in the morning will I direct my prayers unto thee, and will look up." And indeed we should consecrate unto God the freshest and fittest parts of our time, when our bodily senses are most vigorous; and we would do so, (except God by his providence disable us) were our hearts fully set for God, and religion lay with weight upon our spirits.

Some, I confess, cannot receive this injunction, being naturally disabled by prevailing infirmities; but those who can, ought to do so. But oh, how many slothful excuses does the flesh invent to put off duty! We shall injure our health, &c. O the hypocrisy of such pleas! If profit or pleasure calls us up, we have no shifts, but can rise early and sit up late.

O, friends, why has God given you bodies, if not to waste and wear them out in his service, and the service of your own souls! If your bodies must not be put to it, and exercised this way, where is the mercy of having a body? If a stately horse were given you on this condition, that you must not ride or work him, what benefit would such a gift be to you? Your bodies, must and will wear out, and it is better to wear them with working, than with rusting: we are generally more solicitous to live long than to live usefully and serviceably; and it may be our health had been more precious in the eyes of God, if it had been less precious in our own eyes. It is just with God to destroy that health with diseases, which he sees we would cast away in sloth and idleness. Think with thyself, had such a soul as Timothy's or Gaius's been blest with such a body as thine, so strong and vigorous, so apt and able for service, they would have honoured God more in it in a day, than perhaps you do in a year. Certainly this is not love, but laziness; not a due improvement, but a sinful neglect and abuse of the body, to let it rust out into idleness, which might be employed so many ways for God, for your own and others souls. Well, remember death will shortly dissolve them, and then they can be of no more use; and if you expect God should put glory and honour upon them at the resurrection, use them for God now, with a faithful, self-denying diligence.

(3.) It appears by our cowardly shrinking from dangers that threaten them, when the glory of God, our own and others salvation, bid us expose and not regard them. Some there are, that rather than they will adventure their flesh to the rage of man, will hazard their souls to the wrath of God. They are too tender to suffer pain or restraints for Christ, but consider not what sufferings are prepared for the fearful and unbelieving in the world to come, Rev. 21:8. How many sad examples do the church histories of ancient and latter times afford us, of men, who, consulting with flesh and blood in time of danger, have, in pity to their bodies, ruined their souls!

There be but few like-minded with Paul, who set a low price upon his liberty or life for Christ, Acts 20:24. or with those worthy Jews, Dan. 3:28. who yielded their bodies to preserve their consciences. Few of Chrysostom's mind, who told the empress, Nil nisi peccatum timeo, I fear nothing but sin; or of Basil's, who told the emperor, God threatened hell, whereas he threatened but a prison. That is a remarkable rule that Christ gives us, Matt. 10:28. The sum of it is, to set God against man, the soul against the body, and hell against temporal sufferings; and so surmounting these low fleshly considerations, to cleave to our duty in the face of dangers. You read, Gal. 1:16. how in pursuit of duty, though surrounded with danger, Paul would not confer, or consult with flesh and blood, i.e. ask its opinion which were best, or stay for its consent, till it were willing to suffer; he understood not that the flesh had any voice at the council-table in his soul, but willing or unwilling, if duty call for it, he was resolved to hazard it for God.

We have a great many little politicians among us, who think to husband their lives and liberties a great deal better than other plain hearted, and too forward Christians do: but these politics will be their perdition, and their craft will betray them to ruin. They will lose their lives by saving them, when others will save them by losing them, Matt. 10:39. For the interest of the body depends on, and follows the safety of the soul, as the cabin does the ship.

O my friends, let me beg you not to love your bodies into hell, and your souls too for their sakes: be not so scared at the sufferings of the body, as, with poor Spira, to dash them both against the wrath of the great and terrible God. Most of those souls that are now in hell, are there upon the account of their indulgence to the flesh, they could not deny the flesh, and now are denied by God. They could not suffer from men, and now must suffer the vengeance of eternal fire.

(4.) In a word; it appears we love them fondly and irregularly, in that we cannot with any patience think of death and separation from them. How do some men fright at the very name of death! And no arguments can persuade them seriously to think of an unbodied, and separated state. It is as death to them, to bring their thoughts close to that ungrateful subject. A Christian that loves his body regularly and moderately, can look into his own grave with a composed mind, and speak familiarly of it, as Job 17:14. And Peter speaks of the putting off of his body by death, as a man would of the putting off of his clothes at night, 2 Pet. 1:13,14. And certainly such men have a great advantage above all others, both as to the tranquillity of their life and death. You know a parting time must come, and the more fond you are of them, the more bitter and doleful that time will be. Nothing, except the guilt and terrible charges of conscience, puts men into terrors at death, more than our fondness of the body. I do confess, christless persons have a great deal of reason to be shy of death; their dying day is their undoing day: but for Christians to startle and fright at it, is strange, considering how great a friend death will be to them that are in Christ.

What are you afraid of? What, to go to Christ? to be freed of sin and affliction too soon? Certainly this has not been so comfortable a habitation to you, that you should be loth to change it for a heavenly one.

Use third, of exhortation.

To conclude; Seeing there is so strict a friendship and tender affection betwixt soul and body, let me persuade every soul of you to express your love to the body, by labouring to get union with Jesus Christ, and thereby to prevent the utter ruin of both to all eternity.

Souls, if you love yourselves, or the bodies you dwell in, shew it by your preventing care in season, lest they be cast away for ever. How can you say you love them, when you daily expose them to the everlasting wrath of God, by employing them as weapons of unrighteousness, to fight against him that formed them? You feed and pamper them on earth, you give them all the delight and pleasure you can procure for them in this world; but you take no care what shall become of them, nor your souls neither, after death has separated them. Oh cruel souls! cruel, not to others, but to yourselves, and to your own flesh, which you pretend so much love to! Is this your love to your bodies? What, to employ them in Satan's service on earth, and then to be cast as a prey to him forever in hell? You think the rigour end mortification of the saints, their abstemiousness and self-denial, their cares, fears, and diligence, to be too great severity to their bodies: but they know these are the most real evidences of their true love to them, they love them too well to cast them away as you do. Alas! your love to the body does not consist in feeding, and clothing, and pleasing it; but in getting it united to Christ, and made the temple of the Holy Ghost: in using it for God, and dedicating it to God.

I beseech you, brethren, by the mercies of God, to present your bodies living sacrifices to God, which is your reasonable service, Rom. 12:1. The soul should look upon the body as a wise parent upon a rebellious or wanton child, that would, if left to itself; quickly bring itself to the gallows; the father looks on him with compassion and melting bowels, and says, with the rod in his hand, and tears in his eyes, "My child, my naughty, disobedient, headstrong child, I resolve to chastise thee severely. I love thee too well to suffer thee to be ruined, if my care or correction may prevent it." So should our souls evidence their love to and care over their own rebellious flesh. It is cruelty, not love or pity, to indulge them to their own destruction.

Except you have gracious souls, you shall never have glorified bodies: except your souls be united, with Christ, the happiness of your bodies, as well as your souls is lost to all eternity. Know you not that the everlasting condition of your bodies follows and depends on the interest your souls now get in Christ? Oh that this sad truth might sink deep into all our considerations this day; that if your bodies be snares to your souls, and your souls be now regardless of the future state of themselves, and them; assuredly they will have a bitter parting at death, a terrible meeting again at the resurrection, and horrid reflections upon each other, naturally charging their ruin upon each other to all eternity. While they that are in Christ, part in hope, meet with joy, and bless God for each other for evermore.

2 Pet. 1:13,14

Yea, I think it meet, as long as I am in this tabernacle, to stir you up by putting you in remembrance;

Knowing that shortly I must put off this my tabernacle, even as our Lord Jesus Christ hath shewed me.

At the tenth verse of this chapter, the apostle sums up his foregoing precepts and exhortations in one great and most important duty, the "making sure of their calling and election." This exhortation he enforceth on them by a most solemn and weighty motive, ver. 11. "Even an abundant entrance into the everlasting kingdom." No work of greater necessity or difficulty, than to make sure our salvation, no argument more forcible and prevalent, than an easy and free entrance into glory at death, an ε υ θ α ν α σ ι α (euthanasia), a sweet and comfortable dissolution, to enter the port of glory before the wind, with our full lading of comfort, peace, and joy in believing, our sails full and our streamers flying: Oh! how much better is this, than to lie windbound, I mean heartbound, at the harbour's mouth! tossed up and down with fears, doubts, and manifold temptations, making many a board to fetch the harbour, for so much is signified in his figurative and allusive expression, ver. 11.

And for their encouragement in this great and difficult work, he engageth himself by promise to give them all the assistance he can, while God should continue his life; and knowing that would be but a little while, he resolves to use his utmost endeavour to secure these things in their memories after his death, that they might not die with him. This is the general scope and order of the words.

Wherein more particularly we have,

1. His exemplary industry and diligence in his ministerial work.

A TREATISE OF THE SOUL OF MAN

2. Else consideration stunulating and provoking him thereunto.

1. His exemplary industry and diligence in his ministerial work. In which two things are remarkable, viz. (1.) The quality of his work, which was *to stir them up, by putting them in remembrance,* to keep the heavenly flame of love and zeal lively upon the altar of their hearts. He well knew what a sleepy disease the best Christians are troubled with, and therefore he had need to be stirring them up, and awaking them to their duty. (2.) The constancy of his work: *as long as I am in this tabernacle;* i.e. as long as I live in this world. The body is called a tabernacle, in respect of its moveableness and frailty, and in opposition to that house made without hands, *eternal in the heavens.* And it is observable how he limits and bounds his serviceableness to them, by his commoration in his tabernacle or body, as well knowing after death he could be no longer useful to them or any others in this world. Death puts an end to all ministerial usefulness: but till that time he judged it meet, and becoming him, to be aiding and assisting their faith: our life and labour must end together.

2. We have here the motive, or consideration, stimulating and provoking him to this diligence; "knowing that I must shortly put off this tabernacle, even as the Lord Jesus Christ hath shewed me." In which morals he gives an account of, (1.) The speediness; (2.) necessity; (3.) voluntariness of his death, and the way and means by which he knew it. All these must be considered singly and apart, and then valued all together, as they amount to a weighty argument or motive to excite him to diligence in his duty.

(1.) He reflects upon the speediness or near approach of his death. "I must [shortly] put off this my tabernacle;" which is a form of speech of the same importance with that of Paul, 2 Tim. 4:6. "The time of my departure is at hand," my time in the body is almost at an end.

(2.) The necessity of his death: It is not I *may*, but I *must* put off this my tabernacle; yea, I must put it off shortly; for so the Lord hath showed him; Christ had signified it expressly to him, John 21:18,19. And beside this, most expositors think this clause refers to some special vision or revelation which Peter had of the time and manner of his own death; so that besides the natural necessity, or the inevitableness of his death by the law of nature, he was certified of it by special revelation. We have here also,

(3.) The voluntariness of his death; for voluntariness is consistent enough with the necessity of the event. I must put off, or lay down my tabernacle; he says not, I must be torn, or rent by violence from it, but I must *depose, or lay it down.* Camero will have the word here used for death, properly to signify the laying down of one's garments: he made no more of putting off his body than his garment.

Upon the consideration of the whole matter, the speediness of his death which he knew to be at hand; the necessity of it, that when it came he must be gone from, and could be no more useful to them; and his own inclination to be with Christ in a better state, being as willing to be gone, as a weary traveller to be at home; he judged it meet, or becoming him, as he was called of Christ to feed his sheep, as he was gifted extraordinarily for the church's service, full of spiritual excellencies, all which in a short time would be taken away from them by death: I say, upon all these accounts, he could not but judge it meet to be stirring them up, and every way striving to be as useful as he could. Hence the note will be,

Doct. *How strong soever the affections and inclinations of souls are to the fleshly tabernacles they now live in, yet they must put them off; and that speedily.*

The point lies very plain before us in the scriptures. That is a remarkable expression we have in Job 16:22. "When a few years are come, I shall go the way whence I shall not return." In the Hebrew it is, "When the years of number, or my numbered years are come; years so numbered, that they are circumscribed in a very short period of time." When those few years are past, then I must go to my long home, my everlasting abode, never more to return to this world: "The way whence I shall not return;" elsewhere called "the way of all flesh," Josh. 23:15. and "the way of all the earth," 1 Kings 2:2.

"There is no man that hath power over the spirit to retain the spirit; neither has he power in the day of death, and there is no discharge in that war," Eccl. 8:8. By spirit understand the natural spirit, or breath of life, which, as I showed before, connects or ties the soul and body together. This spirit no man can retain in the day of death. *We can* (as one speaks) *as well stop the chariot of the sun when posting to night, and chase away the shadows of the evening, as escape this hour of darkness that is coming upon us.* A man may escape the wars by pleading privilege of years, or weakness of body, or the king's protection, or by sending another in his room; but in this war the press is so strict, that it admits no dispensation, young or old, weak or strong, willing or unwilling, all is one, into the field we must go, and look that last and most dreadful enemy in the face. It is in vain to think of sending another in our room, for no man dieth by proxy? Or to think of compounding with death, as those self-deluded fools did, Isa. 28:15. who thought they had been discharged of the debt by seeing the sergeant: No, there is no discharge in that war. *Nihil prodest ora concludere, et vitam fugientem retinere,* says Hierom on that text; Let us shut our mouths never so close, struggle against death never so hard, there is no more retaining the spirit, than a woman can retain the fruit of her womb, when the full time of her deliverance is come. Suppose a man were sitting upon a throne of majesty surrounded with armed guards, or in the midst of a college of expert and learned physicians, death will pass all these guards to deliver thee the fatal message: Neither can arts help thee, when nature itself gives thee up.

The law of mortality binds all, good and bad, young and old, the most useful and desirable saints, whom the world can worst spare, as well as useless and undesirable sinners, Rom. 8:10. "And if Christ (or though Christ) be in you, the body is dead because of sin." Peter himself must put of his tabernacle, for they are but tabernacles, frail and moveable frames, not built for continuance; these will drop off from our souls, as the shells fall off from the bird in the nest; be our earthly tabernacles never so strong or pleasant, we must depose them, and that shortly; our lease in them will quickly expire, we have but a short term. James 4:14. like a thin mist in the morning, which the sun presently dissipates; this is a metaphor chosen from the air: You have one from the land, where the swift post runs, Job 9:25. So doth our life from stage to stage, till its journey be finished; and a third from the waters, there sail the swift ships, Job 9:26. which weighing anchor, and putting into the sea, continually lessen the land, till at last they have quite lost sight of it: from the fire, Psal. 58:4. The lives of men are as soon extinct as a blaze made with dry thorns, which is almost as soon out as in. Thus you see how the Spirit of God has borrowed metaphors from all the elements of nature, to shadow forth the brevity and frailty of that life we now live in these tabernacles, so that we may say as one did before us, *Nescio an dicenda sit vita mortalis, an vitalis mors;* I know not which to call it, a mortal life, or a living death.

The continuance of these our tabernacles or bodies is short, whether we consider them *absolutely,* or *comparatively.*

1. *Absolutely.* If they should stand seventy or eighty years, which is the longest duration, Psal. 90:10. how soon will that time run out? What are years that are past but as a dream that is vanished, or as the waters that are past away? It is *in fluxu continuo:* there is no stopping its swift course, or calling back a moment that is past. Death set out in its journey towards us the same hour we were born, and how near is it come this day to many of us? It hath us in chase, and will quickly fetch us up, and overtake us; but few stand so long as the utmost date.

2. *Comparatively.* Let us compare our time in these tabernacles, (1.) either with eternity, or with him who inhabits it, and it shrinks up into nothing; Psal. 39:5. "Mine age is nothing unto thee." So vast is the disproportion, that it seems not only little, but nothing at all. Or (2.) with the duration of the bodies of men in the first ages of the world, when they lived many hundred years in these fleshly tabernacles. The length of their lives was the benefit of the world, because religion was then $\alpha \pi \alpha \theta \rho o \pi \alpha \rho \alpha \delta o \tau o \nu$, *apathroparadoton,* a thing handed down from father to son; but certainly it would be no benefit to us that are in Christ, to be so long suspended the fruition of God in the everlasting rest.

The grounds and reasons of this necessity that lies upon all, to put off their earthly tabernacle so soon, are

1. The law of God, or his appointment.

2. The providence of God ordering it suitably to this appointment.

1. The law or appointment of God which came in force immediately upon the fall; Gen. 2:17. "In the day that thou eatest thereof, thou shalt surely die." And accordingly it took place upon all mankind immediately upon the first transgression, Rom. 5:12. *Death entered by sin.* The threatening was not his immediate, actual, personal death in the day that he should eat, but a state of mortality to commence from that time to him and his posterity; hence it is said, Heb. 9:27. "It is appointed to all men once to die."

2. The providence of God ordering and framing the body of man suitably to this his appointment; a frail, weak creature, having the seeds of death in his constitution: Thousands of diseases and infirmities are bred in his nature, and the smallest pore in his body is a door

large enough to let in death. Hence his body is compared to a piece of cloth which moths have fretted, Psal. 39:11. it is become a sorry rotten thing which cannot long hang together. And indeed it is a wonder it continues so long as it doth.

And both these, viz. the divine appointment and providence, are in pursuance of a double design, or for the payment of a twofold debt, which God owes to the first and to the second Adam.

(1.) By cutting off the life, or dissolving the tabernacles of wicked men, God pays that debt of justice owing to the first Adam's sinful posterity, whose sins cry daily to his justice to cut them off. Rom. 6:23. "The wages of sin is death." And indeed it is admirable that his patience suffers ungodly men to live so long as they do, for he endures with much longsuffering, Rom. 9:22. He sees all their sins, he is grieved at the heart with them, his forbearance does but encourage them the more to sin against him; Eccl. 8:11. "Because sentence", &c. yet forbears: "Forty years long was I grieved with this generation," Psal. 95:10. And it is wonderful that he has so much patience under such a load. Habakkuk admired it, Hab. 1:13. "Thou art of purer eyes," &c. Yet he suffers them to spend lavishly upon his patience from year to year, but justice must do his office at last.

(2.) By cutting off the lives of good men, God pays to Christ the reward of his sufferings, the end of his death which was to bring many sons to glory, Heb. ii. 10. Alas! it answers not Christ's end and intention in dying, to have his people so remote from him; John xvii. 24. "He would have them where he is, that they might behold his glory." Two vehement desires are satisfied by this appointment of God, and its execution, viz.

1. Christ's.

2. The saints'.

1. Christ's desires are satisfied; for this is the thing he all along kept his eye upon in the whole work of his mediation; it was to bring us to God, 1 Pet 3:18. Though he be in glory, yet his mystical body is not full till all the elect be gathered in by conversion, and gathered home by glorification, Eph. 1:23. The church is his fullness. He is not fully satisfied till he see his seed, the souls he died for, safe in heaven; and then the debt due to him for all his sufferings is fully paid him, Isa. 53:11. He sees the travail of his soul; as it is the greatest satisfaction

and pleasure a man is capable of in this world, to see a great design which has been long projecting and managing, at last, by an orderly conduct, brought to its perfection.

2. The desires of the saints are hereby satisfied, and their weary souls brought to rest. Oh! what do gracious souls more pant after than the full enjoyment of God, and the visions of his face! the state of freedom from sin, and complete conformity to Jesus Christ! From the day of their espousals to Christ, these desires have been working in their souls. Love and patience have each acted its part in them, 2 Thess. iii. 5. Love has put them into an holy ardour and longing to be with Christ: patience has qualified and allayed those desires, and supported the soul under the delay. Love cries, come, Lord, come; patience commands us to wait the appointed time. This appointed time on which so great hopes and expectations depend, is the time of dissolving these tabernacles; for till then the soul's rest is suspended; and if it were perfectly freed from all other loads and burdens, both of sin and afflictions, yet its very absence from Christ would alone make it restless, for it is with the soul in the body, as it is with any other creature that is off its centre, it does and must gravitate and propend, it is still moving and inclining farther, and feels not itself easy and at rest where it is, be its condition in other respects never so easy. 2 Cor. 5:6. "While we are at home in the body, we are absent from the Lord." You leave a little shadow, or emblem of this in other creatures: You see the rivers, though they glide never so sweetly betwixt the fragrant banks of the most pleasant meadows in their course and passage, yet on they go towards the sea; and if they meet with never so many rocks or hills to resist their course, they will either strive to get a passage through them, or if that may not be, they will fetch a compass, and creep about them, and nothing can stop them till by a central force they have finished their weary course, and poured themselves into the bosom of the ocean. Or as it is with yourselves, when abroad from your habitations and relations: this may be pleasing a little while; but if every day might be a festival, it would not long please you, because you are not at home.

The main motives that persuade gracious souls to abide here, are to finish the work of their own salvation, and further other men's; but as their evidences for heaven grow clearer to themselves, and their capacity of service less to others, so must their desires to be with Christ be more and more enflamed.

A TREATISE OF THE SOUL OF MAN

Now the case so standing, that Christ's condition in heaven, being a condition of desire and longing for the enjoyment of his people there, and all the glory of heaven would not content him without that; and the condition of his people on earth being also a state of longing, groaning, and panting to be with him, and all the pleasures and delights and comforts they leave on earth, will not content them without it: How wise and gracious an appointment of heaven is it, that these our tabernacles shall and must be put off, and that shortly! For hereby a full and mutual satisfaction is given to the restless desires both of Christ's heart and of theirs: See the reflected flames of love betwixt them, in Rev. 22. "The spirit and the bride say, Come. And let him that is athirst come; Behold, I come quickly. Even so, Lord Jesus; Come quickly." Delays make the heart sad, Prov. 13:12. Should our commoration on earth be long, our patience had need be much greater than it is; but under all our burdens here, this is our relief, it is but a little while, and all will be well, as well as our souls can desire to have it.

Inf. 1. Must we put off these tabernacles? Is death necessary and inevitable? Then *it is our wisdom to sweeten to ourselves that cup which we must drink; and make that as pleasant to us as we can which we know cannot be avoided.* Die we must, whether we be fit or unfit, willing or unwilling: It is to no purpose to shrug at the name, or shrink back from the thing. In all ages of the world, death has swept the stage clean of one generation, to make room for another, and so it will from age to age, till the stage be taken down, in the general dissolution.

But though death be inevitable by all, it is not alike evil, bitter, and dreadful to all. Some tremble, others triumph at the appearances of it. Some meet it half way, receive it as a friend, and can bid it welcome, and die by consent; making that the matter of their election, which, in itself, is necessary and unavoidable; so did Paul, Phil. 1:23. But others are drawn, or rent by plain violence from the body, Job 37:1. when God draws out their souls.

• That man is happy indeed, whose heart falls in with the appointment of God, so voluntarily and finely, as that he dare not only look death in the fact, with confidence, but go along with it by consent of will. Remarkable to this purpose, is that which the apostle asserts of the frame of his own heart, 2 Cor. 5:8. "We are confident, I say, and willing rather to be absent from the body, and present with the Lord." Here is both confidence and complacence, with respect to death, θ α ρ ρ ο υ μ ε ν . The word signifies courage, fortitude; or, if you will, an undaunted boldness and presence of mind, when we look the king of terrors in the face. We dare venture upon death, we dare take it by the cold hand, and bid it welcome. We dare defy its enmity, and deride its noxious power, 1 Cor. 15:55. "O death! where is thy sting! And that is not all, we have complacence in it, as well as confidence to encounter it. Ευδοκουμεν, *we are willing;* the translation is too flat, *We are well pleased;* it is a desirable, a grateful thing to us to die; but yet not in an absolute, but comparative consideration, ευδοκουμεν μαλλον, *we are willing rather,* i.e. rather than not see, and enjoy our Lord Jesus Christ; rather than to be here always sinning and groaning. There is no complacency in death; in itself it is not desirable. But if we must go through that strait gate, or not see God, we are willing rather to be absent from the body. So that you see death was not the matter of his submission only, he did not yield to what he could not avoid, but he balances the evils of death, with the privileges it admits the soul into, and then pronounces, ευδοκουμεν, we are content, yea, pleased to die.

We cannot live always if we would, and our hearts should be wrought to that frame, as to say, we would not live always if we could, Job 7:16. "I would not live always;" or *long*, says he. But why should Job deprecate that which was not attainable? " I would not live always; he needed not to trouble himself about that, it being impossible that he should: both statute and natural law forbid it. Ay, but this is his sense: supposing no such necessity as there is, if it were pure matter of election; upon a due balancing of accounts, and comparing the good and evil of death, I would not be confined always, or for any long time to the body. It would be a bondage unsupportable to be here always.

Indeed those that have their portion, their all, in this life, have no desire to be gone hence. They that were never changed by grace, desire no change by death, if such a concession were made to them, as was once to an English parliament, That they should never be dissolved, but by their own consent, when would they say as Paul, "I desire to be dissolved?" But it is far otherwise with them, whose portion and affections are in another world; they would not live always if they might; knowing, that never to die, is never to be happy.

Quest. If you say, *This is an excellent and most desirable temper of soul; but how did these holy men attain it? or what is the course we may take to get the like frame of willingness?*

Sol. They attained it, and you may attain it in such methods as these.

1. They lived in the believing views of the invisible world, and so must you, if ever death be desirable in your eyes, 2 Cor. 4:18. "It is said of all that died comfortably, that they died in faith," Heb. 11:18 You will never be willing to go along with death, except you know where it will carry you.

2. They had assurance of heaven, as well as faith to discern it. Assurance is a lump of sugar, indeed, in the bitter cup of death; nothing sweetens like it. So 2 Cor. 5:1; so Job 19:26,27. This puts roses into the pale cheeks of death, and makes it amiable, 1 Cor. 15:55,56. and Rom. 8:38,39.

3. Their hearts were weaned from this world, and an inordinate affection to a terrene life, Phil. iii. 8. All was dung and dross for Christ; they trampled under foot what we hug in our bosoms. So it is said, Heb. 10:34. "Ye took joyfully the spoiling of your goods, knowing in yourselves," &c. And so it must be with us, if ever we obtain a complacency in death.

4. They ordered their conversations with much integrity, and so kept their consciences pure, and void of offence: Acts 24:16. "Herein do I exercise myself," &c. and this was their comfort at last, 2 Cor. 1:12. "This is our rejoicing," etc. So Job 27:5. "My integrity will I not let go till I die:" Oh! this unstings death of all its terrors.

5. They kept their love to Christ at the height: that flame was vehement in their souls, and made them despise the terror, and desire the friendly assistance of death, to bring them to the sight of Jesus Christ, Phil. 1:28. So Ignatius, *O how I long, &c.* Thus it must be with you, if ever you make death eligible and lovely to you, which is terrible in itself. There is a loveliness in the death, as well as in the life of a Christian: "Let me die the death of the righteous," said Balaam.

Inference 2. Must we put off these tabernacles of flesh? *How necessary is it, that every soul look in season, and make provision for another habitation?* If you must be turned out of one house, you must provide another, or lie in the streets. This the apostle comforted himself with, that "if unclothed, he should not be found naked," 2 Cor. 5:1. a building of God, a house not made with hands. You must turn out, and that shortly, from these earthly habitations. Oh! what provision have you made for your souls against that day? The soul of Adrian was at a sad loss, when he saw he must be turned out of this world; *O animula vagula, blandala, heu quo vadis!* But it was Abraham, Isaac, and Jacob's privilege, that God had prepared for them a city, Heb. 11:16.

I know it is a common presumption of most men, that they shall be in heaven, when they can be no longer on earth. *Presumendo sperant, et sperando pereunt.* But a few moments will convince them of their fatal mistake; their poor souls will meet with a confounding repulse, like that, Matt. 6:22. There is indeed a city full of heavenly mansions prepared for some; but who are they that are entitled to it, and may confidently expect to be received into it? To be sure, not the presumptuous, who make a bridge of their own shadows, and so fall and perish in the waters. Brethren, it is one of the most solemn enquiries you were ever put upon: and therefore I beseech you, see whether your characters set you among those men, or no.

1. Those that are new-born, shall be clothed with their new house from heaven, when death unclothes them of these tabernacles: the *New Jerusalem* has none but new-born inhabitants, 1 Pet. 1:8,4. and Christ tells us, John 3:8. *all others are excluded* Glory is the privilege of grace. Let nature be adorned, and cultivated how it will, if not renewed by grace, there is no hope of glory. You must be born again, or turned back again from the gates of heaven disappointed. You must be regenerated, or damned. This alters the temper of thy heart, and suits it to the life of God, which is indispensably necessary to them that shall live with him. Else heaven would be no heaven to us, Rom. 8:7. and therefore we must be brought this way to it, 2 Cor. 5:5. No privilege of nature, no duties of religion avail without this, Gal. 6:15. If morality, without regeneration, could bring men to heaven, why are not the Heathens there? If strictness in duty, without regeneration, why are not the Pharisees there? Believe it, neither names, nor duties, no, nor the blood of Christ, ever did, or shall bring one soul to glory without it. O then, thou that boastest of a house in heaven, lay thine hand on thy heart, and ask it; Am I a new creature, i.e. Am I renewed, (1.) in my state and condition? 1 John 3:14. past from death to life. (2.) In my frame and temper? Eph. 5:8. "Once darkness, now light in the Lord." (3.) In my practice and conversation? Eph. 2:12,13. 1 Cor. 6:11. If not, my soul is destitute of an habitation in the city of God; and when I die, my body must lie in the lonely house of the grave, that dark vault and prison, and my soul be shut out from God into outer darkness.

2. Those that live as strangers, and pilgrims on earth, seeking a better place, and state, than this world affords them; for them God has made preparations in glory, Heb. 11:13,16. If you be strangers on earth, you are the inhabitants of heaven. Now there be six things included in this character. 1. They look not on this world as their own home, nor on the people of it, as their own people, 2 Cor. 5:8. ε κ δ η μ η σ α ι, *to be unpeopled.* These are none of my fellow-citizens, we must go two ways at death. 2. They set not their affections on things present, as their portion, 2 Cor. 4:18. Psal. 17:13,14. Their bodies are here, their hearts in heaven. 3. Their carriage, and manner of life, not like the men of this world, 1 Pet. iv. 4. ξ ε ν ι ζ ο ν τ α ι. So the rule guides them, Rom. 12:2. and so their course is steered; at least intended, Phil. 3:20. Our τ ο π ο λ ι τ ε υ μ α, *our trade is in heaven.* (4.) Their dialect and language differ from the natives of this world. Their language is earthly, 1 John 4:5,6. but these have a *pure lip,* Zech. 3:9. (5.) Their society, and chosen companions are not of this world, Psal. 16:3. They are a company of themselves, Acts 4:21. (6.) Their spirit, and temper of heart are not after the world, 1 Cor. 2:12. They have *another spirit,* Numb. 14:24. These things discover us to be strangers on earth, and consequently, the men for whom God has prepared heavenly habitations when we die.

3. Those that live and die by faith, shall not fail to be received into a better habitation by death. This is another character of them that shall be received into glory, laid down in the same place, Heb. 11:13. They lived by faith, and when they died, they died embracing the promises, which is characteristic of those that shall dwell in that heavenly city; and implies, (1.) Intimate acquaintance with the promises, they are things well known, and familiarised to them. The word *aspansamenoi, salutantes,* saluting them, is a metaphor, from the manner of parting betwixt two dear and intimate friends. The faith of a Christian embraces the promises in its arms, as dear friends use to do at parting, and says, Farewell, sweet promises, from which I have sucked out so much relief and refreshment in all the troubles of my life; I must now live no more by faith on you, but by sight: O you have often cheered my soul, and been my song in the house of my pilgrimage. (2) It implies the firm credit that a believer gives to things unseen, upon the grounds of the promises, as if he did sensibly take and grasp them in his very arms and bosom. They take Christ, and all the invisible things in the promises, into their sensible embraces, 1 Pet. 1:8. Faith is to them instead of eyes. (3.) It implies the sincerity of a believer's pro-

fession, who dares trust to that at the last gasp, which he professed to believe in the midst of life, and the comforts of this world. As he professed to believe in health, so you shall find his actings, when his eye and heart-strings are cracking, Rom. 14:9. Christ, in the promises, was his professed joy and life, and this is what he grasps at death, and lays his last hold on. (4.) It shows you whence all a believer's comforts come, in life and death. O, it is from the promises, Christ in the promises is the spring of their consolation. This they fetch their comfort from, when the world cannot administer one drop of refreshment to them. There be two great works faith performs for the saints, one in life, the other in death: in life, it is the principle of mortification to their sins; in death, it is the spring of consolation to their hearts; it makes them die while they live, and live while they die.

4. Those that love the person and appearance of Christ, have a mark that sets them among the inhabitants of heaven, and glory, 2 Tim. 4:8. but then this love must be, (1.) Sincere, and without hypocrisy. (2.) Supreme, and above all other beloveds. {3.) Conforming the soul to Christ; if sincere and supreme, it will be transformative. (4.) Longing to be with him. Such love is a mark of souls for whom heaven is prepared.

Inf. 3. Must we put off our tabernacles, and that shortly? *What a spur is this to a diligent redemption, and improvement of time?* This is the use Peter made of it here, and every one of us should make. It was said of Bishop Hooper, he was spare in his diet, spare in his words, but most of all spare of his time. You have but a little time in these tabernacles; what pity is it to waste such out of a little?

(1.) Great is the worth and excellency of time, all the treasures of the world cannot protract, stop, or call back one minute of time. O what is man that the heavenly bodies should be wheeled about by Almighty Power in constant revolutions, to beget time for him! Psal. 8:3.

(2.) More precious are the seasons and opportunities that are in time for our souls; those are the golden spots of time, like the pearl in the oyster-shell, of much more value than the shell that contains it. There is much time in a short opportunity. There is a day on which our eternal happiness depends, Luke 19:41,42. Heb. 4:7.

(3.) Invaluable are the things which God does for men's souls in time. There are works wrought upon men's hearts in a seasonable hour in this life, which have an influence into the soul's happiness throughout eternity. There is a time of mercy, a time of love, viz. of illumination, and conversion; and on that point of time, eternal life hangs in the whole weight of it.

(4.) Lost opportunity is never to be recovered by the soul any more, Ezel. 24:13. Rev. 22:11. To come before the opportunity, is to come before the bird is hatched; and to come after it, is to come when the bird is flown. There is no calling back time, when it is once past. See this in the examples you find, Luke 13:26. Eccl. 9:10.

(5.) It is wholly uncertain to every soul, whether the present day may not determine his lease in this tabernacle and a writ of ejection be served by death upon his soul to-morrow, James 4:16. Luke 12:20.

(6.) As soon as ever time shall end, eternity takes place. The stream of time delivers souls daily into the boundless ocean of vast eternity. *Ab hoc momento pendit aeternitas.* We are now measured by time, hereafter by eternity.

(7.) In eternity all things are fixed and unalterable. We have no more to do, all means and works are at an end, John 9:4. and Eccl. 11:3. "As the tree falls, so it lies." Oh that these weighty considerations might lie upon your hearts, as long as you are in these tabernacles! If they did, (1.) the unregenerate would not so desperately hazard their eternal happiness, by trifling away their precious seasons under the gospel. O! how many aged sinners, grey-headed sinners, hear me this day, who in fifty or sixty years never redeemed one solemn hour, to take their poor souls aside out of the clutter and distracting noise of the world to ask and debate this question with them, *Oh my soul, how stands the case with thee in reference to the world to come!* They have found no time to bethink themselves in what world their souls shall be landed, when time shall deliver them up into eternity. Their whole life has been but a continual diversion from one trifle to another: they have been serious in trifles, and trifled in things most serious; this will afford horrid reflections in the world to come. (2.) The regenerate should not cast away the comfort of their lives, in the evidences of eternal life, at so cheap a rate as they do. May I not say to you as the apostle does, Heb. 5:12. for the time you have had under the gospel you might have attained a rich treasure, both of grace and comfort; *Turpe est esse senex elementarius.* Is it not shameful and inexcusable, to be where you were twenty years past? Oh! let these things sink deep into every soul.

Inf. 4. Must we shortly put off these our tabernacles? *Then slack your pace, am cool yourselves; be not too eager in the prosecution of earthly designs.* O what bustling is here for the world, and for provision for futurity, whereas far less would serve the turn! We need not victual s ship to cross the channel to France, as if she were bound to the Indies. Most men's provisions, at least their cares and thoughts, are far beyond the preparations of their abode in this world. The folly of this, Christ discovers in that parable, Luke 12:19. and on this very account gives him the title of a fool, who provided for years, many years; when poor soul, he had not one night to enjoy these provisions.

Oh the multitude of thoughts and cares this world needlessly devours! We keep ourselves in such a continual hurry and crowd of cares, thoughts, and employments about the concerns of the body, that we can find little time to be alone, communing with our own hearts about our great concernments in eternity. It is with many of us, in respect of our souls, and their great interests, as it is with a man that is deep in thoughts about some subject that wholly swallows him up, he seeth not what he seeth, nor heareth what he heareth of any other matter: his eyes seem to look upon this or that, but it is all one as if he did not. So it was with Archimedes, who was so intent upon drawing his mathematical schemes, that though all the city was in an alarm, the enemy had taken it by storm, the streets filled with dreadful cries, and dead bodies, the soldiers came into his particular house, nay, entered his very study, and plucked him by the sleeve, before he took any notice of it: even so many men's hearts are so profoundly immersed, and drowned in earthly cares, thoughts, projects, or pleasures, that death must come to their very houses, yea, and pull them by the sleeve, and tell them its errand, before they will begin to awake, and come to a serious consideration of things more important.

Inf. 5. If we must shortly put off these tabernacles, *then the groaning and mourning time of all believers is but short; how heavy soever their burden be, yet they shall carry it but a little way.* It is said, 2 Cor. 5:4. "We that are in this tabernacle do groan, being "burdened." Good souls, in this state, are everywhere groaning under heavy pressures. Their burdens are of two sorts, sympathetic, whereby they grieve with, and on the account of others, and so every true member of the church of God ought to sympathise, both with God, Psal. 139:21. "Am not I grieved with them that rise up against thee?" Psal. 13:10. "It is as with a sword in their bones;" and with the people of God, Zeph. 3:18. sorrowful for the solemn assembly; so 2 Cor. 11:29. "Who is offended, and I burn not?" And indeed, it is an argument of rich, as well as true grace, that we can, and do heartily mourn with, and for the interest and people of God, though our own lot in the world, as Nehemiah's, be never so comfortable. Or else our burdens are idiopathic, i.e. such as we ear upon our own proper account and score. And where is the Christian that has not his own burden, yea, many burdens on him at once? Some groan under the burden of sin, Rom. 8:24. Scarce one day are the tears off from some eye-lids on this account. And who groans not under the burden of affliction, either inward upon the soul, Prov. 18:14. Job 6:1,2,3, or outward upon the body, state, relations, &c. These things make the people of God a burden to themselves, Job 7:20,21. Yea, under these burdens they would sink, did not the Lord sustain them, Psal. 55:22.

But God will put a speedy and final end to all these things. When you put off this tabernacle, you put off with it all those burdens, inward and outward. The soul presently feels a great load off his shoulders; it shall never groan more, God shall thenceforth wipe away all tears from their eyes; for why are those burdens now permitted and imposed by the Lord upon you, but (1.) To prevent sin, Hos. 2:6. They are your clogs to keep you from straying. (2.) To purge out sin, Isa. 27:9. (3.) To make you long more for heaven, and the rest to come. But all these ends are accomplished in that day you put off your tabernacles, for then sin is gone, and the rest is come.

Inf. 6. Must you shortly put of those tabernacles? *Then spare them not while you have them, but enjoy them for God with all diligence.* Shortly they shall be useless to you, yea, meat for worms; now they may be serviceable, and their service is their honour: you received them not for such low ends as you employ them for. See 1 Cor. 6:20. "Glorify God in your souls and bodies, which are his:" You expect to have them glorious bodies one day; O then let them be serviceable bodies now! Be not fond of them to that degree many are, who chose rather to have them *eaten up with rust,* than *worm out with service.* It is your present honour to be active, and will be your singular comfort another day. What greater comfort, when you come to put them of at death, than this, that you have employed them faithfully for God.

Inf. 7. Look beyond this embodied state, and learn to live now as you hope to live shortly; begin to be what you expect to be. You know the time is at hand, that you shall live above all bodily concernments and employments, the soul shall be a drudge to the body no more. You shall be as the angels, Matt. 22:30. not marrying, nor giving in marriage, which is, by a *synechdoche,* put for all carnal employments and enjoyments; eat no more, drink no more, sleep no more, buy and sell no more. Now suit yourselves as much as your state and the duties of religion will suffer you to that state before hand. The sum of what I aim at is in 1 Cor. 7:29,30. Be in all your relations as if you had none. Look on those things as if already they were not, which shortly must be none of yours; and both acquaint and accustom your thoughts to the life of separation from the body, which you must shortly leave. Which brings me home to the next point, *viz. The condition of human souls in the state of separation.*

Heb. 12:23

-- Kai pneumasi dikaioon teteleioomenoon. – And to the spirits of just men made perfect.

The particular scope of this context falls in with the general design of the whole gospel, which is to persuade men to a life of holiness. The matter of the exhortation is most weighty, and the arguments enforcing it most powerful: He does not talk, but dispute; he does not say, but prove, that greater and more powerful engagements unto holiness lie upon those who live under the gospel, than upon the people who lived under the law. And thus the argument lies in this context.

If God, at the delivering of the law upon *mount Sinai,* strictly enjoined, and required so great purity and holiness in that people, signified by the ceremonies of two days preparation, the washing of their clothes, abstinence from conjugal society, &c. Exod. 19:10. much more does he require, and expect it in us, who are come under a much more excellent and heavenly dispensation than theirs was.

To make good the *sequel,* he compares the *legal* and *evangelical* dispensations in many particulars, ver. 18, 19,20,21,22,23. giving the gospel the preference throughout the whole comparison.

Hence the privileges of the New-Testament believers are stated, both *negatively* and *positively.*

1. *Negatively,* By showing what we are exempted from.

2. *Positively,* Showing what we are to come unto.

1. *Negatively,* What we are exempted, or freed from; ver. 18, 19,20,21. "We are not come unto the mount that might be "touched," &c.

The sum of all is this, that the promulgation of the law was accompanied with amazing dread and terror. For, after Moses, by command from God, had sanctified the *mount*, and set rails about it, that neither priest nor people, man nor beast, might touch the very borders of it, lest they die; the Lord descended in fire upon the top of the *mountain* the third day, in the morning, with most terrible tokens of divine majesty, to wit, with thunderings, lightnings, dark clouds, and the noise of a *trumpet,* exceeding loud; the *mount* was covered with smoke, as the smoke of a furnace, and flames mounting up into the midst of heaven, the whole mountain shaking and trembling exceedingly: Out of this horrid tempest the awful voice of God was heard, all the people in the camp trembling, Yea, and Moses himself quaking for fear.

This was the manner of the law's promulgation: But to such a terrible dispensation as this we are not come, which is the negative part of our privilege.

2. He opens the positive privileges to which we are come.

(1.) "Ye are come, says he, to mount Sion, not the earthly, but the spiritual Sion. Mount Sion was the place celebrated above all the world for the worship of God, Psal. 87. "All my springs, says God, are in thee." There was the temple, the ark of the covenant, the glory of the Lord dwelling between the *cherubims.* The priests that attended the service of God had their residence there, as the angels have in heaven. Thither the tribes went up from all quarters of Judea, Psal. 84. as the children of God now do to heaven, from all quarters of the world. Judea was the best kingdom in the world; Jerusalem the best city in that kingdom; and Sion the most glorious place in that city. Here Christ taught his heavenly doctrine; near to it he finished his glorious work of redemption. Hence the everlasting gospel went forth into all the world: And, on these considerations, it is put to signify the gospel church, or state in this place, and is therefore called the *heavenly Jerusalem,* in the following words, We do not come to the literal Sion, nor to the *earthly Jerusalem;* but to the gospel-church, or state, which may be called a heaven upon earth, compared with that *literal Jerusalem.*

(2.) Ye are come "to an innumerable company of angels." To *myriads of angels,* a *myriad* is ten thousand, but myriads in the plural number, and set down indefinitely too, may note many millions of angels: And therefore we fitly render it, "to an innumerable company of angels."

A TREATISE OF THE SOUL OF MAN

They had the ministry of angels as well as we, thousands of them ministered to the Lord in the dispensation of the law at Sinai, Psal. 68:17. But this notwithstanding, we are come to a much clearer knowledge, both of their present ministry for us on earth, Heb. 1:14. and of our fellowship and equality with them in heaven, Luke 20:36.

(3.) "Ye are come to the general assembly, and church of the first born, whose names are written (or enrolled) in heaven." This also greatly commends and amplifies the privileges of the New-Testament believers. The church of God in former ages was circumscribed and shut up within the narrow limits of one small kingdom, which was a garden enclosed out of a waste wilderness: But now, by the calling in of the Gentiles, the church is extended far and wide, Eph. 3:5,6. It is become a great assembly, comprising the believers of all nations under heaven; and so speaking of them collectively, it is the general convention or assembly, which is also dignified, and ennobled by two illustrious characters, viz. (1.) That it is *the church of the firstborn,* i.e. consisting of members dignified and privileged above others, as the first born among the Israelites did excel their younger brethren. (2.) That their *names are written in heaven,* i.e. registered or enrolled in God's book, as children and heirs of the heavenly inheritance, as the first born in Israel were registered in order to the priesthood, Numb. 3:40,41.

(4.) Ye are come "to God, the Judge of all." But why to God the Judge? This seems to spoil the harmony, and jar with the other parts of the discourse. No, they are come to God as a righteous Judge, who, as such, will pardon them, 1 John 1:9. *Crown* them, 2 Tim. 4:8. and *avenge* them on all their opt pressing and persecuting enemies, 1 Thes. 1:5,6,7.

(5.) "And to the spirits of just men made perfect." A most glorious privilege indeed; in which we are distinctly to consider.

1. The quality of those with whom we are associated or taken into fellowship.

2. The way and manner of our association with them.

1. The quality of those with whom we are associated, or to whom we are said to be come; and they are described by three characters, viz.

(1.) Spirits of men.

(2.) Spirits of just men.

(3.) Spirits of just men perfected, or consummated.

(1.) They are called spirits, that is, immaterial substances, strictly opposed to bodies, which are no way the objects of our exterior senses, neither visible to the eye, or sensible to the touch, which were called properly souls while they animated bodies in this lower world; but now being loosed and separated from them by death, and existing alone in the world above, they are properly and strictly styled spirits.

(2.) They are the *spirits of just men.* Man may be termed just two ways, (1.) By a full discharge and acquittance from the guilt of all his sins, and so believers are *just* men, even while they live on earth, groaning under other imperfections, Acts 13:39.

Or, (2.) By a total freedom from the pollution of any sin. And though in this sense there is not "a just man upon earth that does good, and sinneth not," Eccl. 7:22. yet even in this sense Adam was just before the fall, Eccl. 7:29. according to his original constitution; and all believers are so in their glorified condition; all sin being perfectly purged out of them, and its existence utterly destroyed in them. On which account,

(a.) They are called the spirits of just men *made perfect,* or consummate. The word perfect is not here to be understood absolutely, but by way of *synecdoche;* they are not perfect in every respect, for one part of these just men lies rotting in the grave: but they are perfected, for so much as concerns their spirit; though the flesh perish and lie in dishonour, yet their spirits being once loosed from the body, and freed radically and perfectly from sin, are presently admitted to the facial vision and fruition of God, which is the culminating point (as I may call it) higher than which the spirit of man aspires not; and attaining to this, it is, for so much as concerns itself, made perfect. Even as a body at last lodged in its centre, gravitates no more, but is at perfect rest; so it is with the spirit of man come home to God in glory, it is now consummate, no more need to be done to malice it as perfectly happy as it is capable to be made; which is the first thing to be considered, viz. the quality of those with whom we are associated.

2. The second follows, namely, the way and manner of our association with these blessed spirits of just men, noted in this expression, [*we are come.*] He says not, *we* shall come hereafter, when

the resurrection had restored our bodies, or after the general judgement; but, *we are come* to these spirits of just men. The meaning whereof we may take in these three particulars.

(1.) We that live under the gospel-light, are come to a clearer apprehension, sight, and knowledge of the blessed and happy estate of the souls of the righteous after death, than ever they had, or ordinarily could have, who lived under the types and shadows of the law, Eph. 3:4,5. And so we are come to them in respect of clearer apprehension.

(2.) We are come to those blessed spirits in our representative, Christ, who has carried our nature into the very midst of them, and whom they all behold with highest admiration and delight. By Christ, who is entered into that holy place where these spirits of just men live, we are come into a near relation with them: for he being the common head, both to them in heaven, and to us on earth, we and they consequentially make but one body or society, Eph. 2:10. whereupon (notwithstanding the different and remote countries they and we live in) we are said "to sit down with them in heavenly places," Eph. 3:5. and 2:6.

(8.) *We are come.* That is, we are as good as come, or we are upon the matter come; there remains nothing betwixt them and us but a puff of breath, a little space of time, which shortens every moment: We are come to the very borders of their country, and there is nothing to speak of betwixt them and us: And by this expression, *we are come,* he teacheth us to account and reckon those things as present which so shortly will be present to us, and to look upon them as if they already were, which is the highest and most comfortable life of faith we can live on earth. Hence the note is,

Doct. *That righteous and holy souls, once separated from their bodies by death, are immediately perfected in themselves; and associated with others alike perfect in the kingdom of God.*

That the spirits of just men at the time of their separation from their bodies do not utterly fail in their beings, nor that they are so prejudiced and wounded by death, that they cannot exert their own proper acts in the absence of the body, has been already cleared in the foregoing parts of this treatise, and will be more fuller cleared from this text.

FLAVEL

But the true level and aim of this discourse is at a higher mark, viz. the far more excellent, free, and noble life the souls of the just begin to live immediately after their bodies are dropped off from them by death, at which time they begin to live like themselves, a pleasant, free, and divine life. So much at least is included in the apostle's epithet in my text, spirits of just men made perfect; and suitable thereto are his words in 1 Cor. 13:10,12. "When that which is perfect is come, then that which is in part shall be done away. For now we see through a glass darkly, but then face to face, now I know in part, but then I shall know, even as also I am known."

These two adverbs, now and then, distinguish the twofold state of gracious souls, and show what it is while they are confined in the body, and what it shall be from the time of their emancipation and freedom from that clog of mortality. *Now* we are imperfect, but *then* that which is perfect takes place, and that which is imperfect is done away, as the imperfect twilight is done away by the opening of the perfect day.

And it deserves a serious animadversion, that this perfect state does not succeed the imperfect one after a long interval, (as long as betwixt the dissolution and resurrection of the body) but the imperfect state of the soul is immediately done away by the coming of the perfect one. The glass is laid by as useless, when we come to see face to face, and eye to eye.

The waters will prove very deep here, too deep for any line of mine to fathom; there is a cloud always overshadowing the world to come, a gloom and haziness upon that state: Fain we would, with our creak and feeble beam of imperfect knowledge, penetrate this cloud, and dispel this gloom and haziness, but cannot. We think seriously and closely of this great and awful subject, but our thoughts cannot pierce through it: we reinforce those thoughts by a sally, or thick succession of fresh thoughts, and yet all will not do, our thoughts return to us either in confusion, or without the expected success. For alas! how little is it that we know, or can know of our own souls now while they are embodied! much less of their unembodied state. The apostle tells us, 1 Cor. 2:9. "That eye has not seen, nor ear heard, neither have entered into the heart of man, the things which God hath prepared for them that love him." And another apostle adds, "It does not yet appear what we shall be," 1 John 3:2.

A TREATISE OF THE SOUL OF MAN

Yet all this is no discouragement to the search and regular enquiry into the future state; for though reason cannot penetrate these mysteries, yet God has *revealed them to us,* (though not perfectly) *by his Spirit.* And though we know not particularly, and circumstantially what we shall be, yet this we know, that "we shall be like him, for we shall see him as he is." And it is our privilege and happiness, that we are come to the spirits of just men made perfect, i.e. to a clearer knowledge of that state than was ordinarily attainable by believers, under former dispensations.

These things premised, I will proceed to open my apprehensions of the separate state of the spirits of just men made perfect, in *twelve propositions:* whereby, as by so many steps, we may orderly advance as far as safely and warrantably we may, into the knowledge of this great mystery, clearing what afterwards shall remain obscure, in the solution of several questions relating to this subject, and then apply the whole, in several uses of this great point: And the first proposition is this:

Proposition 1. There is a twofold separation of the soul from the body: viz. one mental, the other real: Or,

1. Intellectual, by the mind only.

2. Physical, by the stroke of death.

1. Of intellectual, or mental separation, I am first to speak in this proposition; and it is nothing else but an act of the understanding, or mind, conceiving, or considering the soul and body, as separate and parted from each other, while yet they are united in a personal oneness by the breath of life. This mental separation may, and ought to be frequently and seriously made, before death make the real and actual separation; and the more frequently and seriously we do it, the less of horror and distraction will attend that real and fatal stroke, whenever it shall be given. For hereby we learn to bear it gradually, and, by gentle essays, to acquaint our shoulders with the burden of it. *Separation* is a word that has much of horror in the very sound, and uses to have much more in the sense and feeling of it, else it would not deserve that title, Job 8:14. "The kind of terrors," or the most terrible of all terribles: But acquaintance and familiarity abates that horror, and that two ways especially.

(1.) As it is preventive of much guilt.

FLAVEL

(2.) As it gains a more inward knowledge of its nature.

(1.) The serious and fixed thoughts of the parting hour, is preventive of much guilt; and the greatest part of the horror of death rises out of the guilt of sin; "The sting of death is sin," 1 Cor. 15:56. Augustine says, "Nothing more recalls a man from sin, than the frequent meditation of death." I dare not say it is the strongest of all curbs to keep us back from sin, but I am sure it is a very strong one.

Let a soul but seriously meditate what a change death will make shortly upon his person and condition; and the natural effects of such a meditation, through the blessing of God upon it, will be a flatting and quenching of its keen and raging appetite after the ensnaring vanities of this world (which draw men into so much guilt) a conscious fear of sin, and an awakened care of duty. It was once demanded of a very holy man (who spent much more than the ordinary allowance of time in prayer, and searching his own heart) why he so macerated his own body by such frequent and long continued duties! His answer was, *O! I must die, I must die!* Nothing could separate him from duty, who had already separated his soul from his body, and all this world, by fixed end deep thoughts of death.

(2.) Hereby we gain a more inward knowledge and acquaintance with it, the less it terrifies us. A lion is much more dreadful to him that never saw him, than he is to his keeper who feedeth him every day. A pitched battle is more frightful and scaring to a new-listed soldier, that never took his place in the field before, nor saw the dreadful countenance of an army ready to engage, nor heard the thundering noise of cannon, and volleys of shot, the shouts of armies, and groans of dying men on every side, than it is to an old soldier who has been used to such things. The like we may observe in seamen, who it may be trembled at first, and now can sing in a storm.

Scarce any thing is more necessary for weak and timorous believers to meditate on, than the time of their separation. Our hearts will be apt to start and boggle at the first view of death; but it is good to do by them as men use to do by young colts; ride them up to that which they fright at, and make them smell to it, which is the way to cure them. "Look, as bread, says one, is more necessary than other food, so the meditation of death is more necessary than many other meditations." Every time we change our habitations, we should realise therein our great change: our souls must shortly leave this, and be lodged for a longer season in another mansion. When we put off our clothes at night, we have a fit occasion to consider, that we must strip nearer one of these days, and put off, not our clothes only, but the body that wears them too.

Holy Job had, by frequent thoughts, familiarised death and the grave to himself, and could speak of them as men use to speak of their houses and dearest relations, Job 17:14. "I have said to corruption, Thou art my father, to the worm, Thou art my mother and sister." But it needs much grace to bring, and to hold the heart to this work; and therefore Moses begs it of God, Psal. 90:12. "So teach us to number our days"; and David, Psal. 39:4. "Lord, make me to know my end." Yea, the advantages of it have been acknowledged by men, whose light was less, and diversions more than ours. The Jews, for this use and end, had their sepulchres built beforehand, and that in their gardens of pleasure too, that they might season the delights of life with the frequent thoughts of death, John 19:41.

Philip of Macedon would be awakened by his page every morning with this sentence, *memento te esse mortalem:* Remember, O king, that thou art a mortal man. A great emperor of Constantinople, not only at his inauguration, but at his great feasts, ordered a mason to bring two stones before him, and say, "Choose, O emperor, which of the two stones thou wilt for thy tombstone?" Reader, thou wilt find mental separation much easier than real separation: it is easier to think of death, than it is to feel it; and the more we think of it, the less we are like to feel it.

Prop. 2. Actual separation may be considered either in fieri, *in the previous pangs, and foregoing agonies of it; or* in facto esse, *in the last separating stroke, which actually parts the soul and body asunder, lays the body prostrate and dead at the feet of death, and thrusts the soul quite out of its ancient and beloved habitation.*

Let it be considered in the previous pangs and forerunning agonies, which commonly make way for this actual dissolution: and to the people of God, this is the worst and bitterest part of death (except those conflicts with Satan, which they sometimes grapple with on a deathbed) which they encounter at that time. There is (says one) no poinard in death itself, like those in the way or prologue to it. I like not to die, (said another) but I care not if I were dead; the end is better than the way. The conflicts and struggles of nature with death are bitter and sharp pains, unknown to men before, whatever pains they have endured: nor can it be expected to be otherwise, seeing the ties and

FLAVEL

engagements betwixt the soul and body are so strong, as we showed before.

The soul will not easily part with the body, but disputes the possages with Death, from member to member, like resolute soldiers in a stormed garrison, till at last it is forced to yield up the fort royal into the hands of victorious Death, and leave the dearly be loved body a captive to it.

This is the dark side of death to all good men; and though it be not worth naming, in comparison with the dreadful consequences of death to all others, yet in itself it is terrible.

Separation is not natural to the soul which was created with an inclination to the body; it is natural indeed to clasp and embrace, to love and cherish its own body; but to be divided from it, is grievous and preternatural.

The agonies of death are expressed in scripture, by a word which signifies "the travailing pains of a woman", yea, by the sharpest and most acute pains they at that time feel, Acts 2:24.

And yet all are not handled alike roughly by the hands of death; some are favoured with a desirable *euthanasia,* gentle and easy death.

It is the privilege of some Christians to have their souls fetched out of their bodies, as it were by a kiss from the mouth of God, as the Jewish Rabbins use to express the manner of Moses' death. Mr. Bolton felt no pain at his death, but the cold hand of his friend, who asked him what pain he felt. Yea, holy Bayneham in the midst of the flames, professed it was to him as a bed of roses.

Every believer is equally freed from the sting and curse of death; but every one is not equally favoured in the agonies and pains of death.

2. Separation from the body is to be considered *in facto esse,* i.e. in the result and issue of all those bitter pangs and agonies, which end in the actual dissolution of soul and body. "Death, or actual separation, is nothing else but the dissolving of the tie or loosing of the bond of union betwixt the soul and body." "Some call it the privation of the second act of the soul, that is, its act of informing or enlivening the body." Others, according to the scripture-phrase, the departing of

the soul from the body. So Peter stiles it, 2 Pet. 1:15. *Meia ten emen exodon,* after my departure, i.e. after my death. Augustine calls it the laying down of a heavy burden, provided there be not another burden for the soul to bear afterwards, which will sink it into hell.

In respect of the body, which the soul now forsakes, it is called "the putting off this tabernacle," 2 Pet. 1:14. and, "the dissolving the earthly house or tabernacle," 2 Cor. 5:1.

In respect of the *terminus a quo,* the place from which the soul removes at death, it is called our departure hence, Phil. 1:23. or

Our weighing anchor, and loosing from this coast or shore, to sail to another.

In respect of the *terminus ad quem,* the place to which the spirits of the just go at death, it is called our going to, or being with the Lord, Phil. 1:28. To conclude, in respect of that which does most lively resemble and shadow it forth, it is called our falling asleep, Acts 7:60. our sleeping in Jesus, 1 Thes. 4:14. This metaphor of sleep must be stretched no farther than the Spirit of God designed in the choice of it, which was not to favour and countenance the fancy of a sleeping soul after death, but to represent its state of placid rest in Jesus' bosom, if it refer at all to the soul; for I think it most properly respects the body; and then the sepulchres, where the bodies of the saints were laid, got the name of *koimetheria*, dormitories, or sleeping places.

This is its last farewell to this world, never more to return to a low animal life more. Job 7:9,10. "For as the cloud is consumed and vanished away, so he that goeth down to the grave shall come up no more: he shall return no more to his house, neither shall his place know him any more." The soul is no more bound to a body, nor a retainer to the sun, moon, or stars, to meat, drink, and sleep, but is become a free, single, abstracted being, a separate and pure spirit, which the Latins call *lemures, manes,* ghosts or souls of the dead, and my text, *Spirits made perfect;* a being much like unto the angels, who are, *dunameis asomathous*, bodiless beings. An angel, as one speaks, is a perfect soul, a soul is an imperfect angel: I do not say, that upon their separation, they become angels, for they will still remain a distinct species of spirits. Angels have no inclination to bodies, nor were ever fettered with clogs of flesh, as souls were. And by this you see what a vast difference there is betwixt these two considerations of death: how ghastly and affrighting is it in its previous pangs! how lovely and desirable in the issue and result of them! which is but the change of earth for heaven, men for God, sin and misery, for perfection and glory.

Prop. 3. The separation of the soul and body, makes a great and wonderful change upon both, but especially upon the soul.

There is a twofold change made upon man by death, one upon his lady, another upon his soul. The change upon the body is great and visible to every eye. A living body is changed into a dead carcass: a beautiful and comely body into a loathsome spectacle: that which was lately the object of delight and love, is hereby make an abhorrence to all flesh; "Bury my dead out of my sight," Gen. 23:4.

What the sun is to the greater, that the soul is to the lesser world. When the sun shines comfortably, how vegete and cheerful do all things look! how well do they thrive and prosper! the birds sing merrily, the beasts play wantonly, the whole creation enjoyeth a day of light and joy: but when it departs, what a night of horror followeth! how are all things wrapped up in the sable mantle of darkness! or if it but abate its heat, as in winter, the creatures are, as it were, buried in the winding-sheet of winter's frost and snow: just so is it with the body, when the soul shines pleasantly upon it, or departs from it.

That body which was fed so assiduously, cared for so anxiously, loved so passionately, is now tumbled into a pit, and left to the mercy of crawling worms. The change which judgment made upon that great and flourishing city Nineveh, is a fit emblem to shadow forth that change which death makes upon human bodies: that great and renowned city was once full of people, which thronged the streets thereof; there you might have seen children playing upon the thresholds, beauties showing themselves through the windows, melody sounding in its palaces: but what an alteration was made upon it, the prophet Zephaniah describes, chap. 2:14. "Flocks shall lie down in the midst of her, all the beasts of the nations; both the cormorant and the bittern shall lodge in the upper lintels of it: their voice shall sing in the windows; desolation shall be in the thresholds, for he shall uncover the cedar-work."

Thus it is with the body when death has dislodged the soul: worms nestle in the holes where the beautiful eyes were once placed; corruption and desolation is upon all parts of that stately structure. But this being a vulgar theme, I shall leave the body to the dust from whence it came, and follow the soul, which is my proper subject, pointing at the changes which are made on it.

The essence of the soul is not destroyed or changed by the body's ruin; it is substantially the self-same soul it was when in the body. The supposition of an essential change would disorder the whole frame and model of God's eternal design for the redemption and glorification of it, Rom. 8:29,30. But yet, though it undergo no substantial change at death, yet divers great and remarkable alterations are made upon it, by sundering it from the body. As,

1. It is not where it was: it was in a body, immersed in matter, married unto flesh and blood; but now it is out of the body, unclothed and stripped naked out of its garments of flesh, like pure gold melted out of the ore with which it was commixed; or as a bird let out of her cage into the open fields and woods. This makes a great and wonderful change upon it.

2. Being free from the body, it is consequently discharged and freed from all those cares, studies, fears and sorrows to which it was here enthralled and subjected upon the body's account: it puts off all those passions and burdens with it: never spends one thought more about food and raiment, health and sickness, wives and children, riches or poverty, but lives henceforth after the manner of angels, Matt. 22:30. It is now unrelated to, and therefore unconcerned about all these things.

3. In the unbodied state it is perfectly freed from sin, both in the acts and habits; a mercy it never enjoyed since the first moment it dwelt in the body. The cure of this disease was indeed begun in the work of sanctification; but it is not perfected till the day of the soul's glorification. It is now, and not till now, a spirit made perfect; that is, a soul enjoying its perfect health and rectitude: no more groans, tears, or lamentations, upon the account of indwelling sin.

4. The way and manner of its converse with, and enjoyment of God is changed. There are two mediums by which souls converse with God in the body, viz.

(1.) One internal, *to wit*, faith.

(2.) The other external, *to wit*, ordinances.

(1.) If a man walk with God on earth, it must be in the use and exercise of faith, 2 Cor. 5:7. Nor can there be any communion carried on betwixt God and the soul without it, Heb. 11:6.

(2.) The external *mediums* are the ordinances of God, or duties of religion, both public and private, Psal. 63:2. Betwixt these two *mediums* of communion with God, this remarkable difference is found: The soul may see and enjoy God by faith, in the want or absence of ordinances; but there is no seeing or conversing with God, in the greatest plenty and purity of ordinances, without faith, Heb. 4:2.

But in the same moment the soul is cut off from union with the body, it is also cut off from both these ways of enjoying God, 1 Cor. 13:12. Isa 38:11. But yet the soul is no loser; nay, it is the greatest *gainer* by this change. The child is no loser by ceasing to derive its nourishment by the navel, when it comes to receive it by the mouth, a more noble way, whereby it gets a new pleasure in tasting the variety of all delectable food. Hezekiah bemoaned the loss of ordinances upon his supposed deathbed, saying, "I shall not see the Lord, even the Lord in the land of the living:" q.d. Now farewell temple and ordinances; I shall never go any more into his temple, where my soul has been so often cheered and refreshed with the displays of his grace and goodness; I shall never more join with the assembly of his people on earth. And suppose he had not, sure he would have lost nothing, had he then exchanged the temple at Jerusalem, for the temple in heaven; and communion with sinful imperfect saints on earth, for fellowship with angels, and "the spirits of just men made perfect." By this change we lose no more then he loses, who while he stands delightfully contemplating the image of his dearest friend in a glass, has the glass snatched away by his friend, whom he now seeth face to face.

Upon this change of the mediums of communion, it will follow, that the communion betwixt God and the separate soul, excels all the communion it ever had with him on earth, in

(1.) The clearness. (2.) The sweetness. (3.) The constancy of it.

(1.) Its visions of God, in the state of separation, are more clear, distinct, and direct than they were on earth; clouds and shadows are now fled away: The soul now seeth as it is seen, and knoweth as it is known; its apprehensions of God there, differ from those it had here, as the crude and confused apprehensions of a child do, from those we have in the manly state.

(2.) They are also more sweet and ravishing: As our visions are, so are our pleasures; perfect visions produce perfect pleasures: The faculties of the soul now, and never till now, lie level to that rule, Matt. 22:37. The visions of God command, and call forth all the heart and soul, mind, and strength, into acts of dove and delight. It was not so here; if the spirit was willing, the flesh was weak; but there the clog is off from the foot of the will.

(3.) More constant, fixed, and steady. It is one of the greatest difficulties in religion to fix the thoughts and cure the wildness and rovings of the fancy: the heart is not steady with God; and hence are its ups and downs, heatings and coolings; which are things unknown in the perfect state. By all which it appears, the change by dissolution is great and marvellous, both upon the body and soul, but upon the soul more especially

Proposition 4. *The souls of the righteous, at the instant of their separation, are received by the blessed angels, and by them transferred unto the place of blessedness.*

Though angels are by nature a superior order of spirits, differing from men in dignity, as the nobles and barons in the kingdoms of this world, differ from inferior subjects, yet are they made ministering spirits, i.e. serviceable creatures in the kingdom of providence, to the meanest of the saints, Heb. 1:14. And herein the Lord puts a singular honour upon his people, in making such excellent creatures as angels serviceable to them: Luther assigns to them a double office, to wit, to sing the praises of God on high, and to watch over his saints here below. Their ministry is distinguished into three branches: *Nouthetikon,* for admonition or warning; *fulaktikon,* for protection and defence; *Boethetikon,* for succour, help, and comfort. This last office they perform more especially at the soul's departure: Like tender nurses, they keep us while we live, and bring us home in their arms to our Father's house when we die.

They are about our death beds, waiting to receive their precious charge into their arms and bosoms. When Lazarus breathed out his soul, the text says it was "carried by angels into Abraham's "bosom", Luke 16:23. And upon this account, Tertullian calls them *evocatores animarum,* the callers forth of souls. At the transition of

Elijah, they appeared in the form of horses and chariots of fire, 2 Kings 2:11. Horses and chariots are not only designed for conveyance, but for conveyance in state, and truly, it is no small honour to have such a noble convoy and guard to attend our souls to heaven.

Object. If it be demanded, *What need is there of their help or company? Cannot God by his immediate hand and power gather home the souls of his people to himself at death? He inspired them into our bodies without their help, and can receive them again when we expire them, without their aid.*

Sol. True, he can do so; but it has pleased him to appoint this method of our translation, not out of mere necessity, but bounty. Souls ascend not to God in the virtue of the angels' wings, or arms, but of Christ's ascension. Had he not ascended as our head and representative, all the angels in heaven could not have brought our souls thither: He ascended by his own power, and we ascend by virtue of his ascension. It is therefore rather for state and *decurum*, than any absolute necessity, that they attend us in our ascension.

God will not only have his people brought home to him safely, but honourably: They shall come to their Father's house in a becoming equipage, as the children of a king. This puts honour upon our ascension day; that day is adorned by the attendance of such illustrious creatures upon us. It is no small honour which God herein designs for us, that creatures of greater dignity than ourselves, shall be sent from heaven to attend and wait upon us thither.

Yea. that our ascension-day, should, in this, resemble Christ's ascension, is an honour indeed. When he ascended, there were multitudes of these heavenly creatures to wait upon him, Psal. 68:17,18. "The chariots of God are twenty thousand, even thousands of angels; the Lord is among them as in Sinai, in the holy place. Thou hast ascended on high," &c. A cloud was prepared as a royal chariot, to carry up the king of glory to his princely pavilion; and then a royal guard of mighty angels to wait upon his chariot; if not for support, yet for the greater state and solemnity of their Lord's ascension. And O what jubilations of blessed angels were heard that day in heaven! How was the whole city of God moved at his coming! The triumph is not ended to this day, no, nor ever shall.

Now, herein God greatly honours his people, that there shall be some resemblance and conformity betwixt their ascension and

Christ's: Angels rejoice to attend those to heaven, who must be their fellow citizens for ever in heaven! It is convenient also, that those who had the charge of us all our life, should attend us to our Father's house at our death: In the one they finish their ministry; in the other they begin their more intimate society.

Moreover, the angels are they whom God will employ, to gather together his elect from the four winds of heaven, at the great day, Matt. 24:31. And who more fit to attend their spirits to heaven singly, than those who must collect them into one body at last, and wait upon that collective body, when they shall be brought to Christ? Psal. 65:14.

Object. But the sight and presence of angels is exceeding awful and overwhelming to human nature: It will rather astonish and terrify, then refresh and cheer us, to find ourselves, all on a sudden, surrounded, and beset with such majestic creatures. We see what effects the appearance of an angel has had upon good men in this world: "We shall die, (says Manoah) for we have seen God," Judges 13:22. So Eliphaz, "a spirit passed before my face; the hair of my flesh stood up," Job 4:15.

Sol. True, while our souls inhabit these mortal and sinful bodies, the appearance of angels is terrible to them, and cannot be otherwise, partly upon a *natural,* and partly upon a *moral* account. The dread of angels naturally falls upon our animal spirits: They shrink and tremble at the approach of spirits; not only the spirits of men, but of beasts, quail at it. A dog, or an ass is terrified at it, as well as a man, Numb. 22:25. The dread of spirits strikes the animal, or natural spirits primarily; and the mind, or rational soul by consent. There is also another cause of fear in man, upon the sight or presence of angels, viz. a consciousness of guilt. Wherever there is guilt, there will be fear, especially upon any extraordinary appearance of God to us, though it be but mediately by an angel.

But when the soul is freed, both from flesh and sin, and shall enjoy itself in a nature, like to these pure and holy spirits, the dread of angels is then vanished, and the soul will take great content and satisfaction in their company and communion: The soul then finds itself a fit companion for them; looks upon them as its fellow-servants, for so they are, Rev. 19:10. And the angels look upon the spirits of just men, not as inferiors, or underlings, but with great respect, as spirits, in some sense, nearer to Christ than themselves: So that henceforth no dread falls upon us from the presence of these excellent creatures; but each enjoyeth singular delight in each others society. And thus we see in what honourable and pleasing company the souls of the just go hence to their Father's house, and bosom.

Prop. 5. The soul is not so maimed and prejudiced by its separation from the body, but that it both can, and does live, and acts without it: and performs the acts of cogitation and volition, without the aid and ministry of the body.

I know it is objected by them that assert the soul's sleeping till the resurrection, that though its essence be not destroyed by death, yet its operations are obstructed by the want and absence of the body, its tool and instrument. And thus they form their objection.

Object. All that the soul understands, it understands by species; *that is, the images of thins which are first formed in the fantasy. As when we would conceive the nature of a house, a ship, a man, or a beast. We first form the image, or species thereof in our fancy, and then exercise our thoughts about it. But this depending upon bodily organs, and instruments, the separated soul can form no such images. It has no such innate species of its own, but comes into the world an* abrasta tabula, *white paper. And being deprived by separation of the help of senses and fantasms, it consequently understands nothing.*

Thus the soul, in its state of separation, is represented to us as Rounded in its powers and operations, to that degree, which seems to extinguish the very nature of it. But,

Sol. 1. We deny that the soul knows nothing now but by phantasms, and images; for it knows itself, its own nature and powers, of which it cannot possibly feign, or form any image, or representation. What form, shape, or figure, can the fancy of a man cast his own soul into, to help him to understand its nature?

And what shall we say of its understanding during an ecstasy, or rapture? Doth the soul know nothing at such a time? Doth a dull torpor seize and benumb its intellectual powers? No; the understanding is never more bright, clear, apprehensive, and perfect, than when the body, in an ecstasy is laid aside, as to any use or assistance of the mind: The soul for that space uses not the body's assistance, as the very words *ecstasy* and *rapture* convince us.

2. To understand by *species,* does not agree to the soul natural; and necessarily, but by accident, as it is now in union with the body: Were it but once loosed from the body, it would understand better without them, than ever it did in the body by them.. A man that is on horseback, must move according to the motion of the horse he rides, but if he were on foot, he then uses his own proper motion as he pleaseth; so here. But though we grant the soul does in many cases now make use of phantasms, and that the agitation of the spirits, which are in the brain antd heart, are conjunct with its acts of cogitation and intellection: yet, as a searching scholar well observes, the spirits are rather subjects than instruments of those actions; and the whole essence of those acts is antecedent to the motion of the spirits: As when we rise a pen in writing, or a knife in cutting, there is an operation of the soul upon them, before there can be any operation by them: They act as they are first acted, and so do these bodily spirits. So that to speak properly, the body is bettered by the use the soul makes of it in these its noble actions; but the soul is not advantaged by being tied to such a body; it can do its own work without it; its operations follow its essence, not the body to which it is for a time united.

Upon the whole; it is much more absonous and difficult to conceive a stupefied, benumbed, and inactive soul, whose very nature is to be active, lively, and always in motion, than it is to conceive a soul freed frown the shackles and clogs of the body, acting freely according to its own nature. I wish the favourers of this opinion may take heed, lest it carry them farther than they intend, even to a denial of its existence and immortality, and turn them into downright *Somatists* or *Atheists.*

Proposition 6. *That the separated souls of the just having finished all their work of obedience on earth, and the Spirit having finished all his work of sanctification upon them, they ascend to God, with all the habits of grace inherent in them; and all the comfortable improvements of their graces accompanying and following them.*

This proposition is to be opened and confirmed in these four branches.

(1.) When a gracious soul is separated from the body, all its work of obedience in this world is finished. Therefore death is called the "finishing of our course," Acts 20:24. "The night when man works no more", John 9:4. "There is no working in the grave," Eccl. 9:10. for death dissolves the *compositum,* and removes the soul immediately to another world, where it can act for itself only, but not for others, as it was wont to do on earth. "I shall see man no more (says Hezekiah) with the inhabitants of the world," Isa. 38:11. That which was said of David's death, is as true of every Christian, that "having served his generation according to the will of God, he fell asleep", Acts 13:36.

I do not say this lower world receives no benefit at all by them after their death; for though they can speak no more, write no more, pray for, and instruct the inhabitants of this world no more, nor exhibit to them the beauty of religion in any new acts or examples of theirs (which is what I mean by saying *they have finished all their work of obedience on earth);* yet the benefit of what they did while in the body, still remains after they are gone: As the apostle speaks of Abel, Heb. 11:4. "Who being dead, yet "speaketh." This way indeed abundance of service will be done for the souls of men upon earth, long after they are gone to heaven. And this should greatly quicken us to leave as much us we can behind us, for the good of posterity, that *after our decease* (as the apostle speaks, 2 Pet. 1:15.) they may have our words and examples in remembrance. But for any service to be done *de novo,* after death, it is not to be expected: We have accomplished, as a hireling. our day, and have not a stroke more to do.

(2.) As all our work of obedience is then finished by us, so at death all the work of God is finished by his Spirit upon us. The last hand is then put to all the preparatory work for glory, not a stroke more to be done upon it afterwards; which appears as well try the immediate succession of the life of glory, (whereof I shall speak in another proposition) as by the cessation of all sanctifying means and instruments, which are totally laid aside as things of no more use after this stroke is given; *Adepto fine, cessant media,* means are useless when the end is attained. *There is no work* (says Solomon) *in the grave.* How short soever the soul's stay and abode in the belly were, though it were regenerated one day, and separated the next, yet all is wrought upon it, which God ever intended should be wrought in this world, and there is no preparation-work in the other world.

(3.) But though the soul leave all the means of grace behind it, yet it carries away with it to heaven all those habits of grace which were planted and improved in it in this world, by the blessing of the Spirit upon those means: Though it leave the ordinances, it loses not the effects and fruits of them; though they cease, their effects still live

A TREATISE OF THE SOUL OF MAN

"The truth dwelleth in us, and shall be in us for ever," 1 John 2:17. "The seed of God remaineth in us", 1 John 3:9.

Common gifts fail at death; but saving grace sticks fast in the soul, and ascends with it into glory. Gracious habits are inseparable; glory does not destroy, but perfect them: They are the soul's meetness for heaven, Col. 1:12. and therefore it shall not come into his presence, leaving its meetness behind it. In vain is all the work of the Spirit upon us in this world, if we carry it not along with us into that world, seeing all his works upon us in this life have a respect and relation to the life to come.

Look, therefore, as the same natural faculties and powers which the soul had (though it could not use them) in its imperfect body in the womb, came with it into this world, where they freely exerted themselves in the most noble actions of natural life; so the habits of grace, which, by regeneration, are here implanted in a weak and imperfect soul, go with it to glory, where they exert themselves in a more high and perfect way of acting than ever they did here below. The languishing spark of love is there a vehement flame; the faint, remiss and infrequent delight in God is there at a constant, ravishing and transporting, height.

(4.) To conclude, As all implanted habits of grace ascend with the sanctified soul to heaven; (for the soul ascends not thither as a natural, but as a new creature) so all the effects, results, and sweet improvements of those graces which we gathered as the pleasant fruits of them on earth, these accompany and follow the soul into the other world also; "Their works follow them," Rev. 14:18. They go not before in the notion of merits, to make way for them, but they follow or accompany them as evidences and comfortable experiences. I doubt not, but the very remembrance of what passed betwixt God and the soul here, betwixt the day of its espousals to Christ, and its divorce from the body, will be one sweet ingredient in their blessedness and joy, when they shall be singing in the upper region the song of Moses and of the Lamb. They were never given to be lost, or left behind us. And thus you see with what a rich cargo the soul sails to the other world, though if it had no other, it would never drop anchor there.

Prop. 7. The souls of the just when separated from their bodies, do not wander up and down in this world, nor hover about the sepulchres where their bodies lie; nor are they detained in any purgatory, in order to their more perfect purification; nor do they fall asleep in a benumbed stupid state: but do forthwith pass into glory, and are immediately with the Lord.

When once the mind of man leaves the scripture guidance and direction, which is it to what the compass or polestar is to a ship in the wide ocean, whither will it not wander? In what uncertainties will it not fluctuate? And upon what rocks and quicksands must it inevitable be cast? Many have been the foolish and groundless conceits and fancies of men about the receptacles of departed souls.

1. Some have assigned them a restless, wandering life, now here, now there, without any certain dwelling-place anywhere. The only grounds for this fancy, is the frequent apparitions of the ghost or spirits of the dead, whereof many instances are given; and who is there that is a stranger to such stories? Now, if departed souls were fixed anywhere, this world would be quiet and free from such disturbances.

I make no doubt, but very many of these stories, have been the industrious fictions and devices of wicked and superstitious votaries, to gain reputation to their way, speaking lies in hypocrisy, to draw disciples after them. And many others have been the tricks and impostures of Satan himself, to shake the credit of the saints' rest in heaven, and the imprisonment of ungodly souls in hell, as will more fully appear when I come to speak to that question more particularly.

2. Others think, when they are loosed from the body at death, they hover about the graves and solitary places where their bodies lie, as devilling, seeing they can dwell no longer in them, to abide as near them as they can; just as the surviving turtle keeps near the place where his mate died, and may be heard mourning for a long time about that part of the wood. This opinion seeks countenance and protection from that law, Deut. 18:10,11, which prohibits men to consult with the dead; of which restraint there had been no need or use, if it had not been practised; and such practices had never been continued, if departed souls had not frequented those places, and given answers to their questions. But what I said before of Satan's impostures, is enough for the present to return to this also.

3. The Papists send them immediately to purgatory, in order to their more thorough purification. This purgatory Bellarmine thus describes: "It is a certain place wherein, as in a prison, souls are purged after this life, that were not fully purged here, to the intent they may enter pure into heaven; and though the church (says he) hath not de-

fined the place, yet the schoolmen say, it is in the bowels of the earth, and upon the borders of hell." And, to countenance this profitable fable, divers scriptures are by them abused and misapplied, as 1 Cor. 3:15. Matt. 5:25,26. 1 Pet. 3:19. All which have been fully rescued out of their hands, and abundantly vindicated by our divines, who have proved, God never kindled that fire to purify souls; but the *Pope* to warm *his own kitchen.*

4. Another sort there are, who affirm, they neither wander about this world, nor go into purgatory, but are cast by death into a swoon or sleep; remaining in a kind of benumbed condition, till the resurrection of the body. This was the error of Beryllus; and Irenaeus seems to border too near upon it, when he says, "The souls of disciples shall go to an invisible place appointed for them of God, and shall there tarry till the resurrection, waiting for that time: and then receiving their bodies, and perfectly, i.e. corporally, rising again, as Christ did, they shall come to the sight of God."

All these mistakes will fall together by one stroke; for if it evidently appear (as I hope it will) that the spirits of the just are immediately taken to God, and do converse with, and enjoy him in heaven; then all these fancies vanish, without any more labour about them particularly. Now there are four considerations which to me put the immediate glorification of the departed souls of believers beyond all rational doubt.

1. Heaven is as ready and fit to receive them as ever it shall be.
2. They are as ready and fit for heaven as ever they will be.
3. The scripture is plainly for it. And,
4. There is nothing in reason against it.

1. Heaven is as fit and ready to receive them when they die, as ever it shall be. Heaven is prepared for believers, (1.) By the purpose and decree of God, and so far it was prepared from the foundation of the world, Matt. 25:34. (2.) By the death of Christ, whose blood made the purchase of it for believers, and so meritoriously opened the grates thereof, which our sins had barred up against us, Heb. 10:19,20. (a.) By the ascension of Christ into that holy place, as our representative and forerunner, John 14.

2. This is all that is necessary to be done for the preparation of heaven; and all this is done, as much as ever God designed should be

done to it, in order to its preparation for our souls; so that no delay can be upon that account.

2. The departed souls of believers are as ready for heaven as ever they will be: for there is no preparation work to be done by them, or upon them after death, John 9:3. Eccl. 9:10. Their justification was complete before death, and now their sanctification is so too; sin which came in by the union, doing out at the separation of their souls and bodies. They are *spirits made perfect.*

3. The scripture is plain and full for their immediate glorification; Luke 23:48. "Today shalt thou be with me in paradise." Luke 16:22. "The beggar died, and was carried by the angels into Abraham's bosom." Phil. 1:21. "I desire to be dissolved and to be with Christ, which is far better." The scripture speaks but of two ways by which souls see and enjoy God, prize faith and sight; the one imperfect, suited to this life; the other perfect, fitted for the life to come; and this immediately succeeding that, for the imperfect is done away, by the coming of that which is perfect, as the twilight is done away, by the advancing of the perfect day.

4. To conclude; there is nothing in reason lying in bar to it. It has been proved before, that the soul in its unembodied state is capable to enjoy blessedness, and can perform its acts of intellection, volition, &c. not only as well, but much better than it did, when embodied. I conclude therefore, that seeing heaven is already as much prepared for believers as it need be, or can be; and they as much prepared from the time of their dissolution, as ever they shall be; the scriptures also being so plain for it, and no bar in reason against it; all the aforementioned opinions are but the dreams and fancies of men, who have forsaken their scripture-guide; and this remains all unshaken truth, that the spirits of the just go immediately to glory from the time of their separation.

Prop. 8. At the time of a gracious soul's separation from the body, it is instantly and perfectly freed from sin, which, till that time, dwelt in it from its beginning; but thenceforth shall do so no more.

Immediately upon their separation from the body, they are spirits *made perfect,* as my text stiles them; and that epithet *perfect* could never suit them, if there were any remaining root or habit of corruption in them.

The time, yea, the set time is now come, to put an end to all the dolorous groans of gracious souls, upon the account of indwelling sin. What the angel said to Joshua, Zech. 3:3,4, the same does God say of every upright soul, at the time of its separation. "Take away the filthy garments from him, and clothe him with change of raiment, and set a fair mitre upon his head." Thus the garments spotted with the flesh, are taken away with the body of flesh, and the pure unchangeable robes of perfect holiness, clothed upon the soul, in which it appears without fault before the throne of God, Rev. 14:5.

There is a threefold burdensome evil in sin under which all regenerated souls groan in this life; *viz.* (1.) The guilt; (2.) The filth; (3.) The inherence of it in their nature. And there is a threefold remedy or cure of these evils: the guilt of sin is remedied by justification; the filth of sin is inchoatively healed by sanctification: the inherence of sin is totally eradicated by glorification; For as it entered into our persons by the union of our souls and bodies, so it is perfectly cast out by their disunion or separation at death: the last stroke is then given to the work of sanctification, and the last is evermore the perfecting stroke: sin languished under imperfect sanctification in the time of life, but it gives up the ghost under perfected sanctification, from and after death: sanctification gave it its deadly wound, but glorification its final abolition. For it is with our sins, after regeneration, as it was with that beast mentioned, Dan. 2:12. which, though it was "wounded with a deadly wound, yet its life was prolonged for a season." And this is the appointed season for its expiration. For if at their dissolution they are immediately received into glory (as it has been proved they are, in our seventh proposition) they must necessarily be freed from sin, immediately upon their dissolution; because, nothing that is unclean can enter into that pure and holy place; they must be, as the text truly represents them, "the spirits of just men made perfect."

For, if so great holiness and purity be required in all that draw nigh to God upon earth, as you read, Psal. 93:5. certainly those who are admitted immediately to his throne, must be without fault, according to Rev. 7:14,15,16,17.

When a compounded being comes to be dissolved, each part returns to its own principle; so it is here: the spirit of man, and all the grace that is in it, came from God; and to him they return at death, and are perfected in him and by him: the flesh returns to earth, whence it came, and all that body of sin is destroyed with it; neither the one or the other shall be a snare or clog to the soul any more. A Christian in this world, is but gold in the ore; at death, the pure gold is melted out and separated, and the dross cast away and consumed.

Hence three consectaries offer themselves to us.

Consectary 1. That a believer's life and warfare end together. We lay not down our weapons of war, till we lie down in the dust, 2 Tim. 4:7. "I have fought a good fight, I have finished my course." The course and conflict you see are finished together: though they commence from different terms, yet they always terminate together. Grace and sin have each acted its part upon the stage of time, and the victory hovered doubtfully, sometimes over sin, and sometimes over grace; but now the war is ended, and the quarrel decided, grace keeps its ground, and sin is finally vanquished. Now, and never before, the gracious soul stands triumphing like that noble *Argive,*

In vocuo solus sessor, plausorque theatre.

not an enemy left to renew the combat; the war is ended, and with it all the fears and sorrows of the saints.

Consectary 2. Separated souls become impeccable, or free from all the hazard of sin, from the time of their separation: for, there being no root of sin now inherent in them, consequently no temptation to sin can fasten upon them; all temptations have their handles in the corruptions of our natures: did not Satan find matter prepared within us, dry tinder fitted to his hand, he might strike in temptations long enough, before one of his hellish sparks could catch or fasten upon us. Temptations are grievous exercises to believers; they are darts, Eph. 6:16. they are thorns, 2 Cor. 12:7. But the separate soul is out of gun-shot; it were as good discharge an arrow at the body of the sun, as a temptation at a translated soul.

Consectary 3. Separated souls are more lovely companions, and their converses more sweet and delightful than ever they were in this world. It was their corruption which spoiled their communion on earth; and it is their spotless holiness which makes it incomparably pleasant in heaven. The best and loveliest saints have something in them which is distasteful; even sweet briars and holy thistles have their offensive prickles: but when that which was so lovely on earth is made perfect in heaven, and nothing of that remains in heaven, which was so offensive in them on earth; O what blessed, delightful companions will they be! O blessed society! O most desirable companions! let my soul for ever be united to their assembly. I love them under their corruptions; but how shall my soul be knit to them, when it sees them shining in their perfections?

Proposition 9. The pleasure and delights of the separate spirits of the just, are incomparably greater and sweeter than those they did, or at any time could experience in their bodily state.

With what a pleasant face would death smile upon believers! What roses would it raise in its pale cheeks, if this proposition were but well settled in our hearts by faith! And if we will not be wanting to ourselves, it may be firmly settled there, by these four considerations, which demonstrate it.

Consideration 1. *Whatsoever pleasure any man receives in this world, he receives it by means of his soul.* Even all corporeal and sensitive delights have no other relish and sweetness, but what the soul gives them, which is demonstrable by this; that if a man be placed amidst all the pleasing objects and circumstances in the world, if he were in that centre, where he might have the confluence of all the delights of this world; yet if the spirit be wounded, there is no more relish or savour in them, than in the white of an egg. What pleasure had Spira in his liberty, estate, wife and children; these things were indeed proposed and urged, again and again, to relieve him? but instead of pleasure they became his horror: let but the mind be wounded, and all the mirth is marred: one touch from God upon the spirit, destroys all the joy of this world. Nay,

Let but the intention of the mind be strongly carried another way, and for that time, (though there be no guilt or wound upon the soul) the most pleasant enjoyments lose their pleasure. What delight, think you, would bags of gold, sumptuous feasts, or exquisite melody have afforded to Archimedes, when he was wholly intent upon his mathematical lines? By this then it is evident, that the rise of all pleasure is in the mind, and the most agreeable and pleasing objects and enjoyments signify nothing without it: the mind must be found in itself, and at leisure to attend them, or we can have no pleasure from them.

Consid. 2. Of all natural pleasures in the world, intellectual pleasures are found to be most agreeable, and connatural to the soul of man.

The more refined and remote from sense any pleasure is, the more grateful is it to the soul; those are certainly the sweetest delights that spring out of the mind. A drop of intellectual pleasure is valued by a generous and well-tempered soul, above the whole ocean of impure joys, which come to it sophisticated and tinged through the muddy channels of sense.

No sensualists in the world can extract such pleasure out of gold, silver, meat and drink; as a searching and contemplating wind finds in the discovery of truth. Heinsius, that learned library-keeper of Leyden, professed, "That when he had shut up himself among so many illustrious souls, he seemed to sit down there, as in the very lap of eternity, and heartily pitied the rich and covetous worldlings, that were strangers to his delights."

And when Cardan tells us, "That to know the secrets of nature, and the order of the universe, has greater pleasure and sweetness in it, than the thought of man can fathom, or any mortal hope for." "Yea, such beauties, says Plutarch, there are in the study of the *mathematics,* that it were unworthy to compare such baubles and bubbles, as riches with it." "Yea, says another, it were a sweet thing to be extinguished in those studies."

Julius Scaliger was so delighted with poetry, that he protested he had rather be the author of twelve verses in Lucan, than emperor of Germany. And to say truth, "there is a kind of enchanting sweetness in those intellectual pleasures and feasts of the mind; such a delight as hardly suffers the mind to be pulled away from them." These pleasures have a finer edge, a higher gust, a more agreeable savour to the mind than sensitive ones; as approaching much nearer to the nature of the soul, which is spiritual.

Consid. 3. And as intellectual pleasures do as far exceed all sensitive pleasures, as those which are proper to a man, do those which we have in common with beasts: *So divine pleasures do again much more surmount intellectual ones.* For what compare is there betwixt those joys which surprise a scholar in the discovery of the secrets of nature, and those that overwhelm and swallow up the Christian in the discovery of the glorious mysteries of redemption by Christ, and his own personal interest therein.

To solve the *phenomena* of nature is pleasant, but to solve all the difficulties about our title to Christ and his covenant, that is ravishing. Archimedes' *eureka*, " I have found it, was but the frisk, or skip of a boy, to that rapturous voice of the spouse, "My beloved is mine, and I am his." These are entertainments for angels, 1 Pet. 1:11. a short salvation for the season it is felt and tasted, 1 Pet. 1:8. after these delights, all others are insipid and dry. And yet one step higher.

Consid. 4.All that divine pleasure, which ever the holiest and devoutest soul enjoyed in the body, is but a sip or prelibation, compared with those full draughts it has in the unembodied state.

While it is embodied, it rejoiceth in the earnests and pledges of joy; but when it is unembodied, it receives the full sum; Psal. 16:11. "In thy presence is fullness of joy." This fullness of joy is not to be expected, because not to be supported in this world. The joy of heaven would quickly make the hoops of nature fly. When a good man had but a little more than ordinary joy of the Lord poured into his soul, he was heard to cry, Hold, Lord, hold! thy poor creature is but a clay vessel, and can hold no more! These pleasures the soul has in the body, are of the same kind indeed with those in heaven, but are exceeding short of them in divers other respects.

1. The spiritual pleasures the soul has in the body, are but by reflection; but those it enjoys out of the body, are by immediate *intuition*, 1 Cor. 13:12. now in a glass, then face to face.

The pleasures it now has, though they be of a divine nature, yet they are relished by the vitiated appetite of a sick and distempered soul; the embodied soul is diseased and sickly, it hath many distempers hanging about it. Now we know the most pleasant things lose much of their pleasure to a sick man; the separate soul is made perfect, thoroughly cured of all diseases, restored to its perfect health; and consequently, divine pleasures must needs have a higher gust awl relish in heaven, than ever they had on earth.

3. The pleasures of a gracious soul on earth are but rare and seldom, meeting with many and long interruptions. And many of them occasioned by the body, which often calls down the soul to attend its necessities, and converse with things of a far different nature; but from these, and all other ungrateful and prejudicial avocations, the separated soul is discharged, and set free; so that its whole eternity is spent in the highest delights.

4. The highest pleasures of a gracious soul in the body, are but the pleasures of an uncentered soul, which is still gravitating and striving forward, and consequently can be but low and very imperfect, in comparison with those it enjoys, when it is centered and fixed in its everlasting rest. They differ as the shadow of the labourer, for an hour in the day, from his rest in his bed, when his work is ended.

To conclude; the pleasures it has here, are but the pleasures of hope and expectation, which cannot bear any proportion to those of sight and full fruition. O see the advantages of an unbodied state.

Prop. 10. *That gracious souls, separated from the body, do attain to the perfection of knowledge, with more ease than they attained any small degree of knowledge while they dwelt in the body.*

Great are the inconveniences, and prejudices, under which souls labour, in their pursuits after knowledge in this life, *Veritatis in puteo,* Truth lies deep. And it is hard, even with much labour, pains, and study, to pump up one clear notion; for the soul cannot now act as it would, but is fain to act as it can, according to the limitations and permissions of the body, to which it is confined. By heedful observations, and painful researches it is forced to deduce one thing from another, and is too often deceived and imposed upon by such tedious and manifold connections.

Beside, truth is now forced, in compliance with our weakness, and distance from the fountain, to descend from heaven under veils, shadows, and umbrages, thereby to contract some kind of affinity with our fancies and exterior senses first, that so it may with more advantage transmit itself to our understanding. It must come under some vail or other to us, while we are veiled with mortality, because the soul cannot behold it with its native lustre, nor converse otherwise with it.

And hence it was that Augustine made his rational conjecture, Why men used to be so much delighted with metaphors, because they are so much proportioned to our senses, with which our reason in this embodied state, has contracted such an intimacy and familiarity. But when the soul lays aside its vail of flesh, truth also puts off her vail, and shows the soul her naked, beautiful, and ravishing face. It henceforth beholds all truth in God, the fountain of truth. There are five ways by which men attain the knowledge of God, say the schools, four of which the soul makes use of in this world; but the fifth, which is the most perfect, is reserved for the separate state. Men discern God here,

(1.) *In vestigio,* By his footsteps in the works of creation. God hath impressed the marks of his wisdom and power upon the creatures, by which impressions we discern that God has been there. Thus the very heathens arrive to some knowledge of a God, Rom. 1:20. Acts 17:24,27.

(2.) *In umbra,* By his shadow: If you see the shadow of a man you guess at his stature and dimensions thereby. Thus Christ made some discovery of himself to the world, in the *Mosaical* ceremonies, and ancient types and umbrages, Heb. 10:1.

(3.) *In speculo,* in a glass: This gives us a much clearer representation of a person, than either his footsteps or shadow could; this is an imperfect or darker vision of his face, by way of reflection. And thus God is seen in his word and ordinances, wherein, "as in a glass, we behold the glory of the Lord," 2 Cor. 3:18.

(4.) *In Filio,* in his own Son, who is the living image and express character of his Father. Thus we sometimes see a child so lively representing his father in speech, gate, gesture, and every lineament of his face, that we may say,

—*Sic oculos, sic ille manus, sic ora ferebat;*—

"Just so his father, so he went, and just such a on he was".

Thus we know God in the face of Jesus Christ, 2 Cor. 4:6. who is the express image of his Father, Heb. 1:3. and John 14:9. This is the highest way of attaining the knowledge of God in this life. But then, in the unbodied state, we see him,

(5.) *Face to face,* with a direct vision. This is to *see him as he is*. The believer is a candidate for this degree now, but cannot be harvested with it, till he be divested from this body of flesh. Yet the soul, when unbodied, and made perfect, attaineth not to a comprehensive knowledge of God, for it will still remain a finite being, and so cannot comprehend that which is infinite. That question, Job 11:7. "Canst thou find out the Almighty unto perfection?" may be put to the highest graduate in heaven. And yet,

1. To see God face to face, and know him as he is, will be a knowledge of the divine essence itself. To see the divine essence, is to see God as he is; i.e. to see him so perfectly and fully, that the understanding can proceed no farther in point of knowledge, concerning that

great question, *What is God?* Thus no man hath seen or can see God in this world. Even Moses himself could not see God, Exod. 33:18,19, 'But the spirits of the just made perfect, have satisfying apprehensions, though not perfect comprehensions of the Divine essence.

2. In this light they clearly discern those deep mysteries which they here racked their thought upon, but could not penetrate in this life. There they will know what is to be known of the union of the two natures in the wonderful person of our Emmanuel; and the manner of the subsistence of each person, in the most glorious and undivided Godhead, John 14:20. The several attributes of God will then be unfolded to our understandings; for his essence and attributes are not two things, Rev. 4:8,9,10,11. Oh! What ravishing sight will this be!

The mysteries of the scriptures and providences of God will be no mysteries then: Curiosity itself will be there satisfied.

3. This immediate knowledge and sight of God face to face, will be infinitely more sweet, and ravishingly pleasant than any, or all the views we had of him here by faith ever were, or possibly could be. There is a joy unspeakable in the visions of faith, 1 Pet. 1:8. but it comes far short of the facial vision. Who can tell the full importance of that one text, Rev. 22:4. "The throne of the Lamb shall be in it, and they shall see his face?" Oh! for such a heaven (said one) as to get one glimpse of that lovely face! Earth cannot bear such sights. This light overwhelms, and confounds the inadequate faculties of imperfect and embodied souls. But there is *lumen comfortans,* a cheering, strengthening, pleasant light, as the light of *the morning star*, Rev. 2:28.

4. This sight of God will be appropriative and applicative. We there see him as our own God and portion. Without a clear interest in laid, the sight of him could never be beatifical and satisfying. Sight without interest is like the light of a glow worm, light without heat. All doubts and objections are solved and answered in the first sight of this blessed face.

5. To conclude: This perfect, and most comfortable knowledge, is attained without labour by the separate soul. Here every degree of knowledge was with the price of much pains. How many weary hours and aching heads did the acquisition of a little knowledge stand us in! But then it flows in upon the soul easily. It was the saying of a great usurer, *I once took much pains to get a little,* (meaning the first stock) *but now I get much without any pains at all.* Oh lovely state

of separation! That body which interposed, clogged, and clouded the willing and capable spirit, being drawn aside (as a curtain) by death, the light of glory now shines upon it, and round about it, without any interception, or let.

Prop. 11. The separated souls of the just do live in a more high and excellent way of communion with God, in his temple-worship in heaven, then ever they did in the sweetest gospel-ordinances, and most spiritual duties, in which they conversed with him here on earth.

That saints on earth have real communion with God, and that this communion is the joy of their hearts, the life of their life, and their relief under all pressures and troubles in this life, is a truth so firmly sealed upon their hearts by experience, as well as clearly revealed in the word, that there can remain no doubt about it, among those that have any saving acquaintance with the life and power of religion.

This communion with God is of that precious value with believers, that it unspeakably endears all those duties and ordinances to them, which, as means and instruments are useful to maintain it.

At death, the people of God part with all those precious ordinances and duties, they being only designed for, and fitted to the present state of imperfection, Eph. 4:12,13. but not at all to their loss, no more than it is to his that loses the light of his candle by the rising of the sun. A candle, a star is comfortable in the night; but useless when the sun is up, and in its meridian glory. Christian, pray much, hear much, and be as much as thou canst among the ordinances of God, and duties of religion: For, the time is at hand that you shall serve, and wait on God no more this way.

But yet think not your souls shall be discharged from all worship and service of God when you die: No, you will find heaven to be a temple built for worship, and the worship there to be much transcendent to all that in which you were here employed. The sanctuary was a pattern of heaven in this very respect, Heb. 9:23. And, on this very account, it is called *Sion* in my text, and the *heavenly Jerusalem;* as denoting a church state, and the spiritual worship there performed by the spirits of just men made perfect.

Some help we may have to understand the nature thereof, by comparing it with that worship and service which we perform to God here in this state of imperfection, and by considering the agreements

FLAVEL

and disagreements betwixt them. In this they agree, that the worship above and below are both addressed and directed to 'one and the same object, Father, Son, and Spirit; all centres and terminates in God. They also agree in the general quality and common nature, they are both spiritual worship. But there are divers remarkable differences betwixt the one and the other, as will be manifest in the following collation.

1. All our worship on earth is performed and transacted by faith, as the instrument and means thereof, Heb. 11:6. "He that cometh to God must believe," &c. In heaven, faith ceaseth, and sight takes place of it, 1 Cor. 5:7. There we see what here we only believe. There are now before us ordinances, scriptures, ministers, and the assemblies of saints in the places of worship: But if we have any communion with God, by, or among these, we must set ourselves to believe those things we see not. By realising and applying invisible things, we here get sometimes, and with no small pains, a taste of heaven, and a transient glance of that glory. In this service our faith is put hard to it, it must work and fight at once; resolutely act while sense and reason stand by, contradicting and quarrelling with it. And if, with much ado, we get but one sensible touch of heaven upon our spirits, if we get a little spiritual warmth and melting of our affections towards God, we call that day a good day, and it is so indeed.

But in heaven all things are carried at a high rate, the joy of the Lord overflows us without any labour, or pain of ours to procure it.

We may say of it there, as the prophet speaks of the dew and showers upon the grass, "which tarrieth not for man, nor waiteth for the sons of men," Micah 5:7.

2. No grace is, or can be acted here, without the clog of a contrary corruption, Rom. 7:21. "When I would do good, evil is present with me." Every beam of faith is presently darkened by a cloud of unbelief; Mark 9:24. "Lord, I believe, help thou my unbelief." "We often read in the book of experience (says one) what an inconsistent fickle thing the heart is in duties: now it is with us, by and by it is fled away and gone; we know not where to find it. It is constant only in its inconstancy and lubricity." There is iniquity in our most holy things, which needs pardon, Exod. 28:38. Our best duties have enough in them to damn us, as well as our worst sins: But in that perfect state above, grace flows purely out of the soul, as beams do from the sun, or crystal streams from the purest fountain. No impure or imperfect acts proceed from spirits made perfect.

3. Here the graces of the saints are never, or very rarely acted in their highest and most intense degree. When they love God most fervently, there is some coldness in their love. Who comes up to the height of that rule, Matt. 22:37. "Thou shalt love the Lord thy God, with all thy heart, and all thy mind, and all thy strength?" When we meditate on God, it is not in the depth of our thought, without some wanderings and extravagancies; it is very hard, if not impossible, for the soul to stand long in its full bent to God.

But in leaven it doth so, and will do so for ever, without any relation or remission of its fervour. Christ, among the saints and angels in heaven, is as a mighty loadstone cast in among many needles, which leap to him, and fix themselves inseparably upon him. They all act in glory as the fire does here, to the utmost of their power and ability. There is no note lower than "Glory to God in the highest."

(4.) The most spiritual souls on earth, who live most with God, have, and must have their daily and frequent intermissions. The necessities of the body, as well as the defectiveness of their graces, require, and necessitate it to be so. Our hands with Moses will hang down and grow weary. Our affections will cool and fall, do what we can.

But as the spirits of just men made perfect know no remissions in the degree, so neither any intermissions in the acting of their grace: "They shall serve him day and night in his temple," Rev. 7:15. You that would purchase the continuance of your spiritual comforts but for a day, with all that you have in this world, will there enjoy them at full, without any intermitting, through eternity.

5. If the best hearts on earth be at any time more than ordinarily enlarged in spiritual comforts, they need presently some humbling providence to hide pride from their eyes. Even Paul himself must have a thorn in the flesh, a messenger of Satan to buffet him. Bernard could never perform any duty with comfortable enlargement, but he seemed to hear his own heart whisper thus, *Bene fecisti, Bernarde,* O well done, Bernard.

But, in heaven the highest comforts are enjoyed in the deepest humility; and the entire glory is ascribed to God, without any unworthy defalcations. Rev. 9:10. They put not the crown upon their own heads, but Christ's: They cast down their own crowns, and fall down at the feet of him that sitteth upon the throne.

6. All assemblies for worship in this world are mixed; they consist of regenerate and unregenerate, living and dead souls: This spoils the harmony, and allays the comfort of mutual communion. In a congregation consisting of a thousand persons, Ah! how few comparatively are there that are heartily concerned in the duty? But it is not so above. There are ten thousand times ten thousand, even thousands of thousands before the throne, loving, adoring, praising, and triumphing together and not a jarring string in all their harps.

7. Here the worship of God is impure, mixed, and adulterated by the sinful additions and inventions of men. This gracious souls groan under as a heavy burden, sighing and praying for reformation; as knowing they can expect no more of God's presence, than there is of his order and institution in worship. But, above, all the worship is pure, the least pin in the heavenly tabernacle is according to the perfect pattern of the divine will.

8. We have here duties of divers kinds and natures to perform. All our time is not to be spent in loving, praising, and de lighting in God; but we must turn ourselves also to searching, watching, and soul-humbling work. Sometimes we are called to get up our hearts to the highest praise, and then to humble them to the dust for sin and judgments; one while to sing his praises, and another while to sigh even to the breaking of our loins; But the spirits of just men made perfect, have but one kind of employment, viz. praising, loving, and delighting in God. There is no groaning, sighing, searching, or watching-work, in that state.

9. The most illuminated believers on earth have but dark and crude apprehensions *of* Christ's intercession-work in heaven, or of the way and manner in which it is there performed by him. We know indeed that our High priest is for us entered within the vail, Heb. 6:20. That he appears in that most holy place for us, Heb. 9:4. That he there represents his sufferings for us to God, standing before him as a lamb that had been slain, Rev 5:6. That he offers up our prayers with his incense to God, Rev. 8:3.

But the immediate intuition of the whole performance, by the person of Christ in heaven, the beholding of him in his work there, with the smiles and honours, the delight and satisfaction of the Father in his person and work. Certainly, this must be a far different thing, and what must make more deep and suitable impressions upon our hearts than ever the most affecting view of them be faith at this distance, could do.

10. *In such ravishing sights and joyful ascriptions of glory to him that sits upon the throne, and to the Lamb for evermore, all the separated spirits of the just are employed and wholly taken up in heaven, as they come in their several times thither; and will be so employed in that temple-service unto the end of the world, when Christs shall deliver up the kingdom to His Father, and thenceforth God shall be all in all.*

The illustration and confirmation of this assertion we have in these two or three particulars.

(1.) That all the spirits of just men, from the beginning of the world, until Christ's ascension into heaven, did enter into heaven, as a place of rest, as a city prepared for them of God, Heb. 11:16. and did enjoy blessedness and glory there. But yet there seems to be an alteration even in heaven itself, since the ascension of Christ into it, and such an alteration as advances the glory thereof both to angels and saints. "Heaven itself (says one who is now there) was not what it is, before the entrance of Christ into the sanctuary for the administration of his office. Neither the saints departed, nor the angels themselves, were participant of that glory which now they are. Neither yet does this argue any defect in heaven, or the state thereof in its primitive constitution; For the perfection of any state has respect unto that order of things which it is originally suited unto. Take all things in the order of the first creation, and in respect hereunto, heaven was perfect in glory from the beginning, &c.

Whatever was their rest, refreshment and blessedness, whatever were their enjoyments of the presence of God, yet was there no throne of grace erected in heaven, no high-priest appearing before it, no lamb as it had been slain, no joint ascription of glory unto him that sitteth upon the throne, and to the Lamb for ever. *God having ordained some better thing for as, that they without should not be made perfect,* Heb. 11:40.

Now both the angels and saints in heaven, do behold Christ in his priestly office within that sanctuary; a sight never seen in heaven before.

FLAVEL

(2.) This frame of heavenly worship will continue as it is unto the end of the world, and then another alteration will be made in the manner of his dispensatory kingdom; "For then he must deliver up the kingdom to God, even the Father; and then shall the Son also himself be subject unto him that put all things under him, that God may be all in all," as the apostle speaks, 1 Cor. 15:24,28. So that as the present state of heaven is not, in all respects, what it was before Christ's ascension thither; so after the consummation of the mediatorial kingdom, and the gathering of all the elect into glory, it will not in all respects be what now it is.

Christ will never cease to be the immediate head of the whole glorified creation. God having gathered all the elect, both angels and men, unto a head in him, and he being the knot and centre of that collective body, the whole frame of the glorified church would be dissolved, should he lose his relation of a head to it. Yea, I doubt not but he will for ever continue to be the medium of communion betwixt God and his glorified church: God will still communicate himself to us through Christ, and our adherence, love, and delight, will still be through Christ. In a word, whatever change shall be made, the person of Christ shall still continue to be the eternal object of divine glory, praise, and worship, Rev. 22:4.

But when he shall have gathered home all his elect to glory, he will resign his present dispensatory kingdom, and become subject *(as man, and as head of that body which he purchased)* to his Father himself, "that God may be all in all," as it is 1 Cor. 15:28.

(1.) *All in all,* that is, all the saints shall be filled, and abundantly satisfied, in and from God alone; there shall be no emptiness, no want, no complaint: For, as there is water enough in one sea to fill all rivers, light enough in one sun to illuminate all the world; so all souls shall be eternally filled, satisfied and blessed in one God. Surely, there is enough in God for millions of souls. For if there be enough in God for all the angels, Matt. 18:10. yea, enough in God for Jesus Christ, Col. 1:19. there must be enough for all our souls. The capacity of angels is larger than ours; the capacity of Christ is larger than that of angels: He that fills them, can, and will therefore fill us, or be all in all to us.

1 Pet. 3:19

By which also he went and preached unto the spirits in prison.

In the former discourse we have had a just view of heaven, and the spirits of just men made perfect, the inhabitants of that blessed region of light and glory.

In this scripture we have the contrary glass, representing the unspeakable misery of those souls or spirits which are separated by death from their bodies for a time, and by sin from God for ever; arrested by the law, and secured in the prison of hell, unto the judgment of the great day.

A sermon of hell may keep some souls out of hell, and a sermon of heaven may be the means to help others to heaven: the desire of my heart is, that the conversations of all those who shall read these discourses of heaven and hell, might look more like a diligent flight from the one, and pursuit of the other.

The scope of the context is a persuasive to patience, upon a prospect of manifold tribulations coming upon the Christian churches, strongly enforced by Christ's example, who both in his own person, ver. 18. and by his spirit in his servants, ver. 19. exercised wonderful patience and long-suffering as a pattern to his people.

This 19th verse gives us an account of his long-suffering towards that disobedient and immorigerous generation of sinners, on whom he waited an hundred and twenty years in the ministry of Noah.

There are difficulties in the text. Estius reckons no less than ten expositions of it, and says, "It is a very difficult scripture in the judgment of almost all interpreters," but yet I must say, those difficulties are rather brought to it, than found in it. It is a text which has been racked and tortured by popish expositors, to make it speak Christ's local descent into hell, and to confess their doctrine of *purgatory;* things which it knew not.

But if we will take its genuine sense, it only relates the sin and misery of those contumacious persons, on whom the Spirit of God waited so long in the ministry of Noah; giving an account of,

1. Their sin on earth.

2. Their punishment in hell.

1. Their sin on earth, which is both specified and aggravated. (1.) Specified; namely their disobedience. They were sometimes disobedient and unpersuadable; neither precepts nor examples could bring them to repentance. (2) This their disobedience is aggravated by the expense of God's patience upon them for the pace of an hundred and twenty years, not only forbearing them so long, but striving with them, as Moses expresses it; or waiting on them, as the apostle here; but all to no purpose; they were obstinate, stubborn, and impersuadable to the very last.

2. Behold, therefore, in the next place, the dreadful, but most just and equal punishment of these sinners in hell; they are called *spirits in prison,* i.e. the souls now in hell.

At that time when Peter wrote of them, they were not entire men, but *spirits,* in the proper sense, i.e. separated souls, bodiless, and lonely souls: while in the bode, it is properly a soul; but when separated, a spirit, according to scripture language, and the strict notion of such a being.

These spirits, or souls in the state of separation, are said to be in a *prison*, that is, in hell, as the word elsewhere notes, Rev. 20:7. and Jude, ver. 6. Heaven and hell are the only receptacles of de parted, or separated souls.

Thus you have, in a few words, the natural and genuine sense of the place, and it is but a wasting time to repeat and refer the many false and forced interpretations of this text, which corrupt minds, and mercenary pens have perplexed and darkened it withal: That which I level at, is comprised in this plain proportion.

Doct. *That the souls or spirits of all men who die in a state of unbelief and disobedience, are immediately committed to the prison of hell, there to suffer the wrath of God due to their sins.*

Hell is shadowed forth to us in scripture by divers metaphors; "for we cannot conceive spiritual things, unless they are so clothed and shadowed out unto us." Augustine gives this reason of the frequent use of metaphors and allegories in scripture, be cause they are so much proportioned to our senses, with which our senses have contracted an intimacy and familiarity; and therefore God, to accommodate his truth to our capacities, does as it were, this way embody it in earthly expressions, according to that celebrated observation of the Cabbalists,— *Lumen supremum nunquam descendit sine indumento;*—the pure and supreme light never descends to us without a garment or covering. In the Old Testament, the place and state of damned souls are set forth by metaphors taken from the most remarkable places and exemplary acts of vengeance upon sinners in this world; as the overthrow of the giants by the flood, those prodigious sinners that fought against heaven, and were swept by the flood into the place of torment. To this Solomon is conceived to allude, in Prov. 31:16. "The man that wanders out of the way of understanding shall remain in the congregation of the dead;" in the Hebrew it is, he shall remain with the *Rephaims,* or giants. These giants were the men that more especially provoked God to bring the flood upon the world; they are also noted as the first inhabitants of hell, therefore from them the place of torment takes its name, and the damned are said to remain in the place of giants.

Sometimes hell is called Tophet, Isa. 30:33. This Tophet was in the valley of Hinnom, and was famous for divers things. There the children of Israel caused their children to pass through the fire to Moloch, or sacrificed to the devil, drowning their horrible shrieks and ejaculations with the noise of drums.

In this valley also was the memorable slaughter of eighteen hundred thousand of the Assyrian camp, by an angel, in one night.

There, also, the Babylonians murdered the people of Jerusalem at the taking of the city, Jer. 7:31,32. So that Tophet was a mere shambles, the public chopping-block, on which the limbs of both young and old were quartered out, by thousands. It was filled with dead bodies, till there was no place for burial. By all which it appears, that no spot of ground in the world was so famous for the fires kindled in it to destroy men, for the doleful cries that echoed from it, or the innumerable multitudes that perished in it; for which reason it is made the emblem of hell. Sometimes it is called a "lake of fire burning with brimstone," Rev. 19:20, denoting the most exquisite torment, by an intense and durable flame.

And in the text, it is called a *prison,* where the spirits of ungodly men are both detained and punished. This notion of a prison gives us a lively representation of the miserable state of damped souls, and that especially in the following particulars.

First, Prisoners are arrested and seized by authority of law; it is the law which sends them thither, and keeps them there; the *mittimus* of a justice is but the instrument of the law, whereby they are deprived of liberty, and taken into custody. The law of God which sinners have both violated and despised, at death takes hold of them, and arrests them. It is the law which claps up their spirits in prison, and in the name and authority of the great and terrible God, commits them to hell. All that are out of Christ, are under the curse and damping sentence of the law, which now comes to be executed on them, Gal. 3:10.

Secondly, Prisoners are carried, or haled to prison by force and constraint; natural force backs legal authority: the law is executed by rough and resolute bailiffs, who compel them to go, though never so much against their will; this also is the case of the wicked et death: Satan is God's bailiff, to hurry away the law-condemned souls to the infernal prison. The devil has the power of death, Heb. 2:14. as the executioner has of the body of a condemned man.

Thirdly, Prisoners are chained and bolted in prison, to prevent their escape; so are dawned spirits secured by the power of God, and chained by their own guilty and trembling consciences in hell, unto the time of judgment, and the fullness of misery; not that they no torment in the mean time: alas! were there no more but that fearful expectation of wrath and fiery indignation, spoken of by the apostle, Heb. 10:27. It there an inexpressible torment, but there is a further degree of torment to be awarded them at the judgement of the great day, to which they are therefore kept as in chains and prisons.

Fourthly. Prisons are dark and noisome places, not built for pleasure, as other houses are, but for punishments, so is hell, Jude, vs. 6. "Reserved in everlasting chains under darkness," as he there describes the place of torments, yea, *ouster darkness,* Matt. 8:12, extreme or perfect darkness. Philosophers tell us of the darkness of this world, *Non dantur purae tenebrae,* that there is no pure or perfect

A TREATISE OF THE SOUL OF MAN

darkness here, without some mixture of light; but there is not a glade of light, not a spark of hope or comfort shining into that prison.

Fifthly, Mournful sighs and groans are heard in prisons, Psal. 97:11. Let the "sighing of the prisoners come before you," says the psalmist. But deeper sighs and more emphatical groans are heard in hell, " There shall he weeping and wailing, and gnashing of teeth", Matt. 8:12. Those that would not groan under the sense of sin on earth, shall howl under anguish and desperation in hell.

Sixthly, There is a time when prisoners are brought out of the prison to be judged, and then return in a worse condition than before, to the place from whence they came. God also has appointed a day for the solemn condemnation of those spirits in prison. The scriptures call it "the judgment of the great day," Jude, ver. 6. from the great business that is to be done therein, and the great and solemn assembly that shall then appear before God.

But I will insist no longer upon the display of the metaphor; my business is to give you a representation of the state and condition of damned souls in hell, and to assist your conceptions of them, and of their state.

It is a dreadful sight I am to give you this day; lout how much better is it to see, than to feel that wrath? The treasures thereof shall shortly be broken up, and poured forth upon the spirits of men.

You had in the former discourse, a faint umbrage of the spirits of just men in glory; in this you will have an imperfect representation of the spirits of wicked men in hell: and look, as the former cannot be adequate and perfect, because that happiness surpasses our knowledge; so neither can this be so, because the misery of the damned passes our fear.

The case and state of a damned spirit will be best opened in these following propositions.

Proposition 1. *That the guilt of all sin gathers to, and settles in the conscience of every christless sinner, and makes up a vast treasure of his life in this world.*

The high and awful power of conscience belonging to the understanding faculty in the soul of man, was spoken to before, as to its general nature, and that conscience certainly accompanies it, and is inseparable from it, was there showed; I am here to consider it as the seat or centre of guilt, in all unregenerate and lost souls. For, look, as the tides wash up, and leave the slime and filth upon the shore, even so all the corruption and sin that is in the other faculties of the soul settle upon the conscience; "Their mind and conscience (says the apostle) is defiled," Tit. 1:15. It is as it were, the sink of a sinner's soul, into which all filth runs and guilt settles.

The conscience of every believer is purged from its filthiness by the blood of Christ, Heb. 9:14. his blood and his spirit purify it, and pacify it, whereby it becomes the region of light and peace: but all the guilt which has been long contracting, through the life of an unbeliever, fixes itself deep and fast in his conscience; "It is written upon the tables of their hearts, as with a pen of iron," Jer. 17:1. i.e. guilt is as a mark or character fashioned or engraved in the very substance of the soul, as letters are cut into glass with a diamond.

Conscience is not only the principal *engagee,* obliged unto God as a judge, but the principal director and guide of the soul, in its courses and actions, and consequently, the guilt of sin falls upon it, and rests in it. The soul is both the spring and fountain of all actions that go outward from man, and the term or receptacle of all actions inward; but in both sorts of actions, going outward, and coming inward, conscience is the chief counsellor, guide, and director in all, and so the guilt which is contracted either way, must be upon its head. It is the bridle of the soul to restrain it from sin; the eye of the soul to direct its course; and therefore is principally chargeable with all the evils of life. Bodily members are but instruments, and the will itself, as high and noble a faculty or power as it is, moves not until the judgment comes to a conclusion, and the debate be ended in the mind.

Now, in the whole course and compass of a sinner's life in this world, what treasures of guilt must needs be lodged in his conscience? What a magazine of sin and filth must be laid up there? It is said of a wicked man, Job 20:11. "His bones are full of the sins of his youth;" meaning his spirit, mind, or conscience, is as full of sin, as bones are of marrow: yea, the very sins of his youth are enough to fill them: and Rom. 22:5, they are said "to treasure up wrath against the day of wrath," which is only done by treasuring up guilt; for wrath and guilt are treasured up together in proportion to each other. Every day of his life vast sums have been cast into this treasury, and the patience of

God waits till it is full, before he calls the sinner to an account and reckoning, Gen. 15:16.

Prop. 2. *All the sin and guilt, contracted upon the souls arid consciences of impenitent men in this world, accompany and follow their departed souls to judgement, and there bring them under the dreadful condemnation of the great and terrible God, which cuts off all their hopes and comforts for ever.*

"If you believe not that I am he, you shall die in your sins." John 8:24. And Job 20:11. "His bones are full of the sins of his youth, which shall lie down with him in the dust." No proposition lies clearer in scripture, or should lie with greater weight on the hearts of sinners: nothing but pardon can remove guilt; but without faith and repentance there never was, nor shall be a pardon, Acts 10:43. Rom. 3:24,25. Luke 24:46,47. Look, as the graces of believers, so the sins of unbelievers follow the soul whithersoever it goes. All their sins who die out of Christ, cry to them when they go hence, *We are your work and we will follow you.* The acts of sin are transient, but the guilt and ejects of it are permanent; and it is evident by this, that in the great day, their consciences, which are the books of records, wherein all their sins are registered, will lie opened, and they shall be judged by them, and out of them, Rev. 20:12.

Now, before that general judgment, every soul comes to its particular judgment, and that immediately after death: of this I apprehend the apostle to speak in Heb. 9:27. "It is appointed for all men once to die, but after that the judgment." The soul is presently stated by this judgment in its everlasting and fixed condition. The soul of a wicked man appearing before God, in all its sin and guilt, and by him sentenced, immediately gives up all its hope, Prov. 11:7. "When a wicked man dieth, his expectation shall perish; and the hope of the unjust man perisheth." His strong hope perishes, as some read it, i.e. his strong delusion. For, alas, he took his own shadow for a bridge over the great waters, and is unexpectedly plunged into the gulf of eternal misery, as Matt. 7:22.

This perishing, or cutting off of hope, is that which is called in scripture *the death of the soul,* for so long the soul will live, as it has any hope. The deferring of hope makes it sick, but the final cutting off of hope strikes it quite dead, i.e. dead as to all joy, comfort, or expectation of any for ever, which is that death which an immortal soul is capable to suffer. *The righteous hath hope in his death;* but every unregenerate man in the world breathes out his last hope in a few moments after his last breath, which strikes terror into the very centre of the soul, and is a death-wound to it.

Prop. 3. *The souls of the damned are exceedingly large and capacious subjects of wrath and torment; and in their separate state their capacity of greatly enlarged, both by laying asleep all those affections whose exercise is relieving, and thoroughly awakening all those passions which are tormenting.*

The soul of man being by nature a spirit, an intelligent spirit, and, in its substantial faculties, assimilated to God, whose image it bears; it must, for that reason, by exquisitely sensible of all the impressions and touches of the wrath of God upon it. The spirit of man is most tender, sensible, and apprehensive creature: the eye of the body is not so sensible of a touch, a nerve of the body is not so sensible when pricked, as the spirit of man is of the least touch of God's indignation upon it. "A wounded spirit who can bear?" Prov. 18:14. Other external wounds upon the body inflicted either by man or God, are tolerable; but that which immediately touches the spirit of man, is insufferable: who can bear or endure it?

And as the spirit of man has the most delicate and exquisite sense of misery; so it has a vast capacity of receive, and let in the fullness of anguish and misery into it. It can drink up, as one speaks, all the rivers of created good, and its thirst not quenched by such a draught; but after all, it cries, Give, give. Nothing but an infinite God can quiet and satisfy its appetive and raging thirst.

And as it is capable and receptive of more good than is found in all the creatures, so it is capable of more misery and anguish than all the creatures can inflict upon it. Let all the elements, all need on earth, yea, all the devils and damned in hell, conspire and unite in a design to torment man; yet when they have done all, his spirit is capable of a farther degree of torment; a torment as much beyond it, as a rack is beyond a hard bed, or the sword in his bowels is beyond the scratch of a pin. The devils indeed are the executioners and tormentors of the damned; but if that there all they revere capable to suffer, the torment of the damned would be, comparatively, mild and gentle to what they are. Oh, the largeness of the understanding of man, what will it not take into its vast capacity!

But add to this, that the damned souls have all those affections laid in a deep and everlasting sleep, the exercises whereof would be relieving, by ~ emptying their souls of any part of their misery; and all those passions thoroughly and everlastingly awakened, which increase their torments.

The affections of joy, delight, and hope, are benumbed in them, and laid fast asleep, never to be awakened into act any more. Their hope, in scripture, is said *to perish,* i.e. it so perishes, that, after death, it shall never exert another act to all eternity. The activity of any of those affections would be like a cooling gale, or refreshing spring, amidst their torments; but as Adrian lamented himself, *Numquam jocos dabis,* You shall never be merry more.

And as these affections are laid asleep, so their passions are roused, and thoroughly awakened to torment them; so awakened, as never to sleep any more. The souls of men are sometimes jagged and startled in this world, by the works or rods of God, but presently they sleep again, and forget all: but hereafter the eves of their souls will be continually held waking to behold and consider their misery; their understandings will be clear and most apprehensive; their thoughts fixed and determined; their consciences active and efficacious; and, by all this, their capacity to take in the fullest of their misery, enlarged to the uttermost.

Prop. 4. *The wrath, indignation, and revenge of God poured out as the just reward of sin, upon the so capacious souls of the dammed, are the principal part of their misery in hell.*

In the third proposition I showed you, that the souls of the damned can hold more misery than all the creatures can inflict upon them. When the soul suffers from the hand of man, its sufferings are but either by way of sympathy with the body; or if immediately, yet it is but a light stroke the hand of a creature can give: But when it has to do with a sin-revenging God, and that immediately, this stroke cuts off the spirit of man, as it is expressed, Psal. 88:16. The body is the clothing of the soul. Most of the arrows shot at the soul in this world, do but stick in the clothes, i.e. reach the outward man. But in hell, the spirit of man is *the white* at which God himself shoots. All his envenomed arrows strike the soul, which is, after death, laid bare and naked to the wounded by his hand. At death, the soul of every wicked man immediately falls into the hands of the living God; and "it is a fearful thing to fall into the hands of the living God," as the apostle speaks, Heb. x.

31. Their punishment is "from the presence of the Lord, and from the glory of his power," 2 Thess. 1:9. They are not put over to their fellow-creatures to be punished, but God will do it himself, and glorify his power, as well as his justice in their punishment. The wrath of Gull lies immediately upon their spirits, and this is the "fiery indignation which devoureth their adversaries," Heb. 10:27. A fire that licks up the very spirit of man. Who knoweth the power of his anger! Psal. 90:11. How insupportable it is, you may a little guess by that expression of the prophet Nahum, chap. 1:5,6. "The mountains quake at him, and the hills melt, and the earth is burnt at his presence; yea, the world, and all that dwell therein. Who can stand before his indignation? And who can abide in the fierceness of his anger? His fury is poured out like fire, and the rocks are thrown down by him."

And, as if anger and wrath were not worth of a sufficient edge and sharpness, it is called fiery indignation and vengeance, words denoting the most intense degree of divine wrath. For indeed his power is to be glorified in the destruction of his enemies, and therefore now he will do it to purpose. He takes them now into his own hands. No creature can come at the soul immediately, that is God's prerogative, and now he has to do with it himself in fury, and revenge is poured out. "Can your hands be strong, or your heart endure when I shall deal with you?" Ezek. 22: 14. Alas! the spirit quails and dies under it. This is the hell of hells.

What doleful cries and lamenting have we heard from God's clearest children, when but some few drops of his anger have been sprinkled upon their souls, here in this world! But alas! there is no comparison between the anger or fatherly discipline of God over the spirits of his children, and the indignation poured out from the beginning of revenges upon his enemies.

Prop. 5. *The separate spirit of a damned man becomes a tormentor to itself by the various and efficacious actings of its own conscience, which are a special part of its torment in the other world.*

Conscience, which should have been the sinner's curb on earth, becomes the whip that must lash his soul in hell. Neither is there any faculty or power belonging to the soul of man, so fit and able to do it as his own conscience. That which was the seat and centre of all guilt, now becomes the seat and centre of all torments. The suspension of its tormenting power in this world is a mystery and wonder to all that duly consider it. For certainly should the Lord let a sinner's con-

A TREATISE OF THE SOUL OF MAN

science fly upon him with rage, in the midst of his sins and pleasures, it would put him into a hell upon earth, as we see in the doleful instances of Judas, Spira, etc. But he keeps a hand of restraint upon them, generally, in this life, and suffers them to sleep quietly by a grumbling or seared conscience, which couches by them as a sleepy lion, and lets them alone.

But no sooner is the Christless soul turned out of the body, and cast for eternity at the tear of God, but conscience is roused, and put into a rage never to be appeased any more. It now racks and tortures the miserable soul with its utmost efficacy and activity. The mere presages and foreboding of wrath by the consciences of sinners in this world have made them lie with a ghastly paleness in their faces, universal trembling in all their members, a cold sweating horror upon their panting bosoms like men already in hell: But this, all this, is but as the sweating of the stones before the great rain falls. The activities of conscience (especially in hell) are various, vigorous, and dreadful to consider, such are its *recognitions, accusations, condemnations, upbraidings, shamings,* and *fearful expectations.*

1. The consciences of the damned will recognise, and bring back the sin committed in this world fresh to their mind: For what is conscience, but a register, or book of records, wherein every sin is ranked in its proper place and order! This act of conscience is fundamental to all its other acts: for it cannot accuse, condemn, upbraid, or shame us for that it has lost out of its memory, and has no sense of. *Son, remember,* said Abraham to Dives, in the midst of his torments. This remembrance of sins past, mercies past, opportunities past, but especially of hope past and gone with them, never to be recovered any more, is like that fire not blown, (of which Zophar speaks) which consumes him, or the glittering sword coming out of his gall, Job 20:24, etc.

2. It charges and accuses the damned soul; and its charges are home, positive, and self-evident charges. A thousand legal and unexceptionable witnesses cannot confirm any point more than one witness in a man's bosom can do, Rom. 2:15. It convicts, and stops their mouths, leaving them without any excuse or apology. Just and righteous are the judgments of God upon you, says conscience. In all this ocean of misery, there is not one drop of injury or wrong. The judgment of God is according to truth.

3. It condemns as well as charges and witnesses, and that with a dreadful sentence; backing end approving the sentence and judgement of God, 1 John 3:21. Every self-destroyer will be a self-condemner. This is a prime part of their misery.

- - - - Prima est haec ultio, quod se
Judice, nemo nocens absolvitur, improba quamvis
Gratio fallacis praetoris vicerit urnam.

Juv. Sat. 13.

4. The upbraidings of conscience in hell are terrible and insufferable things: To be continually hit in the teeth and twitted with our madness, wilfulness, and obstinacy, as the cause of all that eternal misery which we have pulled down upon our own heads, what is it but the rubbing of the wound with salt and vinegar? Of this torment holy Job was afraid, and therefore resolved what in him lay to prevent it, when he says, Job 27:6. "My heart (i.e. conscience) shall not reproach me so long as I live." O the twits and taunts of conscience are cruel cuts and lashes to the soul!

5. The shamings of conscience are insufferable torments. Shame arises from the turpitude of discovered actions. If some men's secret filthinesses were but published in this world, it would confound them: what then will it be, when all shall lie open, as it will, after this life, and their own consciences shall cast the shame of all upon them? They shall not only be derided by God, Prov. 1:26, but by their own consciences.

Lastly, the fearful expectations of conscience, still looking forward into more and more wrath to come, this is the very sum and complement of their misery. What makes a prison so dreadful to a malefactor but the trembling expectation he there lives under of the approaching assizes? Much after the same rate, or rather after the rate of condemned persons preparing for execution, do these spirits in prison live in the other world. But alas! no instance or similitude can reach home to their case.

Prop. 6. *That which makes the torments and terrors of the damned spirits so extreme and terrible, is, that they are unrelievable miseries, and torments for ever.*

They are not capable either of,

1. A partial relief, by any mitigation, or

2. A complete relief by a final cessation.

1. Not of a partial relief by any mitigation; could they but divert their thoughts from their misery, as they were wont to do in this world, drink and forget their sorrows; or had they but any hope of the abatement of their misery, it would be a relief to them. But both these are impossible. Their thoughts are fixed and determined: to remove them (though but for a moment) from their misery, is as impossible as to remove a mountain. Their sin and misery is ever before them. As the blessed in heaven are *bono confirmati,* so fixed and settled in blessedness, that they are not diverted one moment from beholding the blessed face of God, for they are ever with the Lord: So the damned in hell are *malo obfirmati,* so settled and fixed in the midst of all evil, that their thoughts and miseries are inseparable for ever.

2. Much less can their undone state admit the least hope of relief by a final cessation of their misery. All hope perishes from them, and the perishing of their hope is the plainest proof that can be given of the eternity of their misery. For were there but the remotest possibility of deliverance at last, hope would hang upon that possibility: And while hope lives, the soul is not quite dead. The death of hope is the death of a man's spirit. The cutting off of the soul from God, and the last act of hope to see or enjoy him for ever, is that death which an immortal soul is capable of suffering. "Depart from me, ye cursed, into everlasting fire," is that sentence which strikes hope and soul dead for ever. In these six propositions you have the true and terrible representation of the spirits in prison, or the state of dammed souls. I have not mentioned their association with devils, or the dismal place of their confinement, which, though they complete their misery, yet are not the principal parts of it, but rather accessories to it, or rivers running into the ocean of their misery. The sum of their misery lies in what was opened before, and the improvement of it is in that which follows.

Infer. 1. Is this the state of ungodly souls after death? Then it follows, that *neither death nor annihilation are the worst of evils incident to man.* Aristotle calls death the *most terrible of all terribles,* and the schoolmen affirm annihilation to be a greater evil than the most miserable being: But it is neither so, nor so; the wrath of God, the worm of conscience, are much more bitter than death. The pains of death are natural and bodily pains: The wrath of God and anguish of conscience are spiritual and inward: Those are but the pains of a few hours or days, these are the unrelieved torments of eternity.

And as for annihilation, what a favour would the damned account it! Indeed, if we respect the glory of God's justice, which is exemplified and illustrated in the ruin of these miserable souls, it is better they should abide as the eternal monuments thereof, than not to be at all: but with respect to themselves we may say as Christ does of the son of perdition, Matt. 26:24. "Good had it been for them if they had never been born." For a man's soul to be of no other use than a vessel of wrath, to receive the indignation, and be filled with the fury of God; surely an untimely birth, that never was animated with a reasonable soul, is better than they: For alas! they seek for death, but it flies from them. The immortality of their souls, which was their dignity and privilege above other creatures, is now their misery, and that which continually feeds and perpetuates their flame. Here is a being without the comfort of it, a being only to howl and tremble under Divine wrath, a being therefore which they would gladly exchange with the most contemptible fly, or most loathsome toad, but it cannot be exchanged or annihilated.

Inf. 2. Hence it follows, *thatthe pleasures of sin are dear bought, and costly pleasures.* There is a greater disproportion between that pleasure and this wrath, than between a drop of honey and a sea of gall. Could a man distil all the imaginary pleasure of sin, and drink nothing else but the highest and most refined delights of it all his life, though his life should be protracted to the term of Methuselah's; yet one day or night under the wrath of God would make it a dear bargain. But,

1. It is certain sin has no such pleasures to give you: They are embittered either by adverse strokes of providence from without, or painful and dreadful gripes and twinges of conscience within; Job 20:14. "His meat in his bowels is turned, it is the gall of asps within him."

2. It is certain the time of a sinner is near its period when he is at the height of his pleasure in sin: For look, as high delights in God speak the maturity of a soul for heaven, and it will not be long, before such be in heaven; so the heights of delight in sin, answerably speak the maturity of such a soul for hell, and it will not be long ere it be there. Sin is now a big embryo, and speedily the soul travails with death.

3. According to the measure of delights men have had in sin, will be the degrees and measures of their torments in hell, Rev. 18:7. So much torment and sorrow, as there was delight and pleasure in sin.

4. To conclude, "the pleasures of sin are but for a season", as you read, Heb. 11:25, but the wrath of God in hell is for ever and ever. There is a time when the pleasures of sin cannot be called pleasures to come, but the wrath of God that will still be wrath to come. Oh! consider for what a trifle you sell your souls. When Lysimachus parted with his kingdom for a draught of water, he said when he had drank it, *For how short a pleasure have I sold a kingdom!* And Jonathan lamented, 1 Sam. 14:43. "I tasted but a little honey, and I must die." Satan would not charm so powerfully as he does with the pleasures of sin, if this point were well believed, and heartily applied.

Inf. 3. *What a matchless madness is it to cast the soul into God's prison, to save the body out of man's prison!*

Men have their prisons, and God has his: But because the one is an object of sense, and the other an object of faith, that only is feared, and this slighted all over this unbelieving world, except by a very small number of men, who tremble at the word of God. Now this I say is the height of madness, and will appear to be so in a just collation of both in a few particulars. (1.) Man's prison restrains the body only, God's prison soul and body, Matt. 10:28. The spirits of men (as my text speaks) are the prisoners there. Oh! what a vast odds does this single difference make! A thousand times more than the captivating and binding of the greatest king or emperor differs front the imprisonment of a poor mechanic or vagrant beggar. (2.) In man's prison there are many comforts and unspeakable refreshments from heaven, but in God's prison none, but the direct contrary. You read of the apostles, Acts 16:25, how they sang in the prison: The Spirit of God made them a banquet of heavenly joys, and they could not but sing at it: Though their feet were in the stocks, their spirits were never more at liberty. Algerius dated his letters *from the delectable orchard of the Leonine prison; where,* says he, *flows the sweetest nectar.* Another tells us, Christ was always kind to him: but since he became a prisoner for him, he even overcame himself in kindness. *I verily think,* (says he) *the chains of my Lord are all overlaid with pure gold, and his cross perfumed.* But the worst terrors of the prisoners in hell come from the presence of the Lord, 2 Thes. 1:9. "God is a terror to them. (3.) The cause for which a man is cast into prison by men, may be his duty, and so his conscience must be at last quiet, if not joyful in such sufferings. So was it with Paul, Acts 28:20. "For the hope of Israel am I bound with this chain." This diffuses joy and peace through the conscience into the whole man. But the cause for which men are cast into God's prison, is their sin and guilt, which arm their own consciences against them, and make them, as you heard before, self tormentors, terrors to themselves. What odds is here? (4.) In man's prison the most excellent company and sweet society may be found. Paul and Silas were fellow-prisoners. In queen Mary's days the most excellent company to be found in England was in the prisons: Prisons were turned into churches. But in God's prison no better society is to be found than that of devils and damned reprobates, Matt. 25:41. (5.) In man's prison there is hope of a comfortable deliverance, but in God's prison none: Matt. 5:26. "Thou shalt not come out thence till thou hast have paid the last mite." It is an everlasting prison.

Compare these few obvious particulars, and judge then what is to be thought of that man, who stands readier to cast himself into any guilt, than into the least suffering. What is it but as if a man should over his neck to the sword, to save his hand? The Lord convince us what trifles our estates, liberties, and lives are to our souls, or to the peace and purity of our consciences.

Inf. 4. *What an invaluable mercy is the pardon of sin, which sets the soul out of all danger of going into this prison!.* When the debt is satisfied, a man may walk as boldly before the prison door as he does before his own: They that owe nothing fear no bailiffs. It is the law (as I said before) that commits men to prison, a *mittimus* is but all instrument of law; but the righteousness of the law is fulfilled in them that believe, Rom. 8:4. Yea, they are made the *righteousness of God in him,* 2 Cor. 5:21. There can be no process of law against them. For who shall condemn when it is God that justifies? Rom. 8:33,34. And that Divine Justice might be no bar to our faith and comfort, he adds, It is *Christ that died;* and yet farther, to assure us that his death had made plenary satisfaction to God for all our sins and debts, it is added, *yea, rather, that is risen again:* q.d. If the debts of believers to God were not fully paid and satisfied for by the blood of Christ, how comes it to pass that our Surety is discharged, as by his resurrection he appears to be! Oh believer! your bonds are cancelled, the handwriting that was against you is nailed to the cross, the blood of Christ has done that for you that all the gold and silver in the world could not do, 1 Pet. 1:18,19. "It is a counter-price fully "answering to thy debts," Matt.

20:28. And hence, to the eternal joy of your heart, result three properties of your pardon, which are able to make your eyes gush out with tears of joy while you are reading of it.

1. It is a free pardon to your soul; though it cost Christ dear, it costs you nothing. We have redemption, even "the remission, of sins, according to the riches of his grace," Eph. 1:7. The prospect of it was God's, not yours; the price for it was Christ's blood, not yours, the glory and riches of free grace are illustriously displayed in your forgiveness.

2. It is as full as it is free; a complete and perfect cause produces a complete and perfect erect, Acts 13:39. "Justified from all things." Whatever your sins be for nature, number, or circumstances of aggravations, they cannot exceed the value of the meritorious cause of remission. The blood of Christ cleanses us from all sin.

S. It must be as firm as it is free and full, even an irrevocable pardon for evermore. Christ did not shed his blood at a hazard; the way of justification by faith, makes the promise sure, Rom. 4:16. The justified shall never come again under condemnation.

Oh the unspeakable joy that flows from this spring! Oh the triumphs of faith upon this foundation!

Is it not ravishing, melting, overwhelming, and amazing, to think thus with yourself! Here sit I with a joyful plenary free pardon of sin in my hand, while many, who never sinned to that height and degree I have, lie groaning, howling, sweating, and trembling under the indignation of God, poured out like fire upon their souls in hell. A greater sinner saved, and lesser damned. Oh how unspeakably sweet is that rest into which my terrified and disquieted soul is come by faith! Rom. 5:1. Heb. 4:3. "We which have believed, do enter into rest." Oh blessed calm after a dreadful tempest! This poor breast of mine was lately panting, sweating, trembling under the horrors of wrath to come, terrified with the visions of hell. No other sound was in mine ears, but that of fiery indignation to devour the adversaries. Oh what price can he put upon my *quietus est?* What value upon a pardon, delivered as it were at the ladder's foot! Oh precious hand of faith that receives it! But oh the most precious blood of Christ, which purchased it! If Satan now come with his accusations, the law with its comminations, death with its dreadful summons, I have in a readiness to answer them all.

Here is the law, the wrath of God, and everlasting burnings, the just demerit of sin upon one side, and a poor sinful creature on the other. But the covenant of grace has solved all. An act *of oblivion* is past in heaven, "I will forgive their iniquities, and their sins and transgressions will I remember no more." In this act of grace my soul is included; I am in Christ, and there is no condemnation. Die I must, but damned I shall not be. My debts are paid, my bonds are cancelled, my conscience is quieted: let death do its worst, it shall do me no harm; that blood which satisfied God, may well satisfy me.

Infer. 5. *How amazingly sad and deplorable is the security and stillness of the consciences of sinners, under all their own guilt, and the immediate danger of God's everlasting wrath!*

Philosophers observe that before an earthquake the wind lies, and the weather is exceeding calm and still, not a breath of wind going. So it is in the consciences of many, just before the tempest and storm of God's wrath pours down upon them. What a golden morning opened upon Sodom, and began that fatal day! Little did they imagine showers of fire had been ready to fall from so pleasant and serene a sky as they saw over their heads. How secure, still, and unconcerned are those today, who it may be shall rage, roar, and tremble in hell tomorrow! Caesar hearing of a citizen of Rome who was deep in debt, and yet slept soundly, would needs have his pillow, as supposing there was some strange, charming virtue in it.

It is wonderful to consider what shifts men make to keep their consciences in that stillness and quiet they do, under such loads of guilt, and threatenings of wrath, ready to be executed upon them. It must be strong opium that so stupefies and benumbs their consciences; and upon inquiry into the matter we shall find it to be the effect of,

1. A strong delusion of Satan

2. A spiritual judicial stroke of God.

1. This stillness of conscience, upon the brink of damnation, proceeds from the strong delusions of Satan, blinding their eyes, and feeding their false hopes: He removes the evil day at many years imaginary distance from them, and interposes many a fair day between them and it, and in that interposed season, time enough to prepare for it; without such an artifice as this, his house would be in an uproar, but this keeps all in peace, Luke 11:21. "By presuming he feeds their

hopes, and by their hopes destroys their souls." Some he diverts from all serious thoughts of this day, by the pleasures, and others by the cares of this life; and so that day comes upon them unawares, Luke 21:34.

2. This stillness of conscience, in so miserable and dangerous state, is the effect of a spiritual, judicial stroke of God upon the children of wrath. That is a dreadful word, Isa. 6:10. "Make the heart of this people fat, and make their ears heavy, and shut their eyes." The eye and ear are the two principal doors or inlets to the heart; when these are shut, the heart must needs be insensible, as the fat of the body is. There is a spirit of a deep sleep poured out judicially upon some men, Isa. 29:10, such as that upon Adam when God took a rib front his side, and he felt it not: But this is upon the soul, and is the same as to give up a man to a reprobate sense.

Infer. 6. *The case of distressed consciences upon earth is exceeding sad, and calls upon all for the tenderest pity, and utmost help from men.*

You see the labouring of conscience, under the sense of guilt and wrath, is a special part of the torments of hell, of which there is not a livelier emblem or picture, than the distresses of conscience in this world.

It must be thankfully confessed there are two great differences between the terrors of conscience here, and there: One, in the degrees of anguish, the other, in the reliefs of that anguish. The ordinary distresses of conscience here, compared with those of the damned, are as the flame of a candle to a fiery oven, a mild and gentle fire; or as the sparks that fly out of the top of a chimney, to the dreadful eruption of Vesuvius, or mount Etna. Besides, these are capable of relief, but those are unrelievable. Their hearts die, because their hope is perished from the Lord.

But yet of all the miseries and distresses incident to men in this world, none like those of distressed consciences; the terrors of God set themselves in array, or are drawn up in battalia against the soul, Job 6:4. "While I suffer thy terrors (says Heman) I am distracted," Psal. 88:15. Yea, they not only distract, but cut off the spirit, as he adds, ver. 16. They lick up the very spirit of a man, and none can bear them, Prov. 18:14. For now a man has to do immediately with God; yea, with the wrath of the great and dreadful God. And this wrath, which is the most acute and sharp of all torments, falls upon the most tender and sensible part, the spirit and mind which now lies open and naked before him to be wounded by it. No creature can administer the least relief, by the application of any temporal comfort or refreshment to it. Gold and silver, wife and children, meat and melody, signify no more than the drawing on of a silk stocking to cure the *paroxysms* of the *gout*.

All that can be done for their relief, is by seasonable, judicious, and tender applications of spiritual remedies. And what can be done, ought to be done for them. What heart can hear a voice like that of Job, "Have pity upon me, have pity upon me, O ye my friends; for the hand of God has touched me; and not melt into compassion over them? Is there a word of wisdom in your heart, let your tongue apply it to the relief of your distressed brother. While his heart meditates *terror*, let your meditate his *succour*. It is not impossible but you, who lend a friendly hand to another, may, ere long, need one yourself; and he that has ever felt the terrors of the Almighty upon his soul, has motive enough to draw forth the bowels of his pity to another in the like case.

Alas for poor distressed souls, who have either none about them that understand, and are able and willing to speak a word in season to their weary souls, or too many about them to exasperate their sorrows, and persecute them whom God has smitten. You that have both ability and opportunity for it, are under the strongest engagements in the world to endeavour their relief with all faithfulness, seriousness, compassion, and constancy. Did Christ shed his blood for the saving of souls, and wilt not you spend your breath for them? Shall any man that has found mercy from God, show none to his brother? God forbid. A soul in hell is out of your reach; but these that are in the suburbs of hell are not. The candle of intense sorrow is put to the thread of their miserable life; and should they be suffered to drop into hell, while you stand by as unconcerned spectators of such a tragedy, you will have little peace. Your unmercifulness to their souls will be a wound to your own.

Inf. 7. Be hence informed of the evil that is in sin; be convinced of the evil that is in it, by the eternal misery that follows it.

If hell be out of measure dreadful, then sin must be out of measure sinful: the torments of hell do not exceed the demerit of sin, though they exceed the understandings of men to conceive them. God will lay upon no man more than is right. Sin is the founder of hell; all the miseries and torments there, are but the treasures of wrath which sinners, in all ages, have been treasuring up; and how dreadful soever it be, it is the 'οψωνια, the recompense which is meet, Rom. 6:23. "The wages of sin is death."

We have slight thoughts of sin. *Fools make a mock of sin.* But if the Lord by the convictions of men's consciences did but lead them through the chambers of death, and give them a sight of the wrath to come; could we but see the piles that are made in hell (as the prophet calls them, Isa. 30:33) to maintain the flames of vengeance to eternity; could we but understand in what dialect the damned speak of sin, who see the treasures of wrath broken up to avenge it, surely it would alter our apprehensions of sin, and strike cold to the very hearts of sinners

Cannot the extremity and eternity of hell torments exceed the evil that is in sin? What words then can express the evil of it? Hell flames have the nature of a punishment, but not of an atonement.

O think on this, you that look upon sin as the veriest trifle, that will sin for the value of a penny, that look upon all the humiliations, broken-hearted confessions, and bitter moans of the saints under sin, as frenzy, or melancholy, slighting them as a company of half-witted hypochondriac persons! You that never had one sick night, or sad day in all your life upon the account of sin, let me tell you that breast of you must be the seat of sorrow; that frothy, airy spirit of you must be acquainted with emphatical sobs and groans. God grant it may be on this side hell, by effectual repentance; else it must be there, in the extremity and eternity of sorrows.

Inf. 8. What enemies are they to the souls of men, who are Satan's instruments, to draw them into sin, or who suffer sin to lie upon them!

When there were but two persons in the world, one drew the other into sin; and among the millions of men and women now in the world, where are there two to be found that have in no case been snares to draw some into sin? Some tempt designedly, taking the devil's work out of his hands; others virtually and consequentially, by examples, which have a compelling power to draw others with them into sin. The first sort are among the worst of sinners, Prov. 1:10, the latter are among the lest of saints; see Gal. 2:14, whose conversation is so much in heaven, that nothing falls out in the course thereof, which may not further some or other in their way to hell.

Among wicked men, there are five sorts eminently accessory to the guilt and ruin of other men's souls. (1.) Loose professors, whose lives give their lips the lie; whose conversations make their professions blush. (2.) Scandalous apostates, whose fall is more prejudicial than their profession was ever beneficial to others. (3.) Cruel persecutors, who make the lives, liberties, and estates of men the occasion of the ruin of their consciences. (4.) Ignorant and unfaithful ministers, who strengthen the hands of the wicked, that they should not return from their wickedness. (5.) Wicked relations, who quench and damp every hopeful beginning of conviction and affection in their friends. Of all which I shall distinctly speak in the next discourse, to which, therefore, I remit it at present.

And many there are who suffer sin to lie upon others, without a wise and seasonable reproof to recover them.

O what cruelty to souls is here! The day is coming when they will curse the time that ever they knew you. It is possible you may repent, but then, it may be, those, whose souls you have helped to ruin, are gone, and quite out of your reach. The Lord make you sensible what you have done in season, lest your repentance come too late for yourselves and them also.

Inf. 9. *How poor a comfort is it to him that carries all his sins out of this world with him, to leave much earthly treasure (especially if gotten by sin) behind him?*

It is a poor consolation to be praised where you are not, and tormented where you are; to purchase a life of pleasure to others on earth, at the price of your own everlasting misery in hell. All the consolation, sensual, voluptuous, and oppressing worldlings have, is but this, that they were *coached to hell* in pomp and state, and have left the same *chariot* to bring their graceless children after them, in the same equipage, to the place of torments. There be five considerations provoking pity to them that are thus cast into a miserable eternity, and caution to all that are following after, in the same path.

First, That fatal mistake in the practical understanding and judgement of men deserves a compassionate lamentation, as the cause and reason of their eternal miscarriage and ruin. They looked upon trifles as things of greatest necessity, and the most necessary things as mere trifles; putting the greatest weight and value upon that which little concerned them, and none at all upon their greatest concernment in the whole world, Luke 12:21.

Secondly, The perpetual diversions that the trifles of this world gave them from the main use and end of their time. O what a hurry and thick succession of earthly business and encumbrances filled up their days! So that they could find no time to go alone, and think of the awful and weighty concernments of the world to come, James 5:5.

Thirdly, The total waste and expense of the only season of salvation, about these vanishing, impertinent trifles, which is never more to be recovered, Eccles. 9:10.

Fourthly, That these deluding shadows, the pleasures of a moment are all they had in exchange for their souls, a goodly price it was valued at, Matt. 16:26.

Fifthly, That by such a life they have not only ruined their own souls, but put their posterity, by their education of them in the same course of life, into the same path of destruction, in which they went to hell before them. Psal. 44:18. "Their posterity approve their saying."

Inf. 10. How rational and commendable is the courage and resolution of those Christians who choose to bear all the sufferings in this world from the hands of men, rather than to defile and wound their consciences with sin, and thereby expose their souls to the wrath of God for ever!

That which men now call pride, humour, fancy, and stubbornness, will, one day, appear to be their great wisdom, and the excellency of their spirits. It is the tenderness of their consciences, not the pride and stoutness of their stomachs, which makes them inflexible to sin; they know the terrors of a wounded conscience, and had rather endure any other trouble from the hands of men, than fall by known sin into the hands of an angry God. Try them in other matters wherein the glory of God, and the peace or purity of their consciences are not concerned, and see if you can charge them with stubbornness and singularity, it was the excellency of the spirits of the primitive Christians, that they durst tell the emperor to his face, when he threatened them with torments; "Pardon us, O emperor, you threaten us with a prison, but God with hell." Do we call that ingenuity and good nature which makes the mind soft and tractable to temptations, and will rather venture upon guilt than be esteemed singular?

Salvian tells us of some in his time, who were compelled to "be evil, lest they should not be accounted vile". And was that their excellence? May I not fitly apply the words of Salvian here: "O in what honour and repute is Christ among Christians, when religion shall make them base and ignoble!" He that understands what the punishment of sin will be in hell, should endure all things rather than yield to sin on earth. Indeed, if you that threaten and tempt others to violate their consciences, could bear the wrath of God for them in hell, it were somewhat; but we know there is no suffering by a *proxy* here; they tremble at the word of God, and have felt the burden of guilt, and dare not yield to sin, though they yield their estates and bodies to prevent it.

Inf. 11. *How patiently should we endure the afflictions of this life, by which sin is prevented and purged?*

The discipline of our spirits belong to God the Father of spirits. He corrects us here that we may not be punished hereafter, 1 Cor. 12:32, "We are chastened of the Lord, that we may not be condemned with the world." It is better for us to groan under afflictions on earth, than to roar under revenging wrath in hell. Parents who are wise, as well as tender, had rather hear their children sob and cry under the rod, than stand with halters upon their necks on the ladder, bewailing the destructive indulgence of their parents.

Your chastisements, when sanctified, are preventive of all the misery opened before. It is therefore as unreasonable to murmur against God, because you smart under his rod, as it would be to accuse your dearest friend of cruelty, because he strained your arm to snatch you from the fall of a house or wall, which he saw ready to crush and overwhelm you in its ruins.

If we had less affliction, we should have more guilt. We see how apt we are to break over the hedge, and to go astray from God, with all the clogs of affliction designed for our restraint; what should we do if we had no clog at all? It is better for you to be whipped to heaven with all the rods of affliction, than coached to hell with all the pleasures of the world.

Christian, your God sees, if you do not, that all these troubles are few enough to save you from sin and hell. Your corruptions require all these, and all little enough. "If need be, you are in heaviness", 1 Pet. 1:6. If there be need for it, your dearest comforts on earth shall die, that your soul may live; but if your mortification to them render your removal needless, you and they shall live together. It is better to be preserved in brine, than to rot in honey. Sanctified afflictions working under the efficacy of the blood of Christ, are the safest way to our souls.

Inf. 12. How doleful a charge does the death of wicked men make upon them! From palaces on earth to the prison of hell.

No sooner has the soul of a wicked man steeped out of his own door at death, but the sergeants of hell are immediately upon it, serving the dreadful summons on the law-condemned wretch. This arrest terrifies it more than the handwriting upon the plaster of the wall did him, Dan. 5:5. How are all a man's apprehensions changed in a moment! Out of what a deep sleep are most, and out of what a pleasant dream of heaven are some awaked and startled at death, by the dreadful arrest and summons of God to condemnation.

How quickly would all a sinner's mirth be damped, and turned into howlings in this world, if conscience were but thoroughly awakened! It is but for God to change our apprehensions now and it would be done in a moment: but the eyes of most men's souls are not opened till death has shut their bodily eyes; and then how sudden, and how sad a change is made in one day!

O think what it is to pass from all the pleasures and delights of this world into the torments and miseries of that world; from a pleasant habitation into an infernal prison; from the depth of security to the extremity of desperation; from the arms and bosoms of dearest friends and relations, to the society of damned spirits! Lord, what a change is here; had a gracious change been made upon their hearts by grace, no such doleful change could have been made upon their state by death: little do their surviving friends think what they feel, or what is their estate in the other world while they are honouring their bodies with splendid and pompous funerals. None on earth have so much reason to fear death, to make much of life, and use all means to continue it, as those who will and must be so great losers by the exchange.

Inf. 13. See here the certainly, and inevitableness of the judgement of the great day.

This prison which is continually filling with the spirits of wicked men is an undeniable evidence of it: for why is hell called: prison, and why are the spirits of men confined and chained there but with respect to the judgement of the great day? As there is a necessary connection between sin and punishment, so between punishing and trying the offender; there are millions of souls in custody, a world of spirits in prison; these must be brought forth to their trial, for God will lay upon no man more than is right; the legality of their *mittimus* to hell will be evidenced in their solemn day of trial. God has therefore "appointed a day in which he will judge the world in righteousness, by that man whom he has ordained," Acts 17:31.

Here sinners run in arrears, and contract vast debts; in hell they are seized and committed, at judgment tried and cast for the same. This will be a dreadful day, those that have spent so prodigally upon the patience of God, must now come to a severe account for all; they have past their particular judgment immediately after death, Eccl. 12:7. Heb. 9:27. By this they know how they shall speed in the general judgment, and how it shall he with them for ever, but though this private judgment secures their damnation sufficiently, yet it clears not the justice of God before angels and men sufficiently, and therefore they must appear once more before his bar; 2 Cor. 5:10. In the fearful expectation of this day, those trembling spirits now lie in prison, and that fearful expectation is a principal part of their present misery and torment. You that refuse to come to the throne of grace, see if you can refuse to make your appearance at the bar of justice; you that braved and browbeat your ministers that warned you of it, see if you can outbrave your Judge too as you did them. Nothing more sure or awful than such a day as this.

Inf. 14. How much are ministers, parents, and all to whom the charge of souls is committed, bound to do all that in them lies to prevent their everlasting misery in the world to come!

The great apostle of the Gentiles found the consideration of the terror of the Lord as a spur urging and enforcing him to a ministerial faithfulness and diligence; 2 Cor. 5:11. "Knowing therefore the terror of the Lord, we persuade men." And the same he presses upon Timothy, 2 Tim. 4:1,2. "I charge you therefore, before God and the Lord Jesus Christ, who shall judge the quick and the dead at his appearing, and his kingdom; preach the word; be instant in season and out of season; reprove, rebuke, exhort, with all longsuffering and doctrine." O that those to whom so great a trust as the souls of men is committed, would labour to acquit themselves with all faithfulness therein, as Paul did, warning everyone night and day with tears, that if we cannot prevent their ruin, which is most desirable; yet at least we may be able to take God to witness, as he did, that we are pure from the blood of all men.

Oh! consider, my brethren, if your faithful plainness and unwearied diligence to save men's souls produce no other fruit but the hatred of you now; yet it is much easier for you to bear that, than that they and you too should bear the wrath of God for ever.

We have all of us personal guilt enough upon us, let us not add other men's guilt to our account: to be guilty of the blood of the meanest man upon earth, is a sin which will cry in your consciences; but to be guilty of the blood of souls, Lord, who can bear it! Christ thought them worthy his heart-blood, and are they not worth the expense of our breath? Did he sweat blood to save them, and will not we move our lips to save them? It is certainly a sore judgment to the souls of men, when such ministers are set over them as never understood the value of their people's souls, or were never heartily concerned about the salvation of their own souls.

Matt. 16:26

For what is a man profited, if he shall gain the whole world, and lose his own soul? Or what shall a man give in exchange for his soul?

Difficult duties need to be enforced with powerful arguments. In the 24th verse of this chapter, our Lord presses upon his disciples the deepest and hardest duties of self denial, acquaints them upon what terms they must be admitted into his service: "If any man will come after me, let him deny himself, and take up his cross and follow me."

This hard and difficult duty he enforces upon them by a double argument, viz. From,

1. The vanity of all sinful shifts from it, ver. 25.

2. The value of their souls, which is imported in it, ver. 26.

They may shift off their duty to the loss of their souls, or save their souls by the loss of such trifles. If they esteem their souls above the world, and can be content to put all other things to the hazard for their salvation, making account to save nothing but them by Christianity; then they come up to Christ's terms, and may warrantably and boldly call him their Lord and Master; and to sweeten this choice to them, he does, in my text, balance the soul and all the world, weighing them one against the other, and shows them the infinite odds and disproportion between them: "What is a man profited, if he shall gain the whole world, and lose his own soul? Or what shall a man give in exchange for his soul?,'

What is a man profited? There is a plain meiosis in the phrase and the meaning is, how inestimably and irreparably is a man damnified! what a soul ruining bargain would a man make!

If he should gain the whole world. There is a plain hyperbole in this phrase; for it never was, nor ever will be the lot of any man to be the sole owner and possessor of the whole world. But suppose all the power, pleasure, wealth, and honour of the whole world were bid and offered in exchange for a man's soul; what a dear purchase would it be at such a rate! "What were this, says one, but to win Venice, and then be handed at the gate of it?" As that man acts like a mad man, that goes about to purchase a treasure of gold with the loss of his life; for life being lost, what is all the gold in the world to him? He can have no enjoyment of it, or comfort in it: so here, what is all the world, or as many worlds as there are creatures in its when the soul is lost, if he gain this?

And lose his own soul. The comparison lies here between one single soul and the whole world. The whole world is no price for the poorest, meanest, and most despised soul that lives in it.

By losing the soul, we are not to understand the destruction of its being, but of its happiness and comfort, the cutting it off from God, and all the hopes of his favour and enjoyment for ever. This is the loss here intended, a loss never to be repaired. The whole world can be no recompense for the loss to the soul, if it be but the loss of its purity or peace for a time; much less can it recompense the loss of the soul, in the loss of all its happiness for ever. When a man's chief happiness is finally lost, then is his soul lost: for what benefit can it be, no, how great a misery must it be, to have a being perpetuated in torments for ever? This is *the fine* or *mulct* which is set upon sin, as some render the word. What shall a man gain by such pleasures, for which God will *mulct,* or *fine* him at the rate or price of his own soul? That is, of all the happiness, joy and comfort of it to all eternity.

Or what shall a man give in exchange for his soul? The question aggravates the sense, and amplifies the loss and damage of the man that sells his soul for the whole world. There is no recompense in all the world for the hazard or danger of the soul one hour; nor would a man that understands what a soul and eternity are, put them into danger for ten thousand worlds, much less for one penny, yea, for nothing, as many do: but to barter or exchange it for the world, to take any thing in lieu of it; this is the height of madness. "The way of buying in former times was not by money, but by the exchange of one commodity for another;" and to this custom Brugensis thinks this phrase is allusive. Now, what commodity is found in all the world; or who, that is not blinded by the god of this world, can think that the whole world itself, if all the rocks in it revere rocks of diamonds, and the seas and rivers were liquid gold, is a commodity of equivalent worth to his own soul? Hence two notes arise naturally.

Doct. 1. *That one soul is of more value than the whole world.*

Doct. 2. *How precious and invaluable soever the soul of man is, it may be lost and cast away for ever.*

I begin with the first.

Doct. 1. *That one soul is of more value than the whole world.*

I need not spend much time in the proof of it, when you have considered, that he who bought them, has here weighed and valued them; and that the point before us is the result and conclusion of one that has the best reason to know the true worth of them. That which I have to do is to gather out of the scriptures the particulars; which, put together, make up the full demonstration of the point, And,

1. The invaluable worth of souls appears from the manner of their creation. They were created immediately by God, as has been proved, and that not without the deliberation of the whole Trinity; Gen. 1:26. "Let us make man." For the production of other creatures, it was enough to give out the afford of his command. "Let there be light, let the earth and the waters bring forth;" but when he comes to man then you have no FIAT, *let there be,* but he puts his own hand immediately to it, as to the masterpiece of the whole creation: yea, a council is called about it; *Let us,* implying the just consultation and de deliberation of all the persons in the Godhead about it, that our hearts might be raised to the expectation of some extraordinary work to follow; great counsels and wise debates being both the forerunners and foundations of great actions and events to ensue thereupon. Thus Elihu in Job 35:10, "None saith, Where is God my Makers?" And David, in Ps. 149:2, "Let Israel rejoice in his Makers:" in both places the word is plural. The consultation here is only amongst the divine Persons, no angels are called to this council-table, the whole matter was to be conducted by the wisdom, and effected by the power of God; and therefore there was no need to consult with any but himself, the wisdom of angels being from him: but this great council shows what an excellent creature was now to be produced, and the excellency of that creature man was principally in his soul; for the bodies of other crea-

tures, which were made be the word of his command, are as beautiful, elegant, and neat as the body of man; yea, and in some respects more excellent. The soul then was that rare piece which God in so condescending an expression tells us was created with the deliberation of the Godhead; those great and excellent Persons laid their heads, as it were together to project its being.

And by the way, this may smartly check the pride and arrogance of souls, who dare take it upon them to teach God, as murmurs at his disposals of us. Shall that soul which is the product of his wisdom and counsel, dare to instruct or counsel its maker? But that by the by. You see there is a transcendent dignity and worth in the soul of man above all other beings in the world, by the peculiar way of its production into the number of created beings: no wise man deliberates long, or calls a council about ordinary matters, much less the All-wise God.

2. The soul has in itself an intrinsic worth and excellency, worthy of that divine Original whence it sprang: view it in its noble faculties, and durable powers, and it will appear to be a creature upon which God has laid out the riches of his wisdom and power.

There you shall find a mind susceptive of all light, both natural and spiritual, shining as the candle of God in the inner man, closing with truth, as the iron does with the attractive loadstone; a shop in which all arts and sciences are laboured and formed: what are all the famous libraries and monuments of learning, but so many systems of thoughts, laboured and perfected in the active inquisitive minds of men? Truth is its natural and delectable object; it pursues eagerly after it, and even spends itself and the body too in the chase and prosecution of truth; when it lies deep, as a subterranean treasure, the mind sends out innumerable thoughts, reinforcing each other in thick successions, to dig for, and compass that invaluable treasure, if it be disguised by misrepresentations and vulgar prejudice, and trampled in the dirt under that disguise, there is an ability in the mind to discern it by some lines and features, which are all well known to it, and both own, honour, and vindicate it under all that dirt and obloquy, with more respect than a man will take up a piece of gold, or a sparkling diamond out of the mire: it searches after it by many painful deductions of reason and triumphs more in the discovery of it, than in all earthly treasures; no gratification of sense like that of the mind, when it grasps its prey for which it hunted.

The mind passes through all the works of creation, it views the several creatures on earth, considers the fabric, use, and beauty of animals, the signatures of plants, penetrating thereby into their nature and virtues: it views the vast ocean, and the large train of causes laid together in all these things for the good of man, by God, whose name it reads in the most diminutive creature it beholds on earth.

It can, in a moment, mount itself from earth to heaven, view the face thereof, describe the motions of the sun in the ecliptic, calculate tables for the motions of the planets and fixed stars, invent convenient cycles for the computation of time, foretell, at a great distance, the dismal eclipses of the sun and moon to the very digit, and the portentous conjunctions of the planets, to the very minute of their ingress. These are the pleasant employments of the understanding.

But there is a higher game at which this eagle plays; it reckons itself all this while employed as much beneath its capacity, as Domitian in catching flies; though these be lawful and pleasant exercises, when it has leisure for them, yet it is fitted for a much nobler exercise, even to penetrate the glorious mysteries of redemption, to trace redeeming love through all the astonishing methods, and manifold discoveries of it; and yet higher than all this, it is capable of an immediate sight, or facial vision of the blessed God; short of which it receives no pleasure that is fully agreeable to its noble power and infinite appetite.

View its will, and you shall find it like a queen upon the throne of the soul, swaying the sceptre of liberty in her hand, (as one expresses it) with all the affections waiting and attending upon her. No tyrant can force it, no torment can wrest the golden sceptre of liberty out of its hand; the keys of all the chambers of the soul hang at its girdle, these it delivers to Christ in the day of his power; victorious grace sweetly determines it by gaining its consent, but commits no violence upon it. God accepts its offering;, though full of imperfections; but no service is accepted without it, how excellent soever be the matter of it.

View the conscience and thoughts with their self-reflective abilities, wherein the soul retires into itself, and sits concealed from all eyes but his that made it, judging its own actions, and censuring its estate; viewing its face in its own glass, and correcting the indecencies it discovers there: things of greatest moment and importance are silently transacted in its council-chamber between the soul and God; so remote from the knowledge of all creatures, that neither angels, devils,

A TREATISE OF THE SOUL OF MAN

nor men, can know what is doing, there, but by uncertain guess, or revelation from God. Here it impleads, condemns it, and acquits itself as at a privy session, with respect to the judgment of the great day: here it meets with the latest of comforts, and with the worst of terrors.

Take a survey of its passions and affections, and you will find them admirable: see how they are placed by divine Wisdom in the soul, some for defence and safety, others for delight and pleasure. Anger actuates the spirits, and rouses its courage, enabling it to break through difficulties. Fear keeps centinel, watching upon all dangers that approach us: Hope forestalls the good, and anticipates the joys of the next life, and thereby supports and strengthens the soul under all the discouragements and pressures of the present life: Love unites us to the chiefest good: "He that dwelleth in love, dwelleth in God, and God in him:" Zeal is the dagger which love draws in Gods cause and quarrel, to secure itself from sin, and testify its resentments of God's dishonour.

O what a divine spark is the soul of man! well might Christ prefer it in dignity to the whole world.

3. The worth of a soul may be gathered and discerned from its subjective capacity and inability both of grace and glory. It is capable of all the graces of the Spirit, of being filled with the fullness of God, Eph. 3:19, to live to God here, and with God for ever. What excellent graces do adorn some souls? How are all the rooms richly hanged with divine and costly hangings, that God may dwell in them! This makes it like the carved works of the temple, overlaid with pure gold; here is glory upon glory, a new creation upon the old; in the innermost parts of some souls is a spiritual altar erected with this inscription. *Holiness to the Lord:* here the soul offers up itself to God in the sacred flames of love; and here it sacrifices its vile affections, devoting them to destruction, to the glory of its God: here God walks with delight, even a delight beyond what he takes in all the stately structures and magnificently adorned temples in the whole world, Isa. 66:1,2.

No other soul besides man's is marriageable to Christ, or capable of espousals to the King of glory: they were not designed, and therefore not endued with a capacity for such an honour as this: but such a capacity has every soul, even the meanest on earth, and such honour have all his saints: others may be, but they are betrothed to Christ in this world, 2 Cor. 11:2, and shall be presented without spot before him in the world to cone, Eph. 5:27.

It is now a lovely and excellent creature in its naked, natural state; much more beautiful and excellent in its sanctified and gracious state: but what shall we say, or how shall we conceive of it, when all spots of sin are perfectly washed of its beautiful face in heaven, and the glory of the Lord is risen upon it! when its filthy garments are taken away, and the pure robes of perfect holiness, as well as righteousness, super-induced upon this excellent creature! If the imperfect beauty of it, begun in sanctification, enamoured its Saviour, and made him say, "You have ravished my heart with one of thine eyes, with one of the chains of thy neck;" what will its beauty, and his delight in it be in the state of perfect glorification! As we imagine the circles in the heavens to be vastly greater than those we view upon the globe, so must we imagine in the case before us.

4. The preparations God makes for souls in heaven, speak their great worth and value. When you lift up your eyes to heaven, and behold that spangled azure canopy beset and inlaid with so many golden studs and sparkling gems, you see but the floor or pavement of that place which God has prepared for some souls. He furnished this world for us before he put us into it; but, as delightful and beautiful as it is, it is no more to be compared with the Father's house in heaven, than the smallest ruined chapel your eyes ever beheld, is to be compared with Solomon's temple, when it stood in all its shining glory.

When you see a stately and magnificent structure built, richest hangings and furniture prepared to adorn it, you conclude some great persons are to come thither: such preparations speak the quality of the guests.

Now heaven, yea, the heaven of heavens, the palace of the great King, the presence-chamber of the Godhead, is prepared, not only by God's decree and Christ's death; but by his ascension thither in our nnames, and as our forerunner, for all renewed and redeemed souls. John 14:2. "In my Father's house are many mansions; if it were not so I would have told you: I go to prepare a place for you."

And, where is the place prepared for them, but in his Father's house? The same place, the very same house where the Father, Son, and Spirit themselves do dwell: such is the love of Christ to souls, that he will not dwell in one house, and they in another; but, as he speaks, John 12:26. "Where I am, there shah my servant also be." There is room enough in the Father's house for Christ and all the souls he redeemed to live and dwell together for evermore. His ascension thither was in the capacity of a com man or public person, to take livery and seisin of those many man signs for them, which are to be filled with their inhabitants, as they come thither in their respective times and orders.

5. The great price with which they revere redeemed and purchased, speaks their dignity and value. No wise man will purchase a trifle at a great price, much less the most wise God. Now the redemption of every soul stood in no less than the most precious blood of the Lord Jesus Christ, 1 Pet. 1:18,19. "You know (says the apostle there) that we revere not redeemed with corruptible things as silver and gold, but with the precious blood of Christ, as a lamb without blemish or spot. All the gold and silver in the world was no ransom for one soul; nay, all the blood of the creatures, had it been shed as a sacrifice to the glory of justice, or even the blood which is most dear to us, as being derived from our own; I mean, the blood of our dear children, even of our first-born, the beginning of our strength, which usually has the strength of affection: I say, one of these could purchase a pardon for the smallest sin that ever any soul committed, much less was it able to purchase the soul itself, Mic. 6:6,7. "Thousands of rams, and ten thousand rivers of oil, or our *firstborn* are no ransom to God *for the sin of the soul*. It is only the precious blood of Christ that is a just ransom or counter-price, as it is called, Matt. 20:28.

Now, who can compute the value of that blood? Such was the worth of the blood of Christ, which, by the communication of properties, is truly styled the blood of God, that one drop of it is above the estimations of men and angels; and yet, before the soul of the meanest man or woman in the world could be redeemed, every drop of his blood must be shed; for no less than his death could be a price for our souls. Hence then we evidently discern an invaluable worth in souls: a whole kingdom is taxed, when a king is to be ransomed; the delight and darling of God's soul must die, when our souls are to be redeemed. O the worth of souls!

6. This evidences the transcendent dignity and worth of souls, that *eternity is stamped upon their actions*, and theirs only, of all the beings in this world. The acts of souls are immortal as their nature is; whereas the actions of other animals, having neither moral goodness nor moral evil in them, pass away as their beings do.

The apostle therefore, in Gal. 6:7, compares the actions of men in this world to seed sown, and tells us of everlasting fruits we shall

FLAVEL

reap from them in the next life; they have the sane respect to a future account that seed has to the harvest, "He that soweth iniquity shall reap vanity," *i.e.* everlasting disappointment and misery, Prov. 22:8. and "they that now sow in tears, shall then reap in joy," Prov. 26:5. Every gracious action is the seed of joy, and every sinful action the seed of sorrow; and this makes the great difference between the actions of a rational soul, and those done by beasts: and if it were not so, man would then be wholly swayed by sense and present things, as the beasts are, and all religion would vanish with this distinction of actions.

Our actions are considerable two ways, physically and morally; in the first sense they are transient, in the last permanent; a word is past as soon as spoken, but yet it must and will be recalled and brought into the judgment of the great day, Matt. 12:36. Whatever therefore a man shall speak, think, or do, once spoken, thought, or done, it becomes eternal, and abides for ever. Now, what is it that puts so great a difference between human and brutal actions, but the excellent nature of the reasonable soul? It is this which stamps immortality upon human actions, and is at once a clear proof both of the immortality and dignity of the soul of man above all other creatures in this world.

7. The contentions of both worlds, the strife of heaven and hell about the soul of man, speaks it a most precious and invaluable treasure.

The soul of man is the prize about which heaven and hell contend: the great design of heaven is to save it, and all the plots of hell to ruin it. Man is a borderer between both kingdoms, he lives here upon the confines of the spiritual and material world; and therefore Scaliger fitly calls him *Utriusque mundi nexus*, one in whom both worlds meet: his body is of the earth, earthly; his soul the offspring of the Deity, heavenly. It is then no wonder to find such tugging and pulling, this way and that way, upward and downward, such sallies from heaven to rescue and save it, such excursions from hell to captivate and ruin it.

The infinite wisdom of God has laid the plot and design for its salvation by Christ in so great depth of counsel, that the angels of heaven are astonished at it, and desire to pry into it. Christ in pursuance of this eternal project, came from heaven professedly to seer; and to save lost souls, Luke 19:10. He compares himself to a good shepherd, who leaves the ninety and nine to seek one lost sheep, and having found it, brings it lame upon his shoulder, rejoicing that he has found it, Luke 15:7.

Hell employs all its skill and policy, sets a-work all wiles and stratagems to destroy and ruin it; 1 Pet. 5:8. "Your adversary, the devil goeth about as a roaring lion, seeking whom he may devour." The strong man armed gets the first possession of the soul, and with all his forces and policies labours to secure it as his property, Luke 11:21. Christ raises all the spiritual militia, the very *posse caeli,* the powers of heaven, to rescue it, 2 Cor. 10: 4,5. And do heaven and earth thus contend, think you, *de lana caprina,* for a thing of nought? No, no, if there were not some singular and peculiar excellency and worth in man's soul, both worlds would never tug and pull at this rate which should win that prize. It was a great argument of the worth and excellency of Homer, that incomparable poet, that seven cities contended for the honour of his nativity.

Επλα ωολεις δειριζουσι περι ριζαν Ομηχου
Σμυρια, Ροδοσ, Κολοφων, Σαλαμιν, Χιος, Αργοσ, Αθηναι

Smyrna, Rhodes, Colophon, Salamis, Chius, Argos, and Athens, were all at strife about one poor man, who should crown themselves with the honour of his birth: but when heaven and hell shall contend about a soul, certainly it much more speaks the dignity of it, than the contention of several cities for one Homer.

What are all the wooings, expostulations, and passionate beseechings of Christ's ministers? What are all the convictions of conscience, and the strong impressions made upon the affections? What are all the strokes from heaven upon men in the way of sin? I say, what are all these but the efforts of heaven to draw souls out of the snares of hell?

And what are the hellish temptations that men feel in their hearts, the alluring objects presented to their eyes, the ensnaring examples that are set round about them, but the attempts of Satan, if possible, to draw the souls of men into the same condemnation and misery with himself?

Would heaven and hell be up in arms, as it were, and strive at this rate for nothing? Your soul, O man, how vilely soever you depreciate and slight it, is of high esteem, a rich purchase, a creature of nobler rank than you are aware of. The wise merchant knows the value of gold and diamonds, though ignorant Indians would part with them for glass beads and tinsel toys. And this leads us to

3. The eighth evidence of the invaluable worth of souls, which is the joy in heaven, and the rage in hell, for the gain and loss of the soul of man.

Christ, who came from heaven, and well knew the frame and disposition of the inhabitants of that city, tells us, that "there is joy in the presence of the angels of God over one sinner that repenteth," Luke 15:7,10. No sooner is the heart of a sinner darted with conviction, broken with sorrow for sin, and begins to cry, "men and brethren, what shall I do?" but the news is quickly in heaven, and sets all the city of God a rejoicing at it, as is in the chief city of a kingdom when a young prince is born.

We never read that Christ laughed in all his time on earth; but we read that he once rejoiced in spirit, Luke 10:21. And what was the occasion of that his joy, but the success of the gospel in the salvation of the souls of men? Now, certainly it must be some great good that so affects Christ, and all his angels in heaven at the sight of it, the degree of a wise mans joy is according to the value of the object thereof: No man that is wise will rejoice and feel his heart leap within him for gladness at a small or common thing.

And as there is joy in heaven for the saving, so certainly there is grief and rage in hell for the loss of a soul. No sooner had God, by Paul's ministry, converted one poor Lydia, at Philippi, whither he was called by an immediate express from heaven for that service, but the devil put all the city into an uproar, as if an enemy had landed on their coast; and raised a violent persecution, which quickly drove him thence, Acts 16:9,14,22.

And indeed what are all the fierce and cruel persecutions of God's faithful ministers, but so many efforts of the rage and malice of hell against them, for plucking souls as so many captives and preys out of his paws? for this he owes them a spight, and will be sure to pay them, if ever he get them at an advantage. But all this joy and grief demonstrates the high and great value of the prize which is won by heaven and lost by hell.

9. The institution of gospel-ordinances, and the appointment of so many gospel officers purposely for the saving of souls, is no small evidence of their value and esteem.

No man would light and maintain a lamp fed with golden oil, and keep it burning from age to age, if the work to be done by the light of it were not of a very precious and important nature: what else are the dispensations of the gospel, but loops burning with golden oil to light souls to heaven? Zech. 4:2,3,4, and 12, compared: A magnificent vision is there represented to the prophet, viz. a candlestick of gold with a bowl or cistern upon the top of it, and seven shafts with seven lamps at the ends thereof, all lighted. And that these lamps might have a constant supply of oil, without any accessory human help, there are represented (as growing by the candlestick) two fresh and green olive trees on each side thereof, ver. 8. which do empty out of themselves golden oil, ver. 12, naturally dropping and distilling it into that bowl, and the two pipes thereof to feed the lamps continually. Under this stately emblem you have a lively representation of the spiritual gifts and graces distilled by the Spirit into the ministers of the gospel for the use and benefit of the church, as you find not only by the angel's exposition of it here, but by the Spirit's allusion to it, and accommodation of it in Rev. 11:8,4. See herein what price God puts upon the salvation of souls: Gospel-lamps are maintained for their sakes, not with the sweat of ministers brows, or the expense and waste of their spirits, but by the precious gifts and graces of God's Spirit continually dropping into them for the use and service of souls. These ministerial gifts and graces are Christ's ascension gifts, Eph. 4:8 "When he ascended up on high, he gave gifts unto men; and what are the royal gifts of that triumphant day? Why, he gave some apostles, and some prophets, and some evangelists, and some pastors and teachers, for the perfecting of the saints, for the work of the ministry, for the edifying of the body of Christ." It is an allusion to the Roman triumphs, wherein the conqueror did *spargere missilia,* scatter abroad his treasures among the people. It is reported of the palm-tree, says one, that when it was first planted in Italy, they watered its roots with wine, to make it take the better with the soil: But God waters our souls with what is infinitely more costly than wine, he waters them with the heart-blood of Christ, and the precious gifts and graces of the Spirit; which certainly he would never do if they were not of great worth in his eyes. O how many excellent ministers, who were, as it is said of John, burning and shining lights in their places and generations, have spent themselves, and how many are there who are willing to spend, and be spent, as Paul was for the salvation of souls! God is at great expense for them, and therefore puts a very high value upon them.

Now all this respects the soul of man; that is the object of all ministerial labours. The soul is the terminus *actionum ad intra*, the subject on which God works, and upon which he spends all those invaluable treasures. It is the soul which he aims at, and principally designs and levels all to, and reckons it not too dear a rate to save it at.

No man will dig for common stones with golden mattocks, the instruments that would be worn out being of far greater value than the thing. This may convince us of what worth our souls are, and at what rates they are set in God's book, that such instruments are sent abroad into the world, and such precious gifts and graces, like golden oil, spent continually for their salvation; "Whether Paul, or Apollos, or Cephas, all are yours," 1 Cor. 3:22. i. e, all set apart for the service and salvation of your souls.

10. The great encouragements and rewards God propounds and promises to them that win souls, speak their worth, and God's great esteem of them.

There cannot be a more acceptable service done to God, than for a man to set himself heartily and diligently to the conversion of souls; so many souls as a man instrumentally saves, so many diadems will God crown him with in the great day. St. Paul calls his converted Philippians *his joy and his crown,* Phil. 4:1, and tells the converted Thessalonians, they were his "crown of rejoicing in the presence of Jesus Christ at his coming," 1 Thess. 2:19. There is a full reward assured by promise to those that labour in this great service, Dan. 12:3. "And they that be wise shall shine as the brightness of the firmament; and they that turn many to righteousness, as the stars for ever and ever." The wisdom here spoken of, I conceive not to be only that whereby a man is made wise to the salvation of his own soul, but whereby he is also furnished with skill for the saving of other men's souls according to that, Prov. 11:30. "He that winneth souls is wise:" And so the latter phrase is exegetical of it, meaning one and the same thing with being wise and turning many unto righteousness. And, to put men upon the study of this wisdom, he puts a very honourable title upon them, calling them "mitzdeeqee haraveem", *the justifiers of many,* as in 1 Tim. 4:16. They are said to save others. Here is singular honour put upon the very instruments employed in this honourable service, and that is not all, but their reward is great hereafter, as well as their honour great at present, they "shall shine as the brightness of the firmament, and the stars for ever and every." The firmament shines like a sapphire in itself, and the stars and planets more gloriously again; but those that faithfully labour in this work of saving souls shall shine in glory for ever and ever, when the firmament shall be parched up as a scroll. O what rewards and honours are there to provoke men to the study of saving souls! God will richly recompense all our pains in this work: If we did but only sow the seed in our days, and another enter into our labours, and water what we sowed; so that neither the first has the comfort of finishing the work, nor the last the honour of beginning it; but one did somewhat towards it in the work of conviction, and the other carried it on to greater maturity and perfection; and so neither the one nor the other began and finished the work singly, yet both shall rejoice in heaven together, John 4:36.

You see what honour God puts upon the very instruments employed in this work, even the honour to be saviours, under God, of men's souls, James 5:20. And what a full reward of glory, joy, and comfort, they shall have in heaven; all which speaks the great value of the soul with God. Such encouragements, and suck rewards would never have been propounded and promised if God had not a singular estimation of them.

And the more to quicken his instruments to all diligence, in this great work, he works upon their fears as well as hopes; threatens them with hell, as well as encourages them with the hopes of heaven; tells them he will require the blood of all those souls that perish by their negligence: "Their blood (says he) will I require at the watchman's hands," Ezek. 33:6, which are rather thunderbolts than words, says Chrysostome. By all which, you see, what a weight God lays upon the saving or losing of souls: Such severe charges, great encouragements, and terrible threats had never been proposed in scripture, if the souls of men had not been invaluable precious.

11. It is no small evidence of the precious and invaluable worth of souls, that God manifests so great and tender care over them, and is so much concerned about the evil that befalls them.

Among many others there are two things in which the tender care of God, for the good of souls, is manifested.

(1.) In his tenderness over them in times of distress and danger; as a tender father will not leave his sick child in other hands, but sits up and watches by himself, and administers the cordials with his own hands; even so the great God expresses his care and tenderness. Isa. 57:15. "I dwell in the high and holy place, with him also that is of a contrite and humble spirit, to revive the spirit of the humble, and to revive the heart of the contrite ones." Behold the condescending tenderness of the highest majesty! Is a soul ready to faint and fail, O how soon is God with it, with a reviving cordial in his hand! lest the spirit should fail before him, and the soul which he has made?" as it is, ver. 16. Yea, he put it into Christ's commission, "to preach good tidings to the meek, and to bind up the broken-hearted," Isa. 61:1. and not only inserts it in Christ's commission, but gives the same in solemn charge to all his inferior messengers, whom he employs about them. Isa. 35:3. "Strengthen you the weak hands, and confirm the feeble knees; say to them that are of a fearful heart, Be strong, fear not."

(2.) His special regard to souls is evidenced in his severe prohibitions to all others to do any thing that may be an occasion of ruin to them. He charges it upon all, "That no man put a stumbling-block, or an occasion to fall in his brother's way," Rom. 14:15, that by the abuse of our own liberty, "we destroy not him for whom Christ died," Rom. 14:15. And what does all this signify but the precious and invaluable worth of souls?

12. *Lastly,* It is not the least evidence of the dignity of men's souls, that God has appointed the whole host of angels to be their guardians and attendants.

"Are they not all ministering spirits sent forth to minister for them who shall be heirs of salvation?" Heb. 1:14.

Are they not? It is not a doubtful question, but the strongest way of affirmation; nothing is surer than that they are.

All. Not one of that heavenly company excepted. The highest angel thinks it no disparagement to serve a soul for whom Christ died; well may they all stoop to serve them when they see Christ their Lord has stooped, even to death, to save them. They are all of them.

Ministering spirits. Λαετουργικα πνευμαια, public officers, to whom their tutelage is committed. To them it belongs to attend, serve, protect and relieve them. The greatest barons and peers in the kingdom think it not below them to wait upon the heir apparent to the crown, in his minority; and no less dignity is here stamped by God upon the souls of men whom he calls.

Heirs of salvation. And in some respect nearer to Christ than themselves are; on this account it is, that the angels delight to serve them. Christ's little ones upon earth have their angels, which always behold the face of God in heaven, Matt. 18:10. and therefore says our Lord there, "Take heed you despise not one of those little ones;" they are greater persons than you are aware of. Nor is it enough that one angel is appointed to wait upon all, or many of them, but many angels, even a whole host of them, are sometimes sent to attend upon one of them. As Jacob was going on his way, the angels of God met him; and when he saw them he said, "This is God's host," Gen. 32:1,2.

The same two offices which belong to a nurse, to whom the father commits his child, belong also to the angels in heaven, with respect to the children of God, viz. to keep them tenderly while they are abroad, and bring them home to their Father's house at last. And how clearly does all this evince and demonstrate the great dignity and value of souls? Was it an argument of the grandeur and magnificence of king Solomon, that he had two hundred men with targets, and three hundred men with shields of beaten gold for his ordinary guard every day? And is it not a mark of far greater dignity than ever Solomon had in all his glory, to have hosts of angels attending us? In comparison with one of this guard, Solomon himself was but a worm in all his magnificence.

And now lay all these arguments together, and see what they will amount to. You have before you no ordinary creature: For (1.) It was not produced, as other creatures were by a mere word of command; but by the deliberation of the great council of heaven. And (2.) Such are the high and noble faculties and powers found in it as render it agreeable to, and becoming such a Divine original. Yea, (3.) By reason of these its admirable powers, it becomes a capable subject both of grace here and glory hereafter. (4.) Nor is this its capacity in vain; for God has made glorious preparations for some of them in heaven. (5.) And purchased them for heaven, and heaven for them, at an invaluable price, even the precious blood of Christ. (6.) And stamps immortality upon their actions, as well as natures. (7.) Both worlds contend and strive for the soul, as a prize of greatest value. (8.) Their conversion to Christ is the triumph of heaven, and rage of hell. (9.) The lamps of gospel-ordinances are maintained over all the reformed Christian world, to light them in their passage to heaven. (10.) Great rewards are propounded to all that shall heartily endeavour the salvation of them. (11.) The care of heaven is exceeding great and tender over them. And (12.) the heavenly hosts of angels have the charge of them, and reckon it their honour to serve them. These things, duly weighed, bring home the conclusion with demonstrative clearness, to every man's understanding, *That one soul is of more value than the whole world;* which was the thing to be proved. What remains, is the improvement of this excellent subject, in these following inferences.

Inf. 1. The soul of man, appearing to be a creature of such transcendent dignity and excellency, this truth appears of equal clearness with *it; That it was not made for the body, but the body for it; and therefore it is a vile abuse of the noble and high-born soul, to subject it to the lusts, and enslave it to the drudgery of the inferior and mere ignoble part.*

The very law of nature assigns the mast honourable places and employments, to the most noble and excellent creatures, and the baser and inferior, to things of the lowest rank and quality. The sun, moon and stars are placed by this lair in the heavens; but the *ignis fatuus,* and the glow worm in the fens and ditches. Princes are set upon thrones of glory, the beggars lodged in barns and stables: and if at any time this order of nature is inverted, and the baser suppress and perk over the noble and honourable beings, it is looked upon as a kind of prodigy, in the civil world. And so Solomon represents it, Eccl. 10:7. "I have seen seen servants upon horses, and princes walking as servants upon the earth;" i.e. I have seen men that are worthy of no better employments than to rub horses heels, in the saddle with their trappings; and men who deserves to bear rule, and to govern kingdoms; men, who for their great ability and integrity, deserves to sit at the helm, and moderate the affairs of kingdoms; these have I seen walking as servants upon the earth; and this he calls an evil under the sun, that is, an *ataxy,* confusion, or disorder in the course of nature.

Now there can never be that difference and vast odds between one man and another, as there is between the soul and body of. every man. A king upon the throne is not so much above a beggar that cries at our door for a crust, an the soul is above the body; for the soul of a beggar is of the sane species, original, and capacity of happiness, with the soul of the most illustrious prince; and sometimes greater excellencies of mind are found in the lowest rank and order of men. "Better is a poor and wise child, than an old, and foolish king," Eccl. 4:13, but the soul of the meanest person in the world is better than all the bodies in it; and therefore, to make the noble, and the high born soul a slave, a mere drudge to the vile body, as the apostle calls it, Phil. 3:21. "The body of this vileness;" what is it but to set the beggar on horseback, and make the king lacquey after him on foot!

It was a generous resentment that a Heathen had of the dignity of his own soul, and a very just abhorrence of so vile an abuse of it, when he said, *I am greater, and born to greater things, than that I should be a slave to my body.*

I know there is a debt of duty the soul owes to its own body, and few souls are to be found too careless, or dilatory in the discharge thereof; where one soul needs the spur in this case, thousands need the curb. Most souls are overheated with zeal for the concerns of the flesh, worn out and spent in its constant drudgery, their whole life is but a *serving of divers lusts and pleasures,* as the apostle speaks, Tit. 3:3. Imperious lusts are cruel taskmasters, they give the soul no rest; the more provision the soul brings in to satisfy them, the more they rage, like fire, by the addition of more fuel. What a sad sight is it to see a noble, immortal soul *enslaved,* as the apostle's word is, Tit. 1:7. *to wine? To filthy lucre,* to a thousand sorts of vassalage; like a *tapster* in a common inn, now running up stairs, and then down, at every one's knock and call.

O what a perpetual hurry and noise do thousands of souls live in! so that they have no time to retire into themselves, and think for what end and use they were created and sent into this world. All their thoughts, all their cares, all their studies and labours, are taken up about the perishing, clogging, ensnaring body, which must so shortly fall a prey to the worms. How many millions of poor creatures are there that labour and toil all their life long, for a poor, bare maintenance of their bodies, and never think they have any other business to do in this world!

And how many, of an higher rank, are charmed by a thick succession of fleshly delights and pleasures, into a deep oblivion of their eternal concerns! So that their whole life is but one entire diversion from the great business and proper end of it. James 5:5. "Ye have lived in pleasures on earth," living in them, as the fish does in the water, its proper element, or the eel in the mud. Sometimes it falls out, at the very close of a vain voluptuous life, when you see all their delights shrinking away at the approaches; and appearance of death, that they begin to be a little startled at the change, which is about to be made upon them; and to cry, O what shall we do now! Ah poor souls! is that a time to think what you shall do, when you are just stepping into the awful state of eternity? O that this had been thought on in season! But you could find no leisure for one such thought. Now you begin to wish time had been rescued out of the hands of the cares and pleasures of this life, for better purposes; but it is gone, and never more to be recalled.

Inf. 2. Is the soul so invaluably precious? Then the salvation of the soul is to be the great care, and business of every man in this life.

Where one thought is spent about this question, *What shall I eat, drink, and put on?* a thousand should be spent about that question, "What shall I do to be saved! If a treasure of ten, or twenty thousand pounds were committed to your trust and charge, and for which (in case of loss) you must be responsible, would not your thoughts, cares, and fears, be working night and day about it, till you are satisfied it is safe and out of danger? And then your mind would be at rest, but not before. Your soul, O man, is more worth than the crowns and treasures of all the princes in the world! If all their exchequers were drained, and all their crown-jewels sold to their full value, they could never make up a half ransom for the soul of the poorest and meanest man. This invaluable treasure is committed to your charge; if it be lost, you are lost for ever. That which St. Matthew calls the losing of the soul in my text, St. Luke calls *losing himself;* if the soul be lost, the man is lost. The body is but as a boat fastened to the stern of a stately ship, if the ship sink, the boat follows it.

O. therefore, what thoughts, what fears, what cares should exercise the minds of men, day and night, till their precious souls are out of all danger: Methinks the sound of this text should ring a perpetual alarm in the ears of careless sinners, and make them hasten to the insurance-office, as merchants do, who have great adventures in danger at sea. It was counsel given once to a king, and worthy to be pressed upon all, from the king to the beggar, to ruminate these words of Christ one quarter of an hour every day; "What is a man profited, if he shall gain the whole world, and lose his own soul? Or what shall a man give in exchange for his soul?" Certainly it would make men slacken their pace and cool themselves in their hot and earnest pursuit of the trifles of this world, and convince them, that they have somewhat else to do of far greater importance.

It was not without great and weighty reason, therefore, that the apostle Peter exhorts to all diligence to make our calling and election sure, 2 Pet. 1:10. There are two words in this text of extra ordinary weight, Σπουδασατε, *Give all diligence;* the word is *study*; the utmost intention of the mind, pondering and comparing things in the thoughts, valuing reasons for, and objections against the point before us, this is study; and such as calls for all diligence where the subject matter is (as to be sure here it is) of the greatest importance: And what is the subject matter of all this study and diligence? Why, it is the most solemn of all works that ever came under the hand of man, to make our calling and election sure, firm, stable, or fixed, as a building raised upon a square and strong foundation; or as a conclusion is sure, when regularly drawn from certain and indubitable premises. There can never be too much care, too much study or pains about that which can never be too well secured.

Many souls never spent one solemn hour in a close and serious debate about this matter; others have taken a great deal of pains about it; they have broken many nights sleep, poured out many prayers, made many a deep search into their own hearts, walked with much conscientious watchfulness and tenderness, proposed many a serious case of conscience to the most judicious and skilful ministers and Christians; and after all, the security is not such as fully satisfies. And probably one reason of it may be the great weight wherewith the matters of their salvation lie upon their spirits. O that these soul concerns did bear upon all, as they do upon some! It requires more time, more thoughts, more prayers to make these things sure, than most are aware of.

Inf. 3. *If the soul be so precious, then certainly it is the special care of heaven, that which God looks more particularly after, than any other creature or earth.*

There is an active, vigilant providence that superintends every creature upon earth; there is not the most despicable, diminutive creature that lives in the world, left without the line of providence. God is therefore said to give them all their meat in due season, and for that end they all wait upon him, Psal. 104, who, as a great and provident house keeper orders daily, convenient provisions for all his family, even to the least and lowest among them: The smallest insects and gnats which swarm so thick in the air, and of the usefulness of almost being it is hard to give an account; yet as the incomparably learned Dr. More well observes, these all find nourishment in the world, which would be lost if they did not, and are again convenient nourishment themselves to others that prey upon them.

But man is the peculiar, special care of God; and the soul of man much more than the body. Hence Christ fortifies the faith of Christians against all distrusts of Divine Providence, even from their excellency above other creatures.

Matt. 10:31. "Ye are of more value than many sparrows;" and Matt. 6:26, your heavenly Father feeds the fowls of the air, and are ye not much better than they?" and vs. 30, "he clothes the grass of the field, and shall he not much more clothe you?" and so the apostle, 1 Cor. 9:9. "Does God take care for oxen? or says he it altogether for our sakes? For our sakes, no doubt, this is written." In all which places we have the dignity of man above all animals and vegetables in respect of the natural excellency of his reasonable soul, but especially the gracious endowments of it, which endear it far more to its Maker; this is the very hinge of the argument, and a firm ground for the believer's faith of God's tender care over both parts, but especially the soul. The boldly of a believer is God's creature, as well as his soul; but that being of less value, has not such a degree of care and tenderness expressed towards it, as the soul has: the father's care is not so much for the child's clothes, as it is for the child himself. Besides, the immediate wants and troubles of the soul, which are *idiopathetic,* are far more sharp and pinching than those it suffers upon the body's account, which are but *sympathetic;* and therefore, whenever such an excellent creature as a sanctified soul which is in Christ, or a soul designed to be sanctified, which is moving towards Christ, falls under those heavy pressures and distresses, (as it often does) and is ready to fail; let it be assured, its merciful Creator will not fail to relieve, support, revive, and deliver it, as often as it shall fall into those deep distresses.

Hear how his compassionate tenderness is expressed towards distressed souls. Isa. 49:15, "Can a woman forget her sucking child, that she should not have compassion on the son of her womb? Yea, they may forget, yet I will not forget you."

Sooner shall a *woman,* the more tender sex, forget, (not the nurse child, that only sucks her breast, but) the child, yea, the son of her womb, and that not when grown and placed abroad, but while it hangs upon her breast, and draws love from her hearts as well as milk from her breast, than God will forget a soul that fears him. Let gracious souls fortify their faith, therefore, in the Divine care, by considering with what a peculiar eye of estimation and care God looks upon them above all other creatures in the world: only beware you so eye not the natural or spiritual excellencies of your souls, as to expect mercy for the sake thereof, as if your souls were worthy for whose sake God should do this: no, she non-suited that plea; all is of free grace, not of debt: but he minds us to what reputation the new creation brings the soul with its God.

Inf. 4. *If the soul of man be so precious, how precious and dear to all believers should the Redeemer and Saviour of their precious souls be?*

"Unto you therefore that believe, he is precious," says the apostle, 1 Pet. 2:7. Though he be yet out of our sight, he should never be one whole hour together out of our hearts and thoughts. 1 Pet. 1:8. "Whom having not seen ye love; whom though now ye see him not, yet believing, ye rejoice with joy unspeakable, and full of glory." " The very name of Christ," says Bernard, "is honey in the mouth, melody in the ear, and a very jubilee in the heart." The blessed martyr, Mr. Lambert, made this his motto, None but Christ, none but Christ. Molinus was seldom observed to mention his name without dropping eyes. Julius Palmer, in the midst of the flames, moved his scorched lips, and was heard to say, Sweet Jesus, and fell asleep. Paul fastens upon his name as a bee upon a sweet flower, and mentions it no less than ten times in the compass of ten verses, 1 Cor. 1 as if he knew not how to leave it.

There is a twofold preciousness of Christ, one in respect of his essential excellency and glory; in this respect he is glorious, as the only begotten Son of God, the brightness of his Father's glory, and the express image or character of his person, Heb. 1. The other in respect of his relative usefulness and suitableness to all the needs and wants of poor sinners, as he is *the Lord our righteousness,* made unto us wisdom, righteousness, sanctification, and redemption. None discern this preciousness of Christ but those that have been convinced of sin, and have apprehended the wrath to come, the just demerit of sin, and fled for refuge to the hope set before them; and to them he is precious indeed. Consider him as a Saviour from wrath to come, and he will appear the most lovely and desirable in all the world to your souls: he that understands the value of his own soul, the dreadful nature of the wrath of God, the near approaches of this wrath to his own soul, and the astonishing love of Christ in delivering him from it by bearing that wrath in his place and room, in his own person; cannot choose but estimate Christ above ten thousand worlds.

Inf. 5. How great a trust and charge lies upon them to whom the care of souls is committed, and from whom an account for other men's, as well as their own souls shall certainly be required?

Ministers are appointed of God to watch for the souls of their people, and that as men that must give an account, Heb. 13:17. The word here translated *watch,* signifies such watchfulness as that of shepherds who keep their flocks by night in places infested by wolves, and watch whole nights together for their safety. If a man were a keeper only of sheep and swine, it were no great matter if the wolf now and then carried away one while he slept; but ministers have charge of souls, one of which, as Christ assures us in the text, *is more worth than the whole world.* Hear what one speaks upon this point.

"God purchased the church with his own blood: O what an argument is here to quicken the negligent! And what an argument to condemn those that will not be quickened up to their duty by it! O, says one of the ancient doctors, if Christ had but committed to my keeping one spoonful of his blood in a fragile glass, how curiously should I preserve it, and how tender should I be of that glass! If then he have committed to me the purchase of that blood, should I not carefully look to my charge?"

"What, sirs, shall we despise the blood of Christ? shall we think it was shed for them that are not worthy our care? O then let us hear those arguments of Christ, whenever we feel ourselves grow dull and careless. Did I die for them, and will you not look after them? Were they worth my blood, and are they not worth your labour? Did I come down from heaven to earth, to *seek and to save that which is lost,* and wilt not you go to the next door, or street, or village, to seek them? How small is your labour or condescension to mine? I debased myself to this, hut it is your honour to be so employed."

Let not that man think to be saved by the blood of Christ himself that makes light of precious souls, who are the purchase of that blood.

And no less charge lies upon parents, to whom God has committed the care of their children's souls; and masters that have the guardianship of the souls as well as the bodies of their families; the command is laid express upon you, that they sanctify God's sabbaths, Exod. 20:10, to command your household in the way of the Lord, Gen. 18:19.

O parents, consider with yourselves what strong engagements lie upon you to do all you are capable of doing for the salvation of the precious souls of your dear children. Remember, their souls are of infinitely more value than their bodies; that they came into the world under sin and condemnation; that you were the instruments of propagating that sin to them, and bringing them into that misery; that you know their dispositions, and how to suit them better than others can; that the bonds of nature give you singular advantages to prevail and be successful in your exhortations, beyond what any others have; that you are always with them, and can choose opportunities which others cannot; that you and they must shortly part, and never meet again till you meet at the judgment seat of Christ; that it will be an inconceivably dreadful day to see them stand at Christ's left hand among the cursed and condemned, there cursing the day that ever they were born of such ignorant and negligent, such careless and cruel parents, as took no care to instruct, reprove, or exhort them. O who can think without horror of the cries and curses of his own child in hell, cast away by the very instrument of his being!

Is this the love you bear them, to betray them to eternal misery? Was there no other provision to be made but for their bodies? Did you think you had fully acquitted your duty when you had got an estate for them? O, that God would effectually touch your hearts with a becoming sense of the value and danger of their souls and your own too, in the neglect of that great and solemn trust committed to you with respect to them! And you, masters, consider, though God has set you above, and your servants below, yet are their souls equally precious with your own: they have another Master that expects service from them as well as you. Do not only allow them time, but give them your exhortations and commands not to neglect their own souls, while they attend your business: think not your business will prosper the less because it is in the hand of a praying servant: their souls are of greater concernment than any business of yours can be.

Inf. 6. Are soup so precious? Then certainly the means and instruments of their salvation must be exceeding precious too, and the removal of them a sore judgement.

The dignity of the subject gives value to the instruments employed about it. It is no ordinary mercy for souls to come into such a part of the world, and in such a time as furnishes them with the best helps for salvation. Ordinances and ministers receive their value not from their Author, but from their Object: they have a dignity stumbled upon them by their usefulness to the souls of men, Acts 20:32. The word is the *seed* of life, 1 Pet. 1:23, the regenerating instrument. It is the *bread of life,* cud Job 23:12, more than our necessary food. The word *is a light,* shining in the dark world to direct 'our souls through all the snares laid for them unto glory. It is the soul's cordial in all fainting fits, Psal. 114:50. What shall I say of the word and ordinances of God? The sun that shines in heaven to give us light, the fountains, springs, and rivers that stream for our refreshment, the corn and cattle on the earth, yea, the very air we breathe in is not so useful, so necessary, so precious to our bodies, as the word is to our souls.

It cannot therefore but be a sore judgment, and a dreadful token of God's indignation and wrath, to have a restraint or scarcity of the means of salvation among us; but should there be (which God in mercy prevent) a removal and total loss of those things, wrath would then come upon us to the uttermost. What will the condition of precious souls be when the means of salvation are cut off from them? When that famine, worse than of bread and water, is come upon them? Amos 8:11. When the ark of God (the symbol of his presence) was taken, it is said, 1 Sam. 4:13. "that all the city cried out." When Paul took his leave of Antioch, and told them they should see his face no more, how did the poor Christians lament and mourn, as cut at the heart by that killing word? Acts 20:37,38. It made Christ's bowels to yearn, and move within him when he saw the multitude scattered as sheep having no shepherd, Matt. 9:36.

Matthew Paris tells us, in the year 1072, when preaching was suppressed at Rome, letters were franked as coming from hell, wherein the devil gave them thanks for the multitude of souls sent to him that year. But we need no letters from hell, we have a sad account from heaven, in what a sad state those souls are left, from whom the means of salvation are cut off: "Where no vision is, the people perish," Prov. 29:18. and Hos. 4:6. "My people are destroyed for lack of knowledge."

It is sad when those stars that guide souls to Christ, (as that which the wise men saw did) are set, and wandering stars shall shine in their places. O if God remove the golden candlestick out of its place, what but the desolation and ruin of millions of souls must follow?

We account it insufferable cruelty for a man to undertake the piloting of a ship full of passengers who never learnt his compass; or an ignorant *Empiric* to get his living by killing men's bodies; but much more lamentable will the state of souls be if ever they fall, (which God in mercy prevent) into the hands of Popish guides, *or blind leaders of the blind.*

Inf. 7. If the soul be of so precious a rapture, it can never live upon such base and vile food as earthly things are.

The apostle, Phil. 3:8,9. calls the things of this world *dog's meat;* and judge if that be proper food for such noble and high-born creatures as our souls are. An immaterial being can never live upon material things; they are no bread for souls, as the prophet speaks, Isa. 55:2. "Why do ye spend money, (i.e. time and pains, thoughts and cares) for that which is not bread?" Your souls can no more live upon carnal, than your bodies on spiritual things. Earthly things have a double defect in them, by reason whereof they are called things of nought, Amos 6:18, of no worth or value; they are neither suitable nor durable, and therefore, in the soul's eye, not valuable.

1. They are not suitable. What are corn and wine, gold and silver, pleasures and honours, to the soul? The body, and bodily senses, can find somewhat of refreshment in them; but not the spirit: That which is bread to the body, affords no more nourishment to the soul than wind or ashes, Isa. 44:20. "He feedeth of ashes." "Ashes are that light and dry matter, into which fuel is reduced by the fire;" the fuel, before it was burnt, had nothing in it fit for nourishment, or if the sap or juice that was in it, might in any respect be useful that way, yet all that is devoured and licked up by the fire, and not the least nutriment left in the ashes: And such are all earthly to the soul of man. "I am the bread of life," says Christ, a soul can feed and feast itself upon Christ and the promises; these are things full of marrow and fatness, substantial, and proper soul nutrient.

2. As earthy things are no way suitable to the soul, so neither are they durable. The apostle reduces all earthly things to three heads,

"the lust of the eye, the lust of the flesh, and the pride of life," 2 John 2:16. He calls them all by the name of that which gives the lustre and beauty to them, and pronounces them all fading, transitory vanities, they all pass away; as time, so these things that are measured by time, are *in fluxu continuo,* always going, and at last will be all gone. Now the soul being of an immortal nature, and these things of a perishing nature; it must necessarily and unavoidably follow, that the soul must over-live them all; and if it will do so, what a dismal case are those souls in, for whom no other provision is role, but that of which it cannot subsist, while it has them, no more than the body can upon ashes or wind? And if it could, yet they will shortly fall it, and pass away for ever. So then it is beyond debate, that there lies a plain necessity upon every snag to make provision in time, of things more suitable and durable than earthly treasures are, or the soul must perish, as to its comfort, to all eternity.

Hence is that weighty counsel of him that came to save them, Luke 12:28. "Provide yourselves bags that wax not old, a treasure in heaven that faileth not", i.e. a happiness which will last as long as your souls last. Certainly, the moth-eaten things of this world are no provision for immortal spirits, and yet multitudes think of no other provision for them, but live as if they had nothing to do in this world but to get an estate.

Alas! what are all these things to the soul? They signify somewhat, indeed, to the body, and that but for a little time: for after the resurrection, the bodies of the saints become spiritual in qualities, and no more need these material things than the angels do: It is madness therefore, to be so intent upon cares for the body, as to neglect the soul; but to ruin the soul, and drown it in perdition, for the sake of these provisions for the flesh, is the height of madness.

Inf. 8. *If the soul be so invaluably precious, then it is a rational and well advised resolution and practice, to expose all other things to hazard, yea, to certain loss, for the preservation of the more precious soul.*

It is better our bodies and all their comforts should perish, than that our souls should perish for their sakes. Nature teaches us to offer a hand or arm to the stroke of a sword, to save a blow from the head, or put by a thrust at the heart. It is recorded, to the praise of those three worthies, Dan. 3:28. "That they yielded their bodies, that they might not serve, nor worship any God, except their own God." By this rule, all the martyrs of Christ governed themselves, still slighting and exposing to destruction, their bodies and estates, to preserve their souls, reckoning to save nothing, by religion, but their souls, and that they had lost nothing, if they could save them; "They loved not their lives unto the death," Rev. 12:11.

Then do we live like Christians, when the care of our bodies is swallowed up, and subdued by that of our souls, and all creature-loves by the love of Christ. Those blessed souls hated their own bodies, and counted them their enemies, when they would draw them from Christ and his truths, and plunge their souls into guilt and danger. This was the result of all their delegates with the flesh in the hour of temptation; cannot we live but to the dishonour of Christ, and the ruin of our own souls, by sinful compliance against our consciences? Then welcome the worst of deaths, rather than such a life!

Look into the stories of the martyrs, and you shall find this was the rule they still governed themselves by; a dungeon, a stake, a gibbet, any thing, rather than guilt upon the inner man: death was welcome, even in its most dreadful form, to escape ruin to their precious and immortal souls. One kissed the apparitor, that bolt him the tidings of death. Another being advised, when he came to the critical point, on which his life depended, to have a care of himself: So I will, said he, I will be as careful as I can of my best self, my soul. These men understood the value and precious worth of their own souls; certainly, we shall never prove courageous and constant in sufferings, till we understand the worth of our souls as they did. Consider and conspire these sufferings in a few obvious particulars, and then determine the matter in your own breast.

(1.) How much easier it is to endure the torments of men in our bodies, than to feel the terrors of God in our consciences. Can the creature strike with an arm like God? Oh! think what it is for the wrath of God to cone into a man's bowels like water, and like oil into his bones, as the expression is, Ps. 109:18. Sure there is no comparison between the strokes of God and men.

(2.) The sufferings of the body are but for a moment. When the proconsul told Polycarp that he would tame him with fire, he replied, Your fire shall burn but for the space of an hour, and then it shall he extinguished; but the fire that shall devour the wicked will never quenched. The sufferings of a moment are nothing to eternal strips.

(3.) Sufferings for Christ are usually sweetened and made easy by the consultations of the Spirit; but hell-torments have no relief; they admit of no ease.

(4.) The life that you shall live in that body, for whose sake you leave damned your souls, will not be worth the having; it will be a life without comfort, light, or joy; and what is there in life, separate from the joy and comfort of life?

(5.) In a word, if you sacrifice your bodies for God and your souls, freely offer them up in love to Christ and his truth, your souls will joyfully receive and meet them again at the resurrection of the just; but if your poor souls be now ensnared and destroyed by your fond indulgence to your bodies, you will leave them at death despairing, and meet them at the resurrection howling.

Inf. 9. To conclude, *If the soul be so invaluably precious, how great and irreparable loss must the loss of a soul to all eternity be!*

There is a double loss of the soul of man, the one in Adam, which loss is recoverable by Christ; the other by final impenitence and unbelief, cutting it off from Christ; and this is irreparable anal irrecoverable. Souls lost by Adam's sin, are within the reach of the arms of Christ; but in the shipwreck of personal infidelity, there is no plank to save the soul so cast away; of all losses, this is the most lamentable, yet what more common: O what a shriek does the unregenerate soul make, when it sees whither it must go, and that there is no remedy! Three cries are dreadful to hear on earth, yet all three are drowned, by a more terrible cry in the other world; the cry of a condemned prisoner at the bar, the cry of drowned seamen and passengers in a shipwreck. the cries of soldiers conquered in the field; all these are fearful cries, yet nothing to that of a soul cast away to all eternity, and lost in the depth of hell.

If a man, as Chrysostom well observes, lose an eye, an arm, a hand, or leg, it is a great loss; but yet if one be lost, there is another to help him: for *omnia Deus dedit duplicia*, God has given us all those members double; *Animal vero unam*, but we have but one soul, and if that be damned, there is not another to he saved.

And it is no small aggravation to this loss, that it was a wilful loss; we had the offers, and means of salvation plentifully afforded us; we were warned of this danger, over and over; we were entreated, and beseeched, upon the knee of importunity, not to throw away our souls, by an obstinate rejection of Christ, and grace; we saw the diligence and care of others for the salvation of their souls, some rejoicing in the comfortable assurance of it, and others giving all difference to make their *calling and election sure:* we knew that our souls were as capable of blessedness, as any of those that are enjoying God in heaven, or panting after that enjoyment on earth; yea, some souls that are now irrecoverably gone, and many others who are going after them, once were, and now are not far from the kingdom of God; they had convictions of sin, a sense of their loss, and miserable state; they began to treat with Christ in prayer, to converse with his ministers and people, about their condition, and after all this, even when they seemed to have clean escaped the snares of Satan, to be again entangled, and overcome; when even come to the harbour's mouth, to be driven back again, and cast away upon the rocks. O what a loss will this be!

O thou that created souls with a capacity to know, love, and enjoy thee for ever; who out of thy unsearchable grace sent thine own Son out of thine bosom to seek and save that which was lost, pity those poor souls that cannot pity themselves: let mercy yet interpose itself between them and eternal ruin, awaken them out of their pleasant slumber, though it be at the brink of damnation, lest they perish, and there be none to deliver them.

Doct. 2. *How precious and invaluable soever the soul of man is, it may be lost, and cast away for ever.*

This proposition is supposed, and implied in our Saviour's words in the text, and plainly expressed in Matt. 7:13. "Wide is the gate and broad is the way that leadeth to destruction, and many there be which go in thereat." The way to hell is thronged with passengers; it is a beaten road; one draws another along with him, and scoffs at those that are afraid to follow, 1 Pet. 4:4. *Facilis descensus averni;* it is pleasant sailing with wind and tide. Some derive the word *hell* from a verb which signifies to carry, or thrust in; millions go in, but none return thence: millions are gone down already, and millions more are coming after, as fast as Satan and their own lusts can flurry them onward. You read not only of single persons, but whole nations drowned in this gulf. Psal. 9:17. "The wicked shall be turned into hell, and all nations that forget God." How rare is the conversion of a soul in the dark places of the earth, where the sound of the gospel is not heard?

FLAVEL

The devil drives them in droves to destruction, scarce a man being reluctant or drawing back.

And though some nations enjoy the inestimable privilege of the gospel of salvation, yet multitudes of precious souls perish, notwithstanding, sinking into hell daily, as it were, between the merciful arms of a Saviour stretched out to save them. The light of salvation is risen upon us, but Satan draws the thick curtains of ignorance, and prejudice about the multitude, that not a beam of saving light can shine into their hearts. 2 Cor. 4:8,4. "But if our gospel be hid, it is hid to them that are lost: in whom the god of this world has blinded the minds of them which believe not, lest the light of the glorious gospel of Christ, who is the image of God, should shine unto them."

If our gospel. Ours, not by way of institution, as the authors, but by way of dispensation, as the ministers and preachers of it; and certainly, it was never preached with that clearness, authority, and efficacy by any mere man, as it was by Paul and the rest of the apostles; and yet the gospel so powerfully preached, is by him here supposed to

Be hid.] If not as to the general light and superficial knowledge of it, set as to its saving influence and converting efficacy upon their hearts: this never reaches home to the souls and spirits of multitudes that hear it, but it is never finally so hidden, except

To them that are lost. So that all those to whom the converting and saving power of the gospel never comes, whatever names, and reputations they may have among men, yet this text looks upon them all as a lost generation: They may have as many amiable, homiletic virtues, as sweet and lovely natures, as clear and piercing eyes, in all other things, as any others; but they are such, however,

Whose eyes the god of this world hath blinded. Satan is here called the god of this world, not properly, hut by a mimesis; because he challenges to himself the honour of a god, and has a world of subjects that obey him; and, to secure their obedience, he blinds them, that they may never see a better way or state, than that he has drawn them into. Therefore he is called the ruler of the darkness of this world, who rules in the hearts of the children of disobedience. The eye of the soul is the mind, that thinking, considering, and reasoning power of the soul; this is, as the philosophers truly call it, the το ηγεμονιον, the leading faculty to all the rest, the guide to all the other faculties, which, in the order of nature, follow this their leader: If this be blinded, the wild, which is *caeca potentia,* a blind power in itself, and all affections blindly following the blind, all must needs fall into the ditch. And this is the case of the far greater part of even the professing world. Let us suppose a number of blind men upon an island, where there are many smooth paths, all leading to the top of a perpendicular cliff, and these blind men going on continually, some in one path, and some in another, but all in some one of those many paths which lead to the brink of their ruin, which they see not; it must needs follow, if they all move forward, the whole number will in a short time be cast away, the island cleared, and its inhabitants dead, and lost in the bottom of the sea. This is the case of the unregenerate world; they are now upon this habitable spot of earth, environed with the vast ocean of eternity; there are multitudes of paths leading to eternal misery; one man takes this way, and another that, as it is Isa. 53:6. "We have turned every one to his own way;" one to the way of pride, another to the way of covetousness, a third to the way of persecution, a fourth to the ways of civility and mortality; and so on they go, not once making a stand, or questioning to what end it will bring them, till at last over they go, at death, and we hear no more of them in this world: And thus one generation of sinners follows another, and they that come after approve, and applaud those miserable wretches that went before them, Psal. 49:13. and so hell fills, and the world empties its inhabitants daily into it. Now I will make it my work, out of a dear regard to the precious souls of men, and in hope to prevent (which the Lord in mercy grant) the loss, and ruin of some, under whose eyes this discourse shall fall, to note some of the principal ways in which precious souls are lost, and to put such bars into there, as I am capable to put; and, among many more, I will set a mark upon these following twelve paths, wherein millions of souls have been lost, and millions more are confidently, and securely following after, among which, it is likely, some are within one step, one day, or hour, to their eternal downfall and destruction. There is but one way in all the world, to save, and preserve the precious souls of men, but there are many ways to lose and destroy them: It is here, as it is in our natural birth, and death, but one way into the world, but a multitude out of it. And first,

The first way to hell discovered

1. And to begin where, indeed, the ruin of very many does begin, it will be found, that *ill education is the highway to destruction;* vice need not be planted; if the gardener neglect to dress, sow, and manure his garden, he need not give the weeds a greater advantage;

but if he also scatter the seeds of hemlock, docks, and nettles into it, he spoils it, and makes it fit for nothing. Many parents, and those godly too, are guilty of too many neglects, through carelessness, worldly incumbrances, or fond indulgence; and while they neglect the season of sowing better seed, the devil takes hold of it; if they will not improve it, he will. If they teach him not to pray, he will teach them to curse, swear, and lie. If they put not the bible, or catechism in their hands, he will put obscene ballads into them: and thus the offspring of many godly parents turn into degenerate plants, and prove a generation that know not the God of their fathers. This debauched age can furnish us with too many sad instances hereof. Thus they are spoiled in the bud; simple ignorance in youth, becomes affected and wilful ignorance in age; blushing sins in children become impudent in age; and all this for want of a timely, and prudent preventing care. Others there are of the rude and ignorant multitude, who are bred themselves much like the beasts they daily converse withal; and so they are fitly described, Job 30:6,7. Go into their houses, and you may sooner find in the window, or upon the shelf, a pack of cards, than a bible or a catechism; their beds and tables differ little, or not at all, from the stalls and cribs where beasts lie down and feed, in respect of any worship of God among them; or if, for fashion salve, a few words be huddled over in the evening, when their bodies are tired, the man says something, he scarce knows what, the wife is asleep in one corner, the children in another, and the servants in a third. This is the education multitudes of parents give their children all the week, and when the sabbath comes, the most they learn to know at church, is, where their own seat stands, and that it is necessary to speak with such a neighbour after prayers about such or such a bargain, or business for the next week.

And others there are, who breed their children as profanely, as these do sottishly; teaching them, by their examples, the newest oaths that were last minted in hell, and to revile and scoff all serious godliness, and the sincere professors of it, smiling to hear with what an emphasis they can talk in the dialect of devils, and how wittily they can droll upon godly ministers and Christians.

Such families are nurseries for hell; and though God, by an extraordinary hand of providence, now and then snatches a soul by conversion from among them, as a brand out of the fire; yet generally, they die as they live, going "to the generation of their fathers, where they shall never see light," Psal. 49:19. I know education and regeneration are two things; but I also know one is frequently made the instrument of working the other, and that the favour of what first seasons our youth (generally) abides to odd age," Prov. 22:6. We may observe, all the world over, how tenacious men are of that which is πατροωοραδοτον, delivered to them by their parents. O what a cut must it be to the heart of that father whose son's life shall tell his conscience what a profane son's lips once told his father to his face! "If I have done evil, I have learnt it of you." Had they felt more of your prudent correction, it might have prevented their destruction. Prov. 23:14. "Thou shalt beat hint with the rod, and shalt deliver his soul from hell." That this is a common beaten path to hell, is beyond all question; but how to bar it up, and stop the multitudes that are engaged in it to their own ruin, this is the labour, this is the work. I cannot be large, but I will offer a few weighty considerations.

The first way to hell barred

1. Let all parents consider, what a fearful thing it is to be the instruments of ruining for ever, those that received their beings instrumentally from them, and to seek whose good they stand obliged, by all the laws of God and nature.

In vain are all your cares and studies for their bodies, while their souls perish for want of knowledge. You rejoiced at their birth, but they will have cause to curse the day they were born of you, and say, "Let the day perish wherein I was born, and the night in which I was conceived." You were solicitous for their bodies, but careless of their souls; earnest to see them rich, but indifferent whether they were gracious; you neglected to teach them the way of salvation, but the devil did not neglect to teach them the way of sin. You will one day wish you hall never been parents, when the doleful cries of your damned children shall ring such notes as these in your ears: "O cursed father! O cruel, merciless mother! whose examples have drawn me after you, into all this misery. You had time enough, and motives enough to have warned me of this place and misery while my heart was tender, and my affections pliable: Had it not been as easy to have put a Bible as a play-book before me? To have chastised me when I provoked God by sin, as when I provoked you about a trifle? One word spoken in season might have saved my soul; one reproof wisely given and set on by your example, might have preserved me. Had it not been the same pains to have asked me, child, what will you do to be saved? As, what will you do to live in this world? Or, had I but observed any serious religion in you, had I but found or heard my father or mother upon their knees in prayer, it might have awakened me to a consideration of my condition. In my youth I was shame faced, fearful, credulous, and apt to imitate; had you but had wisdom as other parents have, to have taken hold of any of these handles in time, you had rescued my soul from hell. Nay, so cruel have you been to your own child, that you allowed me no time (if I had had a disposition) for any exercise of religion; yea, you have quenched and stifled the sparks of convictions and better inclinations that sometimes were in my heart. O happy had it been if I had never been born of you, or seen your faces." This must be the result and issue of your negligence, except God, by some other hand (which is no thanks to you) rescue them from their impending ruin.

2. Let all children, whose unhappy lot it is to be born of, and educated by, carnal and irreligious parents, consider, God has endued them with reason, and a conscience of their own, to enable them to make a better choice than their parents did, and that there is no taking sanctuary from the wrath of God in their parents' examples. We read, in 1 Kings 14:13, of a good Abijah, "in whom was found some good thing towards the Lord God of Israel, in the house of Jeroboam." Here was a child that would not follow his wicked father to hell, though he had both the authority of a father, and of a king over him. "You must honour your parents, but still you must prefer your God before them". God will never lay it to your account as your sin, but place it to the account of your duty, and comfort, that you refused to follow them in the paths of sin and destruction. No law of God, no tie of nature binds you to obey their commands, or tread in their steps, farther than they command in God's authority and name, and walk in his ways. Your temptations, indeed, are strong, and disadvantages great; but the greater will the mercy of your deliverance be: It will be no plea for you, at the judgement seat, to say, Lord, my father or mother did so and so, before me, and I thought I might safely follow them; or thus, and thus, they commanded me, and I thought I was bound, by their command, to obey them. Therefore look to your own souls, if they are so desperate as to cast away their own. If some children had not minded their own salvation more than their parents minded it, they had never been saved.

3. Let this consideration work upon the hearts, and bowels of all serious Christians, to pity, and help those that are like to perish under this temptation; and if their parents be so ignorant, that they cannot, or so negligent, that they do not instruct and warn their own

children; you that at any time have an opportunity to help them, have compassion on them, and do it. It is true, they are none of your children by nature; but would it not be a singular honour, and comfort to you, if God should make them so by grace? Thousands of children (and, it may be some of you) are more indebted to mere strangers, upon this account, than to their nearest relations; you know not how much good an occasional word may do them: All have not ability to be so publicly useful this way, as a late worthy minister of our own nation has been, who, in compassion to the dark, and barbarous corners in Wales, where ignorance and poverty shut up the way of salvation to them, at a vast expense procured the translation, and printing of the bible in their own tongue, and freely sent it among them. O you that have the bowels of Christians in you, pity, and help them! What is it, for the saving of a precious soul, to drop a serious exhortation, as you have opportunity, unto them, to bestow a bible, or suitable book upon them? Believe it, these little sums of shillings, and pence, so bestowed, will stand for more, in the *audit-day,* than all the hundreds, and thousands, other ways expended.

The second way to hell discovered

II. A second way to hell, in which multitudes are found hastening to their own damnation, is the way of affected ignorance. The generality of people, even in a land enlightened with the gospel, are found grossly ignorant of Christ, the true and only way to heaven, and of repentance and faith, the only way to Christ; and thus the people perish for want of knowledge, Hos 4:6. If the tree of knowledge had been hedged in from the common people, as it is in Popish countries; and it had been criminal to find a bible in our houses, there might have been some cloak and pretence for our ignorance: But to be stupidly ignorant of the most obvious, plain and necessary truths, and yet bred up among bibles and ministers! O how ominous a darkness is this, foreboding, the blackness of darkness for ever! For if the hiding of the gospel from the hearts of men be a token to them that they are lost souls, how much notional light soever they may have; much more must they be lost to all intents, from whose hearts and heads too it is judicially hidden. They that know not God are in the catalogue of the damned, 2 Thess. 1:8, and if this be life eternal to know the only true God, and Jesus Christ, whom he has sent; then this must be death eternal to be grossly and affectedly ignorant both of God, the eyed, and Christ the way, by the rule of true opposition, John 17:3.

Look over the several countries in the professing world; go into the families of country farmers, day labourers, and poor people, and except here and there a family, or person, into whose heart God has graciously shined; what barbarous, brutish ignorance overspreads them: They converse from morning to night with beasts, though they have souls which are fit companions for angels, and capable of sweet converse with God. The earth has opened her mouth, and swallowed up all their time, strength, thoughts, and sotuls, as it did the bodies of Corah and his company. They know the value of a horse or cow, but know not the worth of Christ, pardon, or their own souls: They mind daily what work they have to do with their hands, but forget all they have to do upon their knees; their whole care is to pay their fine or rent to their landlord, but not a thought who shall pay their debts to God. They are so far frown putting unnecessary business aside to make way for the service of God, that God's service is put aside as an unnecessary business, to make way for the world: The world holds them fast till they are asleep, and will be sure to visit them as soon as their eyes are open, that there may be no vacancy or door of opportunity left open for a thought of their souls, or another life, to slip in: Or, it at any time they think, or speak of these matters, then the world, like Pharaoh, when Israel spake of sacrificing, is sure to speak of more work.

And thus they live and die without knowledge; there is no key of knowledge (as it is fitly called, Luke 11:52.) to open the door of the soul to Christ; he and his ministers, therefore, must stand without; pity they may, but help they cannot, till knowledge open the door: Satan is ruler of the darkness of this world, Eph. 6:12, that is, of all blind and ignorant souls. Ignorance is the chain with which he binds them fast to himself, and till that chain be knocked off by Divine illumination, they cannot be emancipated, and made free of Christ's kingdom; Acts 26:18. "To turn them from darkness to light, and from the power of Satan to God." Ignorance, indeed, incapacitates a man to commit the unpardonable sin; but what is he the nearer while it disposes him to all other sins which damn as well as that? By ignorance it is, that all the essays of the gospel for men's salvation are frustrated; that naked assent is put in the place of saving faith, morality mistaken for regeneration, a few dead duties laid in the room of Christ and his righteousness. Indeed it would fill a greater book than this is, to show the mischievous effects of ignorance, and how many ways it destroys the precious souls of men: but seeing I can speak but little in this place to it, let me bar up this way to hell, if it be possible, by a few serious considerations.

The second way to hell shut up

1. Let the ignorant consider, God has created their souls with a capacity of knowing him and enjoying him as well as others that are famed in the world for knowledge and wisdom. *There is a spirit in man, and the inspiration of the Almighty giveth them understanding.* The faculty is in man, but the wisdom and knowledge that enlightens it from God; as the dial shows the hour of the day when the sun-beams fall upon it. If, therefore, God be sought unto in the use of such helps and means as you have, even the weakest and dullest soul has a capacity of being made wise unto salvation. Psal. 19:7. "The testimony of the Lord is sure, making wise the simple."

Augustine tells us of a man so weak and simple, that he was commonly reputed a fool in all the neighbourhood; and yet says, I believe the grace and fear of God was in him; for when he heard any swear, or take the name of God in vain, he would throw stones at them, and show his indignation against sin by all the signs he could make.

2. You that are so grossly ignorant in the matter of your salvation, are many of you very knowing, prudent, and subtle persons in the affairs of the world. Luke 16:8. "The children of this world are wiser in their generation than the children of light." Had those parts which you have, been improved and heightened by study and observation about spirituals, as they have been about earthly things, you had never been so ignorant or dead-hearted as you are: You might have been as well versed in your bibles, as you are in the almanacs you yearly buy and study. You might have understood the proper seasons of salvation as well as of husbandry. The great and necessary points on which your salvation depends, are not so many or so abstruse and intricate, but your plain and inartificial heads might have understood them, and that with less pains than you have been at for your bodies: What though you cannot comprehend the subtilties of schoolmen, you may apprehend the essentials of Christianity. If you cannot strictly and scholastically define faith, what hinders, if your hearts were set upon Christ and salvation, but you may feel it? Which is more than many learned men do that can define and dispute about it. You cannot put an argument in mood and figure; no matter, if you can by comparing your bibles and hearts together, draw savingly and experimentally this con-

clusion; I am in Christ, and my sins are pardoned. You cannot determine whether faith goes before repentance, or repentance before faith; but for all that you might feel both the one and the other upon your own souls, which is infinitely better. It is not, therefore, your incapacity, but negligence and worldliness that is your ruin.

3. How many are there of your own rank, order, and education, all whose external advantages and helps you have, and all your encumbrances and discouragements they had, who yet have attained to an excellent degree of saving knowledge and heavenly wisdom? How often have I heard such spiritual, savoury, experimental truths, in conference and prayer from plain rustics, such spiritual reasonings about the great concerns of salvation, such judicious and satisfying resolutions of cases depending upon the sensible and experimental part of religion, as have humbled, convinced, and steamed me, and made me say *surgunt indocti,* &c. these are the men that will take heaven from the proud and scornful *ingeniosi* of the world; not many wise, not many learned and acute. Many knowing and learned heads are in hell, and many illiterate and weak ones gone to heaven; and others in the way thither who never had better education, stronger parts, or more leisure than yourselves: So that you are without excuse.

To conclude, Would you heartily seek it of God, and would the Spirit (which he hath promised to give then that ask him) become your teacher, how soon would the light of the saving knowledge of God in the face of Christ shine into your hearts! No matter how ignorant, dull, and weak the scholar be, if God once become the teacher. You are not able to purchase, or want time to read many books; but if once you were sanctified persons, the anointing you would receive from the Father would teach you all things, 1 John 2:27. your own hearts would serve you for a commentary upon a great part of the bible; it would make you of a quick understanding in the fear of the Lord: One drop of your knowledge should be more worth than all learned arts and sciences in the world to you. And is God so far from you, and his illuminating Spirit at such a distance, that there is no hope for you to find him? Is there never a private corner about your houses or barns, or in the fields, where you can turn aside, if it be but a quarter of an hour at a time, to pour out your souls to God, and beg the Spirit of him? Miserable wretch! Is your whole life such a cumber and clutter of cares and puzzles about the world, that you have no leisure to mind God, soul, or eternity? O doleful state! The Lord in much mercy pity and awaken you. Will you not once strive and stumble to save your soul? What, perish, as it were, by consent! How great then is that blindness!

The third way to hell discovered

III. A vast multitude of precious souls are lost for ever by following the examples, and being carried away with the course of this world: It is indeed a poor excuse, a silly argument, that the multitude do as we do; yet, as Junius rightly observes, men's consciences take sanctuary here, and they think themselves safe in it: For thus they reason, *If I do as the generality do, I shall speed no worse than they speed: and certainly God is more merciful than to suffer the greatest part of mankind to perish.* They resolve to follow the beaten road, let it lead whither it will.

Thus the Ephesians, in their unregenerate state, "walked according to the course of this world,: Eph. 2:2. and the Corinthians "were carried away unto dumb idols, even as they were led", 1 Cor. 12:2, just as a drop of water is carried and moved according to the course and current of the tide: For look as every drop of water in the sea is of one and the same common nature, so are all carnal and unsanctified persons; and as these waters being collected into one vast body in the ocean, unite their strength, and make a strong current, this way or that; so does the whole collective body of the unregenerate world, all the particular drops move as the tide moves. Hence they are said "to have received the spirit of this world," 1 Cor. 2:12. One common spirit or principle acts and rules them all; and therefore they must needs be carried away in the same course. And there are two special considerations that seem to determine them by a kind of necessity to do as the multitude do; the one is, that they find it easiest and most commodious way to the flesh, here they meet with quietness and safety: hereby they are exempt from reproaches, losses, persecutions and distresses for conscience sake. Rest is sweet, and here only they think to find it. The other is, the prejudice of singularity, and manifold tribulations they see that little handful that walk counter to the course of the world involved in; this startles them from their company, and fixes them where they are. Against such sensible arguments, it is to no more purpose to oppose spiritual considerations, motives drawn from the safety of the soul, or importance of eternity, than it is for a man to turn the tide or course of a river with his weak breath.

Add to this, That as one sinner confirms and fixes another, wedging in each other, as men in a crowd, who must move as it moves; so they make it their business to render all that dither from them odious and ridiculous: So the apostle notes their practice and Satan's policy in it, 1 Pet. 4:4, wherein they think it strange that ye run not with them into the same excess of riot, speaking evil of you, ξενιζονται; they gaze strangely at them. And that is not all; they not only gaze at them as a strange generation, making them signs and wonders in Israel, as the prophet speaks, but they defame, revile, and speak evil of them, representing them as a pack of hypocrites, as turbulent, factious, seditious persons, the very pests of the times and places they live in; and all this, not for doing any evil against them, but only for not doing evil with them, because *they run not with them into the same excess of riot.* Thus the world smiles upon its own, and derides those that are afraid to follow them to hell, by which it sweeps away the multitude with it in the same course.

The third way to hell shut up

But O! if the Spirit of God would please to set on, and follow home the following considerations to your hearts, you would certainly resolve to take a persecuted path to heaven, though few accompany you therein, rather than swim like dead fishes with the stream into the dead sea of eternal misery.

1. Though you go with the consent and current of the world, yet you go against the express law and prohibition of God: He has laid his command upon you, "not to be conformed to the world," Rom. 12:2. "That you live not the rest of your time to the lusts of men, but to the will of God," 1 Pet. 4:2. "That you follow not a multitude to do evil," Exod. 23:2. "That you go not in the way of evil men." Prov. 4:14. "That you have no fellowship with the unfruitful works of darkness." All these, and many more, are commands flowing from the highest sovereign authority, obliging your consciences to obedience under the greatest penalties; by them your state must be cast to all eternity in the day of judgment. You may make a jest of the precept, but see if you can do so of the penalty.

2. Other men, in all ages of the world, that were as much concerned in the world as you, and valued their lives, liberties, and estates as well as you, have yet got out of the crowd, disengaged themselves from the way of the multitude, and taken a more solitary and suffering path out of a due regard to the safety of their souls: And why should not you love them as well, and care for them as much as ever any that went before you did? Noah walked with God all alone, when all flesh

had their ways. Elijah was zealous for the Lord, when he knew of none to stand by him, but thought he had been left alone; Job was upright with God in the land of Uz; Lot stood by himself, a godly nonconformist, in a vile, debauched Sodom; David was a wonder to many; so was Jeremiah, and those few with him, for signs and wonders in Israel; I demand of your consciences what discouragements have you that these men had not? Or what encouragements had they that you have not? Why should not the salvation of sour souls be as precious in your eyes as theirs was in theirs? Shall you be impoverished and persecuted if you embrace the way of holiness? So were they. Shall you be reproached, scorned, and reviled: So were they. All your discouragements were theirs, and all their motives and encouragements are yours.

3. Is not the way which you have chosen marked out by Christ as the way to destruction? And that which you dare not chase and embrace as the way to life? See the marks he has given you of both in that one text, Matt. 7:13,14. "Enter ye in at the strait gate; for wide is the gate, and broad is the way that leadeth to destruction, and many there be which go in thereat; because strait is the gate, and narrow is the way which leadeth unto life, and few there be that find it." And where now is your encouragement and hope that God will be more merciful than to damn so great a part of the world? If you will do as the many do, dream not of speeding as well as that little flock, separated by sanctification from the multitude, shall speed. You have your choice, to be damned with many, or saved with few; to take the broad, smooth beaten road to hell, or the difficult, suffering, self-denying path to heaven. O then make a seasonable, necessary stand, and pause a while; consider your ways, and turn your feet to God's testimonies: It is a great and special part of your salvation to says ourselves from this untoward generation.

The fourth way of losing the soul opened

IV. Multitudes of souls are daily lost by rooted *habits*, and long continued *custom* in sin. When men have been long settled in an evil way, they are difficultly reclaimed: *Physicians* find it hard to cure a *cacheary,* or ill habit of body; but it is far more difficult to cure an ill custom and habit in sin. Jer. 13:23. "Can the leopard change his spots, or the Ethiopian his skin? Then may ye also do good that are accustomed to do evil. The spots of a *leopard,* and the hue of an *Ethiopian,* are not by way of external, accidental adhesion; if so, washing would fetch them off: But they are innate and contempered, belonging to the constitution, and not to be altered, so are sinful habits and customs in the minds of sinners. By this means it becomes a second nature as it were, and strongly determines the mind to sin. A *tencris assuescere medium est.* It is a great matter to be accustomed to this way, or that, said Seneca; yea, *Caput rei est, hoc vel illo modo, hominem assuefieri,—* It is the very head or root of the matter to be so or so accustomed, says Aristotle. Very much of the strength of sin rises from customary sinning. A brand that has been once in the fire easily catches the second time. Every repeated act of sin lessens fear and strengthens inclination. A horse that took an ill stroke at first breaking, and has continued many years in it, is very difficultly, if ever, to be brought to a better way. What men have been accustomed to from their childhood, they are tenacious of in their old age. Hence it is that so few are converted to Christ in their old age. It was recorded for a wonder, in the primitive times, that Marcus Caius Victorius became a Christian in his old age. Time and usage fix the roots of sin deep in the soul. Old trees will not bow as tender plants do. Hence all essays and attempts to draw men from the course in which they have walked from their youth, are frustraneous and unsuccessful. The drunkard, the adulterer, yea, the self-righteous moralist, are by long continued usage so fixed in their course, and all this while conscience so stupefied by often repeated acts of sin, that it is naturally as impossible to remove a mountain, as a sinner will thus confirmed in his wickedness. However, let the trial be made, and the success left to him to whom no length of time nor difficulty must be objected or opposed.

The fourth way to hell shut up by two considerations

IV. Let it be considered, the longer any man has been engaged in, and accustomed to the way of sin, the more reason and need that man has speedily and without delay to repent and reform his course; there is yet a possibility of mercy, a season of salvation left. How far soever a soul is gone on towards hell, none can say it is yet too late. When Mr. Bilney the martyr heard a minister preaching thus, *O you old sinner, you have gone on in a course of sin these fifty or sixty years; do you think that Christ will accept you now, or take the devil's leavings?* Good God, said he, what a preacher of Christ is here! Had such doctrine been preached to me in my troubles, it had been enough utterly to have discouraged me from repentance and faith. No, no, sinner, it is not yet too late, if at last your heart be touched with a real sense of your sin and danger. The Lord is plain, Isa. 55:7. "Let the wicked forsake his way, and the unrighteous man his thoughts: and let him return to the Lord, and he will have mercy upon him, and to our God, for he will abundantly pardon."

An abundant pardon you need; your sins, by long continued custom and frequent repetitions, have been abundantly aggravated; and an abundant pardon is with God for poor sinners: he will abundantly pardon, but then you must come up to his terns: you must not expect pardon or mercy when your sins have forsaken you, but upon your forsaking them; yea, such a forsaking as includes a resolution or decree in your will to return to them no more, Hos. 4:8. There must be a chance of your way, and that not from profaneness to civility only, which is but to change one false way to heaven for another, or the dirty road to hell for a cleaner path on the other side of the hedge; but a total and final forsaking of every way of sin, as to the love and habitual practice of it; yea, and your thoughts too, as well as your ways. There must be an internal, as well as an external change upon you; yea, a positive, as well as a negative change; a turning to the Lord, as well as a turning from sin; and then how long, soever you have walked in the road towards hell, there will be time enough, and mercy enough to secure your returning soul safe to beaver.

2. Can you not forbear your customary sin, upon lesser motives than the salvation of your soul? And if you can, will you not much more do it for the saving of your precious, immortal soul? Suppose there were but a pecuniary mulet, of an hundred pounds, to be certainly levied upon your estate, for every oath you swear, or every time you are drunk, would you not rather choose reformation than beggary? And is not the loss of your soul a penalty infinitely heavier than a little money? But, as the wise heathen observed, *Ea sola emi putamus, pro quibus pecuniam solvinus; ea gratuita vocamus pro quibus nos ipsos impendimus.* We reckon those things only to be bought, which we part with money for; and that we have those things gratis, for which we pay ourselves. Is nothing cheap in our eyes but ourselves, our souls! Do we call that *gratis*, what will cost us so dear? Darius threw away his messy crown when he fled before Alexander, that it might not hinder him in his flight. Sure your souls are more worth than your money, and all the enjoyments you have in this world. It had been an ancient custom among the citizens of Antioch, to wash themselves in the baths; but the king forbidding its they all presently forbore, for fear of his displeasure: whereupon Chrysostom convinced them of the vanity of that plea for customary sinning. "You see, (says

he), how soon fear can break off an old custom; and shall not the fear of God be as powerful to overmaster it in us, as the fear of man?" O friends, believe it, it "is better for you to cut off a right hand, or pluck out a right eye, than having two hands, or eyes to be cast into hell, where the worm dieth not, and the fire is not quenched."

The fifth way of losing the soul opened

V. The fifth way, by which an innumerable multitude of souls are eternally lost, is by the baits of sensual, sinful pleasures.

Some customary sins have little, or no pleasure in them; as swearing, malice, etc., but others allure, and entice the soul by the sensual delight that is in them: this is the bait with which multitudes are enticed, ensnared, and ruined to all eternity. It is a true and grave observation of the philosopher, "That we are impelled, as it were, to that which is evil, by the alluring blandishments of pleasure." This was the first bait by which Satan caught the souls of our first parents in innocence, Gen. 3:6. "The tree was pleasant to the eye." Pleasure quickens the principles of sin in us, and enflames the desires of the heart after it. Every pleasant sin has a world of customers, and, cost what it will, they resolve to have it. I have read of a certain fruit, which the Spaniards found in the Indies, which was exceeding pleasant to the taste; but nature had so fenced it, and doublet guarded it with sharp and dangerous thorns, that it was very difficult to come at it: they tore their clothes, yea, their flesh, to get it; and therefore called the fruit, *Comfits in hell.* Such are all the pleasures of sin, *consists in hell;* damnation is the price of them, and yet the sensitive appetite is so outrageous and mad after them, that at the price of their souls, they will have them. Thus the wicked are described, Job 21:13. "They spend their days in wealth, and in a moment go down to the grave." That is, their whole stock of time is spent in cares and labours to get wealth, and when they have gotten it, the rest of their life is spent in those sensual pleasures that wealth brings in, or in making provision for the flesh, to fulfil the lusts of it. The rich man, in the parable, fared deliciously every day, Luke 16, where his voluptuous life is described, and in that description, the occasion of his damnation is insinuated. In a pampered and indulged body, is usually found a neglected and starved soul. But how shall the ruin of souls this way be prevented?

The fifth way to hell shut up, by three considerations

1. Consider how the morality of Heathens had bridled their sensual lusts and appetites, and caused them with a generous disdain to repel those brutish pleasures, as things below a man. "What more foolish, what more base," says Seneca, "than to patch up the good of a reasonable soul out of things unreasonable?" "That is the pleasure worthy of a man, not to glut his body, nor to irritate those lasts in whose quietness is our safety." This is the constant doctrine of all the Stoics.

O what a shame is it to hear Heathenism out-brave Christianity! and principles of mere morality enable men to live more soberly, temperately, and abstemiously, than those who enjoy the greatest pattern and highest motives in the Christian religion are found to do? "You embrace pleasure, says the Heathen, but I bridle it; you enjoy it, I only use it; you think it your chief good; I esteem it not so much as good; you do all for pleasure's sake, but I nothing at all an that account." These therefore shall be your judges.

2. Always remember sensual pleasures are but the baits with which Satan angles for the precious soul. There is a fatal hook under them. O if men were but aware of this, they would never purchase pleasure at so dear a rate. "Stolen waters are sweet, and bread eaten in secret is pleasant; but he knoweth not that the dead are there; and that her guests are in the depth of hell," Prov. 9:17,18. Pliny tells us that the mermaids have most enchanting, charming voices, and frequent pleasant, green meadows, but heaps of dead men's bones are always found where they haunt. That which tickles the fancy stabs the soul. If the pain, (as Anacreon well observes) were before the pleasure, no man would be tempted by it; but the pleasure being first, and sensible, and the torment coming after, and, as yet invisible, this allures so many to destruction. "At last it biteth like a serpent, and stingeth like an adder, Prov. 23:32. If sin did sting and bite at first, none would touch it; but it tickles at first, and wounds afterward. O what man that is in his wits would purchase eternal torments for the sensual, brutish pleasures of a moment! "The pleasures of sin bewitch the affections, blind the judgment, stupefy the heart, so that sober and impartial judgment finds no place. The heart is enticed, the lusts are enraged; cost what it will, sinners will gratify their lusts.

3. If you are for pleasure, certainly you are out of the way to it, who seek it in the fulfilling of your lusts. If your hearts were once sanctified and brought under the government of the Spirit, you would

quickly find a far more excellent pleasure in the crucifying of your lusts, than now you seek in the gratification and fulfilling of them. Rom. 8:13. "If ye, through the Spirit mortify the deeds of the body, ye shall live;" i.e. ye shall live the most joyful, peaceful, and comfortable life of all persons in the world, a life of highest delight and true pleasure; for so far as your lusts are mortified, the vigorous, healthful frame, and due temper of your soul is restored, and your evidences for heaven cleared; both which are the springs of all spiritual delight and pleasure. Can any creature-enjoyment, or any beastly lust afford a pleasure like this? Do not you find the life you live in sinful pleasures quite beneath the dignity of a man? and are they not followed with bitter after-reckonings, gripes and flashes of conscience: *Even in the midst of laughter the heart is sad, and the end of that mirth is heaviness:* O ponder seriously what a trifle it is you sell our precious souls for! Is it not a goodly price you value them at? The fugitive, empty, beastly pleasures of a moment, for the torments of eternity.

The sixth way of losing the soul opened

VI. There are also numerable souls lost for ever by the distracting cares of this world which eat up all their time, thoughts, and studies; so that there is no room for Christ, or one serious hour about salvation. It is too true an observation which Sir Walter Raleigh makes upon the common mechanics and poor labourers, their bodies are the anvils of pain, and their souls the hives of unnumbered cares and sorrows, while the voluptuous and rich spend their time and studies in purveying for new pleasures, and filling their heads with projects of that nature. The poorer sort have their heads and hearts filled day and night with anxious thoughts and cares how to get bread, pay their rents or debts, and struggle through the miserable necessities that pinch them on every side; many children, it may be, to provide for, and little or nothing out of which to make it: here is brick that must be made, and no straw to make it of; he borrows here to pay there: debts increase, and abilities decrease; he toils his body all the day, and when his tired carcass calls for rest to enable him for new work tomorrow; the cares of the world invade him on his bed, and keep him sighing or musing there, when, poor man! he had load enough before for one.

And now, what room is there left for salvation work? or how can any spiritual seed that is cast into such a brake of thorns prosper? "The cares of this life, (says Christ) spring up, and choke it," Mark 4:19. Tell not them of heaven and Christ, they must have bread; talk not to them of the necessity or comfort of a pardon, they must pay their debts to men. O the confused buzz and clutter that these thoughts and cares make in their heads! So that no other voice can be heard. And thus multitudes spend their whole lives in a miserable servitude in this world, and by that are cast upon a more miserable and restless state for ever in the world to come; one hell here, and another hereafter. And what shall be done for them? Is there no way for their deliverance? O that God would direct, and bless the following considerations to them, if it may be expected they may at any time get through the brake in which they are involved, and find them at leisure to bethink themselves!

The sixth way to hell shut up, by five considerations

1. Bethink yourself, poor soul! as much as you are involved and plunged in the necessities and distracting cares of this life; others, many others, as poor and necessitous, and every way as much embroiled in the cares of the world as you are, have minded their souls, and taken all care and pains for their salvation, notwithstanding: yea, though millions of your rank and order are destroyed by the snares of the devil, yet God has a very great number, indeed the greatest of any rank of men among those that are low, poor, and necessitous in the world. The church is called the "congregation of the poor," Psal. 74:20, because it consists mostly of men and women of the lowest and most despicable condition in this world; they are all poor in spirit, and most of them poor in purse. "Hearken, my beloved brethren, (says James) has not God chosen the poor of this world, rich in faith, and heirs of the kingdom?" James 2:5.

Now, if others, many others, as much entangled in the necessities, cares, and troubles of the world as you, have yet struggled through all those difficulties and discouragements to heaven; why should you not strive for Christ and salvation as well as they? Your souls are as valuable as theirs, and their discouragements and hindrances as great and as many as yours.

2. Consider your poor and necessitous condition in the world, has something in it of motive and advantage to excite and quicken you to a greater diligence for salvation than is found in a more full, easy, and prosperous state; for God has hereby embittered this word to you, and made you drink deeper of the troubles of it than other men: they have the honey, and you the gall; they have the flower, and you the bran; but then, as you have not the pleasures, so you have not the

FLAVEL

snares of a prosperous condition, and your daily troubles, cares, and labours in it do even prompt you to seek rest in heaven, which you cannot find on earth. Can you think you were made for a worse condition than the beasts? What, to have two hells, one here, and another hereafter? Surely, as low, miserable, and despicable as you are, you are capable of as much happiness as any of the nobles of the world; and, in your low and addicted condition, stand nearer to the door of hope than they do. Ah! methinks these thoughts do even put themselves upon you, when your spirits are overloaded with the cares, and your bodies tired with the labours of this life. Is this the life of troubles I must expect on earth? Has God denied me the pleasures of this world? O then let it be my care, my study, my business to make sure of Christ, to win heaven, that I may not be miserable in both worlds. How can you avoid such thoughts, or put by such meditations which your very station and condition even forces upon you?

3. Consider how all the troubles in this world would be sweetened, and all your burdens lightened, if once your souls were in Christ, and in covenant with God. O what heart's ease would faith give you! What sweet relief would you find in prayer! These things, like the opening of a vein, or tumour when ripe, would suddenly cool, relieve, and ease your spirits; could you but go to God as a Father, and pour out your hearts before him, and cast all your cares and burdens, wants and sorrows upon him, you would final a speedy outlet to your troubles, and an inlet to all peace, all comforts, and all refreshments; such as all the riches, honours, and fullness of this world cannot give: you would then find Providence engage itself for your supply, and issue all your troubles to your advantage; you would suck the breasts of those promises in the margin, and say, all the dainties in the world cannot make you such another feast; you would then see your bread, your clothes, and all provisions for you and yours, in God's promises, when you are brought to an existence, and would certainly find performances as well as promises, all along the course of your life.

4. Say not you have no time to mind another world. God has not put any of you under such an unhappy necessity. You have one whole day every week, allowed you by God and man, for your souls. You have some spare time every day, which you know you spend worse than in heavenly thoughts and exercises, yea, most callings are such as will admit of spiritual exercises of thoughts, even when your hands are exercised in the affairs of this life: besides, there are none of you but have, and must have daily some relaxations and rest from

business; and if your hearts were spiritual, and set upon heaven, you would find more time than you think on, without prejudice to your callings, yea, to the great furtherance of then, to spend with God. I can tell you when and where I have found poor servants hard at work for salvation, labour for Christ, some in the fields, others in barns and stables, where they could find any privacy to pour out their souls to God in prayer. As lovers will make hard shifts to converse together, so will the soul that is devoted to God, and in earnest for heaven; and though your opportunities be not so large, they may be as sweet, as successful, and to be sure sincere, as those whose condition affords them more time, and greater external conveniences than you enjoy. More business is sometimes dispatched in a quarter of an hour in prayer, yea, let me say in a few hearty ejaculations of soul to God, in a few minutes, than in many long and elaborate duties. If you cast in your two mites of time into the treasury of prayer, having no more, you may, as Christ said of the poor widow, *give more than those that cast in of their great abundance of time and talents.*

5. Lastly, Consider, Jesus Christ is no respecter of persons, the poorest and vilest on earth, are as welcome to him as the greatest. He chose a poor and mean condition in this world himself, conversed mostly among the poor, never refused any because of his poverty: "God accepteth not the persons of princes, nor regardeth the rich more than the poor: for they are all the work of his hands", Job 34:19, and that both in respect of their natural constitution, as men, and their civil conditions, as rich or poor men. Riches and poverty make a great difference in the respects of men, but none at all with God. If you be one of God's poor, he will accept, love, and honour you above the greatest (if graceless) person in the world. Poverty is no bar to Christ or heaven, though it be to the respects of men, and the pleasures of this life. Away, then, with all vain pretences against a life of godliness, from the meanness of your outward condition, heaven was not made for the rich, and hell only for the poor. No; how hard soever you find the way thither, I am sure Christ says, *It is hard for a rich man to enter into that kingdom.*

The seventh way of losing the soul discovered

VII. The seventh beaten path to destruction, is by groundless presumption; *praesumendo sperant, et sperando pereunt,* by presumption they have hope, and by that hope they perish.

There are divers objects of presumption, amongst which, these three are most usual and most fatal, viz. that they have,

1. That grace which they have not.

2. That mercy in God they will not find.

3. That time before them which will fail them.

1. Many presume they have that grace in them, which God knows they have not. So did Laodicea, Rev. 3:17. "Thou sayest, I am rich, and have need of nothing, and knowest not that thou art wretched, and miserable, poor, blind, and nakedly." Here is a dangerous conspiracy between a cunning devil, and an ignorant, proud heart, to ruin the soul for ever; they stamp their common grace for special; they put the old creature, by a general profession, into the new creatures habit, and by a confident claim to all the privileges of the children of God.

2. They presume upon such mercy in God, as they will never find; they expect pardoning and saving mercy, out of Christ, in an unregenerate state, when there is not one drop of mercy dispensed in any other way. The whole economy of grace is managed by the Mediator, Jude, ver. 21. All saving mercies come through him, upon all that are in him, and upon no others. God is, indeed, a merciful God, and yet presumptuous sinners will find judgment without mercy, because they are not found in the proper way and method of mercy. Thousands, and ten thousands carve out and dispose of the mercy of God at their own picture, write their own pardons, in what terms they think fit, and if they had God's seal to confirm and ratify them, it were all well, but, alas! it is but a night vision, a dream of their own brain.

3. But especially, men presume upon time enough for repentance hereafter: they question not but there are as fit, and as fair opportunities of salvation to come, as are already past; and in this snare of the devil, thousands are taken in the very prime and vigour of their youth: that age is voluptuous, and loves not to be interrelated with severe and serious thoughts and courses; and here is a salvo fitted exactly to suit their inclination, and quiet them in their way, that they may pursue their lusts without interruption.

I cannot follow the sin of presumption at present, in all these its courses and ways; and therefore will apply myself to the case last mentioned, which is so common to the world.

A TREATISE OF THE SOUL OF MAN

The seventh way to destruction shut up by five weighty considerations

1. I would beg all those young, voluptuous sinners, whose feet are fast held in the snare of this temptation, seriously to bethink themselves, whether they are not old enough to be damned, while they judge themselves too young to be seriously godly. There are multitudes in hell of your age and size; you may find graves in the churchyard, of your own length, and skulls of your own size: men will not spare a nest of young snakes because they are little. If you die christless and unregenerate, it is the same thing, whether you be old or young; there is abundance of young spray, as well as old logs, burning in the flames of hell.

2. If you knew the weight and difficulty of salvation work, you would never think you could begin too soon. Religion is a business which will take up all your time; many have repented they began so late, none that they began so soon. Say not, *the penitent thief found mercy at the last hour*, for his conversion was extraordinary, and we must not hope for miracles: besides, he could never encourage himself in sin, with the hope and expectation of such a miraculous conversion; he was the only example of a sinner that was ever so recovered, in scripture, and this was recorded, not to nourish presumption, but to prevent despair. If ten thousand persons died of the plague, and one only of the whole number infected with it escaped, it is no great encouragement that you shall make the second. O think, and think again, how many thousands now on earth, have been labouring and striving, forty or fifty years together, to make their calling and election sure: and yet, to this day, it is not so sure as they would leave it: they are afraid, after all, time will fail them for finishing, and you think it is too early for beginning so great a work.

3. Others have begun sooner than you, and finished the great and main work, before you have done any thing. Abijah was very young, scarce out of his childhood, "when the grace of God was found in him," 1 Kings 14:18. The fear of God was in Obadiah, when but a youth, 1 Kings 18:12. Timothy was not only a Christian, but a preacher of the gospel, in the morning of his life," 2 Tim. 3:15. What have you to plead for yourselves, which they had not? Or what arguments and motives to godliness had they which you have not? You shall be judged *per pares,* by those of your own age and size; their seriousness shall condemn your vanity.

4. The morning of your life is the flower of your time, the freshest and fittest of all your life for your great work; now your hearts are tender and impressive, your affections flowing and tractable, your heads clear of distracting cares and hurries of business, which come on afterwards in thick successions: "Remember mow thy Creator in the days of your youth, while the evil days come not," Eccl. 12:1,2. If a man has an important business to do, he will take the morning for it, knowing if that be slipped, a crowd and hurry of business will come on afterwards, to distract and hinder him. I presume, if all the converts in the world were examined in this point, it would be found, that at least ten to one were wrought upon in their youth; that is the moulding age.

5. And if this proper, hopeful season be elapsed, it is very unlikely that ever you be wrought upon afterwards: how thin and rare, in the world, are the instances and examples of conversion in old age! Long continued customs in sin harden the heart, fix the will, and root the habits of vice so deep in the soul, that there is no altering of them; your ears then are so accustomed to the sounds of the world, that *Christ* and *sin, heaven* and *hell, soul* and *eternity*, have lost their awful sound and efficacy with you. But it is a question only to be decided by the event, Whether ever you shall attain to the years of your feathers? It is not the uprightly vigour of your youth that can secure you from death. What a madness, then, is it, to put your souls and eternal happiness, upon such a blind adventure? What if your presumption, of so many fair and proper opportunities hereafter, fail you, as it has failed millions, who had as rational and hopeful a prospect of them as you can have: where are you then? And if you should have more time and means, than you do presume upon, are you sure your hearts will be as flexible and impressive as they now are? O beware of this sin of vain presumption, to which the generality of the damned owe their everlasting ruin!

The eighth way of losing the soul opened

VIII. The eighth way of ruining the precious soul, is, by drinking in the principles of Atheism, and living without God in the world.

Atheism stabs the soul to death at one stroke, and puts it quite out of the way of salvation; other sinners are worse than beasts, but Atheists are worse than devils, for they believe, and tremble; these banish God out of their thoughts, and, what they can, out of the world, living as *without God in the world,* Eph. 2:12. It is a sin that quenches all religion in the soul. He that knows not his landlord cannot pay his rent: he that assents not to the being of a God, destroys the foundation of all religious worship; he cannot fear, love, or obey him, whose being he believes not: this sin strikes at the life of God, and destroys the life of the soul.

Some are Atheists in opinion, but multitudes are so in practice; "The fool has said in his heart, there is no God," Psal. 14:1. Though he has engraved his name upon every creature, and written it upon the table of their own hearts; yet they will not read it: or if they have a slight, fluctuating notion, or a secret suspicion of a Deity, yet they neither acknowledge his presence, nor his providence. *Fingunt Deum talem qui nec videt, nec punit,* i.e. They make such a God, who neither sees nor punishes. They say, "How does God know? Can he judge through the dark clouds? Thick clouds are a covering to him, that he seeth not," Job 22:14.

Others profess to believe his being, but their lives daily give their lips the lie; for they give no evidence in practice, of their fear, love or dependence on him: If they believe his being, they vainly show they value not his favour, delight not in his presence, love not his ways, or people; but lie down and rise, eat and drink, live and die without the worship, or acknowledgement of him, except so much as the law of the country, or custom of the place extorts from them. These dregs of time produce abundance of Atheists, of both sorts; many ridicule and hiss religion out of all companies into which they come, and others live down all sense of religion; they customarily attend, indeed, on the external duties of it, hear the word; but when the greatest, and most important duties are urged upon them, their inward thought is, This is the preacher's calling, and the man must say something to fill up his hour, and get his living. If they dare not put their thoughts into words, and call the gospel *Fabula Christi,* the fable of Christ, as a wicked Pope once did; or say of hell, and the dreadful sufferings of the damned, as Galderinus the Jesuit did, *Tunc credam cum illuc venero;* I will believe it when I see it: yet their hearts and lives, are of the same complexion with these men's words: they do not heartily assent to the truth of the gospel which they hear, and though bare assent would not save them, yet their assent, or non-assent, will certainly damn them, except the Lord heal their understandings and hearts, by the light and life of religion. To this last sort I shall offer a few things.

The eighty way to hell shut up by six weighty considerations

1. You that attend upon the ordinances, but believe them no more than so many devised fables, nor heartily assent to the truth of what you hear; know assuredly, that the word shall never do your souls good, it can never come to your hearts and affections in its regenerating and sanctifying efficacy, while it is stopped and obstructed in your understandings in the acts of assent. And thus you may sit down under the best ordinances all your livev, and be no more the better for them, than the rocks are for the showers of rain that fall upon them; Heb. 4:2. "The word preached did not profit them, not being mixed with faith in them that heard it." This is Satan's chief strength and fatness, wherein he trusts; he fears no argument, while he can maintain his post. The devil has no surer prisoner than the Atheist; there is no escaping out of his possession and power, while this bolt of unbelief is shut home in the mind or understanding. A not believed truth never converted or saved one soul from the beginning of the world, nor never shall to the end of it. Those bodies that have the *Boulema,* or dog-appetite, whatever they eat, it affords them no nourishment or satisfaction, they thrive not with the best fare: just so it is with your souls, no duties, no ordinances can possibly do them good; as in argumentation, no conclusion, be it never so regularly drawn, and strongly inferred, is of any force to him that denies principles.

2. If you assent not to the truth of the gospel, you not only make God speak to your souls in vain, which is fatal to them: but you also make God a liar, which is the greatest affront a creature can put upon his Maker; 1 John 5:10. "He that believeth not God, has made him a liar." Vile dust, dare you rise up against the God that made you, and give him the lie? An affront which your fellow creature cannot put up, or bear at your hands. Dare you at once stab his labour, and your own soul? Are not the things that you look on as *romances* and golden dreams, mere artifice, neatly contrived to cheat and awe the world? Are they not all built upon the veracity of God, which is the firmest foundation and greatest security in the world? Has he not intermingled, for our satisfaction, not only frequent assertions, but his asseverations and oath to put all beyond doubt? And yet dare any of you lift up your ignorant blind understandings against all this, and give him the lie? Surely the wrath of God shall smoke against every soul of man that does so, and his own bitter, lamentable, doleful experience shall be his conviction shortly, except he repent.

3. Dare any of you give the thoughts of your hearts as certain conclusions under your hands, and stand by them to the last, and venture all upon them.

Wretched Atheist! Bethink yourself, pause a while, examine your own breast; whatever your vile atheistic thoughts sometimes are, is there not at other times a fear of the contrary? A jealousy that all these things which you deride and sport the wicked fancy with, may, and will prove true at last? When you read or hear that text, John 3:18. "He that believeth not is condemned already;" his mittimus is already made for hell: does not your conscience give you a secret gird, like a stitch in your side? Dare you venture all upon this issue, that if those things you find in the word be true, you will stand to the hazard of them? If that be a truth, Mark 16:16, "He that believeth not shall be damned," you will be content to be damned? Or if, Rom. 8:13 be a truth, That "they who live after the flesh shall die," you will run the hazard, and bear the penalty of eternal death? If Heb. 12:14 prove true, That "without holiness no man shall see God," you will be content to be banished from his presence for evermore? Speak your hearts in this matter, and tell us, do not you live between atheistic surmises, that all these are but cunning artifices, and fears, that at last they will prove the greatest verities.

4. Has not God given you all the satisfaction you can reasonably desire of the undoubted truth and certainty of his word? What would you have which you have not already? Would you have a voice from heaven? The scriptures you read or hear are a more sure word than such a voice would be, 1 Pet. 1:19. Or would you have a messenger from hell? He that believes not the witten word, neither would believe "if one should rise from the dead," Luke 16:81. View the innate characters of the scripture, is it not altogether pure and holy, full of Divine wisdom and awful majesty, and in every respect such as evidences its author to be the wise, holy, and just God, who searches the hearts and reins? Look upon the seals and confirmations of it: has not God confirmed it by divers miracles from heaven, a seal which neither men nor devils could counterfeit? And do not you see the blessing and power of God accompanying it in the conversion and wonderful change of men's hearts and lives, which can be done by no other hand than God's? Say not, the miracles, which confirm the gospel, are but uncertain traditions, and except you yourselves see then done, you cannot believe them. There are a thousand things which you do believe, though you never saw them; and what you require for your

satisfaction, every man may require the same for his; and so Christ must live again in all parts of this world, and repeat his miracles over and over in all ages to satisfy the unreasonable incredulity of those that question their truth, after the fullest confirmation and seal has been given, that is capable to be given, or the heart of man can desire should be given; and if all this should be done, you might be as far from believing as now you are; for many of those that saw and heard the things wrought by Christ contradicted and blasphemed, and so might you.

5. Satan, who undermines your assent to these things, is forced to give his own: he that tempts you to look on them as fables, himself knows and is convinced that they are realities; "The devils also believe and tremble," James 2:19. They know and feel the truth of these things, though it be their great design and interest to shake your assent to them. They know Christ is the Son of God, and that there will be a day in which he will judge the world in righteousness, and that there are torments prepared for themselves, and all whom they seduce from God, Matt. 8:29. If you ungod God, you must unman yourselves: yea, not only make yourselves less than men, but worse than devils.

6. In a word, let your own heart, O Atheist, be judge, whether these be real doubts still sticking in your minds, after you have done all that becomes men to do for satisfaction in such important cases. Or whether they be not such principles as you willingly foment and nourish in your hearts as a protection to your sensual lusts, whose pleasures you would fain leave without interruptions and overawings by the fears of a judgement to come, and a righteous retribution from a just and terrible God! Examine your hearts in that point, and you will soon find the cheat to be in that I here point you to: you have not studied the word impartially, nor brought your doubts and scruples with an humble, unbiased, teachable spirit to those that are wise and able to resolve them, much less prayed for the Spirit of illumination; but willingly entertained whatever atheistic wits invent, or the devil suggests, as a defence against the checks of conscience and fears of hell in the way of sin. You are loath those things should be true which the scriptures speak, and are glad of any colourable argument or pretence to still your own consciences. Is not this the case? The Lord stop your desperate course, your paths lead to hell.

The ninth way of losing the precious soul opened

IX. Precious souls are daily plunged into the gulf of perdition by *profaneness* and *debauchery*. How many every where lie wallowing in the puddle? glorying in their shame, and running into all excess of riot? The hypocrite steals to hell in a private, close way of concealed sin; but the profane gallop along the public road at noon day; "They declare their sin as Sodom, and hide it not;" Isa 3:9. "The show of their countenance testifieth against them." The hypocrite has devotion in his countenance, and heaven in his mouth; you know not by his words and countenance whither he is going; but the profane hide it not, they are past shame, and above blushing at the most horrid impieties. Look, as God has some servants more eminent, forward, and courageous in the ways of godliness than others, men that will not hide their principles, or be ashamed of the ways of godliness in the face of danger; so the devil has some servants as eminent for wickedness who scorn to sneak to hell by concealment of their wickedness, but avow and own it, without fear or shame, in the open sight of heaven and earth. Wherever they come, they defile the air they breathe in with horrid blasphemies and obscene discourses not to be named, and leave a strong scent of hell behind them.

This age has brought forth multitudes of these monsters, the reproach and shame of the nation that bred them. I have little hope to stop any of them in their career and full speed to hell. They have lost the *sense of sin,* the restraints of *shame* and *fear;* and then what is left to check them in their course? I cannot hope that such a discourse as this shall ever come into their hands, except it be to sacrifice it to the flames; yet not knowing the ways of providence, which are unsearchable, and what use God may make upon one occasion or another of these following considerations, I will adventure to drop a few words upon these forlorn sinners, as far as they seem to be gone beyond recovery; beseeching the Lord to make way for these things to their hands and hearts, and make them the instruments of pulling some of them as brands out of the burning.

The ninth way to hell, by profaneness, stopped

1. And first, let it be laid to heart, that though the case and state of many thousand souls be doubtful and uncertain, so that neither themselves nor any other know what they are, or to whom they belong! yet your condition, O profane sinner, is without controversy, miserable and forlorn; all men know whose you are, and whither you are going. The apostle appeals, in this case, to the bar of every man's

reason and conscience, as a thing allowed and yielded by all, Eph. 5:5. "For this ye know, (says he) that no whoremonger, or unclean person, nor covetous man, who is an idolater, has any inheritance in the kingdom of Christ and of God." This is a clear case, there is no controversy about it. Many there be in a doubtful case, but no doubt of these, they are fast and sure in the power of Satan: and as sure as God is a God of truth, they that die in this condition shall never see his face. And to the same purpose again, 1 Cor. 6:9. "Know ye not that the unrighteous shall not inherit the kingdom of God? Be not deceived, neither fornicators, nor idolaters, nor adulterers, nor effeminate, nor abusers of themselves with mankind, nor thieves, nor covetous, nor drunkards, nor revilers, nor extortioners, shall inherit the kingdom of God." *Know ye not?* says he, q.d. "Sure you cannot be so ignorant and blind to think that there is any room in heaven for such wretches as these. If the righteous be scarcely saved, where shall the sinner and ungodly appear? If all strictness, holiness, self-denial, diligence, be all little enough to win heaven, what hope can there be of those that not only cast off all duties of religion, but also cast themselves into all the opposite ways and courses which directly lead to damnation;" He that refused his food endangers his life; but he that drinks poison, certainly and speedily destroys it.

2. As far as you are gone in a course of profaneness, you are not yet gone beyond the reach of mercy and all hopes of salvation, if now at last, after all your debaucheries and profaneness, the Lord touch your hearts with the sense of your sinful and miserable state, and turn your feet to his testimonies. When the apostle, in 1 Cor. 6:9,10, had told us the doom of such men, upon the supposition of their perseverance in that course, yet presently adds, as a motive to their repentance, an example of mercy upon such wretches as these. "And such were some of you, but ye are washed," ver. 11. The golden sceptre of free grace has been held forth to many, as profane and notorious sinners as you, to blaspheming Saul, to a Mary Magdalene, to a Manasseh. It is not the greatness of the sin, but the impenitence and infidelity of the sinner that ruins him. Well, then, there is a certainty of damnation if you go on, and yet a possibility of forgiveness and mercy before you; a mercy in valuable.

3. Nay, this is not all; but in some respect there is more probability and hope of your return and repentance, than there is of many others who have led a more sober, smooth, and civil life than you have done. Your profaneness has more dishonoured God, but the morality

and civility of some men secure them faster in the snare of the devil. They have many things in themselves to build up their presumptuous hopes upon, but you have nothing. It is hard for conviction to reach that man's conscience that has righteousness of his own to trust in; but methinks it should have an easier access to yours, whose notorious courses lay your consciences naked and bare before the word to be wounded by it. Christ's ministry had little success among the Pharisees, who were righteous in their own eyes, but it wrought effectually upon *publicans'* and *sinners.* Hence Christ told them, Matt. 21:31. that "publicans and harlots go into the kingdom of God before them." Publicans were esteemed the worst of men, and harlots the worst of women; yet the one, and the other, as vile as they were, stood fairer for conviction, and consequently for salvation, than those that thought they needed *no repentance.* All this is matter of hope, and runs into a powerful motive and loud call to repentance. "He that has an ear to hear, let him hear."

The tenth way leading to destruction marked

X. Deep and fixed prejudices against godliness, and the sincere professors thereof, precipitate thousands of souls into their own ruin and damnation.

It was not without a weighty reason, that Christ denounced that woe upon the world, Matt. 18:7. "Woe unto the world, because of offences." The poor world will lie ruined by scandals and prejudices; they will take such offences at the ways of godliness, that they will never have good thoughts of them any more. "This sect is everywhere spoken against," Acts 28:22. and so Christians are condemned, δια την φημην, because of the common reproach, as Justin Martyr complained. All the scandals which fall out in the church, see so many swords and daggers put into the hands of the wicked world to murder their own souls withal. Some have sucked in such opinions of the ways of godliness as make them irreconcilable enemies to them, and fierce opposers of them. And from hence are most of the persecutions that befall the people of God. When you see showers of slanders and reproaches going before, expect storms of persecutions coming after. Slanders beget prejudices, and these prepare for persecutions. O how keen and fierce are the minds of many against the upright and innocent servants of God, whom they have first represented to themselves in such an odious dress and character, as the devil has drawn them in, upon their fancies and imaginations! So the primitive Christians were represented to the heathens as monsters, and their conventions in the night, occasioned by the fury of persecutors, were reported to be for lascivious and barbarous ends, to deflower virgins, and murder innocent children: And by this artifice the Heathens were secured against conversion to Christ. This has been the policy of hell front the beginning, and it has prospered so much in the world, that Satan has no reason to change his band. But how may this plot of hell be defeated, and the ruin of souls prevented?

The tenth way of destroying souls shut up by two counsels

1. It will be impossible to prevent the ruin of a great part of the world by prejudices against the ways of godliness, except those who profess them, walk more holily and conformably to the rule and pattern of Christ, whose name is called upon by them. I shall therefore first address my discourse to the professors of religion, beseeching them, in the bowels of Christ, to take pity upon the multitude of souls which are daily ruined and destroyed by their scandals and miscarriages. Did you live according to the rules you profess, "your well-doing would put to silence the ignorance of foolish men," 1 Pet. 2:15. and consequently the ruin of many might be prevented. I remember Bernard, speaking of the lewd and loose life of the priests of his time, sighs out this just and bitter complaint to God about it; *Misera eorum conversatio plebis tuae miserabilis subversio est:* O Low! said he, their miserable conversation is the miserable subversion of your people. O! of how many, who glory in the title of the sons of the church, may Christ say as Jacob did of his two lewd sons, Simon and Levi, "You have troubled me, to make me to stink among the inhabitants of the land," Gen. 34:30.

And how many professors, who pretend to more than ordinary reformation and holiness, do shed soul-blood by their scandalous conversations. Salvian brings in the wicked of his age upbraiding the looseness of Christians, in this manner; "Behold, those men who boast themselves redeemed from the tyranny of Satan, and profess themselves dead to the world, yet are conquered by the lusts of it." And Cyprian, long before his day, brings in the heathens thus insulting over looser Christians: "Where is that catholic law which they believe? Where are the examples of piety and chastity, which they should learn? They read the gospel, yet are immodest; they hear the apostles, yet are drunk." O professors! where are your bowels to the poor souls of sinners? If your neighbour's ox or ass fall into the pit, you are bound to deliver him, if you can; and will you not do as much for a precious soul, as you would do for a beast? Nay, you dig pits, by your scandalous lives, to destroy them. If you sin, there are instruments enough to spread it, and multitudes of souls ready prepared to take the infection. Say not, if they do, the fault is theirs; for though they are principals in the murder of their own souls, by taking the scandal, yet you are accessories in giving it: He is a mad man that will kill himself with a sword, end he no better that will put it into his hand.

O, therefore, if you have any regard to the precious souls of men, live up to the rules of your profession! O, be blameless and harmless, the sons of God without rebuke, in the midst of a perverse and froward generation! Let the heavenliness of your conversation stop those mouths that accuse you as men of a worldly spirit; let them see, by your moderation in seeking it, your patience in losing it, your readiness in distributing it, that it is a groundless calumny under which your names suffer. Let them see, by your apparel, company, and discourses, you are not such proud, lofty spirits, as you are represented to be. Convince them, by your flexibleness to all things that are lawful and expedient, by manifesting, as much as in you lies, that it is the pure bond and tie of conscience, which keeps you from compliance in all other things, and by your meekness in suffering, for such non-compliance, that you are not such turbulent, factious incendiaries, as the wicked world slanderously reports you to be. Convince the world by your exact righteousness in all your civil dealings, and by the lip of truth in all your promises and engagements, that you have the fear of God in your hearts, as well as the livery of Christianity upon your backs. In a word, so live, that none may have just ground to believe the impudent slanders the devil raises in the world against you. Let your light so shine before men, that you may glorify your Father which is in heaven. Without your care and circumspection, the shedding of a world of precious soul-blood can never be prevented.

2. Let me advise and beseech all men to be so just to others, and merciful to their own souls, as not to cast them away for ever, by receiving prejudices against godliness, from the miscarriages of some, who make more than a common profession of it. To prevent this fatal effect of scandal and prejudice at religion, I desire a few particulars may be impartially weighed.

First, Very many of those scandals, bandied up and down the world against the professors of godliness, are devised and forged in hell, as so many traps and snares to catch and destroy men's souls, to beget an irreconcilable aversion and enmity in men to the ways of God. "They devise deceitful matters (says the Psalmist) against them that are quiet in the land," Psal. 35:20. So Jer. 18:18. "Come, say they, let us devise devices against Jeremiah, and smite him with the tongue". And there is as little equity in the credulous receiver, as there is honesty in the wicked forger of these slanders: with one arrow of censure you wound no less than three, viz. the honour of God, your innocent brother, and your own souls: As to the two former wounds, they will in due time be healed; God will vindicate his own name fully, and the reputation of his innocent servants shall be cleared, and repaired abundantly; but, in the mean time, your souls may perish by the wounds prejudices have given, so that you may never be reconciled to godliness and its professors while you live, but turn scoffers and persecutors of them.

Secondly, Examine whether the matters that are changed upon them as their crimes, be not their duties. Sometimes it falls out to be so; and if so, you fight more immediately and directly against God, than men. This was David's case, Psal. 69:10. "When I wept, and chastened my soul, that was to my reproach;" my piety was turned to reproach. They called his tears crocodiles tears, and his fastings, hypocritical shadows of devotion and humility. Thus the very matter of his duty was turned into scorn and reproach. And so it was with the primitive Christians, their very owning of themselves to be Christians was crime enough to condemn them.

Thirdly, If professors of religion do in some things act unbecoming their holy profession, yet every slip and failing in their lives, is no sufficient warrant for you to censure their persons as hypocrites; much less to fall upon religion itself, and condemn it for the faults of them that profess it. There is many an upright heart overtaken by temptation. You see their miscarriages, but you see not their humiliations and self-condemnations before God for them. "Foul, and fearful (says a grave divine) was the scandal of David; and what was the issue? Presently the enemies of God and godliness began to lift their heads, and fall upon David's religion, 2 Sam. 22. They blasphemed the name of God. O! this is he that was so grand a zealot, that the zeal of God's house did eat him up. This is the man, that, out of his transcendent zeal, danced before the ark; this is he that prayed thrice a day, at morning, noon, and night: This is he that was so precise and strict in his family, that a wicked person should not dwell in his house. This your great, precise zealot, has defiled the wife, and murdered the husband. Now you see what his religion is, now you see what comes of this profession of so much holiness and godliness."

O that men would seriously consider their evil in such censures as these! what is all this to religion? Does religion any way countenance, or patronise such practices? Nay, does it not impartially and severely condemn them? It is the glory of the Christian religion, that it is pure and undefiled, James 1:27. These practices flow from no principle of religion, nor are chargeable upon it, for it teaches men the very contrary, Tit. 2:11,12. If I see a Papist sin boldly, or an Arminian slight grace, I justly condemn their principles, in, and with their practices, because Popery sets pardons to sale, and Arminianism exalts nature into the place of grace: But does the doctrine of the gospel lead to any immoralities? Charge it, if you can.

Fourthly, And as senseless a thing it is to condemn all, for the miscarriages and faults of some; which, yet, is the common practice of the world. Are all that profess godliness loose and careless? No; many are an ornament to their holy profession, and the glory of Christianity, and why must the innocent be condemned for the guilty? What is your reason and ground for that? Why might not the enemies of Christianity have condemned the eleven apostles upon the fall of Judas? Had they not as good a warrant for it, as you have for this?

To conclude, You little know what a snare of the devil is laid for your souls, in all those prejudices and offences, you take at the ways and professors of godliness; and what a woe you bring upon your own souls by them. You speak evil of persons and things you know not, and prejudice is like still to keep you in ignorance of them. "Woe to the world (says Christ) because of offences; and "blessed is he that is not offended at me."

The eleventh way of ruining the precious soul opened

XI. The eleventh way, wherein abundance of precious souls perish in the christianised and professing world, is the way of formal hypocrisy in religion, and zeal about the externals of worship. Such a generation of men have, in all ages, mingled themselves with the sincere worshippers of God; and the inducement to it is obvious; the form of godliness is an honour, but the power of it a burden. By the former, earthly interests are accommodated; by the latter, they are frequently exposed and hazarded.

FLAVEL

We find in the Jewish church, abundance of such chaff intermixed with the wheat, which the doctrine of Christ discovered, and purged out of the floor, Matt. 3:9,12. Such were the Pharisees, who were exceeding zealous for traditions, and the external rites and ceremonies of the law, but inwardly full of all filthiness, Matt. 15:7,8,9. Men that honoured the dead, and persecuted the living saints; that reverenced the material temple, and destroyed the living temples; that strained at gnats of ceremonies, and swallowed down the grossest immoralities.

And well had it been, if this generation had ended with the state and time of the church; but we find a prophecy of the increase of these men in the latter days, 2 Tim. 3:5, which is everywhere sadly verified. Religion runs into stalk, and blade, into leaves, and suckers, which should be concocted into pith and fruit: yea, it is of sad consideration, that amongst many high pretenders to reformation, their zeal, which should nourish the vitals of religion, and maintain their daily work of mortification and communion with God, spends itself in some by-opinion, while practical godliness visibly languishes in their conversations. How many are there that hate doctrinal errors, who yet perish by practical ones? Who hate a false doctrine, but, in the mean time, perish by a false heart? It is very difficult to reclaim this sort of men from the error of their way; and thereby save their souls from hell. However, let the means be used, and the success left with God.

The eleventh way to hell, by formality, barred up

1. No sin entangles the souls of men faster, or damns them with more certainty and aggravation, than the sin of formal hypocrisy; it holds the soul fastest on earth, and sinks it deepest into hell. There was no sort of men upon whom the doctrine of Christ and the apostles, had so little success and effect, as the Scribes nod Pharisees; they derided him, when *publicans* and *sinners* trembled, and believed, Luke 16:14,15. The form of godliness wards off all convictions; their zeal for the externals of religion secures them against the fears of damnation, while in the mean time, their hypocrisy plunges them deeper into hell than others that never made such shows of sanctity and devotion: "He shall appoint them his portion with hypocrites;" Matt. 14:51, that is, he shall he punished in hell, as hypocrites are punished, *viz.,* with the greatest, and sorest punishment. Hypocrisy is a double iniquity, and will be punished with double destruction: their ungrounded hopes of heaven serve but to pully up their wretched souls to a greater height

of vain confidence, which gives them the more dreadful jerk in their lamentable, and eternal disappointment.

2. Blind, superstitious zeal, which spends itself only about the externals of religion, usually prepares, and engages men in a more violent persecution of those that are really godly, and conscientious. The Lord opened a great door of opportunity at Antioch to Paul; the whole city came together to attend the discoveries of Christ in the first publication of the gospel, and the poor Gentiles began to taste the sweetness of the gospel; but the devil, perceiving his kingdom begin to totter, immediately stirred up his instruments to persecute the apostles, and drive them out of the country: and who more fit for that work, than the devout, and honourable women? Acts 13:15. These stirred up their husbands, and all they had influence upon, under a fair pretence of zeal for the law, to obstruct the progress of the gospel. *No bird* (says one) *like the living bird, to draw others into the net.* Men of greatest names, and pretensions to religion, if graceless, are the most dangerous instruments the devil can employ to the ruin and extirpation of true godliness. Such a zealot was Paul, in his unregenerate state.

3. Nothing is more common, than to find men hot and zealous against false worship, while their hearts are as cold as a stone in the *vitals,* and *essentials of true religion.* Many can dispute warmly against *adoration of images, praying to angels and saints departed,* who all the while are like those dead images which others worship. Jehu was a zealot against idolatry; and yet the vital power of true godliness was a stranger to his soul, 2 Kings 10:15,16. The Pharisees spared no pains to make a *proselyte,* and yet all the while were the children of the devil themselves, Matt. 23:15.

This was a sad case, yet what more common? The Lord open the eyes of these men, and convince them, in season, that their zeal runs in the wrong channel, and spends itself upon things which shall never profit them. O if they were but as much concerned to promote the love of God, and life of godliness in themselves and others, as they are about some external accidents and appendages of religion, what blessings would they be to the world, and what evidence would they have of their own sincerity?

The twelfth way to hell, opened

XII. The twelfth way to hell, in which many souls are carried on smoothly, and securely, to their own destruction, is, the way of *mere civility* and *moral honesty,* wherein men rest as in a sake state, never doubting but a civil life will produce an issue into an happy death. *Moral honesty* is a lovely thing, and greatly tends to the peace and order of the world; but it is not saving grace, nor gives any man a good title to Christ and salvation. Indeed there can be no grace in that soul in which civility and moral honesty are not found: but these may be found in thousands that have no grace.

That which ruins souls, is not the exercise of moral virtues, but their reliance upon them: they use their morality as a shield to secure their consciences from the convictions of the word, which would show them their sinful and miserable state by nature. Thus the Pharisee, Luke 18:11,12. "God I thank thee, that I am not as other men are, extortioners, unjust, adulterers, or even as this publican;" he blesses himself in the conceits of his own safety and happiness. Let debauched and profane persons look to it, I am well enough; though, alas! poor man, his being less evil, at best, could but procure him a cooler hell, or a milder flame. This was the case of the young man, Matt. 19:28. and like a young man, indeed, he reasons. He sums up all the stock of his civil life, and thinks it strange if that be not enough to make a purchase of eternal life. *What lack I yet?* Alas! poor soul, every thing necessary to salvation: the very first stone was not laid, when he thought the building was finished: And this is the case of multitudes, both young and old; and that which greatly confirms, and settles them in this their dangerous security, is the general, indistinct doctrine of some, who pretend to be guides to the souls of others, the scope of whose ministry aims at no higher mark than to civilise the people, and press moral duties upon them, as if this were all that were necessary to salvation. Nay, it is well if some do not industriously pull down the pale of distinction between morality and regeneration, and tell the world, in plain English, *That there is no reason to put a difference between such as are baptised, and live morally honest, and those that have saving grace; and they that do so, are only a few, who are highly conceited of themselves, and censorious of all others, whom they please to vote formal, and moral.*

This, indeed, is the way to fix them where they are; if Christ had not taken another method with Nicodemus, and his ministers had not pressed *the necessity of regeneration,* and the *insufficiency of moral honesty to salvation,* how thin had the number of true converts been, though, at most they are but a handful in comparison of the *unregenerate!*

O that God would bless what follows, to undeceive and save some poor soul out of this dangerous snare of the devil!

The twelfth way to damnation barred, by three considerations

1. Blind not yourselves with the lustre of your own moral virtues, a life smoothly drawn with civility through the world. For though it must be acknowledged there is a loveliness, and attracting sweetness in morality and civility, yet these things rather respect earth than heaven, and are designed for the conservation of the order and peace of this world, not for your salvation and title to the world to come. Without justice and truth, *kingdoms* and *commonwealths* would become *mountains of prey,* and *dens of robbery.* Where there is no trust there can be no traffic; and where there is no truth, there can be no trust. Civility is the very basis of human society; a world of good accrues to men by it, and abundance of mischief is prevented by it; but it never gave any man *an interest in Christ,* or *a title to salvation.* The Romans and Lacedemonians, who perished in the darkness of heathenism, excelled in morality; there is nothing of Christ or regeneration in these things, how much of excellency soever be ascribed to them. Paul, the Pharisee, was a blameless person, touching the law, and yet, at the same time, not only utterly ignorant of Christ, but a bitter enemy to him, and all that were his. Till you can find another way to heaven than by regeneration, repentance, and faith, never lean upon such a deceitful and rotten prop, as mere civility is.

2. *Civilised nature* is *unsanctified nature* still; and without *sanctification* there is no *salvation,* Heb. 12:14. Civility adorns nature, but does not change it. Moral virtues are so many sweet flowers strewed over a dead corpse, which hide the loathsomeness of it, but inspire not life into it. "Morality hides and covers, but never mortifies, nor cures the corruptions of nature;" and mortified they must be, or you cannot be saved: take the best nature in the world, and let it be adorned with all the ornaments of morality (which they call *homiletic virtues*) and add to these all the common gifts of the Spirit, which are for assistance and ministry; yet all this cannot secure that soul from hell, or be the ground work for a just claim to any promise of salvation: all this is but nature improved, not regenerated. Morality is neither produced as saving grace is, nor works such effects as grace works; there are no pangs of repentance introducing it, it may cost many an aching head, but no aching heart for sin; no such distressed outcries as that, Acts 2:37. "Men and brethren, what shall we do?" Nor

does it produce such humility, self-abasement, heavenly tempers, and tendencies of soul, as grace does. Cheat not yourselves, therefore, in so important a concern as salvation is, with an empty shadow.

3. Civility is not only found in multitudes that are out of Christ, but may be the cause and reason why they are christless: mistake not, I am not pleading the cause of profaneness, nor disputing civility out of the world; I heartily wish there were more of it to be found in every place; it would exceedingly promote the peace, order and tranquillity of the world: but yet it is certain, that the eyes of thousands are so dazzled with the lustre of their own morality, that they see no need of Christ, nor feel any want of his righteousness, and this is the ruin of their souls. Thus Christ brings in the Pharisee with his proud boast, that he is "no extortioner, adulterer, nor unjust, or such an one as that publican," Luke 18:11. O what a saint does he vote himself, when he compared his life with the others! Well, then, beware you be not deceived by thinking you are safe, because you are got out of the dirty road to hell, when, all the while you have only stepped over the hedge into a cleaner path to damnation. *You have had a short account of some few of those many ways in which the precious souls of men are eternally lost: Let us briefly apply it in the following inferences.*

Infer. 1. If there be so many ways of losing the soul, and such multitudes of souls lost in every one of them, *then the number of saved souls must needs be exceeding small.*

The number of the saved may be considered, either *absolutely* or *comparatively:* In the first consideration they appear great, and many, even a great multitude, which no man can number, Rev. 7:9. But if compared with those that are lost, they make but a *small remnant,* Isa. 1:9, *a little flock,* Matt. 12:82. For when we consider how vastly the kingdom of Satan is extended, who is called the *god of this world,* from the world of people who are in subjection to him, how small a part of this earthly globe is enlightened with the beams of gospel-light, and that Satan is the acknowledged ruler of all the rest, Eph. 6:12. But when it shall be farther considered, that out of this spot, on which the light of the gospel is risen, the far greatest part are lost, also: O what a poor handful remains to Jesus Christ, as the purchase of his blood!

It is of trembling consideration, how many thousands of families, amongst us, are mere nurseries for hell, parents bringing forth and breeding up children for the devil; not one word of God (except it be in the way of blasphemy or profaneness) to be heard among them. How naturally their ignorant and wicked education puts them in the course and tide of the world, which carries them away irresistibly to hell; how one sinner confirms and animates another, in the same sinful course, till they are all past hope, or remedy: how the rich are taken with the baits of sensual pleasures, and the poor lost in the brake of distracting, worldly cares, except here and there a soul plucked out of the snare of the devil, by the wonderful power, and arm of God. On the one side, you may see multitudes drowned in open profaneness and debauchery, and, on the other side, many thousands securely sleeping in the state of civility and morality: some key-cold, and without the least sense of religion; others hell-hot with blind zeal, and superstitious madness against true godliness, and the sincere practisers of it. Some living all their days under the ordinances of God, and never touched with any conviction of their sin and misery; others convinced, and making some faint offers at religion; but their convictions (like blossoms nipped with a frosty morning) fall off, and no fruit follows. And as *rubies, sapphires,* and *diamonds* are very few, in comparison of the *pebbles* and *common stones* of the earth; so are true Christians in comparison of multitudes that perish in the snares of Satan.

Inf. *How little reason have the unregenerate to glory, and boast themselves in their earthly acquisitions and successes, while in the mean time, their souls are lost!* They have gotten other things, but lost their souls. It is strange to see how some men, by rolling a small fortune up and down the world (as boys do a snowball) have increased the heap, and raised a great estate; they have attained their design and aim in the world, and hug themselves in the pleased thoughts of their happiness; but, alas, among all the thoughts of their gains, there is not one thought of what they have lost. O if such a thought as this could find room in their hearts, "I have indeed gotten an estate, but I have lost my soul! I have much of the world, but nothing of Christ, gold and silver I have, but grace, peace, and pardon I have not; my body is well provided for, but my soul is naked, empty, and destitute." Such a thought, like the sentence written on the wall, would make their hearts fail within them. What a rapture and transport of joy did the sight of a full barn cast that worldling into! Luke 12:19,20. "Soul, take thine ease, eat, drink, and be merry;" little dreaming that death was just then at the door, to take away the cloth, guest, and all together; that the next hour his friends would be scrambling for his estate, the worms for his body, and the devils for his soul.

O how many have not only lost their souls, while they have been drudging for the world, but have sold their souls to purchase a little of the world! Parted, by consent, with their best treasure for a very trifle, and yet think they have a great bargain of it! Surely, if poor sinners did but apprehend what they have lost, as well as what they have gained, their gains would yield them as little comfort as Judas' money did, for which he sold both his soul and Saviour. Instead of those pleasing frolics of wanton worldlings, what a cold shiver would run through all their bones and bowels, did they but understand what it is to lose a gracious God, and a precious soul, and both eternally, and irrecoverably!

The just God remains still to avenge and punish the sinner; but the favour of God, that friendly look is gone; the peace of God, you heaven upon earth, is gone, the essence of the soul remains still, but its purity, peace, joy, hope, and happiness, these are gone; and these being gone, what can remain, but a tormenting, piercing sight of those things, for which you have sold them?

Infer. 8. *Hence let us estimate the evil of sin, and see what a dreadful thing that is, which men commonly sport themselves with, and make so light of: it is not only a wrong and injury to the soul, but the loss and utter ruin of the soul for ever.*

It is said, Prov. 8:36. "He that sinneth against me, wrongeth his own soul." And if this were all the mischief sin did us, it were bad enough; a wrong to the soul is a greater evil than the ruin of the body or estate, and all the outward enjoyments of this life can be; but to lose the precious soul, and destroy it to all eternity, O what can estimate such a loss! Now the result and last effect of sin is death, the death of the precious soul. Rom 6:21. "The end of those things is death." So Ezek. 18:4. "The soul that sinneth shall die."

Sin does not destroy the being of the soul by *annihilation*, but it does that which the damned shall find, and acknowledge to be much worse; it cuts off the soul from God, and deprives it of all its felicity, joy, and pleasure, which consists in the enjoyment of him. Such is the dolefulness and fearfulness of this result and issue of sin, that when God himself speaks of it, he puts on a passion, and speaks of it with the most feeling concernment. Ezek. 32:11. "As I live, says the Lord, I have no pleasure in the death of the wicked: Turn ye, turn ye, for why will ye die, O house of Israel? q.d. Why will you wilfully cast away your own souls? Why will you choose the pleasures of sin for a season, at the price of my wrath and fury poured out for ever? O think of this, you that make so light a matter of committing sin! We pity those, who, in the depth of melancholy or desperation, lay violent hands upon themselves, and in a desperate mood, cut their own throats; but certainly for a man to murder his own soul, is an act of wickedness as much beyond it, as the value of the soul is above that of the body.

Inf. 4. *What an invaluable mercy is Jesus Christ to the world, who came on purpose to seek and to save such as were lost?*

In Adam all were shipwrecked and cast away: Christ is the plank of mercy, let down from heaven to save some. The loss of souls by the fall, lead been as irrecoverable as the loss of the fallen angels, had not God, in a way above all human thoughts and counsel, contrived the method of their redemption. It is astonishing to consider the admirable harmony and glorious triumph of all the divine attributes, in this great project of heaven, for the recovery of lost souls. It is the "wonder of angels," 1 Pet. 1:12. the "great mystery of godliness," 1 Tim. 3:10. the matter and subject of the triumphant Song of redeemed saints, Rev. 1:5. and well it may, when we consider a more noble species of creatures finally lost, and no Mediator of reconciliation appointed between God and them: this is to save an earthen pitcher, while the vessel of gold is let fall, and no hand is stretched out to save it.

But what is most astonishing, is, that so great a person as the Son of God, should come himself from the Father's bosom, to save us, by putting himself into our room and stead, being made a curse for us, Gal. 3:13. He leaves the bosom of his Father, and all the ineffable delights of heaven, disrobes himself of his glory, and is found in fashion as a man, yea, becomes a worm, and no man; submits to the lowest step and degree of abasement, to save lost sinners. What a low stoop does Christ make in his humiliation to catch the souls of poor sinners out of hell! Herein was love, that God sent his own Son, "to be the propitiation of our sins," 1 John 4:10. and "God so loved the world," John 3:16. At this rate he was content to save lost sinners.

How seasonable was this work of mercy, both in its general exhibition to the world, in the incarnation of Christ, and in his particular application of it to the soul of every lost sinner, by the Spirit! When he was first exhibited to the world, he found them all lost sheep gone astray, every one turning to his own way, Isa. 53:6. He speaks of our lost estate by nature, both collectively, or in general: "we all went astray:" and distributively, or in particular, "Every one turned to his own way;" and in the fullness of time a Saviour appeared.

And how seasonable was it, in its particular application? How securely were we wandering onwards in the paths of destruction, fearing no danger, when he graciously opened our eyes by conviction, and pulled us back by heart-turning grace! No mercy like this: it is an astonishing act of grace. It stands alone!

Inf. 5. If there be so many ways to hell, and so few that escape it, how are all concerned to strive, to the utmost, in order to their own salvation?

In Luke 13:23, a certain person proposed a curious question to Christ; "Lord, are there few that be saved?" He saw a multitude flocking to Christ, and thronging with great zeal to hear him; and he could not conceive but heaven must fill proportionately to the numbers he saw in the way thither. But Christ's answer, ver. 24, at once rebukes the curiosity of the questionist, fully resolves the question propounded, and sets home his own duty and greatest concernment upon him. It rebukes his curiosity, and is, as if he should say,—Be the number of the saved more or less, what is that to you? Strive you to be one of them. It fully solves the question propounded, by distinguishing those that attend upon the means of salvation, into Seekers and Strivers. In the first respect there are many, who by a cheap and easy profession, seek heaven; but take them under the notion of strivers, i.e. persons heartily engaged in religion, and who make it their business, then they will shrink up into a small number; and he presses home his great business, and concern upon him, *Strive to enter in at the strait gate.*

By *gate* understand whatsoever is introductive to blessedness and salvation; by the epithet *strait,* understand the difficulties and severities attending religion; all that suffering and self-denial, which those that are bound for heaven should reckon upon, and expect: and by *striving* understand the diligent and constant use of all those means and duties, how hard, irksome, and costly soever they are. The word αγωνιζεσθε has a deep sense and emphasis, and imports striving, even to an agony; and this duty is enforced two ways upon him, and every man else: First, by the indisputable sovereignty of Christ, from whom the command comes; and also from the deep interest and concern every soul has in the commanded duty. It is not only a simple compliance with the will of God, but what also involves our own salvation and eternal happiness in it: our great duty, and our greatest interest are twisted together in this command; your eternal happiness depends upon the success of it. A man is not crowned except he strive lawfully, i.e. successfully and prevalently. O therefore, so run, so strive, that ye may obtain! If you have any value for your souls, if you would not be miserable to eternity, strive, strive! Believe it, you would find that the assurance of salvation drops not down from heaven in a night dream, as the Turks fable their Alcoran to have done in that *lailato hazili*, night of demission, as they call it; no, no; the righteous themselves are scarcely saved; many seek, but few find. Strive, therefore, as men and women that are heartily concerned for their own salvation; sit not, with folded arms, like so many heaps of stupidity and sloth, while the door of hope is yet open, and such a sweet voice from heaven calls to you, saying, Strive, souls, strive, if ever you expect to be partakers of the blessedness that is here to be enjoyed; strive to the utmost of your abilities and opportunities. Such an heaven is worth striving to obtain, such an hell is worth striving to escape, such an invaluable soul is worth striving to save.

I confess, heaven is not the purchase or reward of your striving: no soul shall boastingly say there, Is not this the glory which my duties and diligence purchased for me? And yet, on the other side, it is as true, that without striving you shall never set foot there. Say not, it depends upon the pleasure of God, and not upon your diligence; for it is his declared will and pleasure, to bring men to glory in the way, though not for the sake of their own striving. As in the works of your civil calling, you know all the care, toil, and sweat of the husbandman, avails nothing of itself, except the sun and rain quicken and ripen the fruits of the earth, and yet no wise man will neglect ploughing and harrowing, sowing and weeding, because these labours avail not, without the influences of heaven, but waits for them in the way of his duty and diligence. Rational hope sets all the world to work. Do they plough in hope, and sow in hope, and will you not pray in hope, and hear in hope? You that know your souls to be hitherto strangers to Christ and the regenerating work of the Spirit; how is it that you take them not aside sometimes out of the distracting noise and hurries of the world, and thus bemoan them?

"O my poor graceless, christless, miserable soul, how sad a case are you in! Others have, but you never felt the burden of sin; thousands in the world are striving and labouring, searching and praying, to make their calling and election sure; while you sit still with folded hands, in a supine regardlessness of the misery that is hastening upon you. Can you endure the devouring wrath of God? Can you dwell with everlasting burnings? Have you fancied a tolerable hell? Or, is it easy to perish? Why do you not cast yourself at the feet of Christ, and cry, as long as breath will last, Lord, pity a sinful, miserable, undone, and self-condemning soul? Lord, smite this rocky heart, subdue this stubborn will, heal and save an undone soul ready to perish: The characters of death are upon it, it must be changed or condemned, and that in a little time. Bowels of pity, hear the cry of a soul distressed, and ready to perish.

And you that do not understand the case and state your souls are in, have you never a bible near you? O turn to those places, 1 Cor. 6:9,10, where you will presently find the more obvious marks and characters God has set upon the children of perdition; and if you find not yourself in that catalogue, among the unrighteous, fornicators, idolaters, adulterers, effeminate, thieves, covetous, drunkards, revilers, extortioners, &c, then turn to John 3:3, and solemnly ask your own soul this question, Am I born again? Am I a new creature, or still in the same condition I was born in? What solid evidence of the new birth have I to rely upon, if I were now within a few grasps of death? Am not I the man or woman who lives in the very same sins which the word of God makes the syrupy tome and characters of damnation? And does not my *conscience* witness against me, that I am utterly void and destitute of all that saving grace, and a mere stranger to the regenerating work of the Spirit, without which there can be no well bottomed hope of salvation? And if so, are not the tokens of death upon me? Am not I a person marked out for misery? And shall I sit still in a state of so much danger, and not once strive to make an escape from the wrath to come? Is this vile body worth so much toil and labour to support and preserve it? And is not my soul worth as much care and diligence to secure it from the everlasting wrath of the great, just, and terrible God? O that the consideration of the wrath to come, the multitudes all the world over preparing as fuel for it, and the door of opportunity yet held open to souls by the hand of grace to escape that wrath, might prevail with your heart, reader, to strive, and that to the uttermost, to secure your precious soul from the impending ruin.

Eph. 5:16

—*Redeeming the time* (or opportunity) *because the days are evil.*

Time is deservedly reckoned among the most precious mercies of this life; and that which makes it so valuable are the commodious seasons and opportunities for salvation which are vouchsafed to us therein: opportunity is the golden spot of time, the sweet and beautiful flower, growing upon the stalk of time. If time be a ring of gold, opportunity is the rich *diamond* that gives it both its value and glory. The apostle well knew the value of time; and seeing how prodigally it was wasted by the most, does therefore in this place, earnestly press all men to redeem, save, and improve it with the utmost diligence. In this, and the former *verse,* we have,

1*st*, The duty enjoined, *Walk circumspectly.*

2*dly*, The *injunction* explained;

1. More generally, *Not as fools, but as wise.*

2. More particularly, *Redeeming the time.*

3. The exhortation strongly enforced with a powerful motive, *because the days are evil.*

Among these particulars, my discourse is principally concerned about the redemption of time, or opportunities, which in this life are graciously vouchsafed us, in order to that which is to come: And here it will be needful to enquire,

1. What the apostle means by *time.*

2. What by the *redemption of time.*

1. Time is taken more largely and strictly according to the double acceptation of the Hebrew word עת which signifies sometimes

time, and sometimes *occasion, season,* or *opportunity,* and accordingly is expressed by χρονος and χαιρος, tempo and *tempestivitas:* the latter is the word here used, and denotes the commodiousness and fitness of some parts of time above others, for the successful and prosperous management and accomplishment of our main and great business here, which is to secure our interest in Christ, and glorify God in a course of fruitful obedience. For these great and weighty purposes our time is graciously lengthened out, and many fit opportunities presented us in the revolutions thereof.

2. By the *redemption of time,* we must understand the study, care, and diligence of Christians, at the rate of all possible pains, at the expense of all earthly pleasures, ease, and gratifications of the flesh, to rescue their precious seasons, both of salvation and service, out of the hands of temptations, which so commonly rob unwary souls of them. Satan trucks with us for our time, as we did at first with the silly Indians for their gold and diamonds, who were content to exchange them for glass beads, and tinsel toys. Many fair seasons are forced, or cheated out of our hands, by the importunity of earthly cares, or deceitfulness of sensual pleasures: at the expense and loss of these, we must redeem and rescue our time for higher and better uses and purposes. We must spend these hours in prayer, meditation, searching our hearts, mortifying our lusts, which others do, and our flesh fain would spend, in sensual pleasures and gratifications of the fleshly appetite. If ever we expect to win the port of glory, we must be as diligent and careful as seamen are, to take every gale that blows, directly or obliquely, to set them forward in their voyage. The note from hence is this:

Doct. *That the wisdom of a Christian is eminently discovered in saving and improving all opportunities in this world, for that world which is to cone.*

God hangs the great things of eternity upon the small wires of times and seasons in this world. That may be done, or neglected in a day, which may be the ground work of joy or sorrow to all eternity. There is a nick of opportunity which gives both success and facility to the great and weighty affairs of the soul as well as body; to come before it, is to seek the bird before it be hatched; and to come after it, is to seek it when it is fled. There is a twofold season, or opportunity of salvation.

1. One was Christ's season for the purchase of it.

2. The other is ours for the application of it.

1. Christ had a season assigned him for the impetration and purchase of our salvation; so you hear his Father bespeaking him, Isa. xlix. 8. "Thus says the Lord, in an acceptable time have I heard thee, and in the day of salvation have I helped you," וְעֵר תעב, *in tempore opportuno voluntatis, vel placito.* It was the wisdom of the Lord Jesus Christ to set in with the Father's time, to comply with his season: and it became a flay of salvation, because it was the acceptable time which Christ took for it.

2. Men have their seasons and opportunities for the application of Christ and his benefits, to their own souls: 2 Cor. 6:1,2. "We then as workers together with God, beseech you also, that you receive not the grace of God in vain; for he says, I have heard thee in a time accepted, and in the day of salvation have I succoured thee. Behold, now is the accepted time, now is the day of salvation." He exhorts the Corinthians not to dally or trifle any longer in the great concerns of their salvation; for now, says he, is your day. Christ had his day to purchase it, and he procured a day also for you to apply it, and this is that day; you enjoy it, you live under it: that golden day is now running: O! see that you frustrate not the design thereof, by receiving the gospel grace in vain.

Now two things concur to make a fit season of salvation to the souls of men.

1. The eternal means and instruments.
2. The agency of the Spirit internally lay, or with those external means.

1. Men have a season of salvation, when God sends the means and instruments of salvation among them. When the gospel is powerfully preached among a people, there is a door opened to them: 2 Cor. 2:12. "When I came to Troas to preach the gospel, a door was opened to me of the Lord." God, as it were, unlocks the door of heaven by the preaching of the gospel: Souls have then an opportunity to step in and be saved.

2. But yet it is not a wide *and effectual door* (as the apostle phrases it, 1 Cor. 16:9) till the Spirit of God joins with, and works upon the heart by those external means and instruments; as the waters of the pool of Bethesda had no inherent senative virtue in themselves, until the angel of the Lord descended and troubled them: but both to-

gether make a blessed season for the souls of men. Then he stands at the door, and knocks, by convictions and persuasions, Rev. 3:20. strives with men as he did with the old world by the ministry of Noah, Gen. 6:3. Now the door of opportunity is indeed opened: but this will not always last; there is a time when *the Spirit ceases to strive,* and when *the door is shut,* Luke 13:25.

There is a season, when by the fresh impression of some *ordinance* or *providence* of God, men's hearts are awakened, and their affections stirred. It is now with the souls of men as it is with fruit trees in the spring, when they put forth blossoms; if they knit and set, fruit follows, if they be nipped and blasted, no fruit can be expected. For all convictions and motions of the affections are to grace, much the same thing as blessings are to fruit, which are but the rudiments thereof, *fructus imperfectus et ordinabilis,* somewhat in order to it; and look, as that is a critical and hazardous season to trees, so is this to souls. I do not say it is in the power of any soul to make the work of the Spirit effectual and abiding, by adding his endeavours to the Spirit's motions; for then conversion would not be the free and arbitrary act of the Spirit, as in John iii. 8, neither would souls be born of God, but of the will of man, contrary to John 1:13. And yet it is not to be thought or said, that men's endeavours and strivings are altogether vain, needless, and insignificant; because, though they cannot make God's grace effectual, his grace can make them effectual; they are our duty, and God can bless them to our great advantage. Now there are, among others, five remarkable essays, efforts, or strivings of a soul under the impression and hand of the Spirit, that greatly tend to the fixing, settling, and securing of that great work on the soul; and it is seldom known any soul miscarries in whom these things are found.

1. Deep, serious, and fixed consideration, which lets conviction deep into the soul, and settles it, and roots it fast in the heart, Psal. 119:59. "I thought on my ways, and turned my feet unto thy testimonies." There are close and anxious debates in those souls in whom convictions prosper to full conversion: they sit alone, and think close to their great and eternal concerns: they carry their thoughts back; to the evils of their life past, then smite on the thigh, and cry, *What have I done?* They run their thoughts forward into eternity, and that to a great depth, and then cry, "What shall I do to be saved?" They deliberate and weigh, in their most advised thoughts, what is to be done, and that speedily, for escaping wrath to come: thus they fix those tender, weak,

A TREATISE OF THE SOUL OF MAN

and hazardous motions, which die away in multitudes of souls; and, in the loss of them, the seasons of salvation are also lost.

2. The first stirrings and motions of the Spirit upon men's hearts, do then become a season of salvation to them, when they are accompanied with spiritual, fervent, and frequent prayer: so it was with Paul, Acts 9:11. "Behold he prayeth." It is a good sign when souls get alone, and effect privacy and retirement, to pour out their fears, sorrows, and requests unto God. It is in the espousals of a soul to Christ, as it is in other marriages; a third person may make the motion, and luring the parties together, but they only between themselves must conclude and agree the matter. Prayer is the first breath which the new creature draws in, and the last (ordinarily) it breathes out in this world. This nourishes and maturates those weak, tender, and first motions after God, and brings them to some consistence and fixedness in the soul.

3. Then do those motions of the Spirit on men's hearts make a season of salvation to them, when they retrain and settle in the heart, and are in them *per modum quietus,* by way of rest and abode, following the man from place to place, from day to day; so that whatever unpleasant diversions the necessities and encumbrances of this world at any time give, yet still they return again upon the heart, and will not vanish or suffer any longer suspension: but in others, who lose their blessed advantage and season, it is quite contrary; James 1:23,24. "They are as one that seeth his natural face in a glass, and goeth away and forgetteth what manner of man he was:" He sees some spot on his face, or disorder in his band, which he purposes to correct; but by one occurrence or another, he forgets what he saw in the glass, and so goes all the day with his spot upon him. This was an evanid light purpose, which came to nothing for want of a present execution; just so it is with many in reference to their great concerns: but if the impression abide in its strength, if it return, and follow the soul, and will not let it be quiet, it is like then to prosper, and prove the time of mercy indeed to such a soul.

4. An anxious solicitude and inquisitiveness about the means and ways of salvation, speaks an effectual door of salvation to be set open to the souls of men, Acts 2:37 and 16:30). "Sirs, what must I do to be saved? Men and brethren, what shall we do?" q.d. we are in a miserable condition: Oh, you the ministers of Christ, instruct, counsel, and show us what course to take! Is there no balm in Gilead? No door

of hope in this valley of Achor? Alas! We are not able to dwell with our own fears, terrors, and presages of wrath to come. Oh for a messenger, one among a thousand, to teach us the way of salvation. Thus the Lord rivets and fixes those motions in some souls, that vanish like a morning mist or dew in others.

5. Lastly, That which secures and completes this work, is the execution of those purposes and convictions, by falling, without delay, to the work of faith and repentance in good earnest, dallying no quote with so great a concern, standing no longer at *shall I? shall I?* when meanwhile time flies away, and opportunities may be lost: but bring their thoughts and debates to a peremptory resolution, as the *Lepers* at Samaria did; and seeing themselves shut up to one only door of hope, there they resolve to take their station, lying at the feet of Jesus Christ, and casting their poor burdened souls upon him, whatever be the issue. When the Spirit of God ripens the first motions to this, and carries them through that critical season thus far, there is an effectual door of opportunity opened indeed: this is an acceptable time, a day of salvation: but oh! how many thousands miscarry in this season, and like trees removed from one soil to another, die in the removal!

But certainly, it is the most solemn and important concern of every soul to watch upon all these scans of salvation, when God comes nigh to them by convictions and notions of his Spirit; and to put the same value upon these things that they do upon their souls, and the salvation of them. This is the door of hope set open, a fresh gale to carry you home to your port of glory. Salvation is now come nigh to your souls; there is but a little between you and blessedness. Arise and happy is that soul which knows and improves its season. To persuade and press men to discern and improve such seasons as these, is the principal work of the preachers of the gospel, and that special work to which I now address myself, in the following motives and arguments.

Arg. 1. And first, who, that has the free exercise of reason, and the sense of a future eternal estate, would carelessly neglect any season of salvation, while he sees all the rational world so carefully attending, and watching all opportunities to promote and secure their lower concerns and designs for the present life?

Is not the saving a man's soul as weighty a concern as the getting of an estate? You cannot but observe how careful merchants are, to nick the opportunity which promises them a good turn; how do poor seamen look out for a wind to waft them to their port, and industriously shift their sails, to improve every flair that may set them on their voyage; how many miles tradesmen will travel to be in season at a fair, to put off, or purchase goods to their advantage: No entertainments, recreations, or importunities of friends can prevail with any of these, to lose a day on which their business depends; all things must give way to their business; they all understand their seasons, and will not be diverted. But, alas! what childish toys are all these, compared with their salvation! What is the loss of a little money to the loss of a man's soul? If a man's life depended upon his being at such a place, by such a precise hour, sure he would not oversleep his time that morning; and had he but the least fear of coming too late, every stroke of the clock would strike to his heart; and yet remissness and carelessness, in such a case as this, is infinitely more excusable than in the matter of salvation. Certainly the solicitude and care of all the world for the interests thereof, yea, your own diligence and circumspection in temporal things, will be an uncontrollable and confounding self-conviction to you in the day of your account, and leave you without plea or apology for your supine neglects of the seasons of salvation.

Arg. 2. The consideration of the uncertainty and slippery nature of these spiritual seasons, must awaken in us all care and diligence to secure and improve them: This nick of opportunity is *tempus labile*, a slippery season; it is but short in itself; and very uncertain: "Today, whilst it is said today (says the apostle) if ye will hear his voice," Heb. 3:15. q.d. You have now a short, uncertain, but most precious and valuable season for your souls, lay hold on it while it is called today; for if this season be let slip, the time to come is called by another name, that is not today, but *tomorrow*. Your time is the *present time*; take heed of procrastinating and putting it off, till that which is called *today,* (which is your *only season*) be past and gone. The precious inch of time, though it be more worth than all the other greater parts and portions of your time, yet it is as much *in fluxu*, in hasty motion, and spending as other parts of time are; and being once lost, is never more to be recalled or recovered. Few men know, or understand it while it is current: other seasons for natural, or civil actions are known and stated, but the time of grace is not so easily discerned, and therefore commonly mistaken, and lost: And this comes to pass partly through,

1. Presumptuous hopes.

2. Discouraging fears.

FLAVEL

1. Presumptuous hopes, which put it too far forth, and persuade us this season is yet to come; that we have time before us, and that *tomorrow* shall be as *today*. "Thus through presumption men hope, and by their presumptuous hopes they perish." This is the ruin of most souls that perish.

2. Discouraging fears put it too far back, and represent it as long since past and gone, while it is yet in being, and in our hands. By such pangs of desperation, Satan cuts the nerves of industry and diligence, and causes souls to yield themselves as by consent for lost, and hopeless, even while the gospel is opening their eyes, to see their sin and misery, which is a part of the work in order to their recovery. Thus the eyes of thousands are dazzled that they cannot discern the season of mercy, and so it slides from them as if it had never been.

God came near to them in the means of their conversion, yea, and nearer in the motions of his Spirit upon their consciences and affections; but they knew not the time of their visitation, and now the things of their peace are hid from their eyes. Had those convictions been obeyed, and those purposes that here begotten in their hearts, been followed by answerable executions of them, happy had they been to all eternity: But their careless neglects have quenched them, and the door is shut and who knows whether it may be opened any more? O dally not with the Spirit of God, resist not his calls! His motions on the soul are tender things; they may soon be quenched, and never recovered.

Arg. 3. Neglect not the seasons of mercy, the day of grace, because opportunity facilitates the great work of your salvation; it is much easier to be done in such a season than it can be afterwards: An impression is easily made on wax, when melted, but stay till it be hardened, and if you lay the greatest weight on the seal, it leaves no impression upon it. Much so it is with the heart, there is a season when God makes it soft and yielding, when the affections are thawed, and melted under the word; conscience is full of sense and activity, the will pliable: Now is the time to set in with the motions of the Spirit; there is now a gale from heaven, if you will take it, and if not, it tarries not for man, nor waits for the sons of men: Neglect of the season is the loss of the soul. The heart, like melted wax, will naturally harden again, and then to how little purpose are your own feeble essays? Heb. 3:15. It is both easy and successful striving when the Spirit of God strives in you, and with you; you are now workers together with God, and such work goes on smoothly and sweetly, that which is in motion is easily moved; but if once the heart is set, you may labour to little purpose.

Arg. 4. The infinite importance and weight of salvation, is alone, instead of all motives and arguments, to make men prize and improve every proper season for it. It is no ordinary concern, it is your life, yea, it is your eternal life; the solemnity and awfulness of such a business as this is enough to swallow up the spirit of man. O what an awful sound have such words as these, Ever with the Lord? Suppose you saw the glory of heaven, the full reward of all the labours and sufferings of the saints, the blessed harvest of all their prayers, tears, diligence, and self-denial in this world; or suppose you had a true representation of the torments of hell, and could but hear the wailings of the damned, for the neglect of the season of mercy, and their passionate, but vain wishes for one of those days which they have lost: Would you think any care, any pains, any self-denial too much, to save and redeem one of these opportunities? Surely you would have a far higher estimation of them than ever you had in your lives.

A trial for a man's whole estate is accounted a solemn business among men, the cast of a dye for a man's life is a weighty action, and seldom done without anxiety of the mind, and trembling of the hand: Yet little these are but children's play compared with salvation work.

Three things put an unspeakable solemnity upon this matter; it is the precious soul, which is above all valuation, that lies at stake, and is to be saved, or lost. The saving or losing of it is not for a time, but for ever; and this is the only season in which it will be eternally saved or cast away. All hangs upon a little inch of time, which, being overslipped and lost, is never more to be recalled or recovered. *Lord! with what serious spirits, deep and weighty considerations, fears, and tremblings of heart, should men and women attend the seasons of their salvation!*

Believe it, reader, since your soul projected its first thoughts, there never was a more weighty and concerning, subject than this presented to your thoughts. O! therefore, let not your thoughts trifle about it, and slide from it as they use to do in other things of common concernment.

Arg. 5. If we set any value on the true pleasure of life, or solid comfort of our souls at death, let us by no means neglect the special seasons and opportunities of salvation we now enjoy.

FLAVEL

These two things, the pleasure of life, and comforts in death, should be prized by every man more than his two eyes, certainly no being at all is more desirable than a being without these. Take away the true, spiritual pleasure of life, and you level the life of man with the beast that perishes; and take away the hope and comfort of the soul in death, and you sink him infinitely below the beasts, and make him a being only capable of misery for ever.

Now there can be no true, spiritual pleasure found in that soul that has neglected and lost his only season of salvation: All the solid delight and comfort of life results from the settlement and security of a man's great concern in the proper season thereof. The true mirth of the *converted Prodigal* bears date from the time of his return, and *reconciliatory to his father,* Luke 15:24. Two things are absolutely prerequisite to the comfort of life, viz. *a change of the state by justification, and a change of the frame and temper of the heart by sanctification.* To be in a pardoned state, is a matter of all joy, Matt. 9:2, and "to be spiritually minded is life and peace" Rom. viii. 6. No good news comes to any man before this; and no bad news can sink a man's heart after this.

And for hope and comfort in death, let none be fond to expect it, till he has first complied with, and obeyed God's call in the time thereof: A careless life never did, nor never will produce a comfortable death. What is more common among all that die, not stupid and senseless, as well as unregenerate and christless, than the bitter, dolorous complaints of their misspent time, and losing their seasons of mercy? *Reader, if you would not feel that anger you have seen and heard others to be in on this account, know the time of your visitation, and finish your great work while it is day.*

Arg. 6. Neglect no season of salvation which is graciously afforded you, because your time is short; death and eternity are at the door. "You know that you must shortly put old these tabernacles," 2 Pet. 1:13,14. that when a few years are come, you "shall go the way whence you shall not return", Job 16: 22. All the living are listed soldiers, and must conflict, hand to hand, with that dreadful enemy death, and there is no discharge in that war, Eccles. 8:8. It will be in vain to say, You are not willing to die; for willing, or unwilling, away you must go, when death calls you. It will be as vain to say, You are not ready; for ready or unready you must be gone when death comes. Your readiness to die would indeed be a cordial to your hearts in death; but then you must improve and ply the time of life, and husband your opportunities diligently; carelessness of life, and readiness for death are inconsistent, and exclusive of each other. The bed is sweeter to none than the hard labourer, and the grave comfortable to none but the laborious Christian. You know nothing can be done by you after death; the *compositum* is then dissolved; you cease to be what you were, to enjoy the means you had, and to work as you did. O therefore slip not the only season you have, both of attaining the end of life, and escaping the danger and hour of death.

The Use

I shall close all with a word of exhortation, persuading (if possible) the careless and unthinking neglecters of their precious time and souls, to awake out of that deep and dangerous security in which they lie fast asleep on the very brink of eternity, and "today, while it is yet called today," to hear God's voice calling them to repentance and faith, and thereby to Christ and everlasting blessedness. "Behold, he yet stands at the door, and knocks," Rev. 3:20. The door of hope is not yet finally shut, there are yet some stirrings at certain times in men's consciences: God comes near them in his word, and in some rousing acts of providence, the death of a near relation, the seizure of a dangerous disease, the blasting and disappointment of a man's great design and project for this world, a fall into some notorious sin; these, and many such like methods of providence, as well as the convincing voice of the word, have the efficacy of an awakening voice to men's drowsy consciences; and if careless sinners would but attend to them, and follow home those motions they make upon their hearts, who knows to what these weak beginnings might rise and prosper? The souls of men are, as it were, embarked in the calls of God, your life is bound up in them; if these are lost, your souls are lost; if these abide upon you, and grow up to sound conversion, you are saved by them. More particularly consider;

1. What a mercy it is, to have your lot providentially cast under the gospel; to be born under, and bred up with the means and instruments of conversion and salvation. We have lived from our youth up, under the calls of God, and within the joyful sound or the gospel; "God hath not dealt so with other nations", Psal. 147:20. Though others should seek the means of life, they cannot find them; and though you seek them not, you can hardly miss them.

2. How great a mercy it is, to have your lines lengthened out hitherto by God's patience under the gospel! That neither that golden lamp, nor the lamp of your life, (both which are liable to be extinguished every moment) are yet put out. Thousands and ten thousands, your contemporaries, are gone out of the hearing of the voice of the gospel, they shall never hear another call; the treaty of God is ended with them; the master of the house is risen up, and the doors are shut. Your neglects and provocations have not been inferior to theirs: but the patience and goodness of God has exceeded and abounded to you beyond whatever it did to them.

3. Bethink yourselves what an aggravation of your misery it will be, to sink into lieu with the calls of God sounding in your ears! To sink into eternal misers, between the tender, out-stretched arms of mercy! This is the hell of hell, the emphasis of damnation, the racking engine on which the consciences of the dammed are tortured. "And you Capernaum, which are exalted to heaven, shall be brought down to hell", Matt. 11:28. Such a fall, after so high an exaltation, is the very strappado which will torment your consciences. Hell will prove a cooler and milder place to the Heathens that never enjoyed your light, means, and mercies in this world, than it will to you. None sink so deep into misery in the world to come, as they that fall from the fairest opportunities of salvation in this world.

4. Let no man expect that God will hear his cries and intreaties in time of misery, who neglects and slights the calls of God in time of mercy. God calls, but men will not hear: the day is coming, "when they shall cry, but God will not hear," Prov. 1:24, 25. "Will God hear his cry, when trouble cometh upon him?" Job 27:9. No; he will not: and this is but a just retribution from the righteous God, whose calls and counsels men have set at nought. But whatever men now think of it, it is certainly the greatest misery incident to men in all the world: for as no words can make another fully sensible what a privilege it is to have the ear, favour, pity, and help of God in a day of straits; so it is impossible for any words to express the doleful state and case of that soul whom God casts off in trouble, and whose cries he shuts out.

5. Beware of neglecting any call of God, because that call you are now tempted to neglect, may be the last call that God ever intends to give your souls. Sure I am, there is a call which will be the last call of God to rebellious sinners, and after that no more calls, but an eternal deep silence: *his Spirit shall not always strive with men;* and the more

motions and calls you have already slighted, the more probable it is that this may be the last voice of God in a way of mercy to your soul: and what if, after this, God should seal up your heart, and judicially harden it? make your will utterly inflexible, and your ears deaf, as he threatens, Isa. 6:10. What an undone, miserable man or woman are you then! Oh! beware of provoking the sorest of all judgments, by persisting any longer in a course of rebellion against light and mercy.

6. While your hearts put off and neglect the calls of God, you can by no means arrive to the evidence and assurance of your election; for your election is only secured to you by your effectual calling, 2 Pet. 1:10. There is no way for men to discern their names written in the book of life, but by reading the work of sanctification in their own hearts Rom. 10:8. I desire no miraculous voice from heaven, no extraordinary signs, or unscriptural notices and informations in this matter: Lord, let me but find my heart complying with all calls, my will obediently submitting to thy commands, sin my burden, and Christ my desire: I never crave a fairer or surer evidence of thy electing love to my soul: and if I had an oracle from heaven, an extraordinary messenger from the other world, to tell me thou lovest me, I have no reason to credit such a voice, while I find my heart wholly sensual, averse to God, and indisposed to all that is spiritual.

7. What reason have you why you should not presently embrace the call of God, and thankfully lay hold only on the first opportunity and season of salvation? Have you any greater matters in hand than the salvation of your precious souls? Is there any thing in this world that more concerns you? If the affairs of this life be so indispensably necessary, and those of the world to come so indifferent; if you think that meat and drink, trade and business, wife, and children are such great things, and Christ, the soul, and eternity, such little things; or if you think salvation to be a work of the greatest necessity, and yet may safely enough be put off to an uncertain time, I may assure you, you will not be long of this mind. How soon are all the mistakes of men in these matters rectified in a few moments after death! Rectified, I say, but not remedied; your opinion will be changed, but not your condition.

8. Do you not every day easily and readily obey the calls of Satan and your own lusts, while God and conscience are suffered to call and strive with you in vain? If Satan or your lusts call you to the tavern, to the world, and sinful pleasures, you speedily comply with

their call, and yield a ready obedience; if pride or covetousness call, or passion and revenge call, they need not call twice; and shall God and conscience call only in vain? Lord, what a creature is man become! If a vain companion call, you have no power to deny him; if God call, you have no ear to hear him.

9. You cannot but observe the obedience and diligence of many others, how seriously, painfully, and assiduously they ply, and follow on the work of their own salvation, and yet are no more concerned in the events and consequences of these things than you are. Does it not trouble you when you compare yourselves with them? Do not such thoughts as these sometimes arise in your hearts upon such observations? "Lord, what a difference is there like to be between their end and mine, when there is so apparent a difference in our course and conversation? Does not God distinguish persons in this world by the frames of their hearts, and tenor of their lives, in order to the great distinction he will make between one and another in the day of judgment? Have not I as precious a soul to save or lose as any of them? What is the matter that I sit with folded arms, while they are working out their salvation with fear and trembling? Why should any man or woman in the world be more careful for their souls than I for mine? Surely its capacity and excellency is equal with theirs, though my care and diligence be so unequal."

10. To conclude, God will shortly give you an irresistible call to the grave, and after that his voice shall call to you in your graves, *Arise, ye dead, and come to judgement:* But woe be to you, woe and alas that ever you were born, if you should hear the call of God to die, before you have heard and obeyed his call to Christ! Will your deathbed be easy to you? Can you with any hope or comfort shoot the gulf of eternity before you have done one act for the security of your own souls from the wrath to come? It is a dreadful thing for a poor christless soul to sit quivering upon the lips of a dying sinner, not able to say, nor yet endure a parting pull from the body, in such a case as it is.

In a word, If that God had made, and will shortly judge you; if the Redeemer that shed his invaluable blood, and now offers you the purchases and benefits of it; if you have any love to, or care of your own souls, which are more worth than the whole world; if you have any value for heaven, or dread of hell, then, for God's sake, for Christ's sake, for your precious soul's sake, trifle with heaven and hell no longer, but be in earnest *to work out your own salvation with fear and trembling.* Could I think of any other means or motives to secure your souls from danger, I would surely use them: could I reach your hearts effectually, I would deeply impress this great concern upon them: But I can neither do God's part of the work, nor yours; it is some ease to me, I have in sincerity, (though with much imperfection and feebleness) done part of my own: The Lord prosper it by the blessing of his Spirit in the hearts of them that read it. Amen.

Also from Benediction Books ...
Wandering Between Two Worlds: Essays on Faith and Art
Anita Mathias
Benediction Books, 2007
152 pages
ISBN: 0955373700

Available from www.amazon.com, www.amazon.co.uk

In these wide-ranging lyrical essays, Anita Mathias writes, in lush, lovely prose, of her naughty Catholic childhood in Jamshedpur, India; her large, eccentric family in Mangalore, a sea-coast town converted by the Portuguese in the sixteenth century; her rebellion and atheism as a teenager in her Himalayan boarding school, run by German missionary nuns, St. Mary's Convent, Nainital; and her abrupt religious conversion after which she entered Mother Teresa's convent in Calcutta as a novice. Later rich, elegant essays explore the dualities of her life as a writer, mother, and Christian in the United States-- Domesticity and Art, Writing and Prayer, and the experience of being "an alien and stranger" as an immigrant in America, sensing the need for roots.

About the Author

Anita Mathias was born in India, has a B.A. and M.A. in English from Somerville College, Oxford University and an M.A. in Creative Writing from the Ohio State University. Her essays have been published in The Washington Post, The London Magazine, The Virginia Quarterly Review, Commonweal, Notre Dame Magazine, America, The Christian Century, Religion Online, The Southwest Review, Contemporary Literary Criticism, New Letters, The Journal, and two of HarperSanFrancisco's The Best Spiritual Writing anthologies. Her non-fiction has won fellowships from The National Endowment for the Arts; The Minnesota State Arts Board; The Jerome Foundation, The Vermont Studio Center; The Virginia Centre for the Creative Arts, and the First Prize for the Best General Interest Article from the Catholic Press Association of the United States and Canada. Anita has taught Creative Writing at the College of William and Mary, and now lives and writes in Oxford, England.

www.anitamathias.com
wanderingbetweentwoworlds.blogspot.com (General and Culture)
thegoodbooksblog.blogspot.com (Reading and Writing)
theoxfordchristian.blogspot.com (Christian)

www.ingramcontent.com/pod-product-compliance
Lightning Source LLC
LaVergne TN
LVHW011910080426
835508LV00007BA/321